Culture and Identity
in the
Luso-Asian
World

The **Nalanda-Sriwijaya Series**, established under the publishing program of the Institute of Southeast Asian Studies, Singapore, has been created as a publications avenue for the Nalanda-Sriwijaya Centre. The Centre focuses on the ways in which Asian polities and societies have interacted over time. To this end, the series invites submissions which engage with Asian historical connectivities. Such works might examine political relations between states; the trading, financial and other networks which connected regions; cultural, linguistic and intellectual interactions between societies; or religious links across and between large parts of Asia.

The **Institute of Southeast Asian Studies (ISEAS)** was established as an autonomous organization in 1968. It is a regional centre dedicated to the study of socio-political, security and economic trends and developments in Southeast Asia and its wider geostrategic and economic environment. The Institute's research programmes are the Regional Economic Studies (RES, including ASEAN and APEC), Regional Strategic and Political Studies (RSPS), and Regional Social and Cultural Studies (RSCS).

ISEAS Publishing, an established academic press, has issued more than 2,000 books and journals. It is the largest scholarly publisher of research about Southeast Asia from within the region. ISEAS Publishing works with many other academic and trade publishers and distributors to disseminate important research and analyses from and about Southeast Asia to the rest of the world.

PORTUGUESE AND LUSO-ASIAN LEGACIES
IN SOUTHEAST ASIA, 1511-2011
VOLUME 2

Culture and Identity
in the
Luso-Asian
World
Tenacities & Plasticities

EDITED BY

LAURA JARNAGIN

ISEAS

INSTITUTE OF SOUTHEAST ASIAN STUDIES
Singapore

First published in Singapore in 2012 by
Institute of Southeast Asian Studies
30 Heng Mui Keng Terrace
Pasir Panjang
Singapore 119614

E-mail: publish@iseas.edu.sg
Website: <http://bookshop.iseas.edu.sg>

The responsibility for facts and opinions in this publication rests exclusively with the authors and their interpretations do not necessarily reflect the views or the policy of the publisher or its supporters.

ISEAS Library Cataloguing-in-Publication Data

Portuguese and Luso-Asian legacies, 1511–2011. Volume 2, Culture and identity in the Luso-Asian world : tenacities and plasticities / edited by Laura Jarnagin.
   Most papers in the volume were originally presented to a Conference on Portuguese and Luso-Asian Legacies in Southeast Asia 1511–2011, Singapore, 28–30 September 2010.
   1. Portuguese—Southeast Asia—History—Congresses.
   2. Portuguese—Asia—History—Congresses.
   3. Southeast Asia—Civilization—Portuguese influences—Congresses.
   4. Asia—Civilization—Portuguese influences—Congresses.
   5. Portuguese—Southeast Asia—Ethnic identity—Congresses.
   6. Portuguese—Asia—Ethnic identity—Congresses.
   I. Jarnagin, Laura.
   II. Institute of Southeast Asian Studies.
   II. Conference on Portuguese and Luso-Asian Legacies in Southeast Asia 1511–2011 (2010 : Singapore)
   III. Title: Culture and identity in the Luso-Asian world : tenacities and plasticities
DS523.4 P81P85   2012

ISBN 978-981-4345-50-7 (soft cover : v. 2)
ISBN 978-981-4345-51-4 (E-book PDF : v. 2)

Cover photo: Close-up of a green parrot's feathers. The green parrot, or *papagaio verde*, is an enduring, centuries-old folk motif found throughout the Lusophone world. Photo © Audrey R. Smith, 2011.

Typeset by Superskill Graphics Pte Ltd
Printed in Singapore by Markono Print Media Pte Ltd

CONTENTS

PART TWO
Cultural Components: Language, Architecture and Music

PART THREE
Adversity and Accommodation

LIST OF FIGURES
AND TABLES

PREFACE

This book, the second of two volumes, is the outgrowth of an interdisciplinary conference entitled "Portuguese and Luso-Asian Legacies in Southeast Asia, 1511–2011", that was held in Singapore and Malacca on 28–30 September 2010, co-sponsored by the Institute of Southeast Asian Studies (ISEAS), Singapore and the Universiti Teknologi MARA (UiTM), Bandaraya Campus, Malacca, Malaysia. Major financial support for the conference was also forthcoming from the Comemorações Portugal/Asia programme of the Government of Portugal, for which we extend our sincerest appreciation.

This event was the brainchild of Ambassador K. Kesavapany, director of ISEAS, who has an abiding commitment to promoting deeper understandings across societies everywhere, and particularly those that comprise the dense and complex cultural *cum* geographical nexus that is Southeast Asia. The coming of the Portuguese by sea into Southeast Asia half a millennium ago marked the opening of a major shift in relations between Asians and Europeans, one that would have a profound impact not only on this region and its peoples, but also on the course of world history. I am especially indebted to Ambassador Kesavapany for bestowing this challenging and rewarding project on me, and for the confidence he has placed in this Brazilianist to make enough of an intellectual transition from the Lusophone Atlantic world to that of the Indian and Pacific oceans in order to do justice to this undertaking.

Special thanks for the many and varied contributions to this conference are hereby extended to Ambassador Jaime Leitão, head of the diplomatic mission to Singapore, Embassy of Portugal in Singapore, for his unwavering enthusiasm, dedication and assistance; to Ambassador Dató Dr Mohd Yusof Ahmad, director of the Institute of ASEAN Studies and Global Affairs (INSPAG), Faculty of Adminstrative Science and Policy Studies (FSPPP), Universiti Teknologi MARA (UiTM), Shah Alam Campus, Malaysia, who orchestrated the Malacca portion of the event with his customary unruffled aplomb and attentiveness; to Dr Peter Borschberg, Department of History, National University of Singapore, for his intellectual guidance, wisdom and wit at many critical junctures; to Dr Geoffrey Wade of the Nalanda-Sriwijaya Centre at ISEAS, for his expansive knowledge of this region and his unvarnished candor in all matters; to Dr Ivo Carneiro, vice-rector of the University of Saint Joseph in Macau, who served as our keynote speaker and proffered many valuable observations about the importance of the contributions made by the scholars whose work appears herein; to the Eurasian Association of Singapore, which hosted a memorable dinner in the unique and special surroundings of the Eurasian Community House; to Mrs Y. L. Lee, head of administration at ISEAS, along with Ms May Wong and Mr Loh Joo Yong of her staff, all of whom bring an exceptional and devoted level of professionalism to project planning and execution; to Dr Roaimah Omar, Faculty of Business Administration, Universiti Teknologi MARA Malacca, who coordinated the Malacca portion of the conference; to Father Luís M. F. Sequeira, vice-rector of the Macao Ricci Institute, and Consul General of Portugal to Macao and Hong Kong, Manuel Carvalho, both of whom employed their good offices in the furtherance of this event in the fine tradition of Portuguese finessing; and to Dr Eul-Soo Pang, visiting professorial fellow at ISEAS, my husband and my colleague, whose counsel, expertise and assistance are always invaluable.

Above all, I would like to express my gratefulness to the conference participants, who hail from a dozen different nationalities, for making this event an exceptional success. Most of them travelled from great distances to attend, and all of them cheerfully endured three long days of intense activity. Their enthusiasm for the interdisciplinary nature of the conference was palpable and infectious, and their individual commitment to making it a success with their contributions was uncharacteristically high, as academic conferences go. It was especially rewarding to know that many individuals were able to meet some of their intellectual counterparts and scholars they admired for the first time (in one instance, capping a thirty-year correspondence). Along with the warm afterglow of this conference, however, we will always carry a deep sense of loss. Dr Glenn Ames, who was the first to submit a proposal, was unexpectedly unable to attend and passed away a few days after our meeting. Befittingly, Volume 1 opens with a tribute to him and the lasting contributions he made to the history of the Portuguese and their legatees in Asia.

Finally, a brief word is in order regarding Portuguese orthography, quotations and translations used throughout this work. For the reader's convenience, most proper names and proper nouns have been converted to the current orthography in the text (for instance, "Afonso de Albuquerque", not the original "Affonso d'Albuquerque"), with a few "judgement call" exceptions. Inevitably, though, given the distinct creole communities and languages that evolved from the Portuguese presence in Asia, it would not be appropriate to modernize the spellings of the names of individuals associated with these groups, although it is not always obvious to know where to "draw the line". However, original spellings of all words in all languages have been retained in quotations and citations. Translations into English of all passages originally in another language have been done by the individual authors themselves, unless stated otherwise.

Laura Jarnagin
The Editor

LIST OF CONTRIBUTORS

Tara Alberts holds the title of Max Weber Fellow at the European University Institue (Italy). She completed her Ph.D. in History at Newnham College, in the University of Cambridge and went on to hold a Research Fellowship at Jesus College, Cambridge. Her primary research interests are in histories of religious change, cultural exchange and beliefs about health and healing in the early modern world. Her doctoral research, also undertaken in Cambridge, examined Catholic mission and conversion to Catholicism in sixteenth- and seventeenth-centuries Southeast Asia. She is currently writing a monograph based on this research.

Alan N. Baxter holds the title of Professor in the Department of Portuguese, Universidade de Macau, Macau S.A.R., China. He received his Masters in Hispanic Linguistics from La Trobe University (Melbourne) and his Ph.D. in Linguistics from the Australian National University. His academic interests include Creole Portuguese (in Asia, in particular), variationist sociolinguistics and language contact. His research has focused on Malacca Creole Portuguese, Macao Creole Portuguese, Afro-Brazilian Portuguese and the Portuguese of the Tongas of the island of São Tomé. His publications include, in addition to scholarly articles, the books *A Grammar of Kristang* (1988), *Maquista Chapado: Vocabulary and Expressions in Macao's Portuguese Creole* (2004, co-authored with Miguel Senna Fernandes), *A Dictionary of Kristang: English* (2004, co-authored with Patrick de Silva), and *O Português Afro-Brasileiro: Afro-Brazilian Portuguese* (2009, co-authored and co-edited with Dante Lucchesi and Ilza Ribeiro). He has taught previously at La Trobe University (Melbourne) and Flinders University (Adelaide), at the University of Lisbon (Portugal), and at the Federal University of Bahia (Brazil).

Hugo C. Cardoso is a linguist who graduated in Portuguese and English Studies from the University of Coimbra before pursuing an MPhil and a Ph.D. in Linguistics at the University of Amsterdam. His research bridges theoretical and fieldwork-based descriptive linguistics, with particular focus on issues of language contact and the formation of Portuguese-lexified creole languages in Asian contexts. He is currently affiliated with the University of Macao's Research Centre for Luso-Asian Studies.

Rita Bernardes de Carvalho obtained a BA in Archaeology from the Universidade Nova de Lisboa (Portugal), a BA in History from Leiden University's Encompass Program, and an MA in Asian Studies (History) in 2006 from the École Pratique des Hautes Études (Paris), where she focused on the Portuguese presence in Ayutthaya during the seventeenth century. She is currently preparing a doctoral dissertation on the construction (and re-construction) of identity in Luso-Asian communities in mainland Southeast Asia, also at the École Pratique des Hautes Études under the supervision of Dejanirah Couto and João Paulo Oliveira e Costa.

Dennis De Witt is an independent researcher and a fifth-generation Dutch Eurasian from Malacca with a keen interest in subjects relating to Dutch influences in Malaysian history. His research on his ancestors has produced family data covering eleven generations through three hundred years and across three continents. He is the author of *Reconnecting through Our Roots* (2006), *History of the Dutch in Malaysia* (2007) (which won the 2009 Dutch Incentive Prize for Genealogy), and *Melaka from the Top* (2010). He has also contributed articles for the *Journal of Malaysian Biographies* (Malaysian National Archives) and is a registered speaker with the Malaysian Tourism Development Council. He has presented numerous papers at seminars and has written articles for various newspapers and magazines. Currently, he is one of the coordinators of the Malaysian Dutch Descendants Project and is the president of the Malaysia-Netherlands Friendship Association.

Vincent Ho (Vincent Ho Wai-kit) graduated from the Department of History of the Chinese University of Hong Kong (CUHK), and is currently teaching at the Department of History of the University of Macau. In the past, he held posts in several government departments in Hong Kong. He also taught world history and Chinese history in secondary school and the advanced diploma curriculum. His current research interest is mainly in Chinese classical texts in East Asia, the overseas Chinese, and the history of Macao, also taking up tourism research, urban research, cultural geography and translation. His translated works include *Chinese Cross Currents* of the Macau Ricci Institute, and various publications found in the *Heritage Hong Kong: Newsletter of the Antiquities and Monument Office*, a Hong Kong government publication.

Laura Jarnagin (Pang) is a visiting professorial fellow at the Institute of Southeast Asian Studies in Singapore and an associate professor emerita in the Division of Liberal Arts and International Studies at Colorado School of Mines (Golden, Colorado) where she served as its director for five years and was a co-founder of its Master of International Political Economy of Resources programme. She is the author of *A Confluence of Transatlantic Networks: Elites, Capitalism, and Confederate Migration to Brazil* (2008). Her current research interests include late eighteenth- and nineteenth-century transatlantic merchant networks and the application of complexity theory to understanding their dynamics. She holds a doctorate in Brazilian history from Vanderbilt University.

Manuel Lobato holds a bachelor's degree in History (1980) and an MA (1993) in History of the Portuguese Discoveries and Expansion. He has been with the Instituto de Investigação Científica Tropical (IICT) in Lisbon since 1993, first as an assistant researcher (to 2004) and subsequently as a titular researcher following the completion of his Ph.D. dissertation, "Trade, Conflict and Religion: Portuguese and Spaniards in the Moluccas (1512–1618)". Since 2008, he has been the vice-director of IICT's History Center and served as the coordinator of IICT's Scientific Council from 2008 to 2010. In addition, he is a lecturer in the Master in Oriental Studies programme at the Institute of Oriental Studies of the Portuguese Catholic University (Lisbon) and of the Asian Studies graduate programme in the Faculty of Arts of the Lisbon University (FLUL). He has held two scholarships from the Fundação Oriente and is the author of two books and more than thirty-five papers on the history of the early presence of the Portuguese in Mozambique and the East African Coast, India, and the Malay-Indonesian Archipelago.

Vicente Paulino is a native of Maliana, East Timor. He received his Licenciado in Communication Sciences in 2007 with a focus on Communication, Culture and Art. In 2009 he completed a master's degree in Communication Sciences with a specialization in Contemporary Culture and New Technologies in the Faculdade de Ciências Sociais e Humanas at the Universidade Nova de Lisboa. He has served as the secretary of RENETIL (Resistência Nacional dos Estudantes de Timor Leste) de Maliana during 1999–2000, was the founder and editor of the *Bulletin kuda Ulun Lian* in Maliana (1999–2001), and was an election observer for the Assembleia Constituinte de Timor-Leste in 2001. From 2007 to 2010, he was also a voting member of the Conselho Fiscal da Associação para Timorense (APARATI) in Lisbon. He has participated in national and international congresses and conferences.

Mário Pinharanda-Nunes holds a BA in Modern Languages and Literature from the Universidade de Lisboa (1990), as well as an MA (2001) and a Ph.D. (2011) in Linguistics from the University of Macao. His doctoral dissertation is entitled "The Tense-Aspect System of Makista, the Portuguese-Based Creole of Macau". He was a visiting lecturer of Portuguese at the Instituto Camões of the Universiti Malaya, Kuala Lumpur (1991–97). From 2001 to 2003 he was appointed by the Instituto Camões as lecturer and attaché for cultural and educational affairs at the Embassy of Portugal in Jakarta. Since 2003 he has been a teaching staff member in the Portuguese Department at the University of Macao. His research interests include the Portuguese-based creoles of Asia (especially Malacca and Macao); language formation and evolution; language variation and change; and naturalistic SLA (second language acquisition). He has published articles on linguistic and sociolinguistic issues concerning Kristang and Makista and has presented related papers at international conferences on Pidgin and Creole languages and language contact.

Roderich Ptak attended schools in both Portugal and Germany in his youth and received his university education in Heidelberg, Beijing, Shenyang, and Guelph (Canada). He holds a Dr phil. in Chinese Studies from Heidelberg (1978), an MA in Economics from Guelph (1981), and a Dr habil. from Heidelberg (1985). He has been a research scholar in Hong Kong and has also conducted research in Toronto. In addition, he has held scholarships and grants from the German Research Foundation (DFG) and other institutions. He began his professional academic career in Heidelberg in 1981, has been a Heisenberg Scholar, and in 1991 was Professor of Chinese Studies at Mainz-Germersheim. Since 1994, he has been the chair of Chinese Studies at Munich. Through the years, he has also taught at universities in Paris, Lisbon and Macao. Presently, his academic interests include the Nanhai region and Macao (historical), and animals in traditional Chinese texts.

Ricardo Roque holds a Ph.D. in History from the University of Cambridge and BA and MA degrees in sociology and historical sociology from the New University of Lisbon. He is currently a Research Fellow at the Institute of Social Sciences, University of Lisbon. He is the author of *Headhunting and*

Colonialism: Anthropology and the Circulation of Human Skulls in the Portuguese Empire, 1870–1930 (2010) and *Antropologia e Império: Fonseca Cardoso e a Expedição à Índia em 1895* (2011); and the co-editor of *Engaging Colonial Knowledge: Reading European Archives in World History* (2011). He is currently working on the history of anthropology and colonialism in East Timor, and on a larger project about colonial mimesis in the late Portuguese empire in Asia and Africa.

Christian Storch has studied musicology, arts management and English literature in Weimar and Jena, Germany. In 2009 he finished his Ph.D. in Weimar on the subject of Alfred Schnittke's piano concertos in terms of authorship theories in music. Since 2010 Storch has been working at the University of Göttingen, pursuing his Habilitation with a research project about the influence of Portuguese musical culture in Southeast Asia in the sixteenth and seventeenth centuries. His main research interests are in the relationship between music and colonialism, the music of Alfred Schnittke and his contemporaries, and early music in the Federal State of Thuringia (Germany). Storch is vice-chairman of the Academia Musicalis Thuringiae as well as member of board of the Deutsche Alfred Schnittke Gesellschaft. His most recent publication is as co-editor (with Amrei Flechsig) of the first volume of a Schnittke Studies book series published with Olms in Hildesheim, Germany (2010).

GLOSSARY

Definitions of the words and terms in this glossary are followed either by the language of origin or a location where the word or term is or was used with reference to the subject matter covered in this book. Most nouns are given in both their singular and plural spellings, as is relevant to their usage in this work. Plurals formed by the simple addition of an "s" or "es" are indicated parenthetically at the end of the singular, such as "*casa(s)*" or *conquistador(es)*; more complex spelllings of plurals are shown separately, such as "*arraial*; pl. *arraiais*".

adat	Culture. (Timor)
aktionsart	In linguistics, the kind of action associated with a verb (as opposed to the time of action). (German)
apertos de mão	Shaking hands. (Portuguese)
arraial; pl. *arraiais*	A Timorese warrior(s), in the context of this work. (Portuguese)
bahasa geragau	Shrimp language. (Bahasa Malaysia)
bahasa serani	Catholic (Eurasian) language. (Bahasa Malaysia)
balão; pl. *balões*	Richly decorated ceremonial Siamese barges. (Portuguese)
bandeira. Flag	(Portuguese)
bandel; pl. *bandéis*	A Portuguese settlement(s) in Southeast Asia. (Portuguese)
bangsal	A warehouse. (Bahasa Indonesia and Bahasa Malaysia)
barcalan	A government official in charge of foreign affairs. (Siam)

barlaque	A matrix of social pacts designed to establish and strengthen family ties in the same geneaological lineage whose practice includes a symbolic exchange of gifts and material goods to connect two lines in a lasting relationship. (Timor)
bastão	Sceptre of office in Timor. (Portuguese)
bastão de rota	A Timorese royal sceptre. (Portuguese)
batuque	Drum playing. (Portuguese)
bei gua	The path of the ancestors. (Timor)
beija-mão	Hand kissing. (Portuguese)
bhineka tungal ika	Unity in diversity. (Timor)
biola	A guitar; see also *viola*. (Bahasa Malaysia)
bumiputera	"Sons of the soil", a legal term in Malaysia denoting someone or some ethnic group that is "native" to the country. (Bahasa Malaysia)
burgerkapitein	A captain of the Civil Guard. (Dutch)
caballero	Literally, a knight; also a term to designate a bulwark or a small fort. (Spanish)
cafre	A term for blacks (individuals of African descent) in colonial Portuguese India. (Portuguese)
cafreal	Of or referring to a *cafre*. (Portuguese)
caixa	Literally, a box; also, in the context of this work, a drum. (Portuguese)
calheta	A small harbour. (Portuguese)
canceira(s)	Payment(s) due to Portuguese officers for their journey. (Portuguese)
cantilene	An insulting song sung almost in parody of a lover's seranade. (Italian)
canto de organo	A four-part song. (Spanish)
canto llano	Plain chant. (Spanish)
capitão-mor	A local commander appointed by the Portuguese crown. (Portuguese)
casado(s)	A married Portuguese man/men. (Portuguese)
casa(s) real(es)	Administrative building(s). (Spanish)
castelo	A castle. (Portuguese)
comando	An administrative district. (Timor)
conquistador(es)	Conqueror(s). (Portuguese)
đạo hoà lan	The Portuguese law. (Vietnamese)
dató(s)	Tetum nobility title(s); literally, "princes of the earth". (Timor and elsewhere in Southeast Asia)

diablete(s)	Dance(s) from Madeira in which performers were clothed and masked as demons. (Portuguese)
diwan	A collector; the name of various public posts in Muslim societies. (Perso-Arabic)
eerste schipvaart	First shipping. (Dutch)
estandela de rotim	A staff made of reed. (Timor)
estilo(s)	A sacred, age-old custom(s) or style(s). (Timor)
fanfang	A quarter of a city or town designated for foreign residents. (Chinese)
fawang	King of the canon; sometimes refers to a priest in classical Chinese descriptions of Macao. (Chinese)
feitoria	Trading post. (Portuguese)
fidalgo-cavaleiro	A nobleman. (Portuguese)
finta(s)	Collective tax(es). (Timor)
fiscaal	Prosecutor. (Dutch)
folía(s)	Dance(s) performed by a large number of people. (Portuguese)
fuerza	A fortress, bulwark, or simple vault. (Spanish)
gastos	Agricultural produce, cattle, and the like, received as provisions, in the context of this work. (Timor)
gigantes	Giant effigies. (Portuguese)
homulac	A ceremonial orator. (Timor)
já	Already; immediately. (Portuguese)
kapitan	A captain. (Dutch)
knua	House. (Timor)
koto	A Japanese psaltery
lipa	A type of traditional Timorese clothing. (Timor)
liural; pl. *liurais*	An executive ruler(s). (Timor)
lorsá	A Timorese warrior song. (Timor)
lua(s)	Literally, "moon(s)"; in the context of this work, Timorese metal disc(s) signifying warrior or headhunter status, as used in this work. (Portuguese)
luas de oiro	Literally, "moons of gold"; in the context of thisi work, golden discs. (Timor)
lulik	Sacred or holy. Also spelled "lulic". (Timor)
macoan	Timorese ceremonial manager of justice; synonymous with *parlamento*. (Timor)
mardika	A free man. (Javanese)

mestiço(s)	An individual of mixed race; in this work, those born of mixed Portuguese and Asian parentage; more properly, *Luso-descendentes*. (Portuguese)
miao	Temples; sometimes used to refer to "churches" in classical Chinese. (Chinese)
mogarim	Jasmine. (Portuguese)
morador, pl. *moradores*	A resident(s). See also *moradores* below for a special meaning in the Timorese context. (Portuguese)
moradores	A company of indigenous irregulars established by the Portuguese. (Timor)
mos indicus	A term that describes a Jesuit manner of preaching in India; in the "India fashion". (Latin)
norteiro	In colonial times, a member of the Catholic and creolophone Indo-Portuguese communities of the Província do Norte (Province of the North), as the Portuguese-held territories along the northwest coast of India were known. (Portuguese)
okul liu lai nalan liu lai na pemerintha	An ethnic group of the Bunak.
ola(s)	A local currency in Maluku. (Maluku)
pacto de sangue	Blood pact. (Portuguese)
paiung	A feminine umbrella. (Timor)
páreas	Tribute. (Portuguese)
parlamento	A Timorese ceremonial manager of justice, in the context of this work; synonymous with *macoan*.
poço	A well. (Portuguese)
português corrompido	Corrupt Portuguese (language). (Portuguese)
presidio	A garrison. (Spanish)
principal, pl. *principais*	A nobleman/noblemen, in the context of this work. (Portuguese)
rai-ten	Tax. (Timor)
regimento	An ordinance. (Portuguese)
régulo	A local Timorese chief or leader. (Portuguese)
reino(s)	A kingdom(s).
romance	A novel. (Portuguese)
rota	A type of reed. (Portuguese)
rotim	A type of reed. (Portuguese)
si	Pagoda or temple. (Chinese)
sobrado	First floor. (Portuguese)
tabedai	A type of dance peculiar to Timor. (Timor)

táis	A type of traditional Timorese clothing. (Timor)
tang	Hall or church. (Chinese)
tébedai	A type of dance peculiar to Timor. (Timor)
topass; pl. *topasses*	Also *topaze(s)*. Variously: (a) a Portuguese-Timorese mestiço group; from volume 1 of this work: (b) the offspring of Portuguese men and South Asian women; (b) the descendants of Portuguese mestizos who married native Sinhalese and Tamil women of Sri Lanka (Ceylon); and (c) possibly, an interpreter, in a Tamil derivation. Topasses were also referred to as "black Christians", and the men often became professional soldiers, leading to the additional meaning of a "hat-wearing mercenary soldier". (Southeast Asia; South Asia)
torre de menagem	In military architecture, the central structure of a medieval castle. (Portuguese)
tumenggung	An official responsible for law and order. (Malacca, possibly of Javanese origin)
tumengó(s)	An ancient title(s), possibly of Javanese origins, based on the term *tumengung*; synonymous with the Portuguese *tumungão* (pl. *tumungões*). (Timor)
uma kain/ahimatan	A descent group. (Tetum)
uma lulik(s)	Sacred house(s). (Timor)
vigário	Vicar. (Portuguese)
vihuela	A guitar; see also *viola*. (Spanish)
vilancete	An Iberian musical genre of the late fifteenth to eighteenth centuries; the same as *villancico* in Spanish. (Portuguese)
villancico	An Iberian musical genre of the late fifteenth to eighteenth centuries; the same as *vilancete* in Portuguese. (Spanish)
viola	A guitar; see also *biola* and *vihuela*. (Portuguese).
vrijzwarten	Free blacks. (Dutch)
wang	King; sometimes used to refer to Catholic priests in classical Chinese descriptions of Macao. (Chinese)
wijkmeester	Ward administrator. (Dutch)
xunan yashi	Senior inspection official. (Chinese)
zhang	3.3 metres (Chinese)

INTRODUCTION:
THE QUALITATIVE PROPERTIES OF
CULTURES AND IDENTITIES

Laura Jarnagin

Culture and Identity in the Luso-Asian World: Tenacities and Plasticities (Volume 2 of *Portuguese and Luso-Asian Legacies in Southeast Asia, 1511–2011*) constitutes the balance of papers associated with September 2010 "Portuguese and Luso-Asian Legacies in Southeast Asia, 1511–2011" conference organized by the Institute of Southeast Asian Studies, Singapore and the Universiti Teknologi MARA, Malacca, Malaysia. Whereas Volume 1 treats the making of the Luso-Asian world in terms of exploring how significantly differing cultures, polities, and societies interacted with one another within the South, Southeast, and East Asian theatres, Volume 2 is concerned with the "living spirit" of the communities and cultures under investigation — that is, the more elusive qualitative properties of Portuguese and Luso-Asian cultures.

The introduction to Volume 1 includes a discussion of two key features of the conference that need to be revisited here briefly, lest the context and intent of this work be misconstrued. The first of these is the selection of the five hundredth anniversary of the Portuguese conquest of Malacca in 1511 as the point of departure for considering half a millennium of actions, interactions, and reactions among the Portuguese, Asians, and Luso-Asians. In the longer treatment of this matter in Volume 1, we make it clear that our intent is not to "commemorate", or to "celebrate", or to attach value judgements to this particular event. Rather, we have sought to create a forum for scholarly reflection, reassessment, and reconsideration of the impact of the Portuguese presence in the Asian theatre.

The second matter that also merits comment is the use of the word "legacies" as an overarching theme. While the term has various connotations, we have employed it in a more open and inclusive sense to refer to "something that has been left, in this case, by an abstract predecessor — the presence of Portuguese and subsequently Luso-Asian peoples in Asia — and that continued for some time or still continues to survive, to be observable, and to be influential at some level of being or existing, well beyond the lifetime of its original agent, albeit with modifications along the way".

As also noted in Volume 1, even though there was no specific theory or concept around which the conference was organized, the general theme of *complexity* was sounded in almost all of the papers presented. By and large, "complexity" is used as a descriptor of the various phenomena observed by our authors, not as the subject of a broader theoretical discussion. And while it would be inappropriate to artificially impose a common conceptual framework *ex post facto*, the fact that this one theme recurs throughout these diverse studies warrants some provisional musings about what might be a fruitful pathway along which to advance our understanding of the qualitative nature of such inherently messy subjects as cultures and identities.

To that end, a few remarks on the rapidly growing body of academic literature concerning the theory of complexity (mostly in the sciences but to an increasing extent in the social sciences)[1] can illustrate how this conceptual framework might capture the essence of the dynamic processes that give cultures and identities their "living spirit". Whereas a full treatment of complexity theory is clearly beyond the scope of this introduction, it is possible to mention a few key features of how complexity "works" and to map some of these to the type of phenomena our authors have investigated.

Above all, complexity theory explains *how* things evolve. In essence, it focuses on how "agents" within a given system interact with their environment by way of continual feedback loops. Was a particular choice or action beneficial? If so — if the feedback was positive — that choice or action is reiterated, unless it ceases to be useful in the context of the system's interaction with the constantly changing environment. In short, agents in a complex system are constantly adapting to changing realities — that is, they themselves are changing, *evolving*, in response to change and to their own internal choices, and are doing so in a non-linear fashion. In order to understand this process, it is especially important to look at the qualitative features of the components of a system and how they interact, and it is in this sense that many chapters in this work make a contribution.

Theorists conceptualize of the dynamism found in complex systems as occurring in a "fuzzy zone" between order and chaos. It is in this zone that innovation and creativity occur, thereby accounting for a system's transformations and ongoing dynamic. Significantly, survival in a complex system is predicated upon agents acting collaboratively with others, that is, upon interdependency and the formation of groups and subgroups. Acting in concert allows individuals to transcend themselves and acquire collective properties that they cannot achieve on their own. In the case of humankind, such properties would include thought, purpose, language, culture, family, and religion. Through bottom-up collaboration and accommodation, networks emerge and a system acquires structures and patterns that have come about through self-organization, not some grand design. But complex systems are not exclusively about collaboration: subgroups within a system also compete, thereby contributing to a system's unpredictability and non-linearity.

Even the most cursory reading of the chapters in both of these volumes readily renders examples of the various characteristics associated with complex systems. For instance, in this volume, one will find many "fuzzy zones" where interactions take place and new realities emerge as a result, such as at the interface between different Catholic laities; in the relationship between Timorese and Portuguese cultures; in the formation and trajectory of creole languages; and in the curious relationship between China and Macao, to name a few. "Evolution" is also a descriptor found in many of these studies, and in one instance, we even witness the withering of one evolutionary branch — a musical one — which, for a number of reasons, lost its dynamic. The slippery topic of identity — one's own, as well as that of "the other" — especially appears to be fertile ground for examining the qualitative features of the components of complex systems. While complexity theory is by no means a "unified theory of everything", it might nevertheless be a useful conceptual tool that can bring additional sophistication to the treatment of the qualitative side of human behaviours and interactions that readers and researchers alike may wish to pursue.

One of the key reasons for choosing so large a canvass as "legacies" and so expansive a time frame as five hundred years for this project was to attract a broad array of scholars and perspectives that could stimulate intellectual cross-fertilization among an international and interdisciplinary gathering of experts. As is true in volume 1, the present volume also comprises contributions by well-established scholars, rising talents, doctoral candidates, and one independent researcher, whose contributions are summarized below.

Volume 2 is organized around three themes: "Crafting Identity in the Luso-Asian World", "Cultural Components: Language, Architecture, and Music", and "Adversity and Accommodation". In each of these sections, readers will find that the cultures and subcultures that precipitated out of the complex mixtures of Europeans, Asians, and Eurasians variously exhibited significant degrees of plasticity — that is, of malleability and changeability — and of tenacity — that is, a retention of cultural patterns, values, and practices. In short, as changing cultural environments presented new options and realities, we find adaptations and modifications of the "new" in combination with adherence to existing ways. In essence, the choices made by different groups and individuals at various points in time are expressions of their interactions with their ever-changing environments — that is, they are the result of feedback loops that either affirmed or negated the value of certain choices open to them.

Part One of this volume, "Crafting Identity in the Luso-Asian World", comprises four chapters that take us into the intersticies of identity formation in the Luso-Asian world of continental Southeast Asia in the sixteenth and seventeenth centuries and of Timor in the nineteenth and twentieth centuries.

In Chapter 1, "Catholic Communities and Their Festivities under the Portuguese Padroado in Early Modern Southeast Asia", Tara Alberts examines popular Catholic festivities in Portuguese Asia in the early modern era and opens a wide window of fresh perspectives onto the process of identity formation and assertion in those communities. Her work includes a rich discussion of the conceptual approaches to events of mass participation in early modern Europe and finds significant parallels in contemporaneous Southeast Asian settings. In her analysis, dichotomous classifications of the nature of public events (orderly/disruptive; ceremonial/chaotic; religious/profane) give way to understanding ritual from the participant's perspective — one in which meanings can blur and overlap along a continuum ranging from formal religious ceremonies to more demotic communal festivities to outright protest and violence. Yet, from this seeming messiness, identities emerge and are expressed, social hierarchies are constructed, and divine favour is sought.

The chapter focuses on Portuguese and Asian Catholic identities and communities in three cosmopolitan, trade-oriented Southeast Asian cities from the late sixteenth to the late seventeenth centuries: Hội An (known as Faifo to Europeans) in Cochinchina; Malacca in the Malay peninsula; and Ayutthaya in Siam. Alberts examines a multifaceted, complex set of religious and secular interfaces in these locales where we find a laity of Portuguese Catholics, mestizo Portuguese Catholics (including those of Afro-Portuguese descent), and non-Portuguese Catholics (such as Japanese, Chinese, and Cochinchinese Christians) who variously competed and cooperated, interacted and distanced themselves from one another. Non-Catholics intrigued by Catholic festivities often joined in for the entertainment of the moment, or eventually converted. Non-Christian local rulers who wished to favour foreigners for strategic or commercial reasons, or else wished to clamp down on the adherents of the foreign faith for disrupting the prevailing social order, variously tolerated or prohibited such festivals. Meanwhile, the mix of clergy from multiple orders (Franciscans, Dominicans, and Jesuits) and of multiple ethnicities (Spanish, Portuguese, Italian, and French) often added to the tensions, with lay groups favouring or reviling one over another.

Competition and cooperation, hostility and amity, and engagement and distancing are all found at these many junctures as lay groups appropriated certain features of Catholicism and invented their own variations on its ceremonies, often incorporating some aspect of their traditional culture and usually blurring distinctions between the religious and the profane in the process. Festivities exposed such modifications, but "public spectacle was an important part of evangelistic methodology in Asia, especially for the Jesuits". Thus, as well as being a declaration of shared Catholic faith, moments of communal celebration "could also reveal the tensions, rivalries, and uncertain alliances between different groups within Catholic communities" despite a superficial assertion of unity under one religion. Further, as is observed in other chapters of this work, Alberts also finds tendencies to conflate being Catholic with being Portuguese. In short, the introduction of a religion new to the cultural environment of these Asian locales by a then-ascendant power inserted a very plastic new variable into the process of identity formation.

Chapter 2, "A 'Snapshot' of a Portuguese Community in Southeast Asia: The *Bandel* of Siam, 1684–86", further confirms the malleabililty and processual nature of identity formation. In it, Rita Bernardes de Carvalho parses the subtleties of identity from what is ostensibly a political text, namely, an account of the Portuguese embassy that Pero Vaz de Siqueira led to Siam. This document and several relevant letters were originally published in Portuguese by Leonor de Seabra in 2003 (with a second edition in 2004), followed by an English translation in 2005. A biographical index of the names appearing in the embassy report accompanies this chapter as an appendix.

By the late seventeenth century, the Portuguese community (*bandel*) in Ayutthaya caused concern in Lisbon. At some 160 years beyond the initial Portuguese presence in the Siamese kingdom, ties to the metropolis were fraying as Portugal's power in the region diminished and the "empire" assumed a distinctly informal character. Nevertheless, the presence of French bishops in this traditionally Portuguese sphere of influence would not go unanswered by the crown, which sent its ambassador, Pero Vaz de Siqueira, from the increasingly independent-minded Macao to investigate and to renew relations with Siam, whose king was then actively expanding his international connections.

Extracting the cases of three individuals from the embassy report, Bernardes de Carvalho reveals the inexactness of what it meant to be "Portuguese" in this culturally fluid environment. Her enquiry explores "the different identitary strategies that drove the *bandel*'s residents to behave in a certain way, letting their actions speak for their feelings about their identity, and trying to grasp the processes that shape identity in the cultural practices, actions, and borders between Portuguese from Ayutthaya and Portuguese coming with the embassy".

The complex shadings involved in crafting and projecting identity emerge from Bernardes de Carvalho's case studies. Amador Coelho survived in Ayutthata by distancing himself from his "Portugueseness" and aligning instead with the ascendant French and with the Siamese court through familial connections. Francisco Barreto de Pina, the long-time headman of the Portuguese settlement, had undergone significant acculturation, having a large family, a Siamese nobility title, and attitudes considered by the Macanese ambassador as being too "casual and indulgent"; hence, Barreto de Pina was dismissed from his position. Burot, a "black New Christian" and petty thief, presents yet another exhibit in the confounding matter of "the relationship between the Catholic faith and Portuguese identity" in which "even missionaries accepted the plasticity of the religious experience in Siam". Given the "considerable cultural distance" that existed between the "Portuguese" of Ayutthaha and Macao that Bernardes de Carvalho exposes, one wonders how Vaz de Siqueira — a native of Macao and probably a mestizo, who held tenaciously to his notions of "Portugueseness" vis-à-vis the *bandel* residents — would have fared under a metropolitan Portuguese cultural microscope.

In Chapter 3, "The Colonial Command of Ceremonial Language: Etiquette and Custom-Imitation in Nineteenth-Century East Timor", Ricardo Roque details a fascinating case of custom-imitation that embodies both cultural plasticities and tenacities in the origins and practice of Timorese ceremonial etiquettes. Using historical and anthropological lenses to scrutinize nineteenth-century Timorese practices that in fact originated in early modern Portuguese customs, Roque demonstrates how the Timorese came to view these as having originated in "their" culture. Just as importantly, Portuguese colonial officials in Timor pragmatically understood that, in order to maintain their own authority, it was necessary to engage in these "indigeneous" practices and customs, known collectively as *estilos*, that had long since ceased to be necessary in the context of contemporary imperial administration.

In early colonial times, the Timorese creatively appropriated and incorporated Portuguese customs into their own ceremonial affirmations of elite power, out of which a politico-jural system of etiquette emerged. By the late nineteenth and early twentieth centuries, the Timorese were still tenaciously practising these same rituals, whereas the Portuguese now considered them repugnant. However, these customs did bridge the "colonial-indigenous divide", simultaneously reinforcing the status of indigenous Timorese potentates *and* sustaining Portuguese authority "beyond its feeble and tiny dimension in Dili". In simple terms, this system of *estilos* became the colonial state, although it "did not safeguard colonial authority from the permanent threat of indigenous hostility".

Tenacity, however, should not be confused with stasis. The system was actively maintained and was adapted to changing realities, thereby constituting a dynamic "social force" that "superseded the most modernizing intentions of colonisers". In their practical application, the *estilos* communicated deference and etiquette in interpersonal situations, and conveyed hospitality when colonial authorities visited Timorese kingdoms, but they also regulated conflict and managed warfare.

Ritual and ceremony have long been understood by anthropologists to lie at the core of indigenous state power in Southeast Asia. For the later periods of Portuguese colonialism, however, the "co-production of colonial and indigenous power, status, and authority" remains understudied, a lacuna that Roque's work begins to fill. In essence, this is a study of a set of two elites — one indigeneous, one foreign — who relied on each other to maintain power in their respective spheres through participation in a common etiquette that was revered by the Timorese and tolerated by the Portuguese.

Roque cautions, however, that this intertwined dependency should not prompt a "celebratory reading" of the phenomenon as an instance of hybridity. In light of the above discussion of complex systems, one could imagine that such features as adaptiveness to local feedback, unpredictability, and the emergence of new states of being might offer an alternative framework within which to consider "the sociopolitical value of ceremonial life at the very juncture of indigenous and colonial cultures, as they emerged in the course of colonial encounters over time".

The role of the Portuguese in the formation of Timorese identity is explored in a different context in Chapter 4, "Remembering the Portuguese Presence in Timor and Its Contribution to the Making of Timor's National and Cultural Identity", by Vicente Paulino. Following a brief review of the Portuguese presence in Timor from colonial times, Paulino demonstrates how the Portuguese presence has influenced the making of the East Timorese nation-state. In addition to considering the results of four-and-a-half centuries of Portuguese influence on Timorese culture, though, he also contrasts this experience with the consequences of twenty-four years of Indonesian occupation (1975–99), which involved the massive destruction of Timorese cultural entities. Additionally, the chapter engages in a comparative analysis of the Timorese national identity and culture with those of Japan and Korea, especially with reference to Japan's occupation of Korea (1910–45).

Timor's system of social organization derives from a composite of some thirty-one ethno-linguistic groups and forty-six kingdoms, the result of waves of primarily Melanesian and Malay migration over time. No one ethnic group has ever dominated, no tradition of a single absolute authority exists, and no single myth evokes the notion of common descent.

Portuguese colonial dominance, as also discussed in Chapter 3, was achieved by a blending of Portuguese administrative policy with the "solid Timorese traditional systems". One of the most important components of these systems is the physical and symbolic role of the "sacred houses", or *knua* — hybrid social spaces accommodating and protecting the individual, the family, and the community. Any construction of a sense of nationhood would thus need to be incorporated into the universe of the *knua*. Conversely, the destruction of sacred houses — in which the Indonesian forces engaged — would deal a severe blow to Timorese identity. The use of the Portuguese language was also disallowed in the education system. Interestingly, though, whereas less than 20 per cent of the Timorese population ever professed being Catholic prior to the invasion, in occupied East Timor 98 per cent soon claimed such an identity.

In Paulino's comparative review of the case of occupied Korea, we find similar tactics employed by the Japanese as by the Indonesians. Among other things, Japanese policies included forcing Koreans to convert to Shintoism (a variant of Confucianism imported into Japan in the sixth century from China) and prohibiting the use of the language. Efforts at obliterating indigenous cultural traditions on the part of relatively short-term occupying forces, though, are generally unsuccessful in the long run. However, given the nature and the longevity of the Portuguese presence in Timor, Paulino concludes that although it did virtually nothing to advance economic development, it has provided an administrative superstructure, bridging multiethnic and multilinguistic differences, within which a new national and cultural identity is emerging.

Part Two of this volume, "Cultural Components: Language, Architecture and Music", examines other types of Portuguese and Luso-Asian legacies that broaden and deepen our understanding of the larger phenomenon of what cultures choose to retain, to relinquish, to adapt, and to modify.

The section comprises a trilogy of linguistic and sociolinguistic studies of Kristang, Makista, and Indo-Portuguese creoles as well as the identification of forts in the Moluccas and the fate of Portuguese music in Southeast Asia.

In Chapter 5, "The Creole Portuguese Language of Malacca: A Delicate Ecology", Alan N. Baxter discusses the current state of the Kristang language, the "last vital variety" of the Portuguese-derived creole languages of East and Southeast Asia. Kristang is neither "sixteenth-century Portuguese", nor is it "broken Portuguese", but rather a distinct yet endangered language that is currently the object of revitalization and maintenance efforts. Baxter discusses several key aspects of this language's interrelationship with its environment, allowing us to view the trajectory of how it was maintained into the twentieth century, what has contributed to its attrition in recent decades, and what its future prospects may be.

Baxter discusses three main factors that account for the survival of Kristang from the early nineteenth century to the present: linguistic reinforcement through a dynamic association of religion, language, and a quasi-ethnic group; the development of a common socioeconomic base in the poorer core community until the late twentieth century; and population dynamics. Kristang is currently undergoing considerable "shrinkage" due to five main factors: (1) generational loss due to the lack of transmission of the language by older generations; (2) diminished fluency among native speakers; (3) greater social status being associated with the use of English and Malay (Bahasa Malaysia); (4) core domain loss, whereby younger generations prefer to use English in both friendship and work domains; and (5) intermarriage with other ethnic groups. A detailed linguistic analysis is then presented that documents how this shrinkage is occurring.

Ultimately, Baxter is optimistic about a revitalization, maintenance, and strengthening programme for Kristang and deems one to be feasible for several reasons. First, a reasonable number of speakers still exists. Second, the language has been extensively documented by professional linguists and members of the community — a prerequisite for any successful revitalization programme. Third, in recent years, the larger Kristang community has come to value its culture in new ways and is also more prosperous, allowing it to consider various options for revitalization. Fourth, the community now recognizes that the language is endangered. Baxter cautions, however, that a successful preservation programme "must be grounded in community-internal dynamics and initiative" while also acknowledging that "external aid and consultancy are very important factors in cultural preservation". Most importantly, however, all parties "must first and foremost be well informed", not simply well intentioned, and should not seek to impose external agendas on the process. Baxter recognizes that language itself is a very plastic artefact and that linguistic changes are natural occurrences. He concludes that, ultimately, "a creole community will do with its culture what it chooses to do. If it chooses to decreolize linguistically and culturally, or if it chooses to acquire some degree of bilingualism in the former colonial language, that is its own business."

In Chapter 6, "Oral Traditions of the Luso-Asian Communities: Local, Regional, and Continental", Hugo C. Cardoso marshals linguistic data that support the growing historical evidence pointing to closer ties among the various Portuguese-dominated territories in Asia than has traditionally been assumed. By analysing a repertoire of songs from the Indo-Portuguese communities of what was once known as the Província do Norte along India's northwest coast (comprising the urban centres of Bassein, Bombay, Chaul, Daman, and Diu), Cardoso exposes not only thematic links with other repertoires collected elsewhere, but linguistic heterogeneity as well, ranging from the "most basilectal creole to the most metropolitan Portuguese".

Of these locations, Diu was under Portuguese rule for the longest period of time (426 years), and today only about 180 speakers of its Indo-Portuguese creole remain. Daman, a Portuguese possession for 403 years, now has about 4,000 native creole speakers, the largest number of the Norteiro locales. Bombay and its surrounding communities were ceded to the British in 1661, and by the early twentieth century, the Portuguese-derived creole in that area had become extinct. The rest of the Província do Norte — including Bassein, Chaul, and Korlai — was annexed by Maratha forces in 1739–40, after which the Catholic population of Chaul relocated to nearby Korlai, which has remained homogenously Catholic and creolophone to the present, with some 760 speakers.

Cardoso identifies several key linguistic features of the Indo-Portuguese creoles that distinguish them from Portuguese, such as a strong preference for world-final stress and an absence of gender and number inflection in nouns, verbs, and adjectives. When these characteristics are set alongside the Norteiro song repertoire, however, its linguistic heterogeneity is revealed: there are songs that are irrefutably part of Diu's local repertoire, but their sociocultural provenance and linguistic profile are clearly not Diuese. Similarly, examples from Korlai reveal lyrics that more closely resemble Portuguese than Korlai Creole.

Once again, the plasticity of language is underscored as this corpus of Norteiro songs reveals that "the poetic material that circulated among the Luso-Asian communities was subject to creative manipulation, recombination, and adaptation to different realities": one place name has been substituted for another; themes have been recombined; and local references have been added in "novel and creative ways". Thus, whereas Cardoso's study documents how songs have been "nativized" in the various Norteiro communities, their linguistic make-up and thematic content also lend further credence to the view that this cultural legacy is the product of an appreciable level of interconnectedness and "a considerable flow of population" across the many Portuguese territories of Asia.

In Chapter 7, "Verb Markings in Makista: Continuity/Discontinuity and Accommodation", these population flows again find linguistic expression as Mário Pinharanda-Nunes examines the aspectual marker *ja* in Makista, the Portuguese Creole of Macao. He tests the hypothesis that Makista was formed gradually by adult speakers in a multilingual context that includes both Chinese and non-Chinese languages. Kristang, the Malacca Creole — itself a product of Portuguese, Malay and possibly Hokkien — served as Makista's substrate, or base language. Portuguese is Makista's superstrate (the language of the dominant group), while Cantonese is classified as its adstrate (a language of close and intense contact). Taken together, these several languages constitute a creole's "feature pool", similar in concept to a gene pool, from which variants can be dropped, selected or modified by speakers of an emerging language. Selected items in turn may then retain, narrow or widen their original functions.

Pinharanda-Nunes places his enquiry in a socio-historical context, noting key factors contributing to Makista's formation that differed from Kristang. For instance, in Malacca, there was greater contact with the large numbers of Chinese speakers resident there from well before the arrival of the Portuguese. By contrast, intense contact with the Chinese community in Macao did not take place until long after the Portuguese settlement was established. In addition, over the centuries, Macao received regular injections of significant numbers of speakers of standard Portuguese, to which greater social prestige and employment prospects were attached (especially from the nineteenth century onwards) than to the local creole.

The theoretical framework presented in this chapter looks at the "feature pool" phenomenon and the linguistic processes of transfer, levelling and congruency. A detailed analysis of the use of *ja* in Makista, with reference to the Portuguese adverb *já* and the Cantonese verbal markers *jó* and *gwó* then follows. Pinharanda-Nunes finds situations of both continuities and discontinuities in transfers from the feature pool into Makista and confirms his original hypothesis. Traits retained from Kristang indicate a "prolonged contact between Macao and Malacca" while the widening use of *ja* underscores the effect of close contact and exposure to standard Portuguese. At the same time, however, "possible correlations between the use of *ja* and some of the functions of the Cantonese markers *jó* and *gwó* also fit concepts of congruency and levelling in the whole process of transfer and use of linguistic elements", thereby affirming increasing contact with Cantonese speakers.

In Chapter 8, "From European-Asian Conflict to Cultural Heritage: Identification of Portuguese and Spanish Forts on Ternate and Tidore Islands", Manuel Lobato successfully identifies some of the architectural legacies of the Iberian presence in the Moluccas in present-day Indonesia, the so-called Spice Islands that were the coveted objects of both Portuguese and Spanish trading in Southeast Asia. Protecting that commerce required forts to be constructed at key sites, although many of these structures lacked "the magnitude of other military architecture erected elsewhere". Nevertheless, they were structures that communicated the presence of foreign power, both physically and symbolically. Yet, today, the local Muslim populace regards these forts as being "highly valuable … in terms of their contributions to collective memories, and also a vehicle to affirm their identity". Through a long and patient process of crossing field data with a vast but often only marginally informative body of literary and archival materials, and despite inaccurate local oral traditions, Lobato has positively identified several fortifications built by Iberians in Northern Maluku, particularly on the islands of Tidore and Ternate.

Of all the forts constructed by the Portuguese in the Malayan Archipelago during the sixteenth century, only three were directly ordered by the crown. The others were more modest structures built at the initiative of individual Portuguese crown representatives, merchants, ships' commanders, missionaries, *casados* (Portuguese married men) and/or mestizo leaders, often with support from local populations. Some ninety-six forts were built throughout the Moluccas — notably on the islands of Ternate, Tidore, Halmahera, Bacan, Seram and Ambon — by local rulers, Europeans and Japanese, of which more than twenty can be identified as Iberian archaeological sites. Portuguese forts were built between 1522 and 1603 and Spanish forts from 1606 to 1637.

Lobato's study takes us through a host of Iberian structures on the neighbouring small islands of Ternate and Tidore, concentrating on the Portuguese fortress of São João Baptista on Ternate, one of the three forts in the region ordered by the crown and thus the one for which greater information exists. But his work also includes the fort of Reis Magos on Tidore in addition to numerous Spanish structures that were variously fortresses, bulwarks and simple vaults. As the data permit, Lobato discusses their architectural design, site selection, building materials, renovations, destructions, takeovers and naming variations. Perhaps most importantly, his study "begins to answer some of the questions posed by the authorities and experts" who are involved in restoration projects on Ternate, which have "aroused some controversy". Like Baxter's entreaty to engage in revitalizations of language only with a firm grounding in solid empirical data, so, too, one would hope for a similar treatment of these architectural legacies as well.

This section concludes with Chapter 9, "The Influence of Portuguese Musical Culture in Southeast Asia in the Sixteenth and Seventeenth Centuries", in which Christian Storch reflects on the under-researched topic of cultural flows and counterflows through music between Portugal and its Asian outposts. Although the long-term impact of formal Portuguese musical tropes was minimal, music nevertheless was to be found "at the intersection of missionary work, urban entertainment and imperial representation".

From the onset of contact between Portugal and Asia, political and religious conquest was reinforced through music. Noisy trumpets, drums and other instruments, although less destructive than cannon, also served to demonstrate power and were employed by the likes of Vasco da Gama, Pedro Álvares Cabral and Afonso de Albuquerque as they established a Portuguese presence in Asia. Music was also used to entice: for instance, Cabral's party included a Franciscan organist whose performances were designed to impress potential trade partners.

Reconstructing this musical legacy, however, is no mean task, given a dearth of primary sources, as Storch discusses. No music manuscripts from the sixteenth or seventeenth centuries are to be found in Goa, Malacca, Macao or Timor, or in Portuguese or Jesuit archives. One known manuscript collection from this era was probably destroyed in the 1755 Lisbon earthquake, although a surviving index from 1649 provides some clues as to what may have been typical of Portuguese musical culture at the time of expansion into Southeast Asia. Similarly, a known treatise by the eccentric composer André de Escobar, who lived in India for several years in the mid-sixteenth century, is also lost, thus depriving us of greater knowledge of the possible counterflow of Indian musical or instrumental influences to Portugal.

The most intense systematic transmission of Portuguese musical cultural, however, would have taken place at the nexus of the Catholic missions and the local populations. Choral singing was introduced into Portuguese Asia as early as 1512, and as of 1514, Goa's Church of Santa Catarina was clearly designed to accommodate musical performance. Franciscans in Goa focused on teaching music to children — a strategy soon adopted by the Jesuits throughout Southeast Asia and in Brazil. Local and Western instruments were combined in the performance of sacred music in Goa, a practice that probably extended throughout Southeast Asia. Thus, in the medium of music, we have another example of how missioinaries sought to make their message more attractive by incorporating local cultural features into the proceeding, thereby blurring cultural lines (see chapters 1 and 2 for related discussions).

By the eighteenth century, Portuguese Asian possessions had lost favour to Brazil, and, concomitantly, the influx of new human capital from the home country dwindled significantly. As other Europeans joined the missionary ranks, the impact of any one nation's music was diluted. In other words, diminished connectedness between Portugal and its Asian territories appears to have translated into discontinuities in the performance of more formal Portuguese music, quite in contrast to the folksong continuities discussed by Jackson (Volume 1) and Cardoso (Volume 2) that are more the product of Portuguese Asia's informal structures.

Part Three, "Adversity and Accommodation", examines how certain Portuguese-derived communities interfaced with resident "others" in Asia, specifically, with the Chinese in Macao (Chapters 10 and 11), and with the Dutch in Malacca (Chapter 12). While the former setting was primarily characterized by accommodation from the outset, with occasional bouts of adversity, the latter context began with adversity that resolved into accommodation.

This section opens with the one chapter in this work that was not originally presented as a paper at the "Portuguese and Luso-Asian Legacies" conference. Rather, it is a contribution by Roderich Ptak that helps round out our understanding of Portugal's Asian presence at Macao, its easternmost anchor. The work was originally published as "Portugal und China: Anatomie einer Eintracht (16. und 17. Jh.)" by the Berlin Deutsches Historisches Museum in 2007 and appears here in English translation.

In Chapter 10, "Portugal and China: An Anatomy of Harmonious Coexistence (Sixteenth and Seventeenth Centuries)", Ptak probes the entity known as Macao, perched at the tip of a peninsula in the Pearl River Delta, where the Portuguese first took up residence in the mid-sixteenth century and remained in control until 1999. Although Fujianese merchants at Malacca probably showed the Portuguese the way to China, we do not know exactly how their foothold was secured. As a reward for dislodging pirates? The result of a bribe? Because the Chinese court needed valuables that the Portuguese could obtain? No known document exists to enlighten us.

Whatever the answer, though, the Portuguese presence at Macao was not the product of military conquest, and, wisely, Portugal never used it as a base from which to attempt greater territorial expansion. To say the least, the ensuing interface between the Portuguese and the Chinese is unusual, and Ptak's examination of its inner dynamic confirms that Macao was neither fish nor fowl: it was not exactly an "autonomous zone" under the Qing, nor a well-integrated diaspora-enclave within the Estado da Índia, nor a variant of a "foreign quarter" on Chinese soil.

Ptak's objective is to analyse the structural principles underlying the nature of the contact between the Chinese and the Portuguese — that is, "the conditions which were to shape certain modes of interaction over a long period of time". In essence, the Portuguese entered the differential equation that was the long-standing commercial rivalry between Fujian and Guangdong provinces as a third variable. On average, central Guangdong benefited more from the Portuguese presence.

Over time, the value of this essentially localized relationship came to be expressed in the classically Chinese concepts of "old privileges" and "good neighbours". Moderation, flexibility and mutual accommodation constituted the *modus vivendi* between "infinitesimal" Macao and the neighbouring Chinese provinces, all geographically distant from their respective centres of power in China and Portugal. "Just how the Chinese provincial officials managed to enforce their local issues ... far up north in Beijing ... we do not know, but that they did so is beyond debate" — as, apparently, the representatives of Portugal were also able to do relative to Lisbon and Goa. In short, maintaining "harmonious coexistence" at Macao routinely trumped the occasional extraneous bouts of adverse political chaff blowing in from abroad.

Here, then, was a structure that had no sharp edges and access to which was left open to every option and all parties. Perhaps this anatomical enquiry has rendered a sponge-like creature, defined by a system of pores and canals through which fluid substances may pass. As Ptak concludes, the "very vagueness" that characterized Macao, and the Portuguese "who truly knew how to contrast pleasantly with the rest of the European powers", made for an "extraordinary strength" in this politically plastic colonial setting.

While a "vagueness" governed regional relations between Macao and its neighbouring Chinese provinces, significant restrictions were placed on the degree of day-to-day interactions between the resident Chinese and the residents of the Portuguese settlement at Macao for an extensive period of time, thereby minimizing opportunities for cultural intercourse. In Chapter 11, " 'Aocheng' or 'Cidade do Nome de Deus': The Nomenclature of Portuguese and Castilian Buildings of Old Macao from the 'Reversed Gaze' of the Chinese", Vincent Ho pries some clues as to how the Chinese regarded the foreign culture in their midst from an examination of the names that the Chinese assigned to structures within the Portuguese walled settlement between the mid-sixteenth and the early nineteenth centuries. Local gazetteers, poems, notes, journals and reports of the Chinese officials and literati are the sources for these rare glimpses.

Ho's study focuses primarily, but not exclusively, on buildings related to the Catholic Church in Macao. The Chinese nomenclature for these structures demonstrates that the Cantonese, Hokkien/Fujianese or perhaps even Tanka names for them were derived in a variety of ways. For instance, St. Paul's Church, located at the main entrance in the wall that separated the Chinese and Portuguese settlements, was called Sanba Men, or Gate of Three Hopes, although "Sanba" ("three hopes" or "three wishes") has "no proper meaning in traditional Chinese usage", nor is it a typical expression or sentiment. Instead, it appears that "Sanba" is an aural cognate of "São Pau", the first two syllables of "São Paulo". Similarly, the three Cantonese versions of the Chinese name for St. Francis's Church — Qie Si Lan, Ge Si Lan and Jia Si Lan — are probably cognates for "Catalonia", the region in Spain that was the home of the first missionary to this church. Otherwise these names also "do not make any sense in Chinese".

Other church-related structures, however, carried names that either reflected their appearance (such as "Temple Covered by Board", or "Temple of Dragon's Whiskers", whose ruined roof was covered by palm fronds) or their function ("Food Supply Temple" in reference to the Holy House of Mercy, or "Clinic Temple", in the case of St. Raphael's Hospital). Still others are less easy to categorize, such as "Waiting Temple" for the cathedral, or "Windy Message Temple" for St. Lawrence's Church.

In general, the information imparted in Chinese records about these buildings is thin. As Ho points out, though, it is difficult to know whether this dearth is due to a lack of greater interest on the part of the Chinese or to restricted access. In either case, although we definitely have glimpses of what the Chinese "saw", a more sustained "gaze" awaits continued scholarly enquiry.

Finally, Chapter 12 takes us back to Malacca, the flashpoint in the history of the Portuguese in Asia that occasioned the "Portuguese and Luso-Asian Legacies" conference and this publication. Here, Dennis De Witt's explores the social interface between the Dutch and the Portuguese Eurasians of Malacca after 1641, which marked the opening of 160 years of Dutch colonial rule in the city. Whereas much of the literature on this subject highlights the adversity that undeniably existed at the outset between these two competing European groups — one Catholic and the other Protestant — De Witt presents documentary evidence of how social accommodation between them evolved over time, in part due to so-called "mixed marriages". While this phenomenon is neither surprising nor unknown, De Witt documents an unexpected twist to it that warrants further investigation. By consulting not only Catholic but also Protestant church registers, as well as Dutch archival material, he reveals cases of single marriages that were solemnized twice in Malacca: once in a Catholic church, once in a Dutch Reformed (Protestant) church.

Although the Dutch attempted to encourage the Malacca Portuguese to remain, given their vast knowledge of and connections into regional trading networks, many left (often at the behest of priests) and settled elsewhere in Portuguese Asia. During the rest of the seventeenth century, Dutch policy concerning the Catholics in Malacca vascillated from tolerance to persecution and often appears to have been primarily the outgrowth of prevailing relations between the Dutch authorities and the Catholic clergy. In secular matters, accommodation and cooperation found greater space in which to flourish: Dutch officials recognized that the Malacca Portuguese provided invaluable intermediary services relative to the local and neighbouring societies.

In the eighteenth century, the Dutch attitude towards the Malacca Catholics became consistently more liberal. Thus, most of De Witt's case studies of "mixed marriages" occurred between the late seventeenth and the late eighteenth centuries. Initially, these alliances were between Protestant Dutch males and Catholic Portuguese Eurasian females; however, as an influx of immigrants from the Netherlands resulted in more Dutch females in the community, this pattern dissipated and marriages between Portuguese Eurasian grooms and brides with Dutch-sounding names are also found in the documentary evidence.

De Witt's research demonstrates that consultation of a broader and more balanced range of sources can make significant contributions to our understanding of the evolving Eurasian social dynamic in Malacca. Why some marriages were celebrated in both Protestant and Catholic churches remains an open question, for instance. Malacca also presents cases of some "Portuguese" assimilating into "Dutch" culture and identities over succeeding generations (often moving first to Indonesia and later to the Netherlands), as well as "Dutch" becoming "Portuguese" and usually continuing to reside in Malacca. De Witt's genealogical gleanings therefore suggest that the social, cultural, religious, political and economic forces that underlay these choices remain fertile ground for additional systematic enquiry and research.

As our last chapter brings us full circle back to Malacca, we should conclude with some final thoughts about anniversary dates. One can certainly engage in all sorts of debates concerning the plethora of events and projects that have been undertaken over roughly the past two decades as the half-millennium watermarks associated with the inception of Portuguese seaborne exploration on a global scale have approached. Their recognition, though, has also spiked normal levels of support for and interest in scholarly research and writing on the multiple dimensions of what Portugal's actions first set in motion centuries ago. In the process, existing interpretations have been reconsidered and new ones put forward, dated rhetorics have been jettisoned and new lexicons compiled, and significant additions have been made to our store of empirical knowledge. In short, the academic world itself has been engaged in a degree of bottom-up "self-reorganization" of understanding how Portuguese and Luso-Asian legacies have evolved, and may continue to evolve. Might these legacies still remain in evidence five hundred years from now, or will they have become just a distant memory?

Note

1   The literature on complexity is vast, but a sampling of works may be presented here. See, for instance, M. Mitchell Waldrop, *Complexity: The Emerging Science at the Edge of Order and Chaos* (New York: Touchstone, 1993); Debra Hammond, *The Science of Synthesis: Exploring the Social Implications of General Systems Theory* (Boulder, CO: University Press of Colorado, 2003); Peter M. Allen, "The Complexity of Structure, Strategy, and Decision Making", in *Evolution and Economic Complexity*, edited by J. Stanley Metcalf and John Foster (Cheltenham, UK: Edward Elgar, 2004); Jürgen Jost, *Dynamical Systems: Examples of Complex Behavior* (Berlin: Springer, 2005); and Gros Claudius, *Complex and Adaptive Dynamical Systems: A Primer* (Berlin: Springer, 2008).

PART ONE

Crafting Identity in the Luso-Asian World

1

CATHOLIC COMMUNITIES AND THEIR FESTIVITIES UNDER THE PORTUGUESE PADROADO IN EARLY MODERN SOUTHEAST ASIA

Tara Alberts

The year 1618 was special for the Catholics of Cochinchina (now part of Vietnam). Portuguese Jesuits had established their mission in the country three years previously and this year another group had arrived to found a new church in the small, bustling trading town of Hội An. The Jesuits brought news of an Extraordinary Jubilee: this would grant Catholics who heard it and met its conditions a plenary indulgence for themselves or their departed loved ones. Local Catholics were joined by visitors from out of town, and the assembled audience of Portuguese, Japanese, Chinese and Vietnamese Christians congregated at the new Jesuit church to hear its publication. So many people came that despite the large size of the church, the congregation filled the building and spilled into the street.[1] Other religious festivals that year, Jesuit Francisco da Pina reported, were celebrated with noteworthy fervour. On each Friday of Lent, large numbers of Christians, especially those from the expanding Japanese quarter of the city, engaged in spiritual exercises, public and private penances, and other devotions, "stripping themselves and clothing themselves anew" — spiritually speaking — ready for Easter. This they celebrated together with "as much internal joy as external". Christmas was greeted with similar communal celebrations, with even some "pagan Japanese" neighbours joining in "with their dances and songs". The latter, we are told, were often inspired to convert to Catholicism in the process.[2]

We can find similar accounts of communal devotions and public Catholic festivities scattered throughout early modern missionary accounts from Southeast Asia. This chapter uses descriptions of such events as the starting point to explore Portuguese and Asian Catholic identities and communities in three cosmopolitan Southeast Asian cities in the late sixteenth and seventeenth centuries: Hội An (known as Faifo to Europeans), Malacca, and Ayutthaya in Siam (Thailand).[3] In each city there was a Portuguese settlement and a number of non-Portuguese Catholic communities. In each locale, these varied communities developed religious devotions that suited the rhythms of their lives and their cultural heritage.

In some cities, such as Portuguese Malacca, where Catholicism had been sown in the furrows of imperial conquest, public religious celebrations could be elaborate and lengthy, and often played an important role in establishing and articulating hierarchies of power and status within colonial society. From smaller parades organized by parish churches or confraternities, to ostentatious Corpus Christi processions winding through the city accompanied by a cacophony of music and fireworks, to special festivities celebrating the translation of a saint's relics or the dedication of new religious buildings, to penitential processions to plead for relief from pestilence or sieges, religious ritual, processions, music, dancing and theatre frequently took over the streets just as it did in Catholic Europe.[4]

Elsewhere — for example in Ayutthaya and Hội An — the public celebration of religious festivals could be tolerated or prohibited by non-Christian rulers who wished to favour foreigners for strategic or commercial reasons, or else wished to clamp down on the adherents of the foreign faith.

As well as serving as a declaration of shared Catholic faith, moments of communal celebration could also reveal the tensions, rivalries and uncertain alliances between different groups within Catholic communities. Issues of contested precedence, rivalry between secular and religious authorities and between the various religious orders, and the stratification of communities along social or racial lines can be glimpsed beneath the surface of asserted unity.

Yet church processions and other celebrations, organized under clerical supervision and oriented around the parish church and the sacraments, were not the only festivities that helped to create and express local identities. In each city we will also encounter several other events organized by members of the laity to counter a perceived threat to their community. In each case the threat came not from non-Christian neighbours or hostile local rulers, but rather from other Catholics, indeed members of the clergy. Responding to such threats could also bring communities together. With music, processions, theatrical use of ritual space, and communal engagement in certain sacraments, lay groups borrowed from the language of religious and civic ritual to exclude perceived interlopers and reassert communal identities.

I have set out to blur the lines between events that we would readily recognize as religious festivities — the Corpus Christi procession, solemn Lenten devotions — and other threatening and sometimes violent collective actions undertaken by the same communities. In this way I suggest a new approach to examining popular festivities in Portuguese Asia.

COMMUNAL DEVOTIONS, EVANGELISM, AND IDENTITY

Da Pina's report from Hội An is typical of seventeenth-century missionary descriptions of popular Catholic festivities in Asia. The nucleus of the festivals would be familiar to European Catholics: these distant communities of Christians were celebrating the same holy days with recognizable rituals of penance, prayer, singing and dancing. Celebrating the boon of the Extraordinary Jubilee, Christians of various nationalities in Hội An joined together to look towards Rome — a celebration which brought them into spiritual unity with their co-religionists in Europe who had participated in similar rituals to share the same papal favour in 1617.[5] Yet these familiar motifs of Catholic devotion are sewn onto an exotic background and embellished with flashes of local colour. From the atmospheric descriptions of the climate, scenery, flora, fauna and people in each region with which missionaries often began their accounts, to the descriptions of spontaneous, novel additions to familiar festivities — such as the Japanese dancers and musicians in Hội An — missionary accounts blended the familiar with the intriguingly different. Such captivating details of life in distant lands attracted a wide readership to the printed versions of these reports.

The jurisdictional structure of the Padroado Church, together with the rhetoric of its missionaries, which depicted the evangelization of Asia as a united project of the church militant, gives a sense of connectedness to the network of Portuguese and convert Catholic communities. They all expressed obedience to the pope, under the jurisdiction of the archbishop of Goa and the bishops of Malacca and Macao, and were served by the missionary orders under licence to the Portuguese crown. They shared a faith that missionary accounts depicted as burning with the same flame in different locations across Southeast Asia, as Catholics celebrated the same festivals.

By describing festivities — rallies, processions, and other extraordinary, communal devotions — which drew large crowds of Christians, missionaries were able to illustrate the success of their missionary strategies. The full church, with congregants spilling into the street, the relocated sermon, delivered in a public square from a hastily constructed pulpit to better accommodate the crowds that had turned up, the exhausted priest, forced to continue leading prayers through the night by a devout (and demanding) congregation: all these tropes served as shorthand to inform the reader of the large numbers of sincere conversions obtained, the piety of the flock, and of the esteem in which the priest and his religious order were held.

However, festivities could also delineate differences. Religious processions involved both the civil and ecclesiastical powers of the city. In Malacca, as in other Portuguese colonial cities, careful choreography was used to express the authority and position of each group, from the captain and his officials to the bishop and cathedral canons, to the heads of the religious orders, members of the main religious confraternities, and important citizens.[6] Key roles in religious processions could be granted to senior members of confraternities, or reserved for city officials or noblemen. Thus during the festivities for Lent in 1580, each Friday processions of up to one hundred penitents were watched by the majority of the inhabitants of the city. The penitents were kept in good order and the procession presided over by members of the Misericórdia, the city's elite confraternity, "with their black wands", which marked their status.[7]

Usually such roles were reserved for Portuguese Christians: Asian converts were frequently excluded. After the fall of Malacca to the Dutch in 1641, Jesuit missionaries Pero Mesquite and Manuel Henriques described organizing clandestine Easter celebrations for remaining Catholics, four leagues up the coast from Malacca city. In the ceremonies on Maundy Thursday, members of the Confraternity of the Rosary took the leading role, and two Portuguese men were chosen to assist Henriques in the rituals in the chapel. Pero Mesquite led the Good Friday processions, where the whole community, "as was the custom of Malacca" divided into men, women and children, and lined up "in order". Barefoot, they followed the priest in a silent march, carrying lit candles. Again, the account specifies that the important roles, such as carrying the crucifix, were given to Portuguese men.[8]

Furthermore, in both Malacca and Ayutthaya, Catholics of different nationalities were accommodated in separate districts, which could result in segregated worship. In Malacca, in the suburb of Upeh, the parish of São Tomé, comprised largely of the South Indians who resided in the ethnic quarter of Kampung Keiling while the parish of São Estevão, was established to oversee the Christian converts of Kampung China who were for the most part from Southern China. The people of the Malay fishing community who lived in the Sabak suburb were part of the parish of São Lourenço.[9] Parish priests, missionaries or confraternities could organize local festivities within each parish.

In Ayutthaya, Japanese, Chinese, Portuguese and Cochinchinese Christians inhabited the respective zones of the city granted to their nations by the kings of Siam. Catholic missionaries had first arrived in the capital in 1555, and by the mid-seventeenth century several religious orders had a permanent presence in the capital.[10] The churches of the Dominicans, Franciscans and Jesuits were all in or around the Portuguese quarter, and congregations could be mixed. But it seems that the Jesuits at least also held special services for Japanese and Cochinchinese Christians in their own languages, perhaps suggesting that groups would attend separate services.

In Hội An, as we have seen, there were also several distinct communities of Catholics. There were Japanese merchants and refugees, tended by Japanese-speaking Jesuits who had also been expelled from the country and who continued many of the pastoral and evangelical strategies developed on the Japanese missions.[11] Favourable trade conditions had also attracted Portuguese and Luso-Asians, some of whom were permanent residents in the town while others were more transient.[12] There were Christians among the Chinese merchants of the city and a rapidly expanding number of Vietnamese converts.

While these groups retained their own identities and some separate festivities, in Cochinchina we see the problems that could arise when "Catholic" became conflated with "Portuguese". As several historians have demonstrated, the offspring of Portuguese men born of Southeast Asian, South Asian, and African women, could assert a Portuguese identity through markers of language, dress, social custom and, perhaps most importantly, religious expression.[13] When Malacca fell to the Dutch in 1641 the majority of the Portuguese of the city fled to Makassar and later Ayutthaya. For these refugees, and for many of the Portuguese who remained in Dutch Malacca, religious festivities were crucial means by which their identity could be preserved. Leonard Andaya has suggested that outsiders sharing in these activities could also attempt to "become" Portuguese, where this conferred some advantage.[14] Yet equivalency between the identities of "Portuguese" and "Catholic" could also be asserted by opponents of evangelization. In Cochinchina, Catholicism was widely known as "the Portuguese Law" (*đạo hoà lan*) but Vietnamese suspicion of the Portuguese could mean that this term was disparaging to the faith.[15] Jesuit Christoforo Borri warned that villagers in Cochinchina had been observed performing a skit in which foolish Vietnamese were "taken into the belly of a Portuguese" through conversion, like some monstrous rebirth.[16]

Yet far from adopting a "Portuguese" identity, it is clear from missionary reports that through their public religious festivities, Cochinchinese converts were involved in recreating Catholic devotions suited to their own needs. Keith Taylor has written on the Viet push south into Cochinchina, undertaken as the Nguyễn lords struggled to establish their independence from the northern Viet polity of Tonkin. He describes the move south as a moment in which "options for being another kind of 'good Vietnamese' could be explored.... This was, in effect, an escape from ancestors, an escape from the past."[17] For a while in the seventeenth century it seemed that this reinvention of identity might include for some communities the creation of a new, Christian religion. These Vietnamese Christians took the initiative to create new public ceremonies of devotion.

In the annual letter for 1628, for example, Jesuit Gaspar Luis reports on the work of Christian Mandarin Paulo Xabim. Real ingenuity was required when it came to the festival season in which mandarins and officials would "spend [in the temples] several entire days and nights in songs, music, and drinking toasts" in honour of the divinities, figures in the nation's past, and the present king.[18] Paulo is presented as the main impetus for the creation of a Christian version of these festivities. His first intention was to centre his new ceremonies on the Eucharist, and so appealed to the Jesuits to say Mass as a part of the ritual. However, as the Jesuits could not say Mass, "due to the serious inconveniences of the place and day on which the festivities were held", he took matters into his own hands. First he erected an altar, "well adorned with ornaments, lights and perfumes in honour of an image of the Virgin, who had her blessed child in her arms".[19] To match the spectacle of the non-Christian festivities, he arranged for more than sixty singers to assemble and perform. He stood before the assembled crowd and explained the significance of the image on the altar, before dropping to his knees to pray. "When this was over", the account continues, he began

> his solemn prostrations, which conformed to the fashion of the Mandarins and were no less splendid than long drawn out. After this, Paulo had all present do the same, adoring the Lord of Heaven, and asking for his favour. Soon music and songs followed, the words being only what Paulo had chosen, their meter interspersing the verses with the repeating sentence, "Thanks to the Lord of Heaven and Earth."[20]

The devotions were an evangelical opportunity, as many curious individuals had come to watch. The ceremony was judged a success: "The festivities ended to great acclaim, and with honour to our holy Law, which was his primary purpose."[21]

However, Cochinchinese authorities were increasingly suspicious of the reluctance of Christian converts to take part in other, non-Christian public ceremonies. Public displays of Catholic devotion by local converts worried some authorities and public declarations of faith seemed to be provocative and dangerous. In 1644 a Cochinchinese Catholic catechist, André, and several other converts were executed for publicly preaching to their countrymen.[22] While the rulers of Cochinchina claimed no authority over the spiritual lives of their subjects, Catholicism, with its new ceremonies and rejection of some forms of traditional public worship, seemed seditious and threatening. The following year all Catholic missionaries were expelled from the country and foreign Christians were limited to private worship in their homes. Dozens of Christians also died in subsequent, sporadic persecutions throughout the seventeenth century.[23]

AMBIGUITY AND DANGER IN RELIGIOUS FESTIVITIES

It was not only non-Catholic rulers who viewed certain religious festivities with some ambivalence. On the one hand, the mass of humanity that attended public events could in itself be a triumphant assertion of a shared and proud identity, in the face of a common enemy. When a jubilee year was declared in Rome in 1600, as was the case during the Extraordinary Jubilee at Hội An, large numbers of Christians participated. Observers in Rome marvelled at the assembled masses: on Christmas Eve the crowds reportedly swelled to two million people and the roads into Rome were flooded with pilgrims. Miracles and conversions reported along the route were offered as proof that the Catholic Church was triumphant against the deprecations of the Protestant reformers: the wider Catholic community stood as one, favoured by God.[24] Similarly, in Malacca, the triumphal processions organized to celebrate the defeat of the Acehnese in 1569 asserted the victory of the Christian community over their Muslim foes.[25]

On the other hand, communal festivities could be ambiguous. The masses could be threatening: commentators described pilgrims in Rome being crushed to death by the crowds and warned that food stocks might be decimated by the influx of visitors.[26] Where crowds gathered, there could be tension and disorder.[27] Even when events did not degenerate into violence, there was potential for things to get out of hand: how far were the clergy in control of these religious devotions? Lance Lazar describes the celebrations organized for Jubilee years as "by nature the mirror image of a mission": rather than missionaries venturing into the provinces, members of the laity did the travelling, pouring into Rome for a week or two of devotional activity.[28]

The pilgrim, rather than the priest, was the active agent who controlled his or her own spiritual experience and without sacerdotal oversight, there was a potential for error to creep in.

While processions, celebrations by confraternities, pilgrimages and public celebrations of local saints could all have spiritual, educative and pastoral benefits, they could also cause disquiet among reformers.[29] There was a need to ensure that festivities were orthodox: to strip out heresy, superstition and profane behaviour, which were all the more visible in these public celebrations. In Portugal, reforming clergy sometimes resorted to relocating relics of popular local saints or attempting to ban certain feast day celebrations when it was considered that these had degenerated into irreligion. Resistance from lay men and women could be fierce and often such reforming efforts were ineffective. In Braga, for example, the initiatives of cleric Baltasar Limpo in the sixteenth century to reform votive celebrations at a local shrine clearly failed: his eighteenth-century successors documented their struggles to reform the same festivities.[30]

Repeated attempts were made in many European countries to ban certain dances or songs from religious celebrations in an attempt to separate the sacred and profane.[31] In Spain, Portugal, and their empires, churchmen debated the propriety of the participation of certain groups in church processions. Dancing and music by African slaves, for example, could be particularly controversial.[32]

Missionary descriptions of mass religious festivities reflect the common concern of Catholic reformers to oversee, regulate and contain such popular expressions of devotion. Yet missionaries' own use of processions and other public festivities as an evangelical tool could also be criticized. The use of public spectacle was an important part of evangelistic methodology in Asia, especially for the Jesuits who had perfected their *mos indicus* (Indian fashion) evangelism — centred on public preaching and processions — in Goa.[33] In Malacca processions of slaves and children were led throughout the city by Jesuit missionaries, ringing bells, striking cymbals and singing catechistical songs to encourage people to come to church. Onlookers were also encouraged to join dramatic night-time processions, during which prayers for souls in purgatory were intoned and acts of penitence — including weeping, self-flagellation and walking barefoot — were carried out.[34] Yet Jesuits in France had been condemned by more austere Catholics for their reliance on processions and other "exterior" signs and instruments of piety, which allegedly encouraged the laity to "play" with religion without effecting internal change, and which could devolve into profanity.[35]

Reformers had a hard time in trying to enforce the line between "orthodox" and superstitious practices in processions and public religious ceremonies in Portuguese Asia. According to Italian Theatine P. Lubelli, for example, public recourse to saints or the Virgin by Catholics in the Portuguese Indies was often highly impious. Rather than honouring the holy, lay Catholics had developed ceremonies that aimed at forcing the saints to intercede. "When they wish for a favour from God through the intercession of some saint, the most Holy Virgin, Saint Anthony, or some other, they give the effigy of that saint a thousand rough handlings and sacrilegious treatments", alleged Lubelli. "For example they bite it indecently on the nose, the face, the ears, the hands etc., and bind it with many chains, hang it outside a window in the sun and the rain, tie it with a rope and throw it in a well or a cistern, and similar things, and they say they do this to oblige that saint to intercede for them to gain that favour."[36] Such traditions were often frustratingly resistant to reform.

Missionaries often found themselves having to defend the public religious celebrations which they had permitted their flock. Italian Jesuit Alessandro Valignano argued for the utility of elaborate processions in Portuguese Asia, despite the expense and disruption that they entailed.[37] He reasoned that Portuguese practices could not be judged by Italian standards: in the Portuguese world, masks, *villanos* (rustic music and dances), and other creative inventions that would seem foreign and strange in Italy were integral to public religious celebrations. Indeed, "the more solemn, the more they are accompanied by dances and jigs of youths and children, and by *folías* [a Portuguese dance performed by a large number of people], and by giant effigies (*gigantes*) and other monstrous representations, and even *villanos* and *diabletes* [dances from Madeira in which performers were clothed and masked as demons]."[38] Great numbers of people were drawn to these events, which confirmed Christian converts in their faith, and impressed pagans and Muslims, many of whom were moved to find out more about the faith.[39] He urged the Father General to allow the Jesuits to continue participating in and organizing such events, not least because were they to pull out, other religious orders would step into the breach, and they "do all this with more disruption and waste, and they organise inferior events".[40]

Such reports were written in response to the criticisms of many visitors to colonial cities such as Goa and Malacca, who often professed shock at the continued "indecency" of religious celebrations. In Europe some condemned Jesuit use of "pagan" imagery — such as *tableaux vivants* representing the gods and virtues of the classical world — in their processions.[41] Similarly, in Asia, some observers accused ecclesiasts of the Padroado of too readily absorbing non-Christian elements into public religious festivities. Italian Discalced Carmelite Agnello dell'Immacolata Concettione reported how "profane" dancing at festivals was the custom "in cities subjected to the Portuguese, and elsewhere in the Indies". He alleged that "free Catholics are permitted to exercise the functions of ecclesiastics in the most solemn processions, even in those in which the Divine Sacrament is carried" and that processions include "profane dances by persons who are masked, and what is of even greater scandal, even pagan dances of the idolaters, used in the festivities of their Pagodas".[42] The state of affairs, he argued, was "truly indecent" as non-Christians learnt nothing about the faith, heretics made fun of the processions, and "idolaters" were simply confirmed in their beliefs and led to scorn Christianity.[43]

Other reformers urged a more perfect separation of the Catholic from the non-Catholic in colonial cities during public festivities. Some argued, for example, that the holy sacrament of the Eucharist needed particular protection during public festivals. In the 1680s, the Papal Congregation of Propaganda Fide — established in 1622 to provide a centralized oversight to all overseas missions — recommended that processions in which the Host was carried should be undertaken cautiously in Portuguese Asia where there were many non-Catholics, lest it be treated irreverently.[44] There was nothing new about such concerns: anxieties over the vulnerability of the sacred to the crowd, and over the potential for holy objects to be ridiculed, attacked or defiled in public surrounded many processions in medieval and early modern Europe.[45]

Irreverence, humour, violence, fun, frivolity and popular invention could be found in the most solemn religious procession. While some missionaries and religious reformers worried that the profane and the sacred had become increasingly confused in public festivities, lay men and women borrowed from both spheres when they engaged in public festivities and displays of identity.[46] On occasion these communal public acts, drawing on traditions of procession and civic ceremony, carnival, and charivari, and reflecting local contexts, could be turned against perceived threats to a community, even priests themselves.

COMMUNAL CEREMONIES AND PROTESTS AGAINST PRIESTS

Several missionaries in Asia complained that they had fallen foul of Portuguese communities that made their displeasure known in a manner which bore echoes or direct quotations from religious festivities. Italian Franciscan Giovanni

Battista Lucarelli di Pisauro came from the Spanish province of San Gregorio Magno in the Philippines and established a Franciscan convent in Malacca in 1581. Although his first public appearance — a sermon in the cathedral — went well, that night groups of men expressed their contempt for this Italian interloper from Spanish lands. They congregated near his residence: parading around, they sang songs that insulted him and questioned his origins. Eventually these night-time musical insults became too much to bear and he moved outside the city to a hill which was "uninhabited for fear of elephants and thieves".[47] Reminiscent of Italian *cantilene* — insulting songs sung almost in a parody of a lover's serenade — the night-time parades also seemed like inversions of the festivities which greeted illustrious and welcome prelates.[48] Rather than a joyous entry, the Portuguese of Malacca had given Lucarelli an ignominious ejection from their community.

On other occasions, the links between religious celebrations and attacks on unwanted missionaries were explicit. In 1663 Italian Theatine Lubelli found it necessary to request that the pope place a "rigorous malediction and excommunication" on those in the Portuguese Indies who spread lies about missionaries and harmed their interests, "in print or writing, and even more through processions, sung masses and sermons, which are often used to authenticate similar falsehoods".[49] Such complaints and criticisms provide useful backdrop to examine in more detail the reaction of Catholic communities in Ayutthaya to the arrival of new French missionaries from 1662.

By the mid-seventeenth century, Rome was determined to assert some control over Catholic missions in Asia, which had hitherto fallen under the Portuguese Padroado. Numerous commentators made trenchant criticisms of Portuguese laxity and lack of evangelic enthusiasm, and argued that centralized oversight over the missions of the East was long overdue. Furthermore, the large numbers of conversions in the Vietnamese polities of Tonkin and Cochinchina, widely publicized in Europe in the 1650s by Jesuit Alexandre de Rhodes, had caused a dilemma.[50] There were not enough priests to minister to these expanding flocks, yet the ecclesiasts of the Padroado Church were reluctant to sanction the ordination of local Christians. In 1658 the Roman Congregation of Propaganda Fide ordained three Frenchmen as bishops and gave them extensive powers as vicars apostolic over mission fields in Southeast Asia and China. A new French religious society, the Société des Missions Étrangères, was set up to send missionaries, directly answerable to the Propaganda, to the East. The first of these missionaries, headed by Bishop Pierre Lambert de la Motte, vicar apostolic of Cochinchina, arrived in Ayutthaya in 1662 and were joined in

1664 by a second group, headed by Bishop François Pallu, vicar apostolic of Tonkin, Laos and southwest China.[51]

At first, these eight newcomers were well received by the Catholic communities of Ayutthaya and this initial *entente cordiale* was represented in public ceremonial. In 1664, the French priests organized an Easter procession and the Jesuits and the Christians of Ayutthaya joined in, bringing musicians to accompany the pageant.[52] King Naraï of Siam (ruled 1656–88) also demonstrated his favour towards the French priests by incorporating them in public ceremony. In 1673 he involved them in the ceremony of Kathin Nam, in which the monarch led a water-borne procession down the canals of Ayutthaya to make a symbolic gift of robes to the Buddhist monks of the kingdom. Naraï stopped his barges in front of the French residence and extended his beneficence to the priests, granting them a tract of land and promising to build them a church.[53]

However, cordial relations between the French and the Portuguese community were short-lived. Lambert de la Motte won no friends with his barbed denunciations of the lifestyles, morals and religious spirit of the Portuguese laity, nor with his public condemnations of the Padroado clergy. Furthermore, as the extent of the powers and jurisdiction claimed by the vicars apostolic gradually became clear, Padroado and Inquisition authorities in Goa condemned them as usurpers of and rebels against the Portuguese crown's Padroado privileges and rights.

This breakdown in relations was marked throughout by public displays. First, Jesuit João Cardoso marched at the head of a delegation of "the principal men of the Portuguese camp" to Lambert de la Motte's house. As *vigário* (vicar) of the vacant bishopric of Malacca, he was head of the exiled Malaccan church, invested with authority from the king of Portugal and the archbishopric of Goa. Cardoso commanded Lambert de la Motte to "show him in writing his powers and from whom he held them".[54] Describing this encounter between representatives of two conflicted jurisdictions, French missionary Bénigne Vachet wryly noted that there could be little hope of Portuguese concessions: "To talk to a Portuguese about the power and authority of his king, is to swell his heart so much that, to defend it, there is no excess to which he will not abandon himself."[55]

The French priests had been instructed by the Propaganda not to reveal initially the letters and privileges which granted the vicars apostolic authority over previously "Portuguese" mission lands. So Cardoso and his party were sent away frustrated. Yet this concealment merely increased suspicions among the Portuguese community against the new missionaries. The French started to fear for their safety: even the head of the Dutch factory invited them to stay in his own house to protect them from the Portuguese. They declined the offer, feeling that "retiring to stay with the heretics, they would have given the Portuguese new subjects for complaints and indignation".[56]

Although tensions between the Portuguese Catholics and the newcomers were rising, the Christians in the Cochinchinese quarter accepted the French missionaries. Learning that Lambert de la Motte was eventually bound for mission in Cochinchina, the Cochinchinese community sent a party to bring the French missionaries out of the Portuguese settlement, to live in their quarter. This was a very public declaration of support for the French, against the condemnations of the Portuguese ecclesiastical hierarchy that hitherto had ministered to this community. Vachet described a delegation of Cochinchinese, "coming in broad daylight to take away [Lambert de la Motte], his companions, their servants and their effects, and they took them into their camp where they built them a house and a chapel on the riverbank".[57]

The Portuguese were furious "to have seen prey which they thought guaranteed, removed before their eyes" and "displayed an inconceivable rage".[58] One of them, "an unthinking and reckless young man, wishing to distinguish himself from the others", gathered together some friends and set off in a boat to the bank beneath the French priests' new residence.[59] Beneath their windows, in an echo of Lucarelli's tormentors in Malacca, he subjected the priests to a midnight serenade. "Strumming his guitar, he started to sing in his language that he wanted to kill a bishop"; one of the priests, François Deydier, "felt his bile rise a little, and got ready to go out and stop him" and had to be restrained by Lambert.[60]

A short time after this, another, more elaborate water-borne procession to the French residence was organized by "another swaggerer, calling himself a relative of the King of Portugal".[61] Reading between the lines of Vachet's disdainful description, we can identify elements common to both religious and civic processions in Portuguese cities. Taking place on Sunday, timed to arrive at the French residence as Vespers was concluded, the procession made a clear assertion of Portuguese spiritual jurisdiction over Ayutthaya: the climax of the procession would see the representative of the Portuguese crown brusquely summon the bishop into his presence in front of the assembled crowd. Portuguese royal authority was thus also upheld: this was a joyous (re-)entry, echoing the processions of kings and their representatives into major cities, in which the civic and religious order was asserted. The leader of the procession "had himself accompanied by a great cortege of servants and slaves. His boat was magnificently adorned: two trumpets at the prow incessantly sounded fanfares, a number of taffeta banners of all colours fluttered all around in the wind [and] he had a royal pavilion."[62] Vachet was not blind to this imagery. "One would have said", he remarked, "that it was another Jean de Paris who was going to do some pompous entry".[63] Jean de Paris, or Jean Perréal, was a famous painter and sculptor who designed several royal entries and other major public ceremonials in Renaissance France.[64]

Yet the pageantry did not have entirely the desired effect and was soon answered by conflicting displays by the Cochinchinese community. The head of the Cochinchinese came to meet the Portuguese delegation with a group of ten or twelve men, "dressed as men of war going to combat" and entered with their swords drawn.[65] Rough-handling and cursing the Portuguese out of the French residence, they ignored the pleas of the bishop for restraint and delivered the delegation back to their boat, sending them on their way with kicks and punches. This tumultuous and degrading end to their procession infuriated the Portuguese who attempted to rally the Dutch to the defence of their honour.[66]

But the Cochinchinese were not finished. The next morning, taking to the water in two boats, the Cochinchinese rowed at speed to the Portuguese camp and paraded up and down the river, swords raised, drums beating out a challenge. Vachet asserts that the Portuguese were so intimidated by this display that they abandoned their homes and sought refuge together in the churches. Their bellicose taunts unmet, the Cochinchinese eventually returned to their quarter. By this account at least, the Portuguese were comprehensively trounced in the war of public representations.[67]

Elsewhere, however, priests of the Missions Étrangères found that public festivities and ceremonies were used to damaging effect by partisans of Padroado missionaries to oppose the new dispensation.

In the Viet polities of Cochinchina and Tonkin, some converts opposed the new French missionaries for what they saw as the unjust treatment of their former Jesuit pastors, and others were displeased by the reforms and changes made to ceremonies and devotions which had developed over the previous centuries. As Nola Cooke has demonstrated, with their austere spirituality, the French priests suffered something of a culture shock when they encountered the divine services of Portuguese Asia.[68] One shocked missionary noted,

> all of these Portuguese of the Indies are accustomed to comedies and mummeries that make up almost all their religious exercises .... the musicians are black mestizos who howl in a manner fit to terrify and put to flight all men of good sense, but which charms those like themselves and often excites them to dance throughout the Blessed Sacrifice which is still made part of their solemnities.[69]

They were also highly critical of the Jesuits for allowing Christians in Tonkin and Cochinchina to continue to participate in ceremonies that honoured their dead ancestors. Like critics of Jesuit strategies of accommodation in China and India, many priests of the Missions Étrangères objected to converts engaging in what seemed to be "pagan" rites.[70] In Hội An and Đà Nẵng, French priest Louis Chervreuil found such ceremonies, and other adaptations permitted by the Jesuits, to be superstitious.[71] His attempts at reform, however, were cut short due to his expulsion from the kingdom, an indignity he blamed on Jesuit machinations.[72]

During the protracted disputes between the Jesuits and the Missions Étrangères priests in Tonkin and Cochinchina, Catholic communities weighed into the controversies with their own public displays. From Tonkin Jacques de Bourges and François Deydier had written to the Propaganda Fide complaining that the Jesuits had encouraged Christians to perform plays ("comédies") in their churches.[73] The French priests disapproved of such practices in general, but in Tonkin and Cochinchina they had extra cause for complaint. In 1683, as a part of the Christmas festivities organized by one community in Tonkin included a "comédie" written by convert Antoine Nho, which lampooned the French missionaries as "wicked scoundrels". The piece was well received and many of the congregation were heard "roundly cursing the Vicars Apostolic, and everyone in general exhorts each other to flee from them".[74] As one of the priests lampooned by the piece glumly noted, it soon became popular in neighbouring villages, and was taken up as a part of their communal festivities, reinforcing the pro-Jesuit sentiment each time it was performed.[75]

Similar complaints were made by French missionaries in Cochinchina who deplored the plays, feasts, musical displays and lay preaching which drew communities together in opposition to the new priests. These Christian plays and parties in the 1680s became so disruptive and insulting towards local sensibilities that they directly contributed to the ruler of Cochinchina's edict of February 1690 which banned rowdy social ills, including gambling, cock fighting and Christianity.[76]

CONCLUSION

The idea that there were separate spheres of "elite" and "popular" religious culture in early modern Christianity has been widely challenged.[77] Yet in some of the scholarly literature addressing festivals and communal activities, while the line between "demotic" and "official" has been blurred by many studies of religious ritual, violence and carnival, it seems that some threshold between these two spheres still lingers. In particular, religious processions organized by the clergy are distinguished from other festivities such as carnival or charivari. In his classic work on crowds, George Rudé had excluded entirely religious festivities from his analysis, judging their participants to be more stable and homogenous.[78] In more recent literature, "congregations" still seem either to exist in a different category from "crowds" or "mobs", or else it seems that they need to undergo some drastic change to allow them to transform from one to another. The "carnivalesque", the "popular", the "demotic" types of festivity, on the other hand, are seen as events which may *easily* erupt into disorder and violence: these are events which are potentially more dangerous and threatening, events in which "ritual" has broken down or taken on new meaning.[79] In Jean-Jacques Wunenburger's analysis, for example, upon becoming part of "the crowd", individuals are enthralled, transported and possessed by the savage, "dionysic experience" of the communal event.[80] This can be distinguished from the experience of participating in a religious gathering which lacks a carnivalesque dimension and so remains inherently more stable.

In many ways, this distinction reflects the language of much of the source material. As historian John Walter wrote of early modern England, "authority was always the first historian of popular protest".[81] Descriptions of the activities of crowds always reach us through the "distorting pens" of contemporary commentators, who had their own, often negative interpretation of events.[82] They decide upon the label for participants — congregation or mob — and offer their own interpretation of the nature of the public event in which they were engaged. In this analysis, the line between "ritual" and "riot" seems clear. Communal activities seem to sit on a clearly defined spectrum, from "officially" organized ceremonies and processions at one end, through more ambiguous festivities like carnival and charivari, to popular upheaval and rebellion at the other.[83]

Yet historians examining events of mass participation in early modern Europe have noted shared themes and commonalities between events which on the surface may seem very different: religious processions, civic ceremonies such as "joyous entries", festivities such as charivari and carnival, and acts of protest, communal violence and rebellion.[84] Furthermore, as historians and other theorists have problematized the modern category of "ritual", it has become harder to assert that early modern participants in these varied events would have drawn hard and fast distinctions between them, despite the wishes of contemporary reformers.[85] Exploring Catholic communities and their festivities in Southeast Asia, this chapter has extended this analysis beyond Europe. By examining the wide range of activities which communities used to create or perform identities, to express or construct social hierarchies, or to obtain divine favour, we can sidestep the over-simple dichotomy between "orderly" and "disruptive" communal festivities, between the ceremonial and the chaotic. We can also see how these categories could overlap, and how the boundaries of orthodoxy could be contested. Most importantly we can shift the focus of analysis from ecclesiastical hierarchy and civic authorities to also take in ordinary men and women who organized and participated in these events. We can examine their role in shaping devotional practices and identities and gain greater insight into the processes that shaped Catholicism and its public expression, as it developed into a global religion.

Notes

1.   "Annua do Collegio de Macao", 1619, Jesuítas na Ásia (hereafter cited as JA), 49–V–7, fol. 168v, Biblioteca da Ajuda, Lisbon (hereafter cited as BA).
2.   Ibid., fols. 168v–69.
3.   *Cf.* Liam Brockey, *Journey to the East: The Jesuit Mission to China, 1579–1724* (Cambridge, MA: Belnapp Press, 2007), pp. 1–2.
4.   See, for example, Francisco Peres to his confreres, Malacca, 2 January 1550, and Peres to his confreres, Malacca, 24 November 1551, in *Documentação para a História das Missões do Padroado Português do Oriente: Insulíndia*, vol. 2, *1550–1562*, edited by Artur Basílio de Sá (Lisbon: Agência Geral do Ultramar, Divisão de Publicações e Biblioteca, 1955), pp. 8 and 61–67. See also Paulo Drumond Braga, "A vida quotidiana", in *História dos Portugueses no Extremo Oriente*, vol. 1, tomo 1, *Em torno de Macau*, edited by A.H. de Oliveira Marques (Lisbon: Fundação Oriente, 1998), pp. 538–39; and R. Cardon, "Portuguese Malacca", *Journal of the Malay Branch of the Royal Asiatic Society* 12, no. 2 (1934): 9. *Cf.*, for example, Edward Muir, *Ritual in Early Modern Europe*, 2nd ed. (Cambridge: Cambridge University Press, 2005); and Miri Rubin, *Corpus Christi: The Eucharist in Late Medieval Culture* (Cambridge: Cambridge University Press, 1991).
5.   Henry Charles Lea, *A History of Auricular Confession and Indulgences in the Latin Church*, pt. 1 (1896; repr., Whitefish, MT: Kessinger Publishing, 2004), p. 233.
6.   Catarina Madeira Santos, *Goa É a Chave de Toda a Índia: Perfil Político da Capital do Estado da Índia (1505–1570)* (Lisbon: Comissão Nacional para as Comemorações dos Descobrimentos Portugueses, 1999), p. 271.
7.   Gomez Vaz to Jesuit Superior General, annual letter from Malacca, 3 December 1580, in *Documenta Indica*, vol. 12, *1580–1583*, edited by Joseph Wicki and John Gomes (Rome: Institutum Historicum Societatis Iesu, 1972), p. 155.
8.   "Anno de 1651[.] [A]o P.e Francisco de Tavora da Comp.ª de JESUS assistente em Roma das Provincias de Portugal e da India. Relação da Nova Missão q' fizerão os PP Pero de Mesquita e M.el Henriques mandados do Coll.º de Macao a Cid.e e fortaleza de Malaca em 1651", 1650s, JA 49–IV–52, fols. 15–15v, BA.

See also Liam Brockey, "Introduction: Nodes of Empire", in *Portuguese Colonial Cities in the Early Modern World* (Aldershot: Ashgate, 2008), pp. 1–14.

9 Kernial Singh Sandhu and Paul Wheatley, "From Capital to Municipality", in *Melaka: The Transformation of a Malay Capital c. 1400–1980* (Kuala Lumpur: Oxford University Press, 1983), 2:532–33.

10 Alain Forest, *Les Missionaries Français au Tonkin et au Siam XVIIe–XVIIIe Siècles: Analyse Comparée d'un Relatif Succès et d'un Total Échec* (Paris: L'Harmattan, 1998), 3:167.

11 Giovanni Fillippo de Marini, *Historia et Relatione del Tunchino e del Giappone: Con la Vera Relatione Ancora d'Altri Regni, e Prouincie di Quelle Regioni, e del loro Gouerno Politico; Con le Missioni Fatteui dalli Padri della Compagnia di Giesù, & Introduttione della Fede Christiana, & Confutatione di Diuersi Sette d'Idolatri di Quelli Habitatori; Divisa in Cinqve Libri, Opera del P. Gio: Filippo de Marini della medema Compagni; Alla Santitá di N.S. Alessandro Papa Settimo* (Rome: Vitale Mascardi, 1665), p. 10.

12 Pierre-Yves Manguin, *Les Portugais sur les Côtes du Viêt-Nam et du Campā: Étude sur les Routes Maritimes et les Relations Commerciales, d'après les Sources Portugaises (XVIe, XVIIe, XVIIIe Siècles)* (Paris: École Français d'Extrême-Oriente, 1972), p. 190; and Lê Thành Khôi, *Histoire du Viêt Nam des Origines à 1858* (Paris: Sudestasie, 1981), pp. 279–82.

13 See especially Leonard Y. Andaya, "The Portuguese Tribe in the Malay-Indonesian Archipelago in the Seventeenth and Eighteenth Centuries", in *Proceedings of the International Colloquium on the Portuguese and the Pacific*, edited by Francis A. Dutra and João Camilo dos Santos (Santa Barbara: Center for Portuguese Studies, 1995), pp. 130–48; and Stefan Halikowski Smith, "No Obvious Home: The Flight of the Portuguese 'Tribe' from Makassar to Ayutthaya and Cambodia during the 1660s", *International Journal of Asian Studies* 7 (Jan. 2010): 1–28. See also Kenneth McPherson, "Staying On: Reflections on the Survival of Portuguese Enterprise in the Bay of Bengal and Southeast Asia from the Seventeenth to the Eighteenth Centuries", in *Iberians in the Singapore-Melaka Area (16th to 18th Century)*, edited by Peter Borschberg (Wiesbaden: Harrassowitz; and Lisbon: Fundação Oriente, 2004), pp. 63–91.

14 Andaya, "The Portuguese Tribe", p. 136.

15 Peter C. Phan, *Mission and Catechesis: Alexandre de Rhodes and Inculturation in Seventeenth-Century Vietnam* (New York: Orbis Books, 1998), pp. 70–71; and Nola Cooke, "Strange Brew: Global, Regional and Local Factors behind the 1690 Prohibition of Christian Practice in Nguyễn Cochinchina", *Journal of Southeast Asian Studies* 39, no. 3 (Oct. 2008): 399.

16 Cristoforo Borri, *Relation de la Nouvelle Mission des Pères de la Compagnie de Jésus, au Royaume de la Cochinchine* (Lille: Pierre de Rache, 1631), p. 102. See also Phan, *Mission and Catechesis*, p. xv.

17 Keith Taylor, "Nguyen Hoang and the Beginning of Vietnam's Southward Expansion", in *Southeast Asia in the Early Modern Period: Trade, Power, and Belief*, edited by Anthony Reid (Ithaca: Cornell University Press, 1993), p. 64.

18 Gaspar Luis, "Annua da missam de Cochinchina anno de 1628", January 1629, JA 49–V–8, fol. 413, BA.

19 Ibid., fols. 413–13v.

20 Ibid., fol. 413v.

21 Ibid.

22 See Alexandre du Rhodes, *La Glorieuse Mort d'André, Catéchiste de la Cochin Chine, Qui a le Premier Versé Son Sang Pour la Querelle de Jésus Christ en Cette Nouvelle Église* (Paris: Sebastien Cramoisy et Gabriel Cramoisy, 1653).

23 Metelle Saccano, *Relation des Progrez de la Foy av Royavme de la Cochinchine és Années 1646 & 1647. Envoiée av R.P. General de la Compagnie de Iesus; Par le P. Metelle Saccano, Religieux de la Mesme Compagnie, Employé aux Missions de Ces Païs* (Paris: Sebastien et Gabriel Cramoisy, 1653).

24 Lea, *A History of Auricular Confession*, pp. 201–2.

25 Manuel Teixeira, *The Portuguese Missions in Malacca and Singapore (1511–1958)*, vol. 1, *Malacca* (Lisbon: Geral do Ultramar, 1961), p. 126.

26 Lea, *A History of Auricular Confession*, pp. 201–2.

27 The historiography addressing this issue in Europe is extensive. See, for example, the pioneering works by Emmanuel Le Roy Ladurie, *Carnival: A People's Uprising at Romans, 1579–1580*, translated by Mary Feeney (London: Scholar Press, 1980); and Natalie Zemon Davis, "The Rites of Violence: Religious Riot in Sixteenth-Century France", *Past and Present* 59 (1973): 51–91.

28 Lance Lazar, *Working in the Vineyard of the Lord: Jesus Confraternities in Early Modern Italy* (Toronto: University of Toronto Press, 2005), p. 142.

29 See, for example, Christopher Black, *Italian Confraternities in the Sixteenth Century* (Cambridge: Cambridge University Press, 2003), pp. 108–13; Marc R. Forster, *Catholic Revival in the Age of the Baroque: Religious Identity in Southwest Germany, 1550–1750* (Cambridge: Cambridge University Press, 2001), pp. 60–151; Jean Delumeau, *Rassurer et Protéger: Le Sentiment de Sécurité dans l'Occident d'Autrefois* (Paris: Fayard, 1989), pp. 90–133; and Charles Zika, "Processions and Pilgrimages: Controlling the Sacred in Fifteenth-Century Germany", *Past and Present* 118 (Feb. 1988): 25–64.

30 Federico Palomo, *A Contra-Reforma em Portugal, 1540–1700* (Lisbon: Livros Horizonte, 2006), pp. 103–4.

31 Louis E. Backman, *Religious Dances in the Christian Church and in Popular Medicine* (London: George Allen & Unwin, 1952), pp. 155–59.

32 See, for example, José Ramos Tinharão, *Os Negros em Portugal: Uma Presença Silenciosa* (Lisbon: Editora Caminho, 1988), pp. 155–58; Jeremy Lawrance, "Black Africans in Renaissance Spanish Literature", in *Black Africans in Renaissance Europe*, edited by T.F. Earle and K.J.P. Lowe (Cambridge: Cambridge University Press, 2005), p. 72; and Jean-Pierre Tardieu, *Destin des Noirs aux Indes de Castille XVIe–XVIIIe Siècles* (Paris: L'Harmattan, 1984), pp. 218–21 and 232–33.

33 See Ines Županov, "Twisting a Pagan Tongue: Portuguese and Tamil in Sixteenth-Century Jesuit Translations", in *Conversion: Old Worlds and New*, edited by

      Kenneth Mills and Anthony Grafton (New York: University of Rochester Press, 2003), p. 120.

[34] "Carta do Padre Baltasar Dias a seus confrades de Portugal", 29 November 1556, in *Documentação para a História das Missões do Padroado Português do Oriente: Insulíndia*, vol. 1, *1506–1549*, edited by Artur Basílio de Sá (Lisbon: Agência Geral do Ultramar, Divisão de Publicações e Biblioteca, 1954), p. 241; and "Carta do Padre Baltasar Dias ao Provincial da Companhia Doutor Miguel Torres", 1 December 1559, in Sá, *Documentação para a História das Missões*, 1:342.

[35] François Cadilhon, "Les processions Jésuites en France au XVIIe et XVIIIe siècles", in *Fastes et Cérémonies: L'Expression de la Vie Religieuse, XVIe–XXe Siècles*, edited by Agostino Marc, François Cadilhon and Philippe Loupès (Pessac: Presses Universitaires de Bordeaux, 2003), p. 199; and Ronnie Po-chia Hsia, *The World of Catholic Renewal*, 2nd ed. (Cambridge: Cambridge University Press, 2005), pp. 224–25.

[36] "Racconto oʼ Relatione del P. Lubelli Chierico Regolare Missionario Apost. co nell'Indie Orientali di molte particolaritaʼ spettanti al buon seruitio della sua missione. Venuta da M. Nuntio di Napoli con sue lettere de 6 . Febrraio 1663", Scritture Originali Riferite nelle Congregazioni Generali (1622–1892) (hereafter cited as SOCG), vol. 231, fol. 227, Archivio Storico de Propaganda Fide (hereafter cited as APF), Vatican City.

[37] Alessandro Valignano to Claude Acquaviva, Cochin, 18 December 1581, in *Documenta Indica*, vol. 13, *1583–1585*, edited by Joseph Wicki (Rome: Institutum Historicum Societus Iesu, 1975), pp. 734–38.

[38] Ibid., p. 735.

[39] Ibid., p. 736.

[40] Ibid., p. 737.

[41] See, for example, Raymond Baustert, *La Quarelle Janséniste Extra Muros, ou, La Polémique Autour de la Procession des Jésuites de Luxembourg, 20 Mai 1685* (Tübingen: Gunter Narr Verlag, 2006), pp. 82–90.

[42] Agnello dell'Immacolata Concettione to the Propaganda Fide, "Memoriale dato del Pr. Agnello (Carm. Scalz.)", Congregazioni Particolari (1622–1864), vol. 30, fols. 272–73, APF.

[43] Ibid.

[44] Franciscum Mariam, "Super rebus missionum", c. 1685, Scritture Riferite nei Congressi, Indie Orientali e Cina, vol. 4 (dal 1685 al 1687), fol. 22 ("Quaesita" and "Notada" number 10), APF.

[45] See, for example, Kathleen Ashley and Pamela Sheingorn, "*Sainte Foy* on the Loose, or, the Possibilities of Procession", in *Moving Subjects: Processional Performance in the Middle Ages and the Renaissance*, edited by Kathleen Ashley and Wim Hüsken (Amsterdam: Rodopi, 2001), pp. 53–67; and Rubin, *Corpus Christi*, pp. 316–46.

[46] *Cf.* David Gentilcore, *From Bishop to Witch: The System of the Sacred in Early Modern Terra d'Otranto* (Manchester: Manchester University Press, 1992).

47 Giovanni Battista Lucarelli de Pisauro, "Viaggio dell'Indie", in *Sinica Franciscana Volumen II: Relationes et Epistolas Fratrum Minorum Saeculi XVI et XVII*, edited by Anastasius van den Wyngaert (Quaracchi, Italy: Claras Aquas, 1933), pp. 69–70.

48 On *cantilene*, see Edward Muir, *Ritual in Early Modern Europe*, p. 109.

49 "Racconto o` Relatione del P. Lubelli", SOCG, vol. 231, fols. 221v–22, APF.

50 Rhodes's works included *Relazione de' Felici Successi della Santa Fede Predicata da' Padri della Compagnia di Giesù nel Regno di Tunchino, alla Santità di N.S. PP. Innocenzio Decimo di Alessandro de Rhodes Avignonese della Medesima Compagnia, e Missionario Apostolico della Sacra Congregatione de Propagande Fide* (Rome: Giuseppe Luna, 1650); *Relation de l'Évangélisation de la Cochinchine* (Paris: Sebastien et Gabriel Cramoisy, 1653); *Divers Voyages et Missions dv P. Alexandre de Rhodes en la Chine, & Autres Royaumes de l'Orient: Auec son Retour en Europe par la Perse & l'Armenie* (Paris: Sebastien et Gabriel Cramoisy, 1653); and *La Glorieuse Mort d'André* (see note 22).

51 The background to these developments is clearly sketched by Françoise Fauconnet-Buzelin, *Aux Sources des Missions Étrangères: Pierre Lambert de la Motte (1624–1679)* (Paris: Éditions Perrin, 2006), pp. 54–75. See also Adrien Launay, *Histoire Générale de la Société des Missions-Étrangères* (1894; repr., Paris: Les Indes Savantes, 2003), 1:14–15; and Goyau, "Les Missions Depuis la Création de la Propagande", in *Histoire Générale Comparée des Missions*, edited by le Baron Descamps (Brussels: M. Hayez, 1932), pp. 376–77.

52 Dick van der Cruysse, *Louis XIV et le Siam* (Paris: Fayard, 1991), p. 182.

53 Ibid., pp. 203–4.

54 "Mémoires de Bénigne Vachet", in *Histoire de la Mission de Siam, 1662–1811: Documents Historiques*, edited by Adrien Launay (Paris: Anciennes Maisons Charles Douniol et Retaux, P. Téqui, successeur, 1920), 1:32.

55 Ibid.

56 Ibid., p. 33.

57 Ibid.

58 Ibid.

59 Ibid.

60 Ibid.

61 Ibid.

62 Ibid.

63 Ibid.

64 See Grete Ring, "An Attempt to Reconstruct Perréal", *The Burlington Magazine* 92 (1950): 255–61.

65 "Mémoires de Bénigne Vachet", in Launay, *Histoire de la Mission de Siam*, 1:33.

66 Ibid.

67 Ibid., p. 34.

68 Cooke, "Strange Brew", pp. 383–409.

69 Anon, "Affaires de Cochinchine, 1689", vol. 736 (Cochinchine: Lettres 04: 1685–91), pp. 305–6, Archives des Missions Étrangère de Paris (hereafter cited as AMEP), cited in Cooke, "Strange Brew", p. 394.

70 On the Chinese and Malabar Rites controversies, see especially Ines G. Županov, *Disputed Mission: Jesuit Experiments and Brahminical Knowledge in Seventeenth-Century South India* (New Delhi: Oxford University Press, 1999); and D.E. Mungello, "An Introduction to the Chinese Rites Controversy", in *The Chinese Rites Controversy: Its History and Meaning* (Nettetal, Germany: Steyler Verlag, 1994), pp. 1–14. Peter C. Phan considers these issues in the context of Vietnam in *Mission and Catechesis*, pp. 78–106.

71 Louis Chevreuil, "Relation de la Cochinchine", 1665, vol. 733 (Cochinchine: Lettres 01: 1663–74), pp. 80–81, AMEP.

72 Louis Chevreuil to directors of MEP Seminary (?), Cambodia, 11 June 1668, vol. 733 (Cochinchine: Lettres 01: 1663–74), pp. 159–60, AMEP.

73 See, for example, vol. 650 (Tonkin: Lettres, 1666–77), p. 91; and vol. 651 (Tonkin: Lettres, 1677–1714), p. 44, AMEP.

74 "Journal du Tonkin[.] Dépuis le commencement de l'Année 1683 Jusqu'en Octobre de l'Année 1684", vol. 656 (Journal du Tonkin 1: 1667–97), p. 110, AMEP.

75 Ibid.

76 Cooke, "Strange Brew", pp. 403–6.

77 See, for example, Robert W. Scribner, "Ritual and Popular Religion in Catholic Germany at the Time of the Reformation", *Journal of Ecclesiastical History* 35 (1984): 47–77; and Gentilcore, *From Bishop to Witch*. Trevor Johnson, "Blood, Tears and Xavier-Water: Jesuit Missions and Popular Religion in the Eighteenth-Century Upper Palatinate", in *Popular Religion in Germany and Central Europe*, edited by Bob Scribner and Trevor Johnson (Basingstoke: Macmillan, 1996), pp. 183–202.

78 George Rudé, *The Crowd in History: A Study of Popular Disturbances in France and England, 1730–1848* (New York: Wiley, 1964).

79 *Cf.* Mark Harrison, *Crowds and History: Mass Phenomena in English Towns, 1790–1835* (Cambridge: Cambridge University Press, 1988), p. 5. See, for example, Knut A. Jacobsen, "Introduction: Religion on Display", in *South Asian Religions on Display: Religious Processions in South Asia and in the Diaspora* (London: Routledge, 2008), pp. 6–7, on "politicization" of religious festivals leading to communal violence; and Thomas A. Boogaart II, "Our Saviour's Blood: Procession and Community in Late Medieval Bruges", in Ashley and Hüksen, *Moving Subjects*, pp. 69–116, on processions as "an independent ritual genre". See also Muir, *Ritual in Early Modern Europe*.

80 Jean-Jacques Wunenburger, "Esthétique et épistémologie de la foule: Une auto-poïétique complexe", in *La Foule: Mythes et Figures; De la Révolution à Aujourd'hui*, edited by Jean-Marie Paul (Rennes: Presses Universitaires de Rennes, 2004), pp. 15–17.

81   John Walter, *Crowds and Popular Politics in Early Modern England* (Manchester: Manchester University Press, 2006), p. 14.

82   Ibid.

83   *Cf.* Jacobsen, "Introduction: Religion on Display", pp. 6–7.

84   For example, Davis, "The Rites of Violence", pp. 51–91; Muir, *Ritual in Early Modern Europe*, pp. 101–17; Philippe Martin, *Les Chemins du Sacré: Paroisses, Processions, Pèlerinages en Lorraine du XVIème au XIXème Siècle* (Metz: Éditions Serpenoise, 1995), pp. 145–46; and Margit Thøfner, *A Common Art: Urban Ceremonial in Antwerp and Brussels during and after the Dutch Revolt* (Zwolle, Netherlands: Waanders Publishers, 2007), pp. 19, 50–51, and 110–11.

85   See especially Philippe Buc, *The Dangers of Ritual: Between Early Medieval Texts and Social Scientific Theory* (Oxford: Princeton University Press, 2001), pp. 1–11; and Caroline Humphrey and James Laidlaw, *The Archetypal Actions of Ritual: A Theory of Ritual Illustrated by the Jain Rite of Worship* (Oxford: Clarendon Press, 1994), pp. 1–3 and 64–74.

2

A "SNAPSHOT" OF A PORTUGUESE COMMUNITY IN SOUTHEAST ASIA: THE *BANDEL* OF SIAM, 1684–86

Rita Bernardes de Carvalho

The Portuguese expansion throughout mainland Southeast Asia, with the exception of Malacca, was characterized primarily by its "private" or "informal" attribute — that is, it was based on the connivance of local authorities rather than on effective territorial occupation by Portuguese forces. Furthermore, the actors on the Portuguese side were, for the most part, merchants and veteran soldiers of the Portuguese Estado da Índia, accompanied by a relatively small number of missionaries from the Dominican, Franciscan and Augustinian orders, as well as Jesuit priests. Since the beginning of the sixteenth century, they had settled in communities of limited numbers, scattered mostly around the main Southeast Asian capitals or important cities. The history of this kind of community, known as a *bandel*, has yet to be fully explored and articulated. This chapter is a step towards this goal, which it takes by analysing certain cultural aspects of the *bandel* of Siam in Ayutthaya at the end of the seventeenth century, after about 160 years of the Portuguese presence in the region. During the seventeenth century, the role of the mestizos in the settlement process became more and more relevant as the Portuguese communities strengthened their connections to the local environment. One cannot address such Portuguese communities without questioning their own notion of "Portugueseness", however, and doing so requires an exploration of themes such as identity construction, cultural practices, and survival strategies.

EXPLORING THE SOCIAL WORLD OF THE SIAMESE-PORTUGUESE BANDEL

In 2003, a description of the embassy that Pero Vaz de Siqueira led to Siam in 1684 was published by Leonor de Seabra, which has recently been translated into English.[1] It is one of the most important documents from the official Portuguese side dealing with Luso-Siamese relations at the end of the seventeenth century. In addition to the official account made by the embassy's secretary, the publication includes several letters pertaining to the mission, making this publication quite a comprehensive source for academic work with its more than 350 pages of documents covering the period 1684–86.

More than a tool for studying how diplomatic strategies worked in the seventeenth-century Portuguese empire, this source has great potential for studying the Portuguese settlement in the Siamese capital of Ayutthaya. An analysis of such a source must go beyond the political perspective, though, and delve into other fields, even when that kind of information is well hidden in the text. To rethink the source and to admit the importance of a political-built narrative for the study of a Portuguese community becomes, then, part of history-making. The image that emerges from this narrative is thus a constructed one. In this sense, the aim of this study is to present a snapshot of the Portuguese settlement in Ayutthaya, using this source as a camera, and seeing the Portuguese settlement through its lenses.

In obtaining such an image of the Portuguese community and analysing the impression that emerges from it, the theme of identity can be satisfactorily addressed. In fact, different behavioural and identitary development rhythms can be observed during the duration of the embassy. In other words, different identitary strategies are adopted by the residents of the *bandel* during several key moments of the embassy. The challenge then becomes to see "identity" as a dynamic process rather than as an enclosed or definable object.

The embassy was embarked upon as a reaction by the Portuguese authorities to the difficulties faced by Estado da Índia such as, among others, the decay of regional influences and the danger to the Padroado[2] brought about by the presence of French bishops in traditionally Portuguese areas of influence. The period between 1684 and 1686 is also when Macao consolidates its role as a regional potency and openly displays a growing independence vis-à-vis the Estado da Índia. Likewise, the period in question was a very important one in Thai history, with King Naraï expanding his connections with foreign countries and the king's favourite, the Greek Constant Phaulkon, engaging in incessant political ruses to consolidate his influence in the kingdom.[3] The publication of this source by Seabra allows scholars to raise new questions on the continuities and disruptions of the Portuguese presence in Asia. In fact, the construction of an image of the Portuguese settlement in Ayutthaya acts as a mirror in the sense that it shows the reflection of the creator of the image in the first place. Considering that the addressee of most of the letters is the king of Portugal or the viceroy in Goa, it was necessary for the resulting image to comply with certain established criteria in order to be fully understood by these two characters, and to (hopefully) please them as well. Bearing this in mind, the perception of the Portuguese who were part of the embassy personnel among the *moradores* (residents) of the Ayutthayan settlement shows a considerable cultural distance between the two Portuguese worlds of Macao and Siam.

The portrait this source reveals is meaningful for the study of identitary processes because it allows us to analyse certain characters that stand out during the duration of the embassy. One of these individuals is Francisco Barreto de Pina, head of the Portuguese community at the time. His role during the diplomatic negotiations and the problems with justice he faced afterwards are relevant for an understanding of the Portuguese community at this juncture. What was his relationship with Siamese authorities? What was the degree of influence he had in governmental spheres, and how did he use it? What were the motivations that drove his behaviour, and how did he ultimately arrange for his survival?

An understanding of identity in the regions that formed the "informal" Portuguese empire has long been a quest for historians, due to the difficulty in addressing a theme as complex in itself as identity. With few sources and specialized secondary works available,[4] plus the fear of being drawn into the pitfalls of Lusotropicalist theory,[5] scholars tend to avoid deep discussions pertaining to identity. The term "informal" empire has been linked with Winius's "shadow empire", a notion that "involves the extension of Portuguese presence far beyond the limits of its effective administrative apparatus".[6] In another article, Winius expands his research to the people who moved in this geographical space, the Portuguese private traders.[7] He chooses to focus on the sociological aspects rather than economic ones and stresses the ambiguities involved in the definition of sociological categories. Finally, he asks "*who*" were the Portuguese that lived, traded and spread around the territories, thereby forming the Portuguese shadow empire.

In 1986, George B. Souza had already provided some clues for understanding the functioning of Portuguese private trade, especially through his use of Dutch sources to track the commercial journeys that Portuguese vessels undertook from Batavia to ports in other parts of Asia.[8] Souza developed the idea of Portuguese country trade in two articles. In one of these, he tried to grasp their movements in the Indian Ocean and South China Sea around 1600, and in another article, he studied the Macao-based Portuguese private traders in the seventeenth and eighteenth centuries.[9] It was Leonard Andaya who introduced the concept of "tribe", bringing to the discussion ethnological elements and notions such as ethnicity and ethnic group. This approach allowed him to conceive of the Portuguese communities as another group, or "tribe", like the ones that already existed in the Southeast Asian region.[10] Andaya has since expanded the question Winius had asked about the nature of the Portuguese identity (*who?*) in a recent article on the *topasses* in the Solor archipelago and Timor, stressing this time the importance of asking "*how* and *why* the notion of 'Portuguese' came to acquire such tremendous power among local communities".[11] In sum, Andaya has laid out a challenge for scholars to try to explain the survival of many Portuguese communities that are still in existence to this day.

This enquiry proposes to go in the same direction, questioning the different identitary strategies that drove the bandel's residents to behave in a certain way, letting their actions speak for their feelings about their identity, and trying to grasp the processes that shape identity in the cultural practices, actions and borders between Portuguese from Ayutthaya and Portuguese coming with the embassy. The methodology adopted here is to gather information about the people living in the Siamese-Portuguese *bandel* in order to contribute to a reconstruction of the social world of the community. I chose to begin by compiling an index of names, starting with the *moradores* of the settlement and including all names (and respective titles) appearing in the source, accompanied by a short biographical notice when possible.[12] This index, which appears as an appendix to this chapter, can be used to select case studies that will illustrate the identitary processes mentioned above. Moreover, the index makes it easier to gather statistical data, such as on who stands out in the documents, and on what occasions they are mentioned. For example, Francisco Barreto de Pina, the head of the Portuguese community, is often mentioned in relation to issues of justice, due to the nature of his function, but also due to his own personal problems with the justice enforced by the Ambassador Pero Vaz de Siqueira.

AMBASSADOR PERO VAZ DE SIQUEIRA AND HIS MISSION

Pero Vaz de Siqueira was a nobleman (*fidalgo-cavaleiro*) born in Macao, the son of Gonçalo de Siqueira de Sousa and an unknown mother. Charles

Boxer opines that Vaz de Siqueira might have been a mestizo[13] because he had several half-brothers also born of unknown mothers. Gonçalo de Siqueira de Sousa was sent to Japan on a diplomatic mission in 1644–47, and Pero accompanied his father on the journey, returning to Goa in 1648. From 1657 to 1669 he served in the Estado da Índia fleet, taking part in the conquest of Coulan (1657) and defending Cochin (1663) on the Malabar Coast. In 1670 Pero Vaz de Siqueira returned to Macao and married Ana Maria de Noronha, who belonged to a rich, well-placed family of merchants. He then became the brother-in-law of Dona Catarina de Noronha, Ana de Noronha's sister and widow of the prominent Portuguese private trader Francisco Vieira de Figueiredo.[14] During the 1680s Vaz de Siqueira carried out his business ventures in Southeast Asian waters, and in 1683 he was chosen by the crown and by the Noble Senate of Macao to conduct three embassies to those regions, namely to Siam, Cambodia and Cochinchina.

In the letter in which the viceroy instructed Pero Vaz de Siqueira on how to conduct the mission,[15] the objectives to be achieved in the three embassies are stated, but in greater detail with respect to the Siamese mission. These objectives were:

1. To reinforce the friendship between Portugal and Siam, Cambodia and Cochinchina ("procurasse muito a conservassão de sua amizade tendo com elles toda a boa correspondençia [sic]")[16] and in particular, [to] give special thanks to the king of Siam, who has been very loving towards the Portuguese nation and its nationals ("particularmente rendereis as graças a El Rey de Sião pello amor que mostra à Nasção [sic] Portugueza, e favores tão geraes que delle reçebem [sic] todos os Vassalos do Prínçepe [sic] nosso Senhor").[17]

2. To expel the French bishops from Siam, Cambodia and Cochinchina. The reasons presented to defend this move were that the French bishops "disturbed and disquieted" the Portuguese. Besides, they were thought to be dangerous, since behind their religious motivations they had the mission of gathering information on the ports, commercial activities and products, with an intended end result of the conquest of the territory by the French government.[18] If the ambassador could not obtain their expulsion from the Southeast Asian kingdoms, he was to at least ask for protection for the Portuguese priests.[19]

3. To obtain trading privileges for Portuguese merchants. This included asking for authorization for Portuguese vessels to trade in the local Asian ports without being charged for more than the usual taxes, and to be treated with respect and friendship. In particular, if the Siamese king

were to ask for authorization to send his vessels each year to Macao, the ambassador was to acknowledge his request, but on two conditions: only one vessel would be permitted per year, and its main cargo should consist of rice.[20]

While in Siam, Vaz de Siqueira had to accomplish several goals. First, he was to expel Amador Coelho from Siam because this resident of the Portuguese settlement had forgotten his "Portuguese blood", behaving like a Frenchman ("esqueçido [sic] do sangue que tem Portuguez se tem feito françez [sic]").[21] Second, he had to gather information about the political situation in Cambodia, and if the country were at war, he was to cancel his mission to that kingdom.[22] Third, as soon as Pero Vaz de Siqueira arrived in Siam, he had to seek advice from the head of the Portuguese community, Francisco Barreto de Pina, because he was a long-term resident of the Siamese kingdom ("porque como há tantos annos assiste no ditto Reino saberá dar rezão do que lhe perguntardes").[23] The ambassador should ask him about the present situation in the country ("do estado das couzas do dito Reino") and show Barreto de Pina the letters and gifts he carried for the king and the *barcalan* (government official in charge of foreign affairs).[24] Pero Vaz de Siqueira was given the order to seek advice from Father Manuel Soares, the superior of the Jesuit mission, on the matters pertaining to the French bishops and missionaries. He was also advised to contact Nicolao da Motta, the reverend father and governor of the bishopric of Malacca, and to praise his juridical actions on the defence of the Padroado Real.[25]

AMADOR COELHO: THE PORTUGUESE WHO "BECAME FRENCH"

The expulsion of Amador Coelho was a central matter in the political manoeuvres of the ambassador and provides a case study of a Portuguese morador acting against official Portuguese interests. Amador Coelho, also known as Amador Coelho de Mello, was a Portuguese born in Macao. Although it is not known when he first arrived in Siam, he was considered an enemy of the Portuguese missionaries because he served as notary of the French bishops, with great prejudice to the Portuguese Padroado. In fact, Coelho is thought to have been an "insurgent" and a "troubled" person who had been worrying the head of the community for a while. In view of this affirmation, it is probable that the viceroy, Francisco de Távora, had already heard about this individual through the letters of Francisco Barreto de Pina.

The viceroy's predecessor, Friar António Brandão, had already given orders to arrest Amador Coelho if by chance he disembarked at Macao. Francisco de Távora reiterated his predecessor's wish, and ordered Pero Vaz de Siqueira to do all possible things to take Coelho to Macao, and from there justice would take its course.[26] While the will to arrest Coelho was strong, the viceroy knew that he could not order his ambassador to do so on Siamese soil, explaining why he often uses the expression "to remove him from Siam" ("tirar de Sião"). This might be due to the favourable position of Amador Coelho in Siamese society, protected by his personal relations with the king's favourite, Constant Phaulkon. Indeed, Coelho's son-in-law, Fernão Nabo Paçanha, was a mandarin of the Siamese king and had a close relationship with Phaulkon, serving as his messenger in his contacts with Vaz de Siqueira.[27] This fact is confirmed by the ambassador, who distrusted Paçanha, believing that he was loyal to Phaulkon and not to the Portuguese prince, Dom Pedro.[28] His opinion was reinforced when on 1 April 1684 (Saturday of Alleluia) a group of thirteen *balões* (ceremonial barges) belonging to Portuguese people came into the vicinity of the Portuguese settlement. In one of those boats was Fernão Nabo Paçanha, who proceeded to support Phaulkon's request that the ambassador's frigate should be treated as any other trading vessel ("barcos chatins"); in other words, its crew, arms and merchandise should be registered when entering Siam, a request with which the ambassador refused to comply.[29]

Ultimately, Amador Coelho was never expelled from Siam, in Vaz de Siqueira's opinion because he did not show up during the whole period the ambassador was in Siamese territory.[30] In reality, it was probably the connections Coelho had in the kingdom that protected him and prevented his arrest. Furthermore, he used his family connections to consolidate his position and his good relations with Constant Phaulkon, through the proximity his son-in-law, Fernão Nabo Paçanha, had with the king's favourite. Indicative of a paradigm of certain Portuguese in Siam not being "loyal subjects of his Highness" Prince Dom Pedro, Coelho managed to assure his survival and his well-being by associating himself with high officials of the Siamese government and offering his services to the emerging foreign power in the region, the French.[31] The allegation that Coelho had forgotten his Portuguese blood and "had become French"[32] points to him being an opportunistic man whose allegiances were chosen in favour of his self-preservation. The French were indeed more and more important in the Siamese political sphere and were a new power to be taken into consideration at the time. Having sensed that, it is only natural that Coelho chose to associate with them. Coelho thus illustrates a stage in the identity process where redefining priorities becomes a real challenge for survival. When allegiances changed, identity had to internalize those adjustments.

FRANCISCO BARRETO DE PINA: A CASE OF CULTURAL ACCOMMODATION AND OFFICIAL CONDEMNATION

The head of the Portuguese community (the *capitão-mor*, a crown-appointed local commander) had a predominant role in the development of the embassy, a role that was consistent with him being one of the most important characters in the life of the *bandel*. A capitão-mor since about 1650, Francisco Barreto de Pina had a large family in Siam.[33] One of his sons, Francisco da Cunha Barreto, was raised in Siam and was an interpreter working for the Siamese kingdom.[34] In 1684, at the time the embassy arrived in Siam, Barreto de Pina was said to be a man of more than seventy years, with a somewhat difficult character. He was pictured as a deceitful person, who constantly changed his opinion on important matters, and to whom the people had never shown any respect.[35] However, he was one of the three men from whom the ambassador had orders to take advice immediately following his arrival in Siamese waters.

On an uncertain date between 25 March and 26 April 1684,[36] the Siamese king gave orders to arrest Barreto de Pina, who was delivered into the Portuguese ambassador's custody on 27 April and stayed behind bars in the embassy's vessel until Vaz de Siqueira returned from Luvo (today's Lopburi), where he had gone to meet King Naraï. Barreto de Pina held a Siamese royal title, which in Vaz de Siqueira's opinion gave the king the legitimacy to arrest him.[37] Suspicion arose quickly that the mastermind behind Pina's arrest was Constant Phaulkon.[38] Nevertheless, complaints against Barreto de Pina by the Christians of the Portuguese settlement had been made earlier, allegedly due to his poor administration of justice.[39] In 1683, and with the support of Barreto de Pina, the Siamese king recruited men among the Portuguese living in the *bandel* to serve in his fleet.[40] Pero Vaz de Siqueira found this situation unacceptable because it would question the authority of the Portuguese crown (in the figure of the *capitão-mor*) over its subjects.

After much insistence, the ambassador was informed of the crimes of which the head of the community was accused, namely his previously mentioned poor judgement in several legal cases, and the treason he committed against the interests of the Siamese king and the city of Macao. This last allegation concerns the episode of the loan requested by the Macanese senate from King Naraï in 1669, part of which was made in the form of goods. Not all of those goods could be sent to Macao immediately, so they were kept in the *bandel* under the chief of the Portuguese community's supervision. The merchandise eventually disappeared, and Barreto de Pina was accused of negligence and, ultimately, treason.[41]

His fate was sealed. Barreto de Pina had to leave office and quit the Siamese territory, accompanying Vaz de Siqueira on his return to Macao.[42] He must have pleaded to be allowed to stay in the kingdom because Pero Vaz de Siqueira even considered leaving Barreto de Pina in Siam, taking into account his poverty ("a muita pobreza do dito") and the family he had in his charge ("e a carga de família com que se acha obrigado").[43] In the end, he spent a great part of his life in Siam, where he had a wife and children, and where he served as chief of the community for thirty-four years. Barreto de Pina was a man between two worlds, living within the Siamese cultural sphere for an extended time, yet having the obligation to answer to Portuguese authorities. He personifies a layer of cultural accommodation, with clear signs of adaptation to the local way of life. As such, he had to juggle two very different judicial models and was accused of being unable to control the "vices" the population of the *bandel* had gradually incorporated into their lives.

Not surprisingly, Barreto de Pina ended up in Macao writing desperate letters to the Portuguese viceroy and the Portuguese king, asking for permission to return to Siam. After a trip to Goa, and a sojourn of three years in Macao working for the Portuguese authorities, he received authorization from the Siamese king to return to the country in 1688.[44]

"BLACK" BUROT: A "SIAMESE NEW CHRISTIAN"

Burot was a resident of the Portuguese settlement, a Siamese who had converted to Christianity. The categories assigned to him were "black", "delinquent", "the apostate", "New Christian" (but not Jewish) and "the sacrilegious black", among others.[45] He was caught stealing an item from the church of São Paulo, a crime for which he was judged and convicted by Francisco Barreto de Pina. His punishment was to have the points of his fingers cut off.[46] Barreto de Pina's authority came from his position as "Minister of the Portuguese and of the Christian people of the bandel". His skills as the administrator of justice were questioned by the people of the Portuguese settlement, who allegedly complained bitterly to Pero Vaz de Siqueira, stating that the punishment was light, and that Burot should have been put to death for what he had done. It is not clear in the source if Burot's punishment should have been given according to Portuguese or Siamese laws. This fact raises an interesting point concerning the practical choices of the *capitão-mor* in applying justice when the criminals were Siamese or Portuguese subjects. The authority of the *capitão-mor* in Burot's case seems to be more closely related to *where* the crime took place (a Catholic church) rather than *who* committed the crime (a Siamese or a Portuguese subject).

Finally, as we have seen earlier, Barreto de Pina was arrested and taken to Macao with the rest of the embassy. At the time, consideration was also given to the possibility of taking Burot to Macao as well, where the viceroy could judge him. This option revealed a deeper issue, expressed by Constant Phaulkon when he ascertained that Burot could not be taken to Macao, given the fact that he remained a subject of the king of Siam, notwithstanding his status as a Christian.

Nowhere is it stated that Burot was Portuguese, or even part of a Portuguese family. However, he lived in the *bandel*; thus, an argument for Portuguese ascendance can be made. His father's name was Thomé Gomez, and there are strong indications that suggest that Gomez was a Christian.[47] If that was the case, how could Burot be a "Siamese New Christian"? He would naturally be called a Christian, if that were his family's tradition. On the other hand, the use of the expression "Siamese New Christian" most probably indicated a recent conversion to that religious faith on the part of Burot and his entire family, but it also raises the question of the legitimacy of considering "Christian" as synonymous with being "Portuguese". How were differences between people living in the same community, sharing the same public spaces, and practising the same religion considered? When did one stop being *just* a Christian and start being a Portuguese (or the other way around)? More importantly, how did this process take place?

Burot's case study opens a whole new world of questions pertaining to the notion of otherness. Who was Burot to the Portuguese living in the Ayutthayan settlement? To what measure did he represent a counterbalance to the notion of being "Portuguese"? Or, on the contrary, how did he enrich that same notion? For the time being, these questions can only be posed, not answered. Burot's case, however, confirms how intricate the matter of identity had become by the seventeenth century.

CONCLUSION

Identity is a manifestly difficult concept to grasp.[48] In fact, I am not even sure we can ever understand it in all its complexity. The duty of the historian, however, is to try. This study is thus an attempt, and a work-in-progress. In this sense, using the index of names I compiled from the source *A Embaixada ao Sião de Pero Vaz de Siqueira (1684–1686)*, I was able to select three case studies, each relating, in theory, to a different stratum of identity.

In the case of Amador Coelho, it has been shown how his loyalties changed, and how working for the French bishops interfered with his "Portugueseness". Francisco Barreto de Pina, on the other hand, was the headman of the Portuguese settlement. He had managed to negotiate his commitments to his Siamese noblility title and his obligations to the Portuguese kingdom, ensuring his survival as the community's *capitão-mor* for more than thirty years. Barreto de Pina is in a deeper layer of acculturation, having a large family in Siam and trying by all means not to be expelled from the country in which he had spent most of his life. However, his casual and indulgent attitudes were interpreted by Pero Vaz de Siqueira as pure incompetence, and the ambassador had no choice but to dismiss him from his position as *capitão-mor*. One of the cases that Barreto de Pina was accused of not dealing with properly was the crime Burot commited in 1679. Burot, a "black New Christian", constitutes our third case study. Here the notions of "Christian" and "Portuguese" mix and demand a deeper analysis of the relationship between the Catholic faith and Portuguese identity in the context of mutual coexistence in the same geographical space — in this case, a Portuguese settlement in Southeast Asia.

In the above snapshot, my analysis reveals a climate of cultural diversity that is predominant among the bandel's residents. The case studies argue for this cultural diversity, and naturally, they also show a diversity of identities in a community that found itself in a constant process of change. In the case of the *bandel* of Ayutthaya, the notion of "being Portuguese" depended on allegiances, on the instinct of self-preservation, on accommodation to local culture(s), and, last but not the least, on a specific way of living the religious experience. Cultural practices, survival strategies, and identity discourses can vary widely; hence the difficulty of defining identity. A much more fruitful approach is to conceive of identity as a process and, following Frederik Barth,[49] to reflect on the Portuguese community as an ethnic group, relating identity construction (and reconstruction) processes with the forms of interaction observed in the sources.

Finally, it is important to stress the formation of identity through differences expressed not in dichotomous "this-or-that" ways, but in more subtle, multiple ways. The interaction between Christianity and "Portugueseness", and the various forms of living the Christian religious experience by the *bandel's* residents, reveal clues about the identification of subgroups in Portuguese communities, each one in different stages of their own idea of Portuguese identity. Therefore, it is not surprising that when the Portuguese embassy, constituted by people from Macao (probably mestizos for the most part), arrived in Siam, they immediately noticed how the

Portuguese from Siam practised their religion.[50] Consequently, they questioned the local Portuguese community's allegiance to the Portuguese crown, the ability of the local Portuguese to serve the king well, and even their right to call themselves Portuguese. Conflicting conceptions of what it meant to be Portuguese and how to practise Catholic rites led to a judgemental attitude on the part of the participants of the embassy which are reflected in their actions: when Pero Vaz de Siqueira returned to Macao, he took with him, in a ship especially built for the occasion, all the people he considered to have committed religious crimes as prisoners of the Inquisition.[51] What for Siqueira was an affront to "true" Catholicism represented to the Portuguese of Siam a logical adaptation to the local context. With few priests and fewer direct migrations from Portugal, it was only natural that a syncretism between local and European religious practices occurred, and that even missionaries accepted the plasticity of the religious experience in Siam. The vicissitudes of religious identity are without a doubt a fruitful path of investigation in the future, and one of the crucial facets of the survival of many Portuguese communities in Southeast Asia, including Siam.

APPENDIX

A Biographical Index of Leonor de Seabra's *A Embaixada ao Sião de Pero Vaz de Siqueira (1684–1686)*, 2nd ed. (Macao: Instituto Português do Oriente and Fundação Oriente, 2004), 379 pp.

Note: The names of all individuals pertaining to the Embassy and their respective titles or designations are included in this appendix, whenever definite identification is possible. The "French Bishops" are mentioned several times in the text, but without specifying exactly who they were; for this reason, those references are not included herein. All names appear in the orthography used in the source.

ACHA, Francisco de (*casado*, resident in Siam, Calvinist), 305, 306.
AMARAL de MENEZES, Belchior (resident and *capitão-mor* of Macao).
    See MENEZES, Belchior Amaral de (resident and *capitão-mor* of Macao).
AMARAL, Miguel (Jesuit priest, attorney general of the Province of Japan), 360.
ANDRÉ, João (participant in the embassy), 114.
ANNUNCIAÇÃO (or ANUNCIAÇÃO), Frei Francisco da (Franciscan priest, ambassador of Portugal to Siam in 1616), 225.
ARANHA, António de Oliveira (participant in the embassy), 114.
ARAÚJO, Manoel de (royal treasurer of the embassy), 114, 120.
AZEVEDO, Rodrigo Homem de (second lieutenant and scribe of the Municipal Office of Macao), 116.

BAPTISTA, João (pilot and captain in Macao), 355.
Barcalão (*barcalan* or "prakalang", governor of the Kingdom of Siam), 64, 68, 70, 74, 84, 89, 90, 111, 126–28, 150, 162, 166, 179, 186, 187, 198, 201, 202, 212–14, 218–22, 224–26, 238, 241, 244, 250, 251, 255, 264, 275, 276, 278, 284–90, 292, 293, 298, 300–04, 312, 315, 316, 330, 334, 336–39, 343–45, 347; brother of the *barcalan*, 206-07; secretary of the *barcalan*, 213, 224; lieutenant of the *barcalan*, 224.
BARRETO, António Botto (possibly the same person as António Preto Barreto, mentioned below), 78.
BARRETO, António Preto (lieutenant to the master of ceremony of the embassy), 114, 120, 126, 130, 131, 146, 147, 178, 280.
BARRETO, Francisco da Cunha (son of Francisco Barreto de Pina), 133, 134, 347.
BARRETO DE PINA, Francisco (*capitão-mor* of the *bandel*; also Francisco Barretto de Pina, Francisco Barretto de Pinna), 64, 67, 71, 74, 75, 81, 83, 84, 90, 92, 93, 97, 126, 131–33, 139–41, 147–50, 167, 170–80, 186–88, 194–96, 198–200, 202, 211, 244, 246, 248, 256, 286, 307–10, 318, 330, 336, 337, 340, 347.
BOR[—]IM, Francisco (English man), 197, 198.

199, 209, 212, 213, 218, 219, 232, 236, 242, 246, 250, 280, 291, 298, 300, 307, 309, 312, 342; report of the embassy by, 112–318.
FREITAS, António de (Portuguese, chief commander of the fortress of Bangkok), 131.
FREYRE, Manoel Rodrigues (captain of the royal banner of the embassy), 113, 120, 152, 194–96, 202, 208, 280(?).

GOMEZ, Thomé (resident of the *bandel* of Siam, father of Burot), 198.
GONÇALVES, Domingos (participant in the embassy), 114.
GUERRA, António Rodrigues da (treasurer of the bull of the Holy Crusade), 108.
GUERRA, António Rodriguez da (resident of the *bandel* of Siam, probably the same person as the above-mentioned António Rodrigues da Guerra), 136.

IGREJA, Bernardino da (Italian Capuchin friar), 100, 107, 158(?).

King of Cambodia, 284, 340, 341.
King of Cochinchina, 86, 87, 341.
King of Siam. *See* NARAI.
King of Tonkin, 87.
Kun Rasaesamut (an officer of the king of Siam), 198.

LANEAU, Louis (also Luis Lancau, a French bishop), 102, 107, 321, 322.
LIGER, João Correa de (captain of the artillery of the frigate *Nossa Senhora do Rosário* during the embassy), 113, 280(?).
LIMA, João de Abreu de (bachelor governor of the bishopric of Malacca), 321.
LOBATO, António (assistant of Joseph Cardozo and previously captain in Macao), 216.

MAGALHÃES, Francisco Coutrim de (also Coutinho; ambassador of Portugal to Siam in 1647), 141.
Maicò (woman, born in Pegu), 197.
MALDONADO, João Baptista (French Jesuit priest), 136, 142, 173, 179, 180, 204, 311.
MARTIR, Pedro (also Pedro Martyr, Pero Martir; Dominican friar, secretary of Constantino Falcão), 61, 62, 78, 79, 92, 94, 106, 110, 111, 161–63, 169, 170, 177, 181, 182, 188, 189, 201, 209(?), 229, 232, 233, 236, 237, 264, 280, 298, 312.
MENEZES, Belchior Amaral de (resident and *capitão-mor* of the City of Macao) 116, 118, 296, 297, 334.
Messia (Christian woman, born in Cochinchina), 198.
MOTTA, Diogo da (also Diogo da Mota, resident in the *bandel* of Siam), 98, 339.

Notes

[1]   Leonor de Seabra, *A Embaixada ao Sião de Pero Vaz de Siqueira (1684–1686)* (Macao: Universidade de Macau, 2003). There is another edition in Portuguese published in 2004 by the Instituto Português do Oriente and Fundação Oriente, *to which all page references in these endnotes refer.* Leonor de Seabra, *A Embaixada ao Sião de Pero Vaz de Siqueira (1684–1686)*, 2nd ed. (Macao: Instituto Português do Oriente, Fundação Oriente, 2004). An English edition was published in 2005: Leonor de Seabra, *The Embassy of Pero Vaz de Siqueira to Siam (1684–1686)*, translated by Custódio Cavaco Martins, Mário Pinharanda Nunes and Alan N. Baxter (Macao: University of Macau, 2005). *All English translations appearing in these endnotes are taken from this 2005 English edition, unless explicitly indicated otherwise.*

[2]   The Padroado Real or Padroado Régio was the right conceded to the king of Portugal by the pope granting Portugal a monopoly over ecclesiastical activities in the Portuguese empire's areas of influence. See Isabel dos Guimarães Sá, "Ecclesiastical Structures and Religious Action", in *Portuguese Oceanic Expansion, 1400–1800*, edited by Francisco Bethencourt and Diogo Ramada Curto (Cambridge: Cambridge University Press, 2007), pp. 255–82, esp. pp. 257–59.

[3]   Jurrien van Goor, "Merchant in Royal Service: Constant Phaulkon as Phraklang in Ayutthaya, 1683–1688", in *Emporia, Commodities and Entrepreneurs in Asian Maritime Trade, c. 1400–1750*, edited by Roderich Ptak and Dietmar Rothermund (Stuttgart: Franz Steiner Verlag, 1991), pp. 445–65.

[4]   George Bryan Souza, *The Survival of Empire: Portuguese Trade and Society in China and the South China Sea, 1630–1754*, 2nd ed. (Cambridge: Cambridge University Press, 2004), p. 35. The first edition was published in 1986.

[5]   For a discussion of Lusotropicalism in the historiography, see Cláudia Castelo, *O Modo Português de Estar no Mundo: O Luso-Tropicalismo e a Ideologia Colonial Portuguesa (1933–1961)* (Lisbon: Edições Afrontamento, 1999). See also Miguel Vale de Almeida, "Portugal's Colonial Complex: From Colonial Lusotropicalism to Postcolonial Lusophony", Queen's Postcolonial Research Forum, Queen's University, Belfast, 28 April 2008, <http://site.miguelvaledealmeida.net/wp-content/uploads/portugal-colonial-complex.pdf> (accessed 16 September 2010).

[6]   George D. Winius, "Embassies from Malacca and the 'Shadow Empire'", in *Proceedings of the International Colloquium on the Portuguese and the Pacific*, edited by Francis A. Dutra and João Camilo dos Santos (Santa Barbara: Center for Portuguese Studies, 1995), p. 170.

[7]   George Winius, "Private Trading in Portuguese Asia: A Substantial Will-o'-the-Wisp", in *Vasco da Gama et l'Inde: Chapelle de la Sorbonne, 11 Mai – 30 Juin 1998*, edited by Maria Helena Mendes Pinto and José Manuel García, translated by Annie Marques dos Santos (Lisbon: Fundação Calouste Gulbenkian; and Paris:

Chancellerie des universités de Paris, 1999), pp. 1–13. This article and the one quoted in the previous note can also be found in a reprint of Winius's works: George Winius, *Studies on Portuguese Asia, 1495–1689* (Aldershot: Ashgate, 2001).

8   Souza, *The Survival of Empire.*

9   *Cf.* George Bryan Souza, "Portuguese Country Traders in the Indian Ocean and the South China Sea, c. 1600", in *European Commercial Expansion in Early Modern Asia,* edited by Om Prakash (Aldershot: Variorum, 1997), pp. 69–80; and George Bryan Souza, "The Portuguese Merchant Fleet at Macao in the Seventeenth and Eighteenth Centuries", in *Rivalry and Conflict. European Traders and Asian Trading Networks in the 16th and 17th Centuries,* edited by Ernst van Veen and Leonard Blussé (Leiden: CNWS Publications, 2005), pp. 342–69.

10   Leonard Y. Andaya, "The Portuguese Tribe in the Malay-Indonesian Archipelago in the Seventeenth and Eighteenth Centuries", in Dutra and Santos, *Proceedings,* pp. 129–48.

11   Leonard Y. Andaya, "The 'Informal Portuguese Empire' and the Topasses in the Solor Archipelago and Timor in the Seventeenth and Eighteenth Centuries", *Journal of Southeast Asian Studies* 41, no. 3 (2010): 391–420. The notion of "tribe" was also employed by Stefan Halikowski Smith when dealing with the Portuguese who migrated from Makassar to other Southeast Asian regions; see Stefan Halikowski Smith, "No Obvious Home: The Flight of the Portuguese 'Tribe' from Makassar to Ayutthaya and Cambodia during the 1660s", *International Journal of Asian Studies* 7, no. 1 (Jan. 2010): 1–28. His work, *Creolization and Diaspora in the Portuguese Indies, 1640–1720: The Social World of Ayutthaya* (Leiden: Brill, 2011), is potentially a great contribution to the debate on this question.

12   See document in appendices. The relevance of such a scholarly tool has been underlined by Kennon Breazeale in his review of the English translation of Pero Vaz de Siqueira's embassy to Siam; see Kennon Breazeale, "Review of Leonor de Seabra, *The Embassy of Pero Vaz de Siqueira to Siam (1684–1686)* (Macao: University of Macau, 2005)", *Journal of the Siam Society* 97 (2009): 234–37.

13   "After returning from Japan in 1647, Gonçalo de Siqueira proceeded to Goa, where he died soon after his arrival, presumably in 1648. He never married, but had several natural children, though whether by European or Asiatic mothers is uncertain." See C.R. Boxer, *The Embassy of Captain Gonçalo de Sequeira de Souza to Japan in 1644–1647* (Macao: Tip. Mercantil, 1938), p. 29.

14   On the life of Francisco Vieira de Figueiredo, see the work of C.R. Boxer, *Francisco Vieira de Figueiredo: A Portuguese Merchant-Adventurer in South-East Asia, 1624–1667* (The Hague: Martinus Nijhoff, 1967).

15   Goa, "Copea da Instrução que o Conde Vice Rey e Capitão Geral da India deu ao Embaixador Pedro Vaz de Siqueira", 12 May 1683, Índia, caixa 58, doc. 98, Arquivo Histórico Ultramarino (hereafter cited as AHU), Lisbon, apud Leonor de Seabra, *A Embaixada,* 2nd ed., pp. 333–42. Also published by Leonor de

Seabra in her article, "Pêro Vaz de Siqueira, mercador e armador nos Mares do Sul da China", *Review of Culture/Revista de Cultura* 11 (2004): 99–113.

[16] Seabra, *A Embaixada*, 2nd ed., p. 334. The 2005 English translation reads: "to seek to preserve their friendship and maintain good relations with [them]."

[17] Seabra, *A Embaixada*, pp. 334–35. The 2005 English translation reads: "You are to personally thank the King of Siam for the devotion towards the Portuguese nation and all the favors received by the vassals of the Prince Our Lord [resident in Siam]."

[18] Seabra, *A Embaixada*, p. 335.

[19] Ibid.

[20] Ibid., p. 336.

[21] Ibid., p. 340. The 2005 English translation reads: "He [Coelho] has forgotten that he has Portuguese blood and has become French."

[22] Seabra, *A Embaixada*, pp. 340–41.

[23] Ibid., p. 337. The 2005 English translation reads: "because, as he [Francisco Barreto de Pina] has been serving in that Kingdom for so many years, he will be able to assist you [the Ambassador] in all matters."

[24] Seabra, *A Embaixada*, p. 337.

[25] Ibid.

[26] Ibid., p. 340. In the original Portuguese: "Dezejo muito tirar de Sião a Amador Coelho que esquecido do sangue que tem Portuguez se tem feito françez, servindo de notário dos Bispos françezes, fazendo de sua pane todas as diligencias a notificações que se offereçem contra os nossos Missionários em prejuizo da regalia, a padroado Real de Sua Alteza, e por ser naturalmente inquieto, e revoltozo tem dado grandes moléstias ao Capitão Mor, e aos nossos Missionários, e como hé tão prejudicial já o Governador meu anteçessor tinha ordenado que se acazo se embarcaçe para Maccao donde hé natural se lancaçe mão delle, e fosse remetido prezo a esta Cidade, e assym vos encomendo que façaes toda a diligencia possivel por verdes se o podeis tirar de Sião, e levá-lo em vossa companhia para Maccao, com algum pretexto fazendo-vos desentendido de seus procedimentos, e depois que estiver em Maccao executará o Capitão Geral a ordem que lhe tenho dado sobre este particular remetendo prezo a esta Cidade, com o que terão os nossos Missionários este inimigo menos no dito Reino." The 2005 English translation reads: "I very much wish to remove Amador Coelho from Siam. He has forgotten that he has Portuguese blood and has become French, serving as notary to the French Bishops, purveying all the diligences and notifications against our Missionaries, harming the exclusive rights and Royal Ecclesiastical Patronage of His Highness. Troublesome and rebellious by nature, he has caused many difficulties for the *Capitão mor* and for our Missionaries. As he is so harmful, the Governor who was my predecessor, had already ordered that if he were to sail to Macau (where he comes from), he should be caught and sent as a prisoner to this city [of Goa]. Thus, I instruct you to take all the possible measures to see if you can remove him from Siam and take him with you to Macau, under

any pretext, without revealing to him that you are aware of his actions. Once in Macau, the *Capitão geral* shall carry out the order that I have issued regarding this matter and will send him as a prisoner to this city [of Goa], and thus our Missionaries in the mentioned Kingdom will have one enemy less."

[27] Seabra, *A Embaixada*, 2nd ed., pp. 159–60 (fols. 266v and 267 of the original embassy report).

[28] Ibid., p. 161 (fol. 267 of the original embassy report). In the original Portuguese: "elle [Paçanha] no seu tanto como leal vassallo que se conhecia ser do Príncipe Nosso Senhor não havia de deixar de obrar o que pudesse na conservação do crédito do dito Senhor, sem embargo de que neste sugeito o Senhor Embaixador tinha descoberto ânimo differente do que erão suas palavras." In the 2005 English translation: "He [Paçanha] also replied that, as a loyal vassal of Our Lord the Prince, he would do all that he could to protect the prestige of the Prince. Although the Ambassador had sensed that [Fernão Nabo Paçanha] was not being true to words, he thanked him warmly for his offer."

[29] Seabra, *A Embaixada*, 2nd ed., p. 134 (fol. 260v of the original embassy report).

[30] Ibid., p. 84 (fol. 228 of the original embassy report).

[31] Ibid., p. 145 (fol. 263 of the original embassy report). This fact is confirmed by the author of the embassy's report, Francisco Fragoso, who harshly criticized the situation: "a mayor desgraça de todos os Portuguezes que vivem no Sião, hé viverem algum tanto esquecidos do brio e crédito portuguez, porque não tratão mais que de sua conservação naquelle Reyno de Sião, e verdadeiramente não sey com que interesses, pois todos passão miseravelmente." The 2005 English translation reads: "The greatest misery of the Portuguese who live in Siam is to have somewhat forgotten Portuguese pride and prestige, for they only care about staying on in that Kingdom, and truly I do not know for what, since they all live miserably."

[32] Seabra, *A Embaixada*, 2nd ed., p. 340. In the original Portuguese, followed parenthetically by the 2005 English translation: "esqueçido do sangue que tem Portuguez se tem feito françez" (he has forgotten that he has Portuguese blood and has become French).

[33] Seabra, *A Embaixada*, 2nd ed., p. 81 (fol. 227v of the original embassy report). In the original Portuguese: "uma família muito grande" (a very large family).

[34] Seabra, *A Embaixada*, pp. 133–34 (fols. 260–60v of the original embassy report). In the original Portuguese: "Francisco Cunha Barretto[,] filho do Capitão mor[,] que servia de língua no Reyno[,] (...) como se criara no Reyno de Sião devia estar esquecido das franquezas e liberdades que em toda a parte do Mundo tinhão os Embaixadores de Sua Alteza [o Príncipe de Portugal]." The 2005 English translation reads: "Francisco da Cunha Barretto, son of the *Capitão mor* who was an interpreter for the [Siamese] Kingdom, (...) as he had been brought up in the Kingdom of Siam he had probably forgotten the privileges and liberties to which the Ambassadors of His Highness [the Prince of Portugal] were entitled to all over the world."

35 Seabra, *A Embaixada*, 2nd ed., pp. 140, 149 and 310 (fols. 262, 264 and 304v, respectively, of the original embassy report). In the original Portuguese, followed parenthetically by the 2005 English translation: "settenta e tantos annos" (seventy-something years of age) (p. 310); "há 34 annos, que assisto por Capitão neste Reyno" (having already served 34 years as *Capitão mor* in this Kingdom) (p. 140); "por natureza hé homem muito fingido, e em poucos instantes varea muitas vezes em matérias de muita consideração" (he is by nature a very dishonest man, and in a short space of time he can change his opinion many times on matters of great importance) (p. 149); and "ninguém lhe teve nunca respeito" (no one ever respected him) (p. 149).

36 Seabra, *A Embaixada*, 2nd ed., pp. 66–67 (fol. 223v of the original embassy report).

37 Ibid., pp. 82–83 and 200 (fols. 227v–28 and 277, respectively, of the original embassy report). The *capitão-mor* could legitimately be arrested because he was a mandarin of the Siamese king. The embassy's secretary, Francisco Fragoso, advises against accepting a royal Siamese title precisely for this reason.

38 Ibid., p. 170 (fol. 269v of the original embassy report).

39 Ibid., pp. 172 and 195 (fols. 270 and 275v, respectively, of the original embassy report). In the original Portuguese, followed parenthetically by the 2005 English translation: "o ditto Capitão mor sobordinado de interesses deixou de fazer o que devia, com que não só mostrou ser ruim ministro, senão táobem mao Christão" (the *Capitão mor*, undermined by personal interests, failed to carry out his duties. Therefore, he not only proved to be a bad minister, but also a bad Christian).

40 Seabra, *A Embaixada*, 2nd ed., p. 83 (fol. 228 of the original embassy report).

41 Ibid. For details on this episode, see information on pp. 196–200 (fols. 276–77 of the original embassy report).

42 Seabra, *A Embaixada*, 2nd ed., p. 71 (fol. 224v of the original embassy report). In the original Portuguese, followed parenthetically by my translation: "só não querendo [el-Rey] consentir que Francisco Barreto de Pina ficasse em seu Reyno nem com o governo dos Portuguezes" (the King granted everything ... except for allowing Francisco Barreto de Pina to remain in his Kingdom neither with the government of the Portuguese); and "por onde me hé necessário levar o dito Francisco Barreto comigo [para] Macao" (I am thereby obliged to take the said Francisco Barreto with me to Macau).

43 Seabra, *A Embaixada*, 2nd ed., p. 75 (fol. 225v of the original embassy report).

44 See Francisco Barreto de Pina to the King D. Pedro II (Carta de Francisco Barreto de Pina ao Rei D. Pedro II), Siam, 10 October 1691, Índia, caixa 38 (old number), doc. 63, AHU, apud Maria da Conceição Flores, "A embaixada de Pedro Vaz de Siqueira ao Sião em 1684", in *Anais de História de Além-Mar*, vol. 3 (Lisbon: Centro de História de Além-Mar da Universidade Nova de Lisboa, 2002), pp. 372–75.

45 It is important to differentiate between the normal use of the expression "New Christian" as referring to a Jew recently converted to Christianity, and the sense in which the above-mentioned expression is used in Burot's case, referring not to a Jew, but simply to a recent convert.

46 Seabra, *A Embaixada*, 2nd ed., p. 194 (fol. 275v of the original embassy report). In the original Portuguese, followed parenthetically by the 2005 English translation: "juntamente entregarão os ditos ministros del Rey de Sião hum negro do dito Reyno por ser Christão que havia cometido, haveria sinco annos [in 1679], hum horrendo sacrilégio como foi abrir o sacrário da Igreja de São Paulo e levar a Ambula das particulas deixando-as todas espalhadas, e como naquelle tempo o dito Capitão mor, como ministro dos Portuguezes, e mais gente Christaã do Bandel, conheceo deste crime e o sentenceou a que lhe fossem ao tal deliquente as pontas dos dedos cortadas sem mais castigo algum" (These Ministers of the King of Siam also handed over a Negro from that Kingdom. He was a Christian who, five years earlier [in 1679], had committed a horrendous crime: he had opened the tabernacle of the Church of São Paulo and taken the ampulla of the holy wafers, and scattered them all about. At the time, the *Capitão mor* was the Minister of the Portuguese and other Christians of the *Bandel*, and informed of this crime, he sentenced that the delinquent should have the tips of his toes cut off, without any further punishment).

47 Seabra, *A Embaixada*, 2nd ed., p. 198 (fol. 276v of the original embassy report).

48 The utility of "identity" as a category of analysis applied to the social sciences is questioned by Cooper in Frederick Cooper, *Colonialism in Question: Theory, Knowledge, History* (Berkeley: University of California Press, 2005); see esp. chap. 3, "Identity" (with Rogers Brubaker), pp. 59–90.

49 Fredrik Barth, ed., *Ethnic Groups and Boundaries: The Social Organization of Culture Difference* (Illinois: Waveland Press, 1998, © 1969).

50 Seabra, *A Embaixada*, 2nd ed., pp. 76 and 100 (fols. 226 and 243, respectively, of the original embassy report). Their observations focused mostly on the Portuguese community's disunity and the residents' disrespect for ecclesiastical matters. In the original Portuguese, followed parenthetically by the 2005 English translation: "está esta Christandade em vesporas de se ver em huma sisma, e dezar[r]anjo que entre esta gentelidade pouco hé necessário para que os Christãos vivão dezonidos, e pouco conforme nas couzas da Igreja" (this Christian community which is on the verge of a rupture and a breakdown, for these Christians easily become disunited and drift away from the teachings of the Church) (p. 76). Also: "porque a nossa gente en [*sic*] Sião nunca teve união, nem obediência só quer viver na liberdade da terra" (because our people in Siam never were united or obedient. They only wish to live within the liberty of the land) (p. 100).

51 See Seabra, *A Embaixada*, 2nd ed., pp. 306 and 314 (fols. 303v and 305v, respectively, of the original embassy report).

3

THE COLONIAL COMMAND OF CEREMONIAL LANGUAGE: ETIQUETTE AND CUSTOM-IMITATION IN NINETEENTH-CENTURY EAST TIMOR[1]

Ricardo Roque

Throughout the nineteenth century, Timor was perceived as Portugal's most remote colonial province, a problematic remnant of the Portuguese maritime empire in Asia. The island was geographically isolated and the administration was militarily weak, economically poor, and enmeshed in multiple political and military conflicts, either between the colonizers and the indigenous, or among colonizers themselves.[2] This marginal, weak and atavistic colonial condition was associated with a ceremonial style of administration. Although the Portuguese governors envisaged an administration modelled on the example of "modern" European and imperial state bureaucracies, territorial occupation, economic order and military organization, the fact was that, in practice, they felt the need to engage and reproduce old *local* institutions and traditions, deeply rooted in the government praxis of the colony. Indeed, the idea of sacred age-old custom — usually under the name of *estilos*[3] — was a main source of legitimacy and normative supervision of colonial domination as "traditional authority".[4] As one governor declared in 1901, the governor's authority could only aspire to indigenous recognition because of and "in accordance with the *estilos*".[5]

Regardless of their being perceived as barbarian, abhorrent, feudal or old-fashioned by nineteenth-century Portuguese, many of these *estilos* of administration could not be easily dismissed or modified in practice without serious consequences for colonial authority. Thus the Portuguese in Timor felt compelled to copy and reproduce a number of locally meaningful ancient sociopolitical customs, norms and ceremonies, of which they were important actors. The origin of many of these *estilos* could be traced to manners and customs introduced in Timor by former Portuguese agents in the early modern period. But by the nineteenth century they were fundamental to the survival of colonial authority *in the present*, and they were not "Portuguese" customs any more. They were a legacy of the past that had been creatively integrated and adopted as lawful by the people and the elites in the Timorese kingdoms. In other words, this legacy had already become a form of "indigenous" ancient custom, and as such was valued by the Timorese.

This chapter explores the pivotal significance of some of these ancient customs and ceremonial practices in nineteenth-century colonial East Timor. Scholars of the Portuguese imperial expansion have already called attention to the significance of ceremonial culture and political rituals in the making of the empire in the early modern period.[6] Yet, in what concerns later historical periods of Portuguese imperialism, ceremonial culture and practices have not been discussed as an active component of Luso-Asian encounters and colonial government. This study contributes to redressing this imbalance, exploring the productive role of ceremonial customs and codified gestures for the co-production of colonial and indigenous power, status and authority in the late imperial period.

In Timor, I argue, ceremoniality was the language and the technology through which both Portuguese and Timorese politico-jural authority and status were constituted and exercised in colonial interactions. It ensured the enactment of command as well as the social communication with and among the colonial and indigenous people and ruling classes, in a variety of situations: during peaceful conjunctive interactions, but also, and importantly, on occasions of political tension, conflict or imminent physical violence. Throughout the nineteenth and early twentieth century, the Portuguese and Timorese jural authority and status constituted an entangled realm, supported by a rich variety of customary rules, rites, objects and signs associated with the exercise of justice, the conduct of war, and generally the rule over worldly affairs. This was a historically fluid, fragile, fractured and contingent entanglement, cut across by dynamics of differentiation and hostility, and from which opposition and violence were not discounted — indeed, they could be constitutive of its functioning.[7] Headhunting rites performed in colonial campaigns fed on the mutual strength of the colonial establishment and the victorious indigenous communities; public labour, warrior service and collective taxes (such as the *finta*) owed to the government formed a ritual tributary system that fed on the Portuguese power in Dili while also strengthening indigenous centres and elites in the kingdoms; and Portuguese national flags, military uniforms, sceptres and a multitude of honours, titles and ranks granted to Timorese lineages of *liurais* (executive rulers) in the course of vassalage oaths helped to sustain, as ancestral tokens of office, the latter's status and authority in the communities.[8]

I will not deal here with the full range of these important expressions of status and authority that stood at the conjunction of indigenous and colonial societies in Timor. My purpose in this work is to concentrate attention on one apparently minor, yet significant, aspect of the entangled ceremonial world of Portuguese-Timorese affairs. I refer to the minute care paid by both the European and indigenous agents to the rightful performance of ancient stereotyped behaviours and deference gestures in their mutual dealings: the *etiquette* performed in colonial interactions in relation to persons of certain status and authority positions, in accordance to custom, to the *estilo* — to every norm, rite, tradition or gesture acknowledged as lawful in colonial Timor.

ETIQUETTE AND THE NOTION OF CUSTOM-IMITATION

It is one hypothesis of this study that managing etiquette in colonial interactions was critical for the communication and regulation of authority, social hierarchy and political tension. Etiquette regulated the relationships with authorities and persons of rank, holding together the circuits of deference upon which superior power and status were sustained. Army officers and indigenous aristocracy; army officers and missionaries; governors and indigenous kings and noblemen; and the commoners as regards every person or thing perceived to be an embodiment of higher authority, were to observe in their relations a certain number of modes of behaviour, dress codes, linguistic manners, spatial locations, use of material objects and so on. As such, managing etiquette was critical for those (Timorese and Portuguese alike) who claimed higher status and authority in colonial Timor. The mutual observance of etiquette implied the bodily expression of deference. These were gestures "expressing the status of an individual" and "represent[ing] an assent to the unequal distribution of rewards and facilities", to be owed to a person of status by people of equal or lower standing.[9]

As a ceremonial mode of "stereotyped behaviour", etiquette represented, as Edward Shils observed, an "appreciation of the charismatic qualities embodied in great authority, power, and eminence".[10] Therefore, etiquette mattered not only to maintain the micro-sociological order of social interactions. In that it expressed an acknowledgement of power and social hierarchy in human relations, etiquette was crucial to the wider regulation of status and authority at both a societal and a cross-cultural level in colonial Timor. Etiquette simultaneously expressed and made possible the central elements of jural authority, across the colonial-indigenous divide. In addition, it was an important aspect in the regulation of conflicts and violence — to the extent that, in some instances, as I shall suggest, the greater the political tension or the sense of imminent physical threat, the more important was the rightful performance of etiquette for the actors involved.

The emphasis on the continued adoption of etiquette (and, more generally, of *estilos*) configured a form of imitation, one way of performing the social in Portuguese-Timorese colonial interactions through the insistence upon (re)enacting lawful customs and manners, allegedly of ancient origin. In effect, in exploring etiquette and its circuits of deference, it is also my purpose in this chapter to articulate the ceremonial nature of power and status with the function of imitation in the creation of social ties and authority in intercultural colonial interactions. I here draw on the sociologist Gabriel Tarde's insights about the "social force" of *custom-imitation*, that is: "imitative radiations emanated from ancient inventions", such as lawful or sacred norms and behaviours reproduced in the present but inherited (or understood as inherited) from the past.[11] Accordingly, I shall suggest that the Portuguese and the Timorese involvement with the enactment of *locally and mutually significant* customary rules and practices — such as etiquette — crucially mattered for configuring the social and the political in colonial relationships over time. Although it is not within the scope of this chapter to historically examine the dynamics between repetition and difference, or imitation and innovation, in etiquette behaviour, it needs to be noted that, as Tarde argued, processes of imitation and processes of innovation are interdependent and complementary. Therefore, the custom-imitation practices here described in connection with ceremonials and etiquette in Timor should be understood as historically contingent and dynamic; they were not a static system.

In the wider context of nineteenth- and twentieth-century imperial Portugal, the notion of custom-imitation might more immediately lead us to consider the centrality of the Age of Discoveries as model and example in the imagination of the "Third Portuguese Empire".[12] In that historical context, in particular, in the wake of nationalist-imperialist ideologies, the "Age of Discoveries" grew into major historical reference for the contemporary construction of a new Portuguese empire in Africa and Asia.

Then, Portuguese colonial agents were called to revive in their actions the ancestral glories of heroes and explorers of a mythic golden past of imperial splendour. Nevertheless, with the notion of custom-imitation it is not to this mythical ideological vision of the Portuguese imperial past to which I want to draw attention. As used here, the notion of custom-imitation emphasizes, first, the colonial *locality* of the re-edition of ancient customary behaviours and traditions, and, second, the fact that these behaviours bear some kind of *reciprocal* European-indigenous cultural meaning and political significance. Finally, it draws attention to the primordial importance of inherited gestures, norms, and objects in the making of the social and the political among the Timorese and Portuguese, and, as such, to the importance of shared stylized behaviours for the generation of society between colonizers and colonized people. Some of these locally and reciprocally meaningful customs could be traced to the activity of the Portuguese missionaries and military in Timor in the seventeenth and eighteenth centuries. Vassalage oaths, for example, possibly dated back to the early days of missionary activity. Yet, I believe, the mythical imagery of the Discoveries — however important to shape the grand narrative of the Third Portuguese Empire — was here of secondary practical consequence in shaping the local contours of colonial situations. In Timor, instead, the actual observance of customs and traditions considered significant at the local levels of the colony, of each Timorese *reino* (kingdom), or even of the specific occasion of social interaction ruled over the conduct of governors, officers and other officials in their relations, and in their relationships with the Timorese. Many of these customs then went unnoticed in metropolitan circles; many were ideally undesired by Portuguese officials and officers. But they were nonetheless preserved, for they seemed to constitute a "social force" that, in concrete interactions, superseded the most modernizing intentions of colonizers. Etiquette was one expression of such social force, one variety of those customs perceived as ancestral that seemed to require dedicated reproduction in the present.

I will deal particularly with the period from the 1860s to the early 1900s, as this was a moment when the enactment of past local political ceremonials and traditions came visibly to the fore in the definition of a colonial government style in East Timor — especially (but not exclusively) during the governorship of Celestino da Silva (1894–1908). The study begins with a brief examination of the significance of ceremoniality in the colonial theories of government and authority in East Timor. The next section looks at different manifestations of etiquette in the interactions between Portuguese officers, governors, and Timorese commoners and jural authorities. I will here explore gestures of deference in communal rites of hospitality, in interpersonal interactions and in the ceremonial expressions of warfare and confrontation.

COLONIAL CEREMONIALITY AS
STYLE OF GOVERNMENT

In Timor, stereotyped ceremonials and bodily gestures were a form of politics, a way of enacting central symbolic powers. With regard to the Portuguese establishment, particularly, ceremonial action, to paraphrase Clifford Geertz, had *become* the colonial state.[13] The management of *estilos* and etiquette constituted a paramount technology of rule, and the principal idiom of status and political communication with, and between, those who were acknowledged as hierarchically superior. This praxis of state-ruling, centred on the performance and observance of stereotyped gestures and objects, configured a government style that can be designated as *ceremoniality*: a mode of governance whose strategic rationality was the manoeuvring of stereotyped behaviour, etiquette codes and ritual occasions. The importance of ritual action and objects in the constitution of jural authority in Timor, for example, was interpreted by Governor Celestino da Silva in 1901 as an expression of the historical precedence of Portuguese colonization in the very creation of the authority of the *liurais* as *reis* (kings) and of the Timorese polities as *reinos* (kingdoms). His peculiar theorizing of the "origins of power" in Timorese political organization — certainly not shared by all colonial observers and not equivalent to certain indigenous theories of diarchic authority and origins of power — emphasized how jural power in Timor was a charismatic emanation from the Portuguese governor.[14] On the ritual occasions of vassalage, the titles and emblematic object embodiments of (Portuguese) jural power (particularly the flag and specially made sceptres) were delegated to the Timorese *liurais*, on the occasion of their ceremonial appointment as vassals of Portugal, and to colonels and *reis* in the communities: "The capacity of the *régulo* (local chief) to administer justice derives from the power that the governor granted him on occasion of proclaiming him régulo, receiving his [vassalage] oath, and handing him the sceptre of office [*bastão*], sign of the invested powers."[15]

For the Portuguese, this was a government style that was in harmony with Timorese views on power, status and authority. As such, it was accounted for by its colonial practitioners as a mirror-image of Timorese attitudes towards power and social hierarchy. "Because they [Timorese] are inclined to the fantastic and the supernatural", one colonial observer noted in 1897, "it is convenient that the pomp of the cults touches their spirits by means of the senses".[16] The attention thus paid to the conduct of ceremonials in political affairs by the Portuguese was understood as a response to an indigenous demand — actions meaningful and efficient because they expressed *conformity* with a Timorese special concern with "exteriority", status display and "pompous cults". A similar "propensity" of the "Timorese princes" for "vanity", the futility of war, and status display had also been noticed by Dominican friars in the seventeenth century.[17] It is possible that this local attachment to the dramatization of status — in objects, gestures, rites — amounted to a Timorese version of regional conceptions of power, namely of traditional Javanese concepts based in status display and the centralization of charisma.[18] Javanese influence could indeed be felt in the social stratification of the Timorese kingdoms. The class of *tumungões* or *tumegós* — an ancient title possibly of Javanese origins (after the term *tumenggung*) — corresponded by the 1900s to a sort of "less powerful *datós*" (Tetum nobility). They could rule villages, command armies in war, or serve as counsellors to the king.[19] By the 1900s, this class maintained political and administrative influence, at least in some kingdoms of the eastern part of East Timor.[20]

Whatever their "colonial" or "pre-colonial" origins, it seemed clear to the Portuguese that ceremonial moments, objects and the self-exhibition of status carried intense meaning in Timorese culture as indication of power and social ranking. Accordingly, careful attention was devoted to the imitative practice of past norms and behaviours. In concrete interactions, this occurred with greater intensity whenever the persons involved — Timorese and/or Portuguese — were perceived as holders of special authority and status: Portuguese governors, army officers, and missionaries; and Timorese liurais (also designated kings or *régulos* in colonial language), and Timorese noblemen (the *principais* and *datós*). The people, as well as the elites, were very keen on the repetition of rehearsed gestures that expressed the sense of social distance and power. Etiquette behaviour was among these significant gestures.

DEFERENCE AND THE PRACTICE OF ETIQUETTE IN COLONIAL ENCOUNTERS

Colonial rule was a complex world of ritual observances and codes of behaviour, an art of manoeuvring ceremoniality. Etiquette codes regulated the circuits of deference and respect, the acknowledgement of power and hierarchy in interactions. Codified deference gestures expressed and regulated the hierarchical relationships between commoners and persons of status. In what follows I shall pay attention to the performance of deference associated with two main forms of colonial encounters: *conjunctive* occasions of communal display of hospitality and subordination towards the authorities, usually associated with the passage of colonial authorities through the territories of Timorese communities; and *disjunctive* occasions of collective display of hostility and opposition towards the colonial government, usually associated with moments of confrontation and warfare. Both these two forms of colonial encounters were to be regulated by modes of etiquette. Accordingly, I will also look at the general significance of etiquette in interpersonal encounters — regardless of the conjunctive, disjunctive or routine character of the encounters — with or between persons of status and holders of office and authority. I shall start with the latter, and then will look at the specific expressions of etiquette on collective manifestations of hospitality and hostility. The sociopolitical significance of etiquette came into view in the minute gestures of courtesy that, so often in the everyday routines of administration, were to regulate the expression of power and social rank in interpersonal encounters. Some Portuguese officers and governors, as we will now see, would not neglect this significance in their government praxis.

Deference and Etiquette in Interpersonal Encounters

Encounters, either private or public, between persons of status were inherently ceremonial, and thus inherently political. The governor, army officers, missionaries, *régulos*, and *datós* should mutually observe certain codes of behaviour. Deference gestures and bodily appearances should express recognition of social ranking and authority. As such, etiquette included attitudes and behaviours performed *between* the Portuguese officials and the indigenous authorities; *and* attitudes and behaviours performed *among* the Portuguese officials themselves — between military officers and missionaries, for example — and which could as well be consequential for ordering status and power. To interfere with the appropriate etiquette that ought to rule the dealings between the Portuguese and Timorese, or between the Portuguese themselves, was an issue of reciprocal political, social and symbolic significance. To fail, break or change the codified performances in actual interactions could have important consequences for the maintenance of social standing and the legitimacy of authority.

Hand kissing is a paradigmatic example of the importance of etiquette gestures in interpersonal encounters. The significance of observing this custom with respect to authority holders was followed by the people regardless of the condition of the recipients of deference being either "Portuguese" or "Timorese". The *beija-mão* (hand kissing), possibly a custom introduced by the Portuguese in former times, for example, was a widespread deference gesture reserved by the commoners to the principal authorities.[21] To "kiss the hand" was a gesture of reverence expressing the highest status, and nineteenth-century accounts point to their ordinary use by the Timorese people in their dealings with Timorese kings, the colonial governor and the Catholic missionaries.

The Timorese people — certainly not the *régulos* — did not usually apply it to army officers, a fact that reveals the relatively subaltern position of the officers in the local status structure of authority. Possibly, *lesser* variations of the usual hand-kissing gesture performed in relation to governor and missionaries could occasionally be applied to Portuguese army officers, another indication of the lower status of the latter as regards the perceived subject centre of Portuguese jural power — the governor — but also as regards the Portuguese figures of ritual or spiritual power — the missionaries.

In contrast, *apertos de mão* (shaking hands) was apparently the gesture normally exchanged between persons of status of equal or proximate ranking. The fact that this was presumably a gesture used between the Timorese *liurais* and the Portuguese officers in command of the districts suggests that the former saw themselves in equal (or at least never inferior) status position with regard to the army officers. Kings and colonels could consider themselves as equals in status to the governor in Dili because their ultimate source of jural power — just like the governor's — resided in an invisible entity, the El-Rei (king of Portugal). The *régulos*, as Celestino da Silva acknowledged, thought of themselves as "representatives of His Majesty El-Rei in the domain of the land", *direct* delegates of the King, not the governor, who, like them, was seen as a subordinate of His Majesty, sometimes holding the same military rank as the *régulos*, if not lower.[22]

Gestures of deference should express recognition of higher ranking in status and power position, such that much care should be taken in the management of etiquette. The Portuguese sensed that a deficit in deference gestures from commoners or *régulos* could mean a shortfall of colonial power. By the same token, an incorrect or offensive observance of etiquette in the relationships with indigenous authorities (or even in the relationships between authorities, for example, military officials and missionaries) could weaken or endanger the Portuguese power, leading the Timorese to show attitudes of hostility, rather than friendly hospitality, towards the Portuguese journeying through the kingdoms. In this light it is significant that, in 1895–96, while trying to find an explanation for the massacre of a Portuguese military column and the tragic death of all the European officers in the Cová and Fatumean kingdoms, one reason invoked in the official report of the events for explaining the indigenous violence was the offensive behaviour of the Portuguese commanding officer towards the aristocracy and the people of these kingdoms. In reaching Cová and Fatumean, and supposedly convinced that behind the resistance of the carriers and ill-dispositions of the population were the manoeuvres of *principais* of Cová and the *régulo* of Fatumean, the Portuguese commandant, Captain Câmara, decided to harshly punish the rulers and noblemen. The

Cová carriers were dismissed and the Fatumean and Cová kingdoms fined. In addition, Câmara publicly whipped the *principais*, broke their swords — an act of great offence to their status ("constitutes one of the gravest offences that one can do the indigenous people", the official report noted) — and put them and the *régulo* under arrest in the government station of Fatumean. In short, the fact that the ceremonial codes of etiquette that regulated the interactions between the Portuguese delegate and indigenous authorities were broken on this occasion was claimed as cause of the outbreak of Timorese hostility and violence that followed.[23]

A deficit in deference gestures from commoners or *régulos* could cause a shortfall of Portuguese "prestige"; similarly, an incorrect or offensive observance of etiquette in the relationships with indigenous authorities (or even in the relationships between authorities, e.g., military officials and missionaries) could weaken the Portuguese position. Therefore, the correct management of appearance and courteous behaviour was perceived by the colonizers as a careful political matter in Portuguese-Timorese relations, an issue that required proper supervision. In 1860, in his instructions for the officers who were to be in charge of the new district organization of the colony, Governor Afonso de Castro recommended the district commandants to be "polite in the dealings with the [Timorese] Kings or Regents, treating them with all the deference owed to an equal, and as equals they should be considered".[24] In the 1890s, Governor Celestino da Silva was especially concerned with the politics of the management of etiquette. He issued a set of special instructions to be adopted by military officers in the interior districts, including a number of recommendations about etiquette. In his *Instructions to the Military Commandants* published in 1896, he suggested the best attention of army officers to the Timorese gestures of deference and courtesy. A rule of reciprocity, for instance, was to be maintained in what concerned the exchange of presents. Although theoretically the reception of presents from the *régulos* was to be avoided, in practice, Celestino da Silva recommended, presents had to be reciprocated, "when from its refusal political inconveniences are foreseen".[25] Army officers should not show disrespect for indigenous authorities in public, but should also be vigilant such that the deference owed to *régulos* was not offensively superior to the deference owed to Portuguese representatives. "Because the natives are in the habit of displaying, principally in our presence, great consideration and respect for their chiefs", the governor advised, "the military commandants should proceed so that, without humiliating those same chiefs, those demonstrations do not become excessive and lead them to consider themselves as superior to our authorities."[26] In addition, military officials and missionaries were instructed to show mutual courtesy in their transactions. In the interior, the use of a uniform by the army officers in their dealings with authorities was further recommended as a rule of important political implications. In the *Instructions* the governor recommended:

> Never receive the missionaries at the district [*comando*] houses and secretaries without the best attentions, and without previously dressing yourselves appropriately, abstaining from visiting them in case they do not proceed in the same way; but, without by any means breaking up official relations, you should not let the public understand that any sort of disagreement or indifference exists; for this reason you shall always compliment them in public ... Do not forget that the natives observe carefully and with indefatigable insistence the actions of military authorities and clergy; that they make judgements on the basis of appearances ...; that manners less courteous and respectful between the various authorities are commented by them always to the detriment of our prestige.[27]

Etiquette and the Administration of Hospitality: The Colonial Authorities' Visits to the Kingdoms

An important manifestation of indigenous etiquette were communal occasions in which gestures of deference and tribute were supposed to express the people's "respect" and ceremonial subordination towards the hierarchical superiors and acknowledged holders of important offices. In colonial accounts, this appears in relation to the Portuguese authorities' visits to the kingdoms, situations in which the conjunctive connections to the Portuguese and the ceremonial subordination towards the colonial representatives of authority were to be dramatized in rites of reception and ceremonials of hospitality.

It was on these types of occasions that demonstrations of deference towards the Portuguese authority achieved greater visibility and intensity. Vassalage was one of those communal occasions, but here I wish to mention another important institution of the colonial circuits of deference: the visits of authorities to the kingdoms, and the collective etiquette of hospitality that pertained to how colonial authorities were to be welcomed while on journey in the kingdoms. Public gestures of deference and tribute normally occurred upon occasion of Portuguese authorities — colonial officers, governors and missionaries — visiting the kingdoms' territories. These visits took place according to stereotyped situations. They were also followed by more or less varied ritualized gestures of deference, which included dances and songs, gifts and forms of tribute, and the exhibition of sacred objects and regalia.

For instance, by virtue of *estilo*, as he went passing through the villages, a Portuguese army officer and his party carrying what was designated as *caixa e bandeira* (drum and flag) was entitled to request tribute from the people and their *datós* in the form of produce and cattle as provisions for him and his party, but also to request tribute in the form of manpower, calling carriers to accompany him or warriors (*arraiais*) to join him on the warpath. On these occasions, the *gastos* (agricultural produce, cattle, and so forth, received as provisions) and the *canceiras* (payment due to the officers for their journey) seem to have been the tributes owed to the Portuguese jural representative, namely (but not exclusively) as he went passing through the villages for collecting the *finta* tax.[28] Likewise, a missionary on a journey in a kingdom should be honoured with the company of the local *régulo* and a personal ceremonial party, and was also entitled to receive provisions as a form of tribute from the villages at their passage.

Eventually less frequent than the passage of missionaries or officers, the visits of the colonial governor to the kingdoms were special ceremonial moments of collective tribute and deference. They gave the impression of an important stately occasion. In fact, to the extent that they configured an intense public invocation of the core elements of politico-jural power, the governor's visits appeared as state rituals: special ceremonial occasions in which the charismatic or sacred qualities perceived as constitutive of the jural power of colonial governors were publicly performed, celebrated and put at stake. Colonial accounts, perhaps unsurprisingly, thus tend to put considerable emphasis on the Timorese rites of hospitality and accompanying signs of ceremonial subordination, as if *per se* they communicated and guaranteed harmonious colonial hegemony to the Portuguese in Dili. However, as we shall see later below, the etiquette of hospitality and the gestures of subservience that came into view on these occasions did not preclude hostility and opposition.

People from various settlements, sometimes different kingdoms, would come together to receive the governor. There were customary feasting, songs, drum-playing (*batuque*) and dances (*tabedai*). The men were arrayed in war dresses and held their swords in the air while dancing.[29] *Liurais* would bring presents or even offer buffaloes for sacrifice to the governor and his party on these occasions. The *liurais* and the *datós* would come along with their families to greet the governor, bringing presents, parading in Portuguese old military uniforms and displaying the material emblems of jural authority; afterwards, they would continue to accompany him during the rest of his journey through the kingdom.[30] One of the most important of such emblems, the Portuguese flag, kept under special care in a bamboo and/or guarded in the *uma luliks* (sacred houses), could be publicly shown and specially raised at the sight of the governor.[31] But the flag was not the only object removed from the *uma lulik* for these special occasions. Other items of European origin were also used and displayed. Umbrellas, uniforms, and particularly the *bastão* (sceptre or staff of office handed over by the Portuguese governor on vassalage rites, and thereafter a fundamental token of Timorese jural authority and status) were also ritually made visible. Whenever they came to the presence of the colonial governor, indigenous aristocracy and royalty exhibited their ancient *lulik* objects of war and justice: swords, sceptres and headhunters' emblems (golden discs or "moons" known as *luas de oiro*). If they had one, they would wear a Portuguese military uniform, eventually outdated.[32] In 1909, after accompanying the governor, Eduardo Marques, on one such visit, the Portuguese colonial judge and poet Alberto Osório de Castro described with literary verve the obsequious gestures and the accompanying ceremonial display of the ancestral heirlooms that bear on the indigenous jural rulers' lineage authority and status:

> The old régulos of Cailaco and Deribate come to pay their homage, in the company of their principal women, their dignitaries, their ceremonial *tébedais*, with animal presents brought in on flowery litters. The Deribate one is grave. The Cailaco one shows towards the Governor, who had met him years ago when he was still a presumptive heir, a good intelligent smile. And how picturesque it is his navy officer's uniform from, at least, the time of Dom João VI [prince regent of Portugal, 1799–1815, and king of Portugal, Brazil, and the Algarves, 1815–26], dolmen upon his chest, as if they were *luas* [Timorese metal discs, signifying warrior or headhunter status], hanging as medals, the corners of the ancestral bicorn on the shoulders and decorated with dolmen as well! One of the dignitaries held the royal paiung[,] which for the effect is a feminine umbrella, with crepe and black glass beads. Another dignitary brings the royal rota sceptre [*bastão de rota*] of Malacca with a silver handle, and another brings the *rotim* staff [*estadela de rotim*] of Canton. The old régulo going barefoot conveys a charming barbarian dignity.[33]

The ostentatious aspect of these ceremonial encounters and the public display of deference and respect towards Portuguese people and things left a strong impression on some colonial governors. Governor Alfredo Lacerda e Maia, who went on a visit to the Western kingdoms in 1886, came back persuaded of the importance of the governors' visits to the kingdoms as a true technique of rule, able in its own right to extend colonial authority to the interior and pacify the usual hostility of those distant kingdoms. In 1886, reporting on his visit to Aipelo, Liquiçá and Maubara, Lacerda e Maia wrote: "The presence of the governor always represents for them a magic influence, even when they have been ill-treated by the commandants, even when prior misconducts have caused them distrust."[34] Thus impressed with these manifestations, the Portuguese could take Timorese etiquette and rites of reception as signs of uncontested colonial power, perceiving the visits as a technology of ceremonial rule in their own right. However, the same kingdoms and *régulos* that one day showed respect towards Portuguese rulers could raise arms against them just a few days, weeks or months later. Exuberant gestures of deference could coexist with, or be followed by, feelings and manifestations of enmity, for etiquette, too, had a role to play in hostile encounters. It is to this facet of etiquette that I now turn.

Etiquette and the Regulation of Hostility: Courteous Customs and Manners in Warfare

Etiquette mattered for sustaining status and authority in Timorese-Portuguese relations; it was also important to regulate hostility in colonial interactions. It was thus not limited to conjunctive occasions of public deference, or even to the interpersonal dealings with and between persons of status; it was a critical aspect of conflict management. In fact, as the governor's above concern with etiquette management reveals, managing etiquette was perceived as critical to the preservation of friendly relationships with the indigenous aristocracy and commoners, thus helping to prevent indigenous ill-disposition towards the Europeans. Moreover, the Timorese, too, seemed to value etiquette as a means to secure friendliness and prevent conflict. In this light, not only was etiquette important for maintaining stable hierarchies, it was also important to routinely administer political tension and even military confrontations. In effect, it might be hypothesized that as the occasion grew problematic, or prone to violence, the more important it was to resort in practice to pre-established etiquette conventions: the higher the tension among people who were recognized enemies, the more significant was the accuracy of ceremonial interactions.

In the indigenous administration of justice and conduct of war, the importance of etiquette was acknowledged in special positions. Every kingdom had a ceremonial manager of justice designated as the *macoan*, or the *parlamento*, in charge of the regulation of ceremonials and social conventions in jural matters.[35] An example of the importance of etiquette in situations of hostility was the oratory ceremonials that preceded combat. These ceremonials helped to legitimate a state of hostility but could also, on occasions, help to impede actual bloodshed. The value of etiquette in the regulation of military conflicts was thus attested by the existence of a "ceremonial orator", the *homulac*, in charge of the speeches and exchange of arguments prior to combat.[36] The *homulac* could state the motives for engaging in the war, declaim a history of the affairs that justified the dispute, and try to bring the parties into agreement. Sometimes, his skills were enough to stop the fighting. Significantly, this was not simply an activity of inter-indigenous fighting; it was also an integral part of Portuguese warfare customs in Timor. In effect, the *homulacs* also played their role by the side of the Portuguese in colonial campaigns. In 1896, for instance, Second Lieutenant Francisco Duarte gave permission to the *régulo* of Maubili and the *principal* (a nobleman) Maucura to perform the oratory ceremonials in the name of the government before launching an attack on Timorese enemy villages. Their speech justified the war and, in return for obedience, they offered the governor's clemency. In Duarte's words: "each one at a time, in clear and sounding voice, enumerated the government's motives for doing war against them; they reminded them of the setbacks suffered by the government since long ago, the treachery of 1869, etc., etc., and finally upbraided their active participation in the massacre of last year [1895]."[37]

Hostility and etiquette, therefore, were not opposites. Etiquette was one important means in the management of jural affairs and politico-military tensions and confrontations. But they were not opposites in yet another sense. Signs of respect towards colonial authorities could coexist with manifestations of enmity towards the same authorities. Although at war with the Portuguese establishment in Dili, gestures of deference could still be selectively preserved in relation to the highest representatives of the Portuguese powers (such as the governor), or simply in relation to Portuguese authorities for whom the Timorese occasionally held a special consideration. The social force of the custom-imitation of etiquette could then appear in the most extraordinary occasions. Two stories reported as "fantastic" in late nineteenth-century colonial accounts may illustrate this point. In 1887, in the aftermath of Governor Lacerda e Maia's enigmatic assassination by the Timorese irregular troops of *moradores* (a company of indigenous irregulars established by the Portuguese) in Dili, the parish priest of Dili, Father João Gomes Ferreira, was able, by sheer force of his bodily presence, to save the life of the Portuguese government secretary who was about to be killed by a great number of infuriated *moradores*.[38] Allegedly, the rebels did not dare to touch him, and thus the official's life was spared. Yet another fantastic story — this time concerning the figure of the governor — was reported by Celestino da Silva in 1901, relating to his visit to the Atabai battlefield in 1899. Besieged in their villages for a month, the Atabai people offered ferocious resistance to the government troops. The governor then decided to pay a visit in person to the commanding officer and check on the progress of the combat: "when I arrived", wrote Celestino da Silva,

> I ordered Lieutenant Figueiredo to cease fire, and I got off my horse and went in the direction of the rebels' trenches, which were well guarded, and as I got close to the sentinels who were protected behind the rocks and the trenches they stood up from their defensive posts and removed their kerchiefs, as sign of respect for the governor, for the "father" ... . Not even one rebel considered the idea of killing me, of disrespecting me, though they could have done it safely and with advantage! They sent a principal to speak to me, and I began by demanding the delivery of two firearms and respective ammunition that they had taken from two dead soldiers killed in the assault; they handed them back to me! I spoke to them as I wished, and gave them 24 hours to lay their arms down and surrender, and promised absolute pardon, and I left .... They did not surrender! They fought like heroes until the 6th of August![39]

Showing deference through etiquette and practising hostility through violence were not mutually exclusive. Respect for the Portuguese authority did not mean that this same Portuguese power went unchallenged and uncontested. Acting against Dili, the government, specific officers, or even specific governors, did not mean that deference and etiquette as regards special figures of colonial authority should not be followed. Opposing the Portuguese forces in battle, for instance, could be compatible with the continuance of customary codes and etiquette gestures that concerned the recognition of certain Portuguese persons and things as embodiments of higher powers.

CONCLUSION

The notions of ritual and ceremonial have been at the core of anthropological understandings of indigenous state power in Southeast Asia.[40] To establish ritual connections with ancestors has also been conventionally described as one definitional trait of indigenous or traditional societies, particularly in Timor.[41] However, as regards Portuguese colonial government in Timor, the role of ceremonial, and the value of customs, objects and manners of ancestral origin cannot be ascribed simply to a presumably separate "indigenous" culture. Their significance resides at the intersection of the European and indigenous worlds. This chapter has suggested that one needs to look at the sociopolitical value of ceremonial life at the very juncture of indigenous and colonial cultures, as they emerged in the course of colonial encounters over time. In Timor, where the Portuguese had been firmly settled since the seventeenth century, the command of a peculiar ceremonial language was critical to the colonial project until a late period. Vassalage rites, social protocols, status signs and objects ensured communication with local rulers, and became the means through which the Portuguese government authority — *but also* the politico-jural authority with which the Timorese *liurais*, as *régulos*, were endowed — could be effectively exercised. In the late nineteenth century, the Portuguese could regret their dependence on the everyday reproduction of these mechanisms, criticizing them as undesirable and out of fashion. Yet, they pragmatically sensed that without the artful imitation of the practices and institutions of Timor's colonial past, "colonialism" in the present was not possible. They were a legacy without which colonial authority could not survive; and a legacy that could not be sustained without Portuguese and Timorese mutual engagement with imitation of the past. In order to energize both the Portuguese establishment and the sociopolitical authority of the Timorese ruling classes, this legacy of customs and manners required practical maintenance by both the colonizers and the indigenous people in their interactions; it required constant care to be put in the rightful enactment and reactivation of old customs, norms and behaviours — a sociological process that I have here designated, after Gabriel Tarde, as the engagement with custom-imitation.

The observation of minute gestures and etiquette rules was an important element of these meaningful practices of custom-imitation. It expressed higher status and authority in concrete public and private interactions and as such helped to sustain the existence of Portuguese authority, beyond its feeble and tiny dimension in Dili. Regardless of their more or less volatile condition, etiquette was perceived by clear-minded colonial observers as an important aspect of government practices, a sensitive matter in concrete political and social relations with the Timorese, particularly with the indigenous upper classes. Yet, as the Portuguese, too, could sense, the enactment of reputedly old customs and manners, and the mastery of this ceremonial language did not guarantee a peaceful state of affairs: etiquette and deference were not straightforward signs of indigenous submission; they did not run counter to Timorese critique and hostility. The very same kingdom (Maubara), for example, whose people and leaders had showed such respect for Governor Lacerda e Maia's passage in 1886 were credited to be "treacherous" vassals by tradition; and just a few years later in 1893, the people of Maubara would not hesitate to raise arms against Dili. Similarly, in 1895, the Western kingdoms that, just a few months earlier, had paid vassalage to the government and the king of Portugal, would not hesitate in killing and decapitating the same Portuguese officers to whom they had presented their vassalage. Custom-imitation remained important in ritual moments of conjunction and celebration, but also when crisis and disruption were imminent. Hostility and etiquette, just like hospitality and deference, maintained close connections. Etiquette and ceremonial instantiated hierarchy and authority; they also helped to tame social tensions, regulate conflict, and manage warfare. Deference gestures could emerge even in situations of feud, without contradicting the continuance of war and enmity. Thus, on its own, etiquette and custom-imitation did not safeguard colonial authority from the permanent threat of indigenous hostility. Enacting the legacy was not enough, for, although intense and majestic, the status, authority and symbolic power of Portuguese agents that came into existence in one ceremonial moment, could just as easily melt into the air on the day after.

Notes

1   An earlier version of this chapter was presented at the conference "Portuguese and Luso-Asian Legacies in Southeast Asia, 1511–2011", held at Singapore and Malacca in September 2010. I thank the participants at this conference and particularly Hugo C. Cardoso for comments during the discussion of the paper. This essay is a product of the project "Colonial Mimesis in Lusophone Asia and Africa", funded by the Foundation for Science and Technology, Portugal (Ref. PTDC/CS-ANT/101064/2008).

2   This paragraph summarizes points made at greater length in Ricardo Roque, "The Unruly Island: Colonialism's Predicament in Late Nineteenth-Century East Timor", in *Parts of Asia*, Portuguese Literary & Cultural Studies 17/18, edited by Cristiana Bastos (Dartmouth: University of Massachusetts Dartmouth Center for Portuguese Studies and Culture, 2010), pp. 303–30; and Ricardo Roque, *Headhunting and Colonialism: Anthropology and the Circulation of Human Skulls in the Portuguese Empire, 1870–1930* (Basingstoke: Palgrave Macmillan, 2010), pp. 1–14.

3   The expression "estilo" was used in Tetum-Dili, but it was originally a Portuguese term with a juridical meaning, partially preserved in colonial Timor. In colonial usage, "estilos" referred not only to rites associated with spiritual affairs but also to sets of norms, rites and behaviours established by tradition that expressed the exercise of jural power as well as the embodiments of authority and charisma (in persons, material objects or immaterial entities).

4   As such, Portuguese authority in Timor could be seen as a variant of Weber's "traditional" type of legitimate domination: "Authority will be called traditional if legitimacy is claimed for it and believed in by virtue of the sanctity of age-old rules and powers." Max Weber, *Economy and Society* (Berkeley: University of California Press, 1979), 1:226.

5   Celestino da Silva to Minister and Secretary of Navy and Overseas Affairs, 25 January 1901, Macau and Timor, ACL_SEMU_DGU_1R_002_Cx 11, 1901–04, Arquivo Histórico Ultramarino (hereafter cited as AHU).

6   For a recent example, see Stuart B. Schwartz, "Ceremonies of Public Authority in a Colonial Capital: The King's Procession and the Hierarchies of Power in Seventeenth-Century Salvador", *Anais de História de Além-Mar* 5 (2004): 7–26.

7   Thus, celebratory readings as "hybridity" or as benevolent amalgamations of the ceremonial interconnections discussed herein must be avoided. I elaborate on this critique, from the point of view of a mutual parasitism approach in Roque, *Headhunting and Colonialism*, chaps. 1, 2 and 3.

8   Ibid.

9   Edward Shils, *Center and Periphery: Essays in Macrosociology* (Chicago: University of Chicago Press, 1975), pp. 245 and 268. The notion of etiquette developed herein draws on Shils's definition of the term as analytically distinct from the notions of ceremony and ritual. For Shils, these three notions belong to a continuum of modes of "stereotyped behaviour"; however, they differ in their cognitive content and degree of proximity to the sacred or charismatic elements of collective life. But on the sociological importance of courteous behaviour and etiquette in structuring authority and hierarchy in Europe, see also Norbert Elias's classic study, *The Court Society* (Oxford: Blackwell, 1983).

10   Shils, *Center and Periphery*, pp. 154–55.

11   Gabriel Tarde, *Les lois de l'imitation*, 2nd ed. (1895), p. 32, <http://classiques. uqac.ca/classiques/tarde_gabriel/lois_imitation/tarde_lois_imitation_1.pdf> (accessed September 2010).

12   This dimension of what I call here "custom-imitation" has been observed and analysed by previous historiography of the late Portuguese colonial empire. *Cf.*, for example: Valentim Alexandre, *Velhos Brasis, Novas Áfricas: Portugal e o Império (1808–1975)* (Porto: Afrontamento, 2000); Omar R. Thomaz, *Ecos do Atlântico Sul: Representações sobre o Terceiro Império Português* (Rio de Janeiro: Editora da Universidade Federal do Rio de Janeiro, 2002).

13   *Cf.* Clifford Geertz, *Negara: The Theatre State in Nineteenth-Century Bali* (Princeton: Princeton University Press, 1980), p. 13. The importance of "political rituals" in state administration in colonial and imperial contexts has been underscored by various studies. Hobsbawm and Ranger's volume *The Invention of Tradition* was seminal in bringing to the imperial historians' attention the importance of ritual in European colonial administration in Asia and Africa. Eric Hobsbawm and Terence Ranger, eds., *The Invention of Tradition* (Cambridge: Cambridge University Press, 1992).

14   This colonial view needs to be contrasted with indigenous diarchic theories of power, in which ritual powers (claimed to be an exclusive possession of the Timorese holders) ranked higher than the jural or political powers that could be shared with, or be somehow connected to, the Portuguese. But *cf.* Elizabeth Traube, *Cosmology and Social Life: Ritual Exchange among the Mambai of East Timor* (Chicago: University of Chicago Press, 1986); and Roque, *Headhunting and Colonialism*, chap. 2.

15 Silva to Minister and Secretary of Navy and Overseas Affairs, 25 January 1901.

16 Bento da França, *Macau e os seus Habitantes: Relações com Timor* (Lisbon: Imprensa Nacional, 1897), p. 278; *cf.* pp. 242–43.

17 Cited in Afonso de Castro, *As Possessões Portuguezas da Oceania* (Lisbon: Imprensa Nacional, 1867), p. 20.

18 See Geertz, *Negara*, pp. 16–17; Benedict Anderson, "The Idea of Power in Javanese Culture", in *Culture and Politics in Indonesia*, edited by Claire Holt (Ithaca: Cornell University Press, 1972), pp. 1–70.

19 In the fifteenth century, prior to the arrival of the Portuguese, Timor island had been under the sphere of influence of the Javanese Majapahit empire. On Tumungões, compare Alberto Osório de Castro, *A Ilha Verde e Vermelha de Timor* (Lisbon, 1943; repr., Lisbon: Cotovia, 1996), p. 191; Afonso de Castro, "Notícia dos usos e costumes dos povos de Timor", *Anais do Conselho Ultramarino*, unofficial section (1863): 29.

20 In 1901, one governor referred to the " 'Tumegós', who are old men, counsellors to the *régulo* in some states in the East". Silva to Minister and Secretary of Navy and Overseas Affairs, 25 January 1901.

21 Compare José Simões Martinho, *Timor: Quatro Séculos de Colonização Portuguesa* (Porto: Livraria Progredior, 1943), p. 229; J.A. Fernandes, *Timor: Impressões e Aspectos* (Porto: Tip. A Tribuna, 1923), p. 21; and Castro, *A Ilha Verde*, pp. 170–71.

22 Celestino da Silva to Minister and Secretary of Navy and Overseas Affairs, 5 June 1897, Macao and Timor, ACL_SEMU_DGU_1R_002_Cx 10, 1897–1900, AHU.

23 See Albano de Magalhães, João Mariano de Lamartine Rocha, Belarmino Lobo, José Maria d'Assumpção Ozório, and César Máximo dos Santos, Relatório da Comissão para o Governador de Timor sobre o desastre de Fatumean, 5 October 1895, AC, P-1547, Arquivo Histórico de Macau (hereafter cited as AHM), Macao. On this episode, see also Roque, *Headhunting and Colonialism*, chap. 7.

24 Governor Afonso de Castro, Portaria nº 58, 2 August 1860, enclosed in Afonso de Castro to Minister and Secretary of Navy and Overseas Affairs, 4 April 1863, Macao and Timor, ACL_SEMU_DGU_005_Cx 29, 1863, AHU.

25 José Celestino da Silva, *Instruções para os Commandantes Militares* (Macao, 1896), p. 5.

26 Ibid., p. 7.

27 Ibid., p. 4.

28 The values of these subsidiary tributes, rather than being fixed beforehand, were discretionarily set down by the authorities, becoming a personal asset of their offices. For detailed descriptions of the complexity of these chains of tribute, involving *régulos*, *datós* and army officers, see Silva to Minister and Secretary of Navy and Overseas Affairs, 25 January 1901; Castro, *As Possessões*, p. 377; and José dos Santos Vaquinhas, "Timor: Usos – superstições de guerra", *Boletim da Sociedade de Geografia de Lisboa* 4 (1884): 490–91.

[29] Significantly, the ceremonials celebrating the arrival of Portuguese authorities were qualified in colonial accounts with the term "estilo" (as in "batuque do estilo", that is, customary drumming). Fernandes, *Timor*, pp. 25–26.

[30] For other descriptions of governors' visits to the interior kingdoms in this period, see also Fernandes, *Timor*, pp. 19–22; Alfredo de Lacerda e Maia to Governor of Macao and Timor, 15 April 1886, AC, P-653, AHM.

[31] José dos Santos Vaquinhas, "Timor: I", *Boletim da Sociedade de Geografia de Lisboa* 4, no. 7 (1883): 328.

[32] The practice might date at least to the eighteenth century. Then, indigenous kings could dress "the Portuguese way" on feasting days or when visiting the governor in Dili. *Cf.* Artur Teodoro de Matos, *Timor Português, 1515–1769: Contribuição para a sua História* (Lisbon: Instituto Histórico Infante Dom Henrique, 1974), p. 27. The propensity of indigenous aristocracy for status display and power was eventually observed by the Dominican missionaries in the seventeenth century. See Castro, *As Possessões*, p. 20.

[33] Castro, *A Ilha Verde*, pp. 79–80.

[34] Alfredo de Lacerda e Maia to Governor of Macao and Timor, 15 April 1886.

[35] For the *macoan*, see Matos, *Timor Português*, p. 107; for the *parlamento*, see Fernandes, *Timor*, pp. 33–34. See also França, *Macau*, p. 233.

[36] Vaquinhas, "Timor", p. 478. For the Atoni oratory ceremonials that preceded combat, *cf.* H. Schulte-Nordtholt, *The Political System of the Atoni* (The Hague: Nijhoff, 1971), pp. 331–32.

[37] Francisco Duarte, "Commando Militar de Thiarlelo, 31 August 1896", in *Relatório das Operações de Guerra no Districto Autónomo de Timor no Anno de 1896 Enviado ao Ministro e Secretário de Estado dos Negócios da Marinha e Ultramar*, by José Celestino da Silva (Lisbon: Imprensa Nacional, 1897), p. 51.

[38] The event became legendary thereafter within ecclesiastical circles, as alleged evidence of the superior "prestige of the missionaries among the natives" *vis-à-vis* the government representatives. *Cf.* Abílio José Fernandes, *Esboço Histórico e do Estado Actual das Missões de Timor e Refutação dalgumas Falsidades contra Elas Caluniosamente Afirmadas por um Ex-Governador de Timor* (Macao: Tipografia Mercantil, 1931), p. 41; Manuel Teixeira, *Macau e a sua Diocese: Missões de Timor* (Macao: Tipografia da Missão do Padroado, 1974), pp. 99–104.

[39] Silva to Minister and Secretary of the Navy and Overseas Affairs, 25 January 1901.

[40] *Cf.*, for example, Geertz, *Negara*; Stanley Tambiah, *Culture, Thought and Social Action: An Anthropological Perspective* (Cambridge, MA: Harvard University Press, 1985); Margaret J. Wiener, *Visible and Invisible Realms: Power, Magic, and Colonial Conquest in Bali* (Chicago: University of Chicago Press, 1995); and Graeme McRae, "Negara Ubud: The Theatre-State in Twenty-First-Century Bali", *History and Anthropology* 16, no. 4 (2005): 393–413. G.C. Bentley, "Indigenous States of Southeast Asia", *Annual Review of Anthropology* 15 (1986): 275–305.

[41] *Cf.* James Fox, ed., *The Flow of Life: Essays in Eastern Indonesia* (Cambridge, MA: Harvard University Press, 1980).

4

REMEMBERING THE PORTUGUESE PRESENCE IN TIMOR AND ITS CONTRIBUTION TO THE MAKING OF TIMOR'S NATIONAL AND CULTURAL IDENTITY

Vicente Paulino[1]

Culture is the memory of a people that never dies.

"Manifesto Maubere", Fernando Sylvan

Culture is a framework of human adventure, a result of time and space, an attempt to contemplate, understand and transform it in pursuit of an ideal of harmony and perfection. A healthy relationship with nature and with the community in which it is housed are the crucial elements of any culture. The true subject of culture is man himself on the basis of "tradition". Thus, for the sake of continuity, every human community shapes its own assets so that these are preserved.

Culture cannot exist without society and, likewise, no human society can exist without its culture, because culture is the soul of the human being in all of its branches. In other words, despite cultural variations that distinguish human communities and "because of its cultural legacy, the man moved away from the animal, but has become closely dependent on men. So in order to become a man, it is essential for him to live his life socially and under the influence of all stimuli which provides him with his family and his tribe."[2] Stuart Hall defines culture as a set of structures of meaning, or a process that has to do with the implementation of joint practice and depends "on its participants interpreting meaningfully what is happening around them, and making sense of the world, in broadly similar ways".[3]

This chapter will seek to remember the Portuguese presence in Timor and its contribution to the formation of the cultural and national identity of East Timor. First, it describes the initial contacts established by merchants, sailors and Portuguese missionaries with the island of Timor and its people, then goes on to address the cultural traits of the Timorese. Second, this study will examine the results of the long-term Portuguese influence over some 450 years, contrasting these with the consequences of twenty-four years of Indonesian occupation that caused the massive destruction of cultural Timorese entities, among them the "sacred houses". Third, it will engage in a comparative analysis of Timorese national identity and culture with those of Japan and Korea.

EAST TIMOR, THE ISLAND OF SANDALWOOD

The island of Timor, as part of the far-flung Portuguese seaborne empire, was the richest in sandalwood in the Asian region. It was the sandalwood that attracted the attention of the Portuguese to the island. But this had long been the history of the island of Timor, which was an ancient land considered to be a meeting place for different groups of traders from around the world. The existence of the island was noted in fourteenth-century Chinese geography, which saw it as the "the end of the world". The name of Timor was famous for its sandalwood and still alludes to tropical fragrance.

The first reports about the existence of the island of Timor are contained in brief references in Chinese, Javanese and Arab literature. From the Chinese literature, the oldest reference concerns the sandalwood trade and consists of twelve to twenty lines of text, repeating almost verbatim the same wording until the end of the sixteenth century, when they started reporting the Portuguese presence on the island.[4] Javanese chronicles have been reporting on Timor since the fourteenth century but are even more laconic, merely citing specifically the island's name in the list of who sent tribute to the Majapahit kingdom in East Java, which ruled the area from the late thirteenth until the beginning of the sixteenth century.

First driven by mere curiosity, then out of interest, the Portuguese established their presence on Timor around 1514–15. The first expedition took place on board a junk named the *Luso-Malay*.[5] According to a report drafted in 1514 for the king of Portugal, Dom Manuel I, from the captain of Malacca, Afonso Lopes da Costa, successor of Jorge de Brito, that reveals the direct contacts with the island of Timor: "os nossos junques que varo pera banda de Timor e Malaquo" (our boats that went close to Timor and Malacca). From this and other fragmented documentation such as price figures for sandalwood that appear in correspondence sent from Malacca, we know today that the Portuguese exchanged Malacca cotton cloth and metal objects for sandalwood, honey and wax in Timor.

In the second half of the sixteenth century there are references to regularly scheduled services departing not only from Malacca but also Macao, because China was the main consumer of sandalwood. During the commercial expeditions, Dominican missionaries travelled to the island of Solor, to the north of Timor, and were responsible for building the first Portuguese fortress in that strategic region. While the merchants were engaged in the sandalwood trade, the clergy made multiple conversions and spread the Christian faith to the surrounding islands. From the Solor fortress, the Portuguese — merchants, adventurers, and missionaries — often sighted Timor. But whether or not they actually visited it remains a matter of some conjecture. According to McIntyre, Timor was sighted and marked on a chart, but the actual landing was made at Solor. This author considers it possible that a number of degraded or deported convicts were unloaded at Solor and thus comprised the genesis of the Solor-Timor colony.[6]

In 1595, Portugal and the Netherlands were in armed conflict. The Netherlands won the war, and Portugal lost the strategic regions of Batavia and the Moluccas, including the island of Solor. In 1613 the Portuguese moved their headquarters for the captaincy to the island of Flores. But the territorial clashes between the two settlers — Portugal and the Netherlands — did not stop, resulting in the fall of Malacca, which was taken by the Dutch in 1641. The seat of the captaincy was built in 1646 in Kupang, today part of the Republic of Indonesia, in West Timor. In 1652 it fell to the Dutch as well, and the captaincy was then moved to Lifau.

Contact between the two peoples — the Portuguese people and Timorese — consisted of an intermingling of feeling and culture: in other words, the Portuguese lived in harmony with the local people, marrying East Timorese women who were descendants of the noble families. Thus, one can say that the specificity of the Portuguese presence was promoted or reinforced by the democratization of human societies through intermarriage and assimilation, and whose policy was aimed at reinforcing the cultural ties between the two peoples.

TIMORESE CULTURE AND ITS SYSTEM OF
SOCIAL ORGANIZATION

East Timor's history before the arrival of the Portuguese was marked by successive waves of migration. The modern East Timorese are a composite of different cultural traditions, predominantly Melanesian and Malay, giving it great cultural heterogeneity, which also gave rise to the existence of various ethno-linguistic groups that still persist to this day. As described by Elizabeth Traube:

> This history of diversity is reflected in Timorese oral traditions. Each of the peoples of Timor represent themselves as being descended either from original, autochthonous inhabitants of the land, or from ancestral invaders who are traced back to a mythic homeland overseas. Interethnic relations are represented in terms of a distinction between insiders and outsiders ...[7]

There is no consensus among various authors regarding the exact number of East Timorese ethno-linguistic groups and their subdivisions. However, everyone seems to agree on the existence of a wide variety of these ethno-linguistic groups.[8]

East Timor was part of an island grouped into two great realms that separately ruled over the island of Timor: the realm of Belos (meaning "nice"), consisting of forty-six kingdoms and that covered the current territory of East Timor, and the realm of Servião, consisting of sixteen kingdoms that covered the current territory of West Timor. The kingdoms were independent from one another and were governed by a *liurai* (king). The *liurais* were appointed from the noble families and exercised power in a manner similar to the feudal lords in medieval Europe.

The *liurais* and the community's chiefs enjoyed the status of being *datós*, that is, the "princes of the earth", with paternal-like powers to protect those who welcomed their protection within a kingdom. The *datós* had the power to represent their people in foreign affairs and to pursue the receipt of tax (*rai-ten*) in exchange for authorizing the cultivation of a parcel of land.

In general, these were the political and social systems that the Portuguese found when they arrived in Timor. Afonso de Castro noted that even before Western civilizations entered Timor, "the man [of Timor] had abandoned the woods [and the] wandering, nomadic life, and had settled on farmland. The tribe had become the village, and the village had established relations with other neighbouring villages forming a state. Miserable little states, but with all the elements that constitute the nation."[9] In the context of what constitutes a nation-state, even in those remote days, in the opinion of Afonso de Castro, there was already an "infantile" nation, constituted by small republics each governed, if not by written laws, at least by the customs and traditions, or what are denominated the *estilos* (styles), their *adat* (culture).[10] This characteristic has been observed in the Bunak ethnic group *okul liu lai nalan liu lai na pemerintah*.

Always outnumbered, the Portuguese colonial authority did not seek to destroy the Timorese political and social system; on the contrary, the Portuguese blended their administrative policy into the already solid Timorese traditional systems in order to exercise dominion over the territory. To intensify and accelerate colonial power over the territory in the eighteenth century, Governor Coelho Guerreiro equated the hierarchies of traditional power with the colonial military ranks by assigning military patents to local Timorese chiefs. This integration of the local aristocracy into the bureaucratic system of the colonial state allowed for cultural assimilation and political identity that would result in a "Timor Portuguese", with the advantages of access to a Western educational system, at least for the children of local elites.

House and *Knua*

We assume herein the notion of the house or *knua* as a hybrid social space or place of crossing symbolic representation (the personal representation of "family" and the social representation of "community"). The *knua* is represented by sacred objects that are present throughout the course of social interactions.

The *knua* is constituted by multiple borders. These borders are both horizontal (male/female) and vertical (the male represents heaven and the female symbolizes the earth). This concept varies according to the myths of origin of the different ethno-linguistic groups that constitute East Timorese society. Nonetheless, of note is the peculiarity that the houses reserve specific symbolic places for animals.

The learning of sociopolitical systems begins in the house, and it is fundamental to understanding the structure of identity and the ethno-symbolic Timorese nation. The house is a physical space from which man builds his family, social and cultural life. It therefore represents the memory of the ancestors and has important symbolic value.

Ruy Cinatti, in his work *A Arquitectura Timorense* (*Timorese Arquitecture*), makes a detailed survey of the Timorese ethnological universe, based on studies undertaken during his stay in East Timor. He notes the existence of a "symbolic cosmic world expressed in the village and in the home",[11] and James J. Fox, in his study *The Flow of Life: Essay on Eastern Indonesia*, identifies a set of social categories of the various ethnic groups of eastern Indonesia based on the cosmological significance of "house" and considers women as a component of the "flow of life".[12]

The *knua* is the centre of cultural contacts and the breeding place for the family and for social relationships. It is the political and economic centre. It constitutes as a sort of super-family imaginary, and it is the basis of the nation.[13] Thus the house can be classified into three imaginary dimensions: community, nation-state and world, which are all rooted in the notion of home as defining and representing identity.

The community is a member of the super-family house and an imaginary element required for the formation of national identity. The nation-state as the sovereign body of a country provides all relations with the "community house" and the "world" in order to maintain their national identity and lead to the development of policy that can sustain all the needs of the "community house". Further, it is not possible to build the "community house" and the nation/state without the "world" or a "habitat/territory". If the world did not exist, man could not build his community house; indeed, not even his own human individuality could exist. So the world is the birthplace or home of humanity.

The nation is seen as a "house" to the extent that it is "an existential unity of humanity that circumscribes a sacred unity, actions, and ritual processes which position and articulate processes of identification and belonging".[14] The "house" or *knua* in this sense is the connecting link between the family and community. According to Anne-Marie Thiesse, "the nation has been intellectually constructed as an unchanging body, always identical to itself through the vicissitudes of history".[15] The original groups are associated with the founders of specific villages, and the offspring of the group live as one *uma kain/ahimatan* or "descent group",[16] a phenomenon which in the Bunak ethnic group is known as "tita oto kere, tita deu uen" ("together in one fire, together in one roof/house", or, in Portuguese, "juntos num só fogo, juntos num só tecto/casa").[17] In other words, the ancestors' ongoing presence is revealed in the living structure of human society, for example, and is also found in the landscape and the unknown spaces occupied by many peoples, especially by strangers, all linked to each other, which thereby relates the habitat areas with their human households, the houses themselves, and their interiors.

This universe of the "sacred house" represents an ethnic heritage and collective memory. With the Portuguese presence began a new identity with the formation of a powerful mestizo group, the *topasses*. This new group was incorporated into the social structure and into the existing kinship relations,

FIGURE 4.1
The Function of the Sacred House

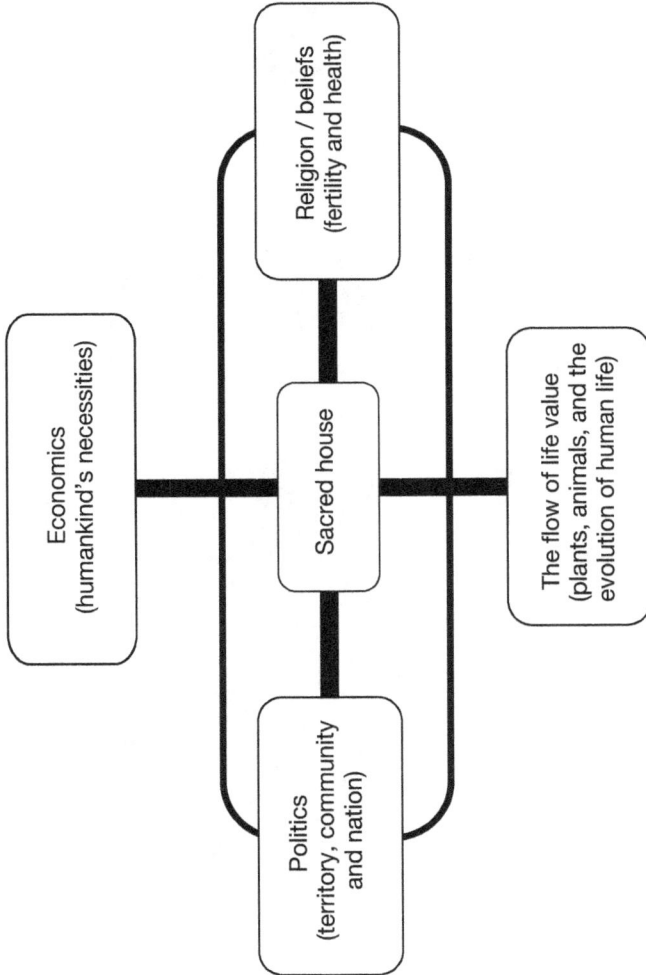

FIGURE 4.2
Representation of the Symbolic Metaphor "House"

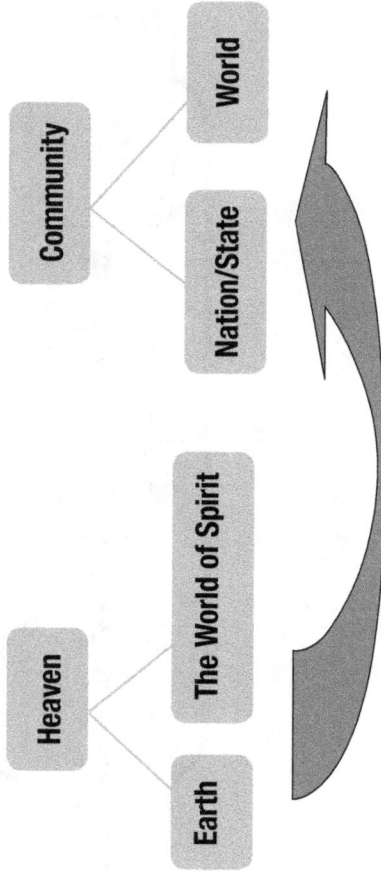

and founded new houses that were inserted into the circuit of existing exchanges.[18]

The discussions about the patriotic nature of the people in general after 1974 utilized traditional values and ideas as they are related to the house and were aimed at supporting the revolutionary doctrine and its strategy of establishing its own identity. Generally, the symbolic value of the sacred house continued to be respected by the Timorese people, although the national liberation war was destroying their physical structure. For this reason, the sacred house is the nation's own background. In the modern state, the National Parliament is the sacred house of the people, and the nation is considered the "collective house of all Timorese".[19]

The sacred house and sacred objects are very important for the Timorese because they are bases of their faith and the symbolic representation of the value of human life. Each ritual follows the ancient codes of representation called "estilos" or "styles" which date back to times immemorial. In the context of interpreting rituals, ritualistic practices must be respected and faithfully conserved, and on certain occasions, carried out by the groups of the community.

However, whatever the style or ritual required, animals are sacrificed, which is a way of granting a position of legitimacy to certain people to strengthen moral values and consolidate new visions of the world. Therefore, the rituals have to be performed regularly. This repetition helps people to understand the meaning of the rituals and share the sentiments of solidarity in a climate of social cohesion.

East Timor's Multiethnicity

East Timor's multiethnic composition is illustrated by the coexistence of some thirty-one ethno-linguistic groups and forty-six "kingdoms". There has never been a dominant ethnic group per se, and in the same way there was no absolute authority, not even a single myth that eventually evoked an ethnic descent common to all peoples of the territory now known officially as Timor-Leste, or, in English, East Timor.

The multiethnic composition of East Timor, since ancient times, was formed on the basis of mythology and systems of alliance by marriage. According to Marc Augé, this practice

> creates an alliance between two groups A and B. The children of the marriage may be linked to one or the other of these two groups or by reason of the marriage covenant. The symbols to which we allude

(the bones, the meat, the food, and the mystical influence) differentiate permanent incorporation from partial incorporation, as well as from incorporation into an alliance.[20]

These variables are visible in Timorese corporate alliances.

The alliances by marriage are established by the complex system of *barlaque*. This practice is, first, a kind of matrix of social pacts to establish and strengthen family ties in the same genealogical lineage, and second, a symbolic exchange of gifts and material goods that connect two lines in a lasting relationship.

In the East Timorese multiethnic composition, there is a record of memories and traditions that throughout time have been shared and passed on orally through families and local communities. Among the various ethnic groups, traces of a common cultural practice are noted that used the Tetum language as the vernacular instrument that made its disseminatioin possible. It is worth acknowledging that, in terms of the diffusion of this "collective culture", much of this can be attributed to the presence and actions of the Catholic Church in Timor, not only in terms of the diffusion of its own values, but also in the transversal crossing of the values of each kingdom.

THE PORTUGUESE AND INDONESIAN PRESENCE IN EAST TIMOR: A COMPARATIVE ANALYSIS

Today, East Timor is an independent multilingual nation with many limitations and facing many challenges, which in practice makes its independence still very tenuous. Low levels of development are still present, a recurring theme that is the consequence of four-and-a-half centuries of Portuguese exploitation, with practically no developmental returns, cobbled together with another twenty-four years of Indonesian military occupation, which had substantial structural impacts on the territory.

Despite being part of the Portuguese empire for such a long period of time, this association contributed almost nothing to the development of the territory. On the other hand, while physical development was minimal, the Portuguese language and the Catholic religion were key to the development of a unique culture, a hybrid of indigenous cultures imbued with Chinese and Malay influences, present in the territory since the thirteenth century as a result of the sandalwood trade, which today is all but extinct.

As an overseas province, East Timor was kept isolated without any significant investment in development being undertaken, either due to the geographical remoteness of the island, or because of the limited prospects for economic and political returns for Portugal. An example of such developmental alienation is seen by the establishment of the first official school in Timor as having taken place only in 1915 (four centuries after the initial occupation of the territory). In terms of a politico-administrative context, the Portuguese adopted more of an assimilation policy than other "colonizing" *conquistadores* (conquerors) and were concerned to a point to bring the Western (Christian) faith to the Timorese. According to Portuguese colonial and missionary historical records, "the Catholic religion, alongside the Portuguese language, constitutes a genuine heritage that the East Timorese retain from the Portuguese colonial presence. It is not difficult to argue that, on arrival, the Catholic religion was a strange belief to a population that is mostly animist. However, this strange belief prompted a reaction in the host that received it, as if it were a pearl that Timorese jealously guard today as part of the core values of their national identity."[21]

Nonetheless, until the Indonesian invasion in 1975, and according Geoffrey Gunn, the number of Christians in East Timor was small: "throughout 450 years until the date of 1975, the percentage of Catholicism never rose to more than 15 to 20 per cent of the population".[22] The reasons for that being, first, that "it was certainly not the wish of the people of Timor to embrace the Christian faith, nor the will of its kings to become the subjects of the King of Portugal";[23] and second, according to Afonso de Castro, "for Timor, being a Christian means being the subject of His majesty the King of Portugal[;] this is the important point for policy. The conversations in Timor took greater advantage of politics than of religion. Portugal would acquire subjects, but the [Catholic] Church hardly increased the number of faithful since most of the converts were Christians in name only."[24] Finally, because the hierarchical powers of the Catholic missions in East Timor were forced to accommodate themselves to the many traditional practices, the number of qualified priests capable of doing so was always small.

With the Indonesian occupation, the number of Catholics increased significantly to 98 per cent. It is in this sense that the Catholic faith is seen as a symbol of Timorese national identity, because it allowed Timorese resistance against Indonesian culture and gave the country its own religious identity.

Unlike Portuguese colonization, Indonesian occupation from 1975 to 1999 was marked by investment in infrastructure and education in order to win the sympathy of the Timorese. The Indonesian strategy was to disrupt Timorese identities and the Portuguese cultural heritage of East Timor, with the aim of creating structures of submission. During this period, the Indonesian Government built many public schools in East Timor.

In order to ensure territorial control, the Indonesian regime tried to replace the Portuguese language with the Indonesian language. To this end, Indonesia sent teachers to the field, promoting an education of subservience to the new regime.

Thus, the "Indonesianization" of the East Timorese was an attempt to create a sense of cultural and psychological identification and belonging with the rest of the multiethnic Republic of Indonesia. In terms of administrative policy, Indonesia tried to impose a new entity in the Timorese territory as well, by maintaining the boundaries set by Portugal and Holland, and declaring it to be called Timor-Timur (TIM-TIM) and designating it as a first-level province.

With regards to the local authority's administrative composition, the Indonesian regime also maintained the divisions left by the Portuguese colonial authority, although it changed their names. The political strategy of the Indonesian Government was to adopt a developmental strategy that tried to modernize the territory and encourage the population to leave the mountainous areas and reside along the coastal zones instead.

By promoting development, the regime was actually attempting to sever the bonds between the people and their ancestral and sacred lands by moving them to other regions in the territory, thus attempting to instill in the Timorese one of its foundation tenets, the concept of *bhineka tungal ika* (unity in diversity). It also tried to better control the movements of the Timorese Resistance movement, led by the FALINTIL (Liberation Armed Forces).

As Geoffrey Hull has noted, "the fact that the Portuguese language survived persecution proves that it is an integral part of national culture (unlike Dutch, which disappeared completely after Indonesia's independence)".[25] The Timorese people believe the Portuguese language is an important element of their cultural identity. This is demonstrated by several factors that are interrelated with the Timorese culture and were sometimes reinforced as being a form of resistance against Indonesian occupation: a mixture of the two peoples of Timor and Portugal: the influence of the Catholic Church in being close to the people's cultural roots and its role in spreading the Portuguese language (through liturgy) and education; the duration of the Portuguese presence (four-and-a-half centuries) and the construction of a collective memory; the comparatively violent character of the invasion of East Timor by other nations (first by Japan during the Second World War, and later by Indonesia) relative to the more moderate administration of the territory that was implemented by the Portuguese during colonial times; and, finally, the Portuguese connections that supported the Timorese resistance movement and the consequent awakening of a sense of national unity, functioning as a weapon of cultural struggle.

For the Timorese, Portuguese cultural influence in Timor was *proposed and not imposed*, which was very contrary to the Indonesian influence that was imposed through language, military presence, and the strategic demographic and economic strength of the neighbouring country. As argued by Ruy Cinatti, the East Timor people were not "conquistado" (conquered) by the sword, but rather by the water and salt of Christian civilization:

> The Timorese are said to have been conquered by water and not by the sword … the missionaries were not prepared for a role that demanded, above all, the knowledge of the values that informed the gentile personality … . [S]omething remained and was promoted despite it all, and that may have been the spirit of individual liberty that the Christian faith always inspired. The missions were the great educators of the Timorese people and they were responsible for validating the Portuguese presence.[26]

The Catholic religion was accepted by the Timorese people independently of any relationship with traditional culture. This means that before the imposition of Indonesian identity, Timor already had a cultural, political, and religious identity that was historically constituted.

Throughout the history of the territory, there were several rebellions of the kingdoms that did not intend to follow the wishes of the "Coroa Portuguesa" (Portuguese crown). But in order to control theses rebellions, Portugal used a policy of "devide et impera" (divide and conquer), using other Timorese kingdoms to do Portugal's bidding against their neighbouring kingdoms.

For this, the Portuguese empire established a political strategy, termed "alliance and mutual respect"; however, the alliances were not respected by the Portuguese colonial agents. For this reason, there were many revolts against the Portuguese presence in Timor. This can be seen in the history of the conspiracy by Timorese kings of the Camenasse kingdom that was the result of a blood pact ceremony.[27] According to Geoffrey Gunn, the Cailaco rebellion (1719–69) is worthy of attention not only as an example of heroic defence by the kingdoms of central Timor against the injustice of paying *fintas* (collective taxes), a situation that persisted until the very seat of Lifau was transferred to Dili, but also because, as noted by Basílio de Sá, this is one of the few episodes in Timor history that is abundantly and thoroughly documented.[28]

One of the main reasons that led Timorese kingdoms to fight against the Portuguese presence was that some missionaries and men of the governor of East Timor under the flag of the Portuguese monarchy tried to exert absolute power. They did this by initiating a political campaign to bring the Portuguese monarch's centralized power to bear against the feudal aristocracy of the Timorese kingdoms by virtue of the imposition of tax increases.

The Portuguese political strategy was to use some Timorese kingdoms loyal to Portugal to defend, control and defeat their kind who were against the Portuguese presence in Timor. In this sense, commenting on Abílio Araújo's argument, Gunn, in *Timor Loro Sae: 500 Anos*, writes: "these *liurais* were rewarded by the Portuguese with the rank of major or lieutenant colonel in the army of the 'segunda linha' [second line]."[29] As *datós* and *liurais* surrendered, the first to do so were rewarded with land acquired at the expense of their rivals or rebel kingdoms.[30] Of course, many *datós* and *liurais* were killed during the riots, and many others were prisoners. To replace them, they created new *liurais*, not according to traditional methods or the laws of ethnic succession, but according to the Portuguese criterion of "loyalty".

According to Geoffrey Gunn, the effectiveness of the Portuguese presence in Timor was due to their ability to cement alliances whose purpose was to impose a shifting mutual alliance between allies.[31] Alliances were reinforced by a ritual *pacto de sangue* (blood pact) or alliances with elites; in the process, thereby fostering a unified Timorese whose purpose was to form a Lusitanian imaginary identity. Indeed, in a story by Ruy Cinatti in "Brevíssimo Tratado da Província de Timor", based on the account given in 1669 by William Dampier, an English navigator, the East Timorese were proud not only of their religion but also the fact that the Portuguese had accepted them because of the "sangue lusitano que lhes corre nas veias" (Lusitanian blood that runs through their veins), warning that serious harm would befall anyone who doubted this claim.[32] This is an identity that operated "almost" reciprocally with the display of *lulic* (sacred object) flags.[33]

Regarding Lusitanian identity in Timor, Mexican journalist Fernando Medina Ruiz, in his newspaper *El Sol de México*, explains that "Timor, lighthouse of Christianity in the immensity of the Malay Archipelago, is the most remote Lusitanian province." He added: "With the conquest of Malacca, on 15 August 1511 [the region] was opened to the Portuguese [including] the spice islands of Timor, where sandalwood came from, so valued in the East and around the World." The journalist concludes his speech by praising the process of Portuguese missions in the land of Timor: "Today, East Timor continues its quiet, fruitful work and every day, more than ever, [as] Lusitania earth and Christianity."[34]

COMPARISON OF JAPANESE AND
TIMORESE CULTURAL IDENTITY

The most noticeable similarity between Japan and East Timor concerns the traditional rituals and other cultural popular events that symbolize national unity, albeit with rather different applications that enabled the two countries a clear, continued and persistent identity. In a nutshell, José Yamashiro recalled that the Japanese culture during the Meiji era was defined by what it had inherited from classical and feudal culture. The Meiji period has been characterized by Japanese historians as one of "enlightened rule" when Japan introduced large-scale Western cultural products (profound social, economic and political changes) that were to become the basis of their entry into modern capitalist society. The first step the Meiji emperor took in this direction was to foster a sense of nationalism and unity. Meanwhile, the emperor wanted to see Japan stand firm in the preservation of the multiple cultural identities that were so valued by its ancestors. Until then, according to Japanese historical documents, most Japanese identified themselves as being loyal to the Meiji emperor and considered him to be a symbol of national unity.[35]

The social and political structures headed by the imperial family, Shintoism, the worship of ancestors, the traditional arts and many other cultural features were preserved, strengthened and renewed. The Japanese — from premodern times to the end of World War II and even until today — consider the Shinto religion and other traditions as symbols of national unity and the solidarity of groups native to Japan.

The educational policy in Japan during the Meiji era was promoted along with the rules of patriotism based on military doctrines: "unquestioning obedience and sacrifice", although with a few changes to the rules of conduct, according to Maria Christensen. For instance, by 1876 samurai were forbidden to carry their traditional swords, and the warrior class evolved into bureaucrats.[36] Peasants who had previously been forbidden to carry arms were conscripted into a centralized army. The old class system of Japan was abandoned. This structural change in the politics of decision making supervised by the Meiji emperor completely changed Japan's traditional image. For example, by the end of this period, more than a third of the world's supply of silk came from Japan, and the percentage of exports carried out by Japanese-built and -owned ships rose from 7 per cent in 1893 to 52 per cent by 1913.

The development of Japan is based on the adoption of two foreign cultures, namely, religion and science. The first was influenced by Chinese culture, from the sixth century, followed by the entry of Western culture in the mid-nineteenth century (discounting the minimal and restricted impact of the Portuguese and Dutch presences in Japan variously between the mid-sixteenth and mid-nineteenth centuries). Japan continued to elaborate cultural traits because for most Japanese, culture is an essential element for the development of the country; even in recent times, one sometimes sees electronic products, automobiles and clothing, labelled "made in Japan or copied in Japan".

Notably, in East Timor, since Portuguese colonial times, and during five years of Japanese occupation, twenty-four years of Indonesian rule, and until today, the soul of the Timorese people still has not "been absorbed by an evolution that is taking place for four centuries of contact with the civilizing people [Europeans]";[37] instead, they have preserved their languages, customs and mythology. The East Timorese people have a shared history that lies within their own territory and in the world, asserting themselves as having their own idiosyncrasies (which makes them a different people), while at the same time they are aware that, as part of humanity, they "are all the same", that is, human.[38]

In Japan (still in the Meiji period, particularly in pre-war times), the Shinto rituals and other festivals were presented publicly by public entities, with the intention of invoking the gods' spirits to protect the Japanese nation and its people. In East Timor, the Timorese soul is constituted through symbolic power to be sacred and through the use of the discourse of the warrior. A Timorese becomes strong — that is, one Timorese sings a song to warriors predisposing them to action — because he believes that in this way they will be victorious. The Timorese warrior song is known as *lorsá*.

When the Timorese heroes sing the *lorsá*, they immediately create body movements, the intensity and extent of the "collective pathos", and every man who goes to war is a hero and receives the title "Açu-ua'in".[39] The enhancement of self-value and of the cause manifests itself in all versions of the *lorsá* verses, especially in how the relationship between winner and loser is treated, as seen in Table 4.1.

There are other similarities: the Japanese and the East Timorese are animists, that is, both peoples believe in the presence of spirits everywhere. In Japan, this body of beliefs is called Shinto, which means the "way of the spirits". In East Timor, these beliefs have several names, but collectively are called *lulik* (sacred or holy), and in the Bunak ethnic group case, the body is associated with the story of "Bei Gua" (the path of the ancestors). As Cinatti has observed, "the home of East Timorese from Lospalos has numerous similarities with its counterpart of the Bronze Age in Japan".[40]

The following are Cinatti's words that legitimize the description of the house by Osório de Castro, a Portuguese judge who worked in Timor:

TABLE 4.1
Lorsá Verses Depicting Winner-Loser Relationships

Loro mane nacsán iha ami leten,	Sobre nós raiou o sol-homem,	The sun-man dawned on us,
Natutu iha ami úlun;	Brilhou sobre nossas cabeças;	He shone over our heads;
Loro feto tur tan imi,	Em vós poisou o sol-mulher,	On yours landed the sun-woman,
Monu tan imi.	Sobre vós tombou.	Who fell upon you.
Ne'e duni loron ida ôhin,	Por isso, neste dia,	Therefore, on this day,
uain ida ôhin,	nesta data,	on this date,
Ami fera imi rain,	Devastámos vossas terras,	We ravaged your lands,
Têri imi ulun;	Decepámos vossas cabeças;	We chopped off your heads;
Ulun monu ba rai,	Cabeças caídas na arena,	Drooping heads in the arena,
Tetec ih arai,	Amontoadas no chão,	Piled on the floor,
Lian laec ona,	Já silenciosas,	Already silent,
Lian côtu ona.	Já emudecidas.	Already muted.

Source: Jorge Barros, "O Lorsán", *Seara: Boletim Eclesiástico da Diocese de Díli* 15, no. 2 (1963): 50–51.

"The Governor showed me that he had taken to showing a sketch of a singular 'uma Lulic' (sacred house) from the kings of Laga, who said to me that it reminded them of the rustic buildings of Japan's hinterlands sitting above stilts, holding in the middle an open wooden platform, with a roof shaped as an irregular truncated pyramid .... going up a ladder to a door with carved ornaments, of a half-toke on the shutters, of a snake in the other. The construction of the roof finishings was decorated with large shells."[41]

The "International Religious Freedom Report 2006" document asserts that 96 per cent of the Japanese population professes one of the following religions: Shintoism (51 per cent), Buddhism (44 per cent) or Christianity (1 per cent); however, according to Kisala, only 30 per cent the population identifies itself as belonging to any religion.[42] Religion in Japan is syncretic by nature, and this results in a variety of practices, such as parents and children celebrating Shinto rituals in the family, students praying before exams, couples celebrating their wedding in a Christian church, and funerals being held at Buddhist temples.

Such cultural practices are similar to those of Timorese society. For example, Timorese couples celebrate their weddings in a church, but before that, a marriage is formalized with a traditional sacred ritual. This cultural practice is based on the exchange of gifts and material goods between the bride and groom's families. This traditional wedding is reinforced by the *barlaque* system. Funerals are similarly conducted in a mixture of systems in which the traditional funeral rites and Christian rites are complementary.

Japanese culture was greatly influenced by Chinese culture, while Timorese culture has been strongly influenced by Portuguese culture, but also by Melanesian and Polynesian culture; it has also assimilated practices from other cultures as seen in the dance of the candles, which has Philippine, Malay and Indonesian origins. The Japanese and Timorese cultures also have their own distinctive and unique aspects, as seen in architecture (innovative woodwork), the plastic arts and even painting.

COMPARISON OF KOREAN AND TIMORESE CULTURAL IDENTITIES

In Korean history, we can find similarities and parallels that can be drawn between it and the history of East Timor, particularly with respect to the establishment of Korea's cultural and national identity. Despite differences in intensity and in space, the two countries — Korea and East Timor — share some common features in their social and political organization and in the establishment of culture and identities. Both have been weakened by colonialism. Korea was colonized by the Japanese, and East Timor was colonized by the Portuguese and occupied by both Japan (1941–45) and Indonesia (1975–99).

The greater similarities noticeable between the two countries, however, are the importance of the Christian presence in the struggle against colonial powers, albeit with some differences. Regarding language, there are also similarities: the Japanese language did not expand within the Korean territory because the Korean people did not accept Japanese language identity. In fact, the Koreans had their own unique linguistic identity. In East Timor, both Tetum (the indigenous language) and Portuguese were the important elements for the Timorese people during the Indonesian occupation and were used as unifying elements of the Timorese in opposition to Javanese culture. Later, the two languages — Tetum and Portuguese — became recognized as the official languages of East Timor by the Timorese Parliament.

Korea was colonized by Japan between 1910 and 1945. According to Lee, Japan's goal was to eradicate the Korean culture and substitute it with Japanese culture — that is, an attempt at the "Japanization" of the Korean people, forcing them to adopt Japanese-style manners and converting them to the Shinto religion. Japan prohibited Korean leaders from developing their own political and academic research about Korean history and linguistic identity. This experience was also shared by the East Timorese because the Indonesian regime banned the use of Portuguese and closed schools, such as the Externato São José de Balide, in Dili, the capital.

Koreans used religion as an important weapon to save their country and used it to prevent Japanese cultural domination. But Confucianism and Buddhism were unable to counter the Japanese religious and colonist culture. The Christian religion was regarded as an important element of strength to prevent the cultural assimilation sought by Japan; hence, Christianity is recognized alongside Confucianism and Buddhism as an important symbol of Korean national unity. According to Harris, today it is difficult to miss the way in which Koreans conduct themselves, the way in which they speak, the way in which they hold a cup when pouring, the way they smile, laugh and cry — everything, in short, that defines them on a social level. Confucianism still remains an integral element in the way Koreans act much more than it does in China, for example, where Confucianism died an ugly death in the aftermath of the Communist revolution.[43]

The Korean political strategy of resistance was manifested by the population in much the same way as by the Timorese resistance fighters, preventing assimilation of the culture put forward by the Indonesian regime. For the Timorese majority, the Catholic religion was and is part of the matrix of their cultural and national identity, including the Portuguese language (and culture) as well as the original Timorese culture. With this religion, the Timorese peoples preserved many features of their identity. That is why there was not a contradiction between the actions of the Catholic Church, the traditional belief systems, and the power of local authorities; in fact, they were regarded as reinforcing the spiritual power of all the Timorese peoples. This is demonstrated by the existence of crucifixes, statues of saints and bells in the sacred houses, alongside other objects such as flintlock rifles and sticks.

Today, the Westernization of popular culture (and traditional culture) tends to be synonymous with neomercantilism, materialism, violence and sensuality, in comparison with traditional Timorese and Korean cultures, which are beginning to lose the space in which they can exist little by little. Because of rapid modernization, there has been an increase in the individualistic spirit and hedonism. In fact, these tendencies lead to a certain cultural identity crisis in the industrialized countries (as in the case of Korea, an emerging industrialized economy) and in developing countries (as in the case of East Timor). In these circumstances, the two countries face the same challenges, and that is the reformulation of their cultural identity within the globalization phenomena.

CONCLUSION

This study has endeavoured to document how the Portuguese presence in Timor contributed to the making of the country's national and cultural identity. It has also sought to compare the East Timorese experience with defining its national and cultural identity with two other Asian countries, namely, Japan and Korea.

The emergence of the Timorese nation-state and the making of the national project had their genesis in a process of administrative unification established by Portuguese colonization in a medium that encouraged the creation of a set of identities having a homogenous character and distinct cultural traditions. The young state of East Timor is constituted by multiple cultural identities and multiple linguistic identities, which coexist in the territory.

Some Timorese say the Portuguese presence did not substantially affect the local customs such as the consecrations of new dwellings (house or sacred house), the *barlaque* practices, funeral ceremonies, and other ritual practices often crowned by symbolic ritual celebration. Rather, the contention is that the Portuguese influence was integrated into Timorese traditions.

The "sacred house" by virtue of its aggregate and identitary force, is both a valued physical — and, more importantly — non-physical heritage of East

Timor. For this reason, the "sacred houses" as collective places are where rituals are structured. The sacred houses remain both a familial (intimate) and social arena, that is to say, they promote and safeguard the individual, the family and the community flow of life. Most sacred houses were destroyed by the Indonesian military, but they continue to be important symbolic places for the Timorese people because, for them, the "sacred houses" are analogous to a synagogue or a church in Western cultures.

This chapter also looked at how Korea and East Timor were the targets of colonization. The methods and strategies used by Japan, Portugal and Indonesia were also similar, particularly in terms of the initial military conquest and repression. In the case of Korea, Japan forced Koreans to convert to the Japanese religion of Shintoism, prohibited the Korean population from speaking its own language, and forced them to adopt Japanese names. Likewise, Portugal, for its part, prohibited the wearing of the Timorese *táis* or *lipa* (two kinds of Timorese traditional clothing). Indonesia prohibited the Portuguese language from being used in the education system and imposed a system of "Indonesianization" of the Timorese under the motto of "bhineka tungal ika" (unity in diversity) and the five principles of the Pancasila (the Indonesian state philosophy).

Most of the phenomena that took place in the countries cited are not unique in either time or in space, especially with respect to the modernization of Asian countries, particularly Japan and Korea. In other countries, a chain of similar events also led to major changes of existing structures, including sociopolitical and economic ones, which allowed these countries to become bigger and better.

This study concludes with a quotation from one of Portugal's greatest poets of the middle of the twentieth century, Fernando Pessoa, who wrote, "Minha patria é a lingual portuguesa" (my home is the Portuguese language). Paraphrasing Pessoa's dictum, one could also say: "minha patria é a minha cultura" (my motherland is my culture).

Notes

[1]   The research for this work was supported by Fundação Calouste Gulbenkian. In addition to thanking the conference sponsors for making my participation in the event possible, I would also like to extend my thanks to the conference coordinator, Professor Laura Jarnagin Pang, and to Emanuel Braz for reviewing the English translation of the text.
[2]   Robert Clark, *O Nascimento do Homem* (Lisbon: Edição Gradiva, 1995), p. 28.

3   Stuart Hall, *Representation: Cultural Representation and Signifying Practices* (London: Sage, 1997), p. 2.

4   See Luís Filipe Thomaz, *País dos Belos: Achegas para a Compreensão de Timor-Leste* (Lisbon: Instituto Português do Oriente, 2008).

5   See Artur Teodoro de Matos, *Timor Português 1515–1769: Contribuição para a sua História* (Lisbon: Instituto Histórico Infante Dom Henrique, 1974); Eduardo dos Santos, *Kanoik: Mitos e Lendas de Timor* (Lisbon: Serviço de Publicações da Mocidade Portuguesa, 1967); and Artur Basílio de Sá, *A Planta de Cailaco* (Lisbon: Agência Geral das Colónias, 1949).

6   Kenneth Gordon McIntyre, *The Secret Discovery of Australia: Portuguese Ventures Two Hundred Years before Captain Cook* (Medindie, Australia: Souvenir Press, 1977).

7   Elizabeth Traube, *Cosmology and Social Life: Ritual Exchange among the Mambai of East Timor* (Chicago: University of Chicago Press, 1986), p. 24.

8   See James J. Fox, "Tracing the Path, Recounting the Past: Historical Perspectives on Timor", in *Out of the Ashes: Destruction and Reconstruction of East Timor*, edited by James J. Fox and Dionísio Babo Soares (Adelaide: Crawford House Publishing, 2000), pp. 1–29; Apolinário Guterres, "A identidade cultural timorense: Desafios de futuro", in *Estudos Orientais: O Oriente, Hoje, do Índico ao Pacífico*, edited by António Augusto Tavares (Lisbon: Faculdade de Ciências Sociais e Humanas, Universidade Nova de Lisboa, 1994); and Geoffrey Hull, "The Languages of East Timor: 1772–1997: A Literature Review", in *Studies in Languages and Cultures of East Timor*, vol. 1, edited by Geoffrey Hull and Lance Eccles, (Campbeltown, NSW: Language Acquisition Research Centre, University of Western Sydney, Macarthur, 1999).

9   Afonso de Castro, *As Possessões Portuguezas na Oceania* (Lisbon: Imprensa Nacional, 1867), p. 17.

10   Ibid., pp. 17–18.

11   Ruy Cinatti, António de Sousa Mendes, and Leopoldo Castro de Almeida, *A Arquitectura Timorense* (Lisbon: Instituto de Investigação Científica Tropical, Museu de Etnologia, 1987), p. 38.

12   Nuno Canas Mendes, *A Multidimensionalidade da Construção Identitária em Timor-Leste: Nacionalismo, Estado e Identidade Nacional* (Lisbon: Instituto Superior de Ciências Sociais e Políticas, 2005), p. 109.

13   Anthony Smith, *A Identidade Nacional*, translated by Cláudia Brito (Lisbon: Edição Gradiva, 1997), p. 25.

14   Armando Marques Guedes, "A complexidade estrutural do nacionalismo timorense", paper presented at the international conference "Ásia do Sul e do Sudeste em Perspectiva [Séculos XX–XXI]", Instituto Superior de Ciências Sociais e Políticas, Lisbon, 2002, p. 5.

15   Anne-Marie Thiesse, *A Criação das Identidades Nacionais* (Lisbon: Temas e Debates, 2000), p. 229.

16   Sofi Ospina and Tanja Hohe, "Traditional Power Structures and the Community

Empowerment and Local Governance Project: Final Report", report, presented to CEP/PMU, ETTA/UNTAET and the World Bank, Dili, 2001, p. 19.

[17] Lúcio Manuel Gomes de Sousa, "As casas e o mundo: Identidade local e nação no património material/imaterial de Timor-Leste", paper presented at "Etnografia: Actas do III Congresso Internacional", Cabeceira de Basto, Portugal, 13–14 July 2007.

[18] Mendes, *A Multidimensionalidade*, pp. 112–13.

[19] Ibid., p. 115.

[20] Marc Augé, *A Construção do Mundo: Religião, Representação e Ideologia* (Lisbon: Edições 70, 2000), p. 21.

[21] Vicente Paulino, "Identidade e Representação: Uma Abordagem da Cultura Timorense", master's thesis, Universidade Nova de Lisboa, 2009, pp. 44–45; and Vicente Paulino, "Timor entre a fé e a cultura", talk presented to the grupo 3 nós de jovens de Carnide, Casa dos Irmãos Maristas, Lisbon, 2 October 2008.

[22] Geoffrey Gunn, *Timor Loro Sae: 500 Anos* (Macao: Livros do Oriente, 1999), p. 40.

[23] Abílio Araújo, *Timor Leste: Os Loricos Voltaram a Cantar* (Lisbon: Trama, 1977), p. 82.

[24] Ibid., pp. 82–83.

[25] Geoffrey Hull, "Língua, identidade e resistência", *Camões: Revista de Letras e Cultura Lusófonas* 14 (Jul.–Sept. 2001): 80–92.

[26] Mendes, *A Multidimensionalidade*, p. 316.

[27] Sá, *A Planta de Cailaco*, p. 15.

[28] Gunn, *Timor Loro Sae*, pp. 104–08.

[29] Ibid., p. 204.

[30] Araújo, *Timor Leste*, p. 3.

[31] Geoffrey Gunn, "Língua e cultura na construção da identidade de Timor-Leste", *Camões: Revista de Letras e Cultura Lusófonas* 14 (July–September 2001): 21.

[32] Ruy Cinatti, "Brevíssimo tratado da Província de Timor", *Revista Shell* 346 (Jul.–Sept. 1963).

[33] Gunn, "Língua e cultura", p. 21; and Luís Filipe Thomaz, *Babel Lorosae: O Problema Linguístico de Timor-Leste* (Lisbon: Cadernos Camões, 2002), p. 131.

[34] Fernando Medina Ruiz, untitled editorial, *Seara: Boletim Eclesiástico da Diocese de Díli* 2, no. 54 (1967): 1.

[35] José Yamashiro, *História da Cultura Japonesa* (São Paulo: IBRASA, 1986).

[36] Maria Christensen, "The Meiji Era and the Modernization of Japan", <http://www.samurai-archives.com/tme.html> (accessed 11 November 2010).

[37] Jorge Barros, "A alma Timorense", *Seara: Boletim Eclesiástico da Diocese de Díli* 10, no. 1 (1958).

[38] Paulino, "Identidade e Representação", p. 40.

[39] Jorge Barros, "O Lorsán", *Seara: Boletim Eclesiástico da Diocese de Díli* 15, no. 2 (1963): 48–49.

40   Ruy Cinatti, *Motivos Artísticos Timorenses e a sua Integração* (Lisbon: Instituto de Investigação Científica Tropical, Museu de Etnologia, 1987), p. 164.

41   Cited in Cinatti, *Motivos Artísticos*, p. 164.

42   U.S. Department of State, Bureau of Democracy, Human Rights, and Labor, "International Religious Freedom Report 2006", <http://www.state.gov/g/drl/rls/irf/2006/71342.htm> (accessed 6 December 2010); and Robert J.J. Wango, *The Logic of Nothingness: A Study of Nishida Kitarō* (Honolulu: University of Hawai'i Press, 2005).

43   Don Moen, "Korean Hybridity: The Language Classroom as Cultural Hybrid", *Journal of Intercultural Communication* 20 (May 2009).

PART TWO

Cultural Components: Language, Architecture and Music

5

THE CREOLE PORTUGUESE LANGUAGE OF MALACCA: A DELICATE ECOLOGY[1]

Alan N. Baxter

Today's Malacca Creole Portuguese (MCP) are the descendants of Portuguese, Indo-Portuguese, Malayo-Portuguese and diverse camp followers present in Malacca at the time of the Dutch takeover, in 1641. Admixed over the years with Chinese, Indian, Malay, Dutch, Sri Lankan, Filipino and English elements, they survive as a separate ethnic group, concentrated in Malacca in the suburb of Hilir. Their Creole Portuguese language is the last vital variety of a group of East and Southeast Asian Creole Portuguese languages, formerly spoken in many other locations throughout these regions.[2] Although this community has displayed remarkable adaptability and resilience in the face of history, today even a conservative appraisal must conclude that Malacca Creole Portuguese shows clear signs of endangerment.

This chapter discusses key aspects of the ecology of this language, considering three areas: (1) maintenance of Malacca Creole Portuguese[3] until the twentieth century; (2) evidence of sociolinguistic and linguistic attrition; and (3) the question of revitalization and maintenance of the language and the role of assessors and external agencies. In the latter respect, the chapter concludes with some concrete proposals.

KEY FACTORS IN LINGUISTIC SURVIVAL

Among the factors facilitating the survival of the Kristang language into the twentieth century, three stand out: first, linguistic reinforcement through a dynamic association of religion, language and quasi-ethnic group; second, the development of a common socioeconomic base in the poorer core community until the late twentieth century; and third, population dynamics.

Roman Catholicism and the Portuguese Language

A symbiosis between the "Portuguese" language and Roman Catholicism is believed to have been one key factor in the survival of Kristang[4] during the centuries after the Portuguese period.[5] The role of religion to facilitate language maintenance in adverse contexts has been noted in research on language maintenance by Dorian.[6] In Portuguese Asia, this connection developed through the missionary representation of Catholicism through the Portuguese language, as is evident in the word "Kristang", which has traditionally meant the language, the religion and the ethnic group.

Today, one of the clearest manifestations of the bond between language and religion in Kristang culture is the confraternity of the Irmang di Greza or "Brothers of the Church", founded by the Dominicans in the seventeenth century. A significant domain of Kristang language, the Irmang di Greza played a key role in maintaining Catholicism for the "Portuguese" population during the periods of prohibition under the Dutch.[7] The confraternity continues to be predominantly Kristang, its members being largely strong speakers of the language.

From the eighteenth century, the Catholic Church provided linguistic reinforcement through pastoral and liturgical use of "Portuguese", and, partially, through education. Many priests were trained in the seminaries of Goa and Macao, and would have had exposure to, or knowledge of, Asian varieties of Creole Portuguese. To judge from documents from the nineteenth century, we surmise Creole Portuguese to have been used by priests in some functions, along with an essentially metropolitan Portuguese.

Elderly Kristangs in 1980–83 reported that the priests prior to the Second World War, resident in Malacca since the nineteenth century, were fluent speakers of "Kristang". Rêgo's 1942 study provides evidence of Creole texts used by the Portuguese Mission until the Second World War,[8] and early numbers of the *Boletim Eclesiástico da Diocese de Macau* provide evidence that the priests used the Creole in additional cultural events organized with the community. Thus, for example, Friar Rufino do Espírito Santo Affonso writes that a play in Kristang is to be included in the Easter celebrations: O programa será alterado, representando-se tambem a farça Preguiça e Mentira, que acabei de traduzir no christão de Malaca. (The programme will be altered; the play "Idleness and Lies", which I have just translated into Malacca Kristang, will also be staged.)[9]

Portuguese and Indo-Portuguese Taught

Further linguistic reinforcement may have occurred in schools in the nineteenth century. In the early nineteenth century some schools were organized by the Portuguese Mission.[10] The Malacca Free School and the London Missionary Society ran Portuguese language schools between 1826 and 1834.[11] Instruction of the Portuguese children was conducted initially in "their own language", and subsequently in English.[12]

The London Missionary Society used both "Indo-Portuguese" (namely, Creole Portuguese)[13] and Portuguese.[14] Three of its schools operating in 1831 are referred to as Indo-Portuguese schools, and Creole Portuguese materials were printed at the Malacca Mission.[15] Indeed, the Society was even sensitive to the nature of Malacca Creole Portuguese, as one missionary observed: "The Malacca Portuguese do not speak the Madras Indo-Portuguese[.] It is that of Ceylon which approaches nearest to *our* [emphasis in original] local dialect."[16]

Later, at the end of the nineteenth century, a boys' school and a girls' school were again run by the Portuguese Mission;[17] the latter school was later administered by the Cannossian nuns.[18] Indirect evidence, based on records of the schools and testimonies of elderly speakers in 1980, suggests that these mission schools taught Portuguese, the girls' school being partly staffed by nuns from Macao.[19]

It is difficult to say the extent to which education may have reinforced Kristang. However, the fact that Portuguese still had a semi-official status in the nineteenth-century Dutch and British administrations, and had retained some use in legal and commercial areas well into the nineteenth century,[20] suggests that teaching could have added reinforcement to the general presence of Portuguese language influence. The use of "Portuguese" in education in the latter nineteenth century and early twentieth century, and in the church until the Second World War, may also have provided Kristang some additional lexical reinforcement.

In sum, the connection between Roman Catholicism and membership of the Creole community would appear to have been a significant contributor to the maintenance of Kristang into the twentieth century. However, there are another two very significant factors: demography and socioeconomic status.

The Effect of Demography and Socioeconomic Status

In the early stages of Dutch Malacca, the "Portuguese" constituted the largest local ethnic group in the town area.[21] They retained a reasonably high socioeconomic position, and shipping involving Malacca-based "Portuguese" continued throughout the Dutch period, largely with ports where Luso-Asian communities existed.[22] Strength of numbers and socioeconomic status would have aided language maintenance.[23]

Nevertheless, by the beginning of the nineteenth century, the economic status of the bulk of the Creoles had changed radically. As an 1827 census reports,

> the Siranies or native Portugueze … are now dwindled to no more than 2239 souls. … These people are all poor and many live in wretched houses erected in that part of Malacca called Banda Hilir. It is by these men that the Inhabitants are so largely supplied with fish — but with few exceptions they are constantly out in small sampans following this precarious livelihoods… . [they are] Roman Catholics, and are regularly supplied with priests … by the two colleges at Goa and Macao… . They speak a language peculiar to themselves which may be dominated [sic] as Creole Portugueze … [24]

This excerpt mentions elements that certainly have been instrumental in the language's survival: the Catholic religion, the connection with priests from Portuguese India and Macao, a common socioeconomic profile in fishing and poverty, and density of population in the Hilir area.[25] Later in the nineteenth century, and throughout the twentieth century, the impact of education, the spread of English, and employment opportunities elsewhere in the colony led to an exodus of Kristangs to areas of growth. Nevertheless although gradually acquiring English and other local employment opportunities (often as lower public servants), the core Kristang-speaking community in Malacca maintained much of its inward-looking characteristics of the early period.

The clustering of demographic and socioeconomic characteristics was further strengthened in 1933. Under an initiative of the Catholic Church, aided by the British Administration, a large number of poorer creoles from the central town areas of Bunga Raya and Trankera, and many from the Praya Lane and Hilir areas, were resettled at a twenty-eight acre location in Hilir, on the coast south of the town. This nucleus became known as the Portuguese Settlement or Padri sa Chang, "The Priest's Land".[26] The resettlement created a large Kristang speech community, with a concentration of low-income families, many devoted to fishing. Three decades later, this community displayed strong inward focusing in kinship and friendship relations, a high degree of intermarriage, and a high proportion of extended families with elderly Kristang speakers present,[27] tendencies still evident in the 1980s.[28] This ghetto effect doubtless has aided language retention.

CHANGES IN KRISTANG SOCIOLINGUISTICS IN THE TWENTIETH AND TWENTY-FIRST CENTURIES

In the twentieth century, especially in the latter half and into the early twenty-first century, several changes have conditioned the cultural and linguistic ecology of the community. Significant changes have occurred in relation to the religion, the socioeconomic profile of the community and patterns of language use.

On the one hand, several changes relating to the Portuguese Mission in the second half of the twentieth century influenced the Kristang culture and had consequences for the language. The introduction of regional Portuguese music and dance to the community, in the early 1950s, is a notable example. I return to this point at the end of the chapter.

Alterations in the demography of the Catholic congregation of the Portuguese Mission have made the Kristangs a minority at the traditional Portuguese church, Saint Peter's Church, among a majority of Chinese and Indian parishioners. However, the most significant change in relation to the Catholic Church came about after Malaysian independence: restrictions were imposed on the entry of foreign priests into Malaysia. Today, there are no more Portuguese-speaking priests in Malacca, nor are there any local priests who speak Kristang.

On the other hand, the last four decades have seen radical changes in the socioeconomic profile of Padri sa Chang. These have had important implications for the survival of the Kristang culture and language, both positively and negatively. While Kristangs still migrate for work, there is a now a stronger trend towards local employment. Industrial growth around Malacca and in the tourism and hospitality industry is significant. Also, since the late 1970s, there has been a steady growth of the restaurant business within Padri sa Chang, a trend that was given an extra boost in the wake of public concern surrounding an environmental conflict: the negative effects for the fishermen caused by a land reclammation project along the Banda Hilir coast at that time.[29]

The controversy increased awareness on the part of politicians and the wider public concerning a community that was seen as something of an historical relic. There were two unexpected consequences. First, the Portuguese Settlement was given a "Portuguese-style" building to house restaurants and to provide a venue where cultural shows were initially staged.[30] These changes generated alternative employment within the Portuguese Settlement and created new settings in which Kristang is used. Moreover, it has served as a new basis for self-awareness. The Kristang cultural identity now has a renewed value within and beyond the community. This development has also led to a constant influx of tourists and locals into the community, bringing a greater presence of both Malay and English. The second consequence of the growing public awareness regarding Padri sa Chang was that the Kristangs caught the attention of the United Malay National Organization (UMNO), the ruling party of the Barisan Nasional coalition. In Malaysia, the Malays have certain social and economic privileges, as defined by *bumiputera* "sons of the soil" status, enshrined in the New Economic Policy of 1970.[31] In 1991, some of these privileges were extended to the Kristangs,[32] yet conditional on three factors: Malaysian citizenship, Roman Catholic religion and the ability to speak Kristang.[33] This change of status has contributed both to increased self-regard and to change in socioeconomic conditions for Padri sa Chang.

Changes in Language Use: A Shift to English, and Recent Pressure from Malay

The shift towards English as the dominant language of Malaysian Portuguese Eurasians began in the mid-nineteenth century. The shift continued throughout the British period as schools were established and employment became available in clerical and auxiliary positions in Malacca and elsewhere. English was a prestige language, a key to employment; Kristang was not.

This process fostered the growth of an English-dominant Portuguese Eurasian middle class in urban centres, which gradually shifted to English. The middle-class group viewed the traditional Malacca Kristang-speaking community as low prestige. The effect of such attitudes would have been to facilitate a breakdown in transmission of Kristang in the core community in Malacca. Certainly, during fieldwork in the 1980s, the prestige of English was readily apparent.[34] Many families had English as the home language, Kristang being used only if elderly Kristang-speakers resided in the same household. Direct evidence of a widespread failure to transmit Kristang was common. The following comments from an elderly Kristang-dominant grandmother reflect this:

Yo	lo	papiá	neta		netu,	papiá	Kristang.	Mas,
1s	FUT	speak	granddaughter	grandson	speak	Kristang.	But,

papiá	Kristang	olotu	ngka	mutu	chadu	la,	...	kauzu	olotu
kristang	3pl		NEG	very	clever	EMPH	...	because	3pl

sa	mai	pai	tudu	ke	papiá	inggres.	Yo	papiá	kristang
GEN	mother	father	all	want	speak	English.	1s	speak	Kristang

olotu	*membe*	*kere*	*respostá*	*inggres.*
3pl	sometimes	want	reply	English.

(I speak to my grandchildren in Kristang. But they are not very clever at speaking Kristang! ... because their parents both want to speak English. I speak Kristang to them; sometimes they want to reply in English.)[35]

Other interviewees reported that parents had transmitted Kristang early in the informant's life only to change to an almost exclusive home use of English when the informant attended school.

With the independence of Malaysia, Malay became the official language and replaced English as the main language of education.[36] Nevertheless, the strong position of English in the Padri sa Chang community has not altered. The position of Malay, however, is interesting. Although the Kristangs have always spoken colloquial vehicular Malay, and have been educated in formal Malay since the early 1970s, the language formerly was not commonly heard within the community. Nevertheless, it was present in lexical loans into Kristang. Participant observation during the last three years suggests that Malay is having a stronger effect among younger Kristangs.

The Kristang Language under Threat: Sociolinguistic Surveys Showing Language Loss in Padri sa Chang

Four notable sociolinguistic surveys have been conducted over the last fifteen years by Nunes (1996), David and Noor (1999), Sudesh (2000) and Lee (2004).[37] Each of these studies points to shrinkage in Kristang language use, with a strong shift towards English. Five factors point to this:

1. *Generational loss.* A shift away from Kristang as a mother tongue was made clear in Nunes's 1996 study of 225 speakers, with low mother tongue status evident in the 16–20 years (23 per cent mother tongue) and 21–30 (38 per cent mother tongue) age-groups, in conjunction with an already weak mother tongue index in the 50+ years age-group (75 per cent).[38] These results were echoed in Lee's 2004 survey of eighty-five households, with speakers from different age groups self-reporting very low presences of best/fluent speakers in their own age-groups: 7–12 years (1.2 per cent), 13–20 years (1.2 per cent), 21–30 years (0 per cent), 31–40 years (18.8 per cent), 41–50 years (37.6 per cent) and 51+ years (40 per cent).[39]

2. *Fluency.* In David and Noor's 1999 survey of sixty-two respondents from sixty-two households, only 46 per cent claimed full fluency in Kristang, while 30.2 per cent claimed average spoken fluency. A further 23.8 per

cent stated they had no fluency at all. (Contrasting with this are the results regarding English and Malay: 62.9 per cent claimed full fluency in English, and a further 29 per cent claimed average spoken fluency. Nevertheless, in this survey, full fluency in Malay was still rated lower than that in Kristang: 32 per cent claiming full fluency in Malay and 50 per cent claiming average fluency.)[40]

3. *Status.* Both the surveys of David and Noor (1999) and Sudesh (2000) yielded the following status ranking: 1: English; 2: Malay.[41]

4. *Core domain loss.* In the *home domain,* both of these studies found that only the oldest age group reported using Kristang alone.[42] The other age groups used both Kristang and English. Sudesh's study registered a preference for English in the two youngest age-groups surveyed.[43]

In the *friendship domain,* David and Noor found that, in their sample of five age groups, the oldest group used Kristang alone in friendships within the Settlement, whereas the youngest group used a mixture of Kristang and English but had no friendships exclusively in Kristang. The middle age groups were found to have some friendships exclusively in Kristang and others in a mixture of English and Kristang.[44] Using a different method, Sudesh found a preference for Kristang in his two older age groups and a preference for English in his two younger groups.[45]

In the *work domain,* Sudesh found that English dominates in the domain outside of Padri sa Chang.[46] However, as noted by Chan in 1969 and Baxter in 1988, Sudesh too finds that Kristang is strong in the work domain within Padri sa Chang.[47] This augers well with the substantial growth in employment within the confines of the community.

5. *Intermarriage with other ethnic groups.* David and Noor, as well as Lee, report that marriage to non-Kristang speakers is now significant, in contrast with the traditional Kristang tendency to intermarry.[48] Lee's 2004 survey of eighty-five households revealed twenty-two non-Kristang spouses, yielding a 25.9 per cent rate of out-marriage. Of these predominantly female spouses, Lee found that only 22.7 per cent can understand and speak Kristang and 59 per cent can understand but not speak Kristang. The remaining 27.3 per cent can neither understand nor speak Kristang. Most significantly, Lee noted that 86.4 per cent of non-Kristang parents never used Kristang with their children and 25 per cent of non-Kristang parents use Kristang "not much of the time".[49] Marriage out of the Kristang community is a further cause of Kristang language decline within the home, leading to a shift in the mother tongue of children in this setting. The traditional linguistic assimilation dynamic of the Kristang community evident over the centuries seems no longer significant.

The most alarming finding is that all three studies show evidence of a shift between the language use patterns of the oldest and the youngest groups. Generational transmission is breaking down. Ominously, the language is being maintained mostly by the presence of older Kristang speakers. Yet, as noted above, according to Lee, the older speakers represent the smallest section of the population, and fluent speakers are a minority that largely overlaps with the oldest age group. Hence, it is only a matter of time before the Kristang-speaking elders disappear. When this occurs, a shift to English seems inevitable.

These sociolinguistic changes in the Kristang community have reflexes in the language itself. In the following section, some tendencies found in language data from the 1980s,[50] 1990s,[51] and 2000s[52] will be outlined. These concern lexical "shrinkage" in Kristang in the twentieth century, and the entry of words from Malay and English.

CHANGES IN THE KRISTANG LANGUAGE

Rêgo (1942; updated in 1998 as Rêgo and Baxter) recorded a lexicon of 835 single words from native speakers in Malacca in the 1930s.[53] A comparison with the list in Baxter and da Silva (2004) shows that 78 items have been lost over six decades, and another 13 have changed meaning.[54] The rate of loss over sixty years is in the order of 9.3 per cent, whereas the rate of semantic shift is in the order of 1.5 per cent.

Loss is also observable if we compare the 971 items noted in Hancock's 1973 work with Baxter and da Silva's 2004 list.[55] In this case, loss involves 68 words whereas 15 words have changed meaning, a 7 per cent loss rate and a 1.5 per cent rate of semantic shift. These preliminary figures suggest that the language is now receding at a faster rate than in previous decades.

Other evidence of "shrinkage" in the lexicon was noted during of the preparation of Baxter and da Silva's 2004 Kristang dictionary. Some 204 words were classified as "archaic" because they were rare, or only vaguely recalled. This amounts to 8.3 per cent of the dictionary's 2,429 single word entries.[56] However, there were a number of other words that were excluded because, although people had heard the word before, they could not assign it a meaning. These included, for example, *strabaladu* "afflicted, distressed", *nozamintu* "mourning", *muchadu* "full, swollen", words which were recorded by Rêgo.[57] On the other hand, some words have been lost because their referents are obsolete. For example, *askung* "glove", is no longer used because gloves are no longer part of Kristang reality.[58]

Table 5.1, derived from my 2005 article, "Kristang (Malacca Creole Portuguese): A Long-Time Survivor Seriously Endangered", presents examples of obsolete words which in the current language are represented by other terms, sometimes by phrases. All items on the left of the table have been lost.

TABLE 5.1
Some Words Lost from the Kristang Lexicon since 1942 and 1973

SOURCE		CURRENT EQUIVALENT	
Rêgo 1942			
asniá	to fool about	*brinká dodu*	(lit.) play fool
compania	company	*jenti kompanyá*	(lit.) person accompany
emado	glutton	*pustemadu*	glutton, gluttonous
fermosura	beauty	*buniteza*	beauty
nescitá	to need	*prësizu*	to need
Hancock 1973			
kidá	to care for	*biziá (kuidadu)*	(lit.) to watch over, care
ripará	to see	*olá*	to see
sanggrá	to bleed	*sai sanggi*	(lit.) to emit blood
spoza	wife	*mulé*	(lit.) woman
tang	so (Adv.)	*bong bong*	(lit.) good good, very
		isorti	(lit.) this type
úniku	unique, alone	*justu ungua*	(lit.) just one
		onsong sa	(lit.) alone + GEN

Source: Alan N. Baxter, "Kristang (Malacca Creole Portuguese): A Long-Time Survivor Seriously Endangered", *Estudios de Sociolingüística* 6, no. 1 (2005): 25–26.

Malay and English Words in Kristang Discourse

The influence of Malay and English is seen in two main ways: first, the presence of non-Kristang words in competition with equivalent Kristang words; and second, the presence of non-Kristang words which have no equivalent in Kristang. Both are natural tendencies when languages are in close contact, and they traditionally contribute to the development of a language's lexicon.

The presence of Malay influence is especially notable with frequent adverbs, conjunctions and prepositions. Table 5.2[59] exemplifies this with a small set of of Kristang and Malay function words at three points in time: 1942 (Rêgo), 1973 (Hancock) and 2004 (Baxter and da Silva).[60]

Here, it is assumed that these Kristang (< Portuguese) words were present in 1942 and in 1973, yet perhaps not recorded by Rêgo or Hancock.

TABLE 5.2
Some Adverbs, Conjunctions and Prepositions at Three Points in Time

Lexical Item	KRISTANG				MALAY			
		Rêgo 1942	Hancock 1973	Baxter & de Silva 2004		Rêgo 1942	Hancock 1973	Baxter & de Silva 2004
same	*igual*	✓		✓	*sama*	✓	✓	✓
always	*sempri*		✓	✓	*slalu*		✓	✓
only	*namás*	✓		✓	*seja*	✓		✓
too	*taming*	✓	✓	✓*	*pun*	✓	✓	✓
or	*ke*			✓	*atu, atau*		✓	✓
but	*mas*	✓		✓	*tapi*		✓	✓
if	*kantu*	✓		✓	*kalu*		✓	✓
	si	✓	✓	✓*				
for	*para, par, pa*	✓	✓	✓	*pada*			✓
	padi		✓	✓				
until	*ati*	✓	✓	✓*	*sampe*	✓	✓	✓

Note: * Infrequent and not widely known.
Source: Alan N. Baxter, "Kristang (Malacca Creole Portuguese): A Long-Time Survivor Seriously Endangered", *Estudios de Sociolingüística* 6, no. 1 (2005): 27.

For the Malay words, in most cases, the absence of the Malay equivalent term in the 1942 and 1973 lists may mean the word was not a notable variant.[61] As such, it seems that there has been an increase in the Malay items competing with Kristang items in Table 5.2. Today, Kristang *taming* "too", *si* "if", and *ati* "until" are extremely infrequent. However, Malay *atu/atau* "or", *tapi* "but", *kalu* "if" and *pada* "for", none of which were reported in 1942, are very common currently.

A recently detected use in the Kristang of younger speakers points to the introduction of a further frequent Malay preposition, namely, *di* "at, in, on", substituting certain functions of the otherwise strong Kristang preposition *na* "at, in, into, on", as in the following exerpt from an interview recorded in 2009:

> **Researcher:**
> Bos podi dá sabé ku yo ki angkoza bos ta prendé agora na universiti?
> (Can you tell me what you are studying now at university?)[62]
> **Informant (female, 20 years):**
> Yo ta prendé di Multi-media University di Bukit Beruang.
> (I am studying at the Multimedia University in Bukit Beruang.)[63]

New influence of Malay syntactic structure may also be readily observed, as in the following written example from a community pamphlet, where we see the presence of a Malay passive structure:

> Isti bairu agora di choma "Padri sa Chang"
> (This village area is called "Padri sa Chang".)

Kristang does not have a generalized passive structure, and the traditional Kristang way of stating this sentence would be:

> Isti bairu agora jenti choma "Padri sa Chang"
> (This village area is called [= lit. people call/one calls] "Padri sa Chang".)

Proportions of English and Malay Items in Kristang Discourse

My 2005 work on Kristang noted that competing and non-competing forms from Malay and English were found widely distributed across fluent speakers in interviews in the early 1980s.[64] Reflexes of the shift to English are in evidence. Table 5.3 presents a sample of totals of first occurrences of Malay and English words[65] in the discourse of four female speakers in 1981.[66]

In this table, English words clearly prevail over Malay words. English dominates both in the domains of competing words (that is, where there is an equivalent word in Kristang) and of non-competing words (that is, where there is no equivalent in Kristang).

The preference for English is also confirmed in Table 5.4, which presents the results of a translation-elicitation exercise[67] whereby informants proposed Kristang equivalents of five English kinship terms. Informants proposed English terms either exclusively or as their first suggestion together with a second suggestion of the traditional Kristang item. It is noticeable that the

TABLE 5.3
A Sample of Four Female Speakers Showing "Competing" and "Non-Competing"
Words from English and Malay during 1+ Hours of Kristang Discourse

	FEMALE SPEAKER AGE			
LANGUAGE	**38 years**	**29 years**	**23 years**	**19 years**
English non-competing	20 (38%)	47 (46%)	32 (51%)	25 (34%)
English-competing	18 (35%)	38 (37%)	19 (30%)	28 (38%)
English total	**38 (73%)**	**85 (83%)**	**51 (81%)**	**53 (72%)**
Malay non-competing	6 (12%)	6 (6%)	5 (8%)	7 (10%)
Malay-competing	8 (15%)	11 (11%)	7 (11%)	13 (18%)
Malay total	**14 (27%)**	**17 (17%)**	**12 (19%)**	**20 (28%)**
Total Non-Kristang	**52**	**102**	**63**	**73**

Source: Alan N. Baxter, "Kristang (Malacca Creole Portuguese): A Long-Time Survivor Seriously Endangered", *Estudios de Sociolingüística* 6, no. 1 (2005): 28.

TABLE 5.4
Results of a Translation-Elicitation Exercise for Kin Terms

	FEMALE SPEAKER AGE								
	67	65	63	38	30	22	19	18	**WORD SELECTED**
grandfather	x	x	x	x		x			*abo machu*
					x		x	x	*grempa*
	x								*pa gren*
grandmother	x	x	x	x		x			*abo femi*
					x		x	x	*grema*
	x								*ma gren*
uncle	x	x	x	x		x			*tiu*
			x	x	x	x	x	x	*angkl*
aunt	x	x	x	x		x			*tia*
			x	x	x	x	x	x	*enti*
brother-in-law	x	x	x	x	x	x			*kunyadu*
							x	x	*bradinlo*

Source: Alan N. Baxter, "Kristang (Malacca Creole Portuguese): A Long-Time Survivor Seriously Endangered", *Estudios de Sociolingüística* 6, no. 1 (2005): 29.

variation displayed by the "older" speakers is resolved by the younger speakers by replacing the Kristang terms with English terms.

Recent Evidence of European Portuguese Influence

An increased presence of the Portuguese language, through contact with Portuguese tourists, journalists, and perhaps through classes in European Portuguese, during the last decade, shows some signs of influence on the language. At this stage, it is too early to say whether these influences will be lasting. Furthermore, my observations here are not based on a structured quantified study, but rather on participant observation of certain individuals during the last year. Table 5.5 shows a small set of Kristang items and European Portuguese items that are currently in variation for some speakers.

TABLE 5.5
Variation Showing Modern European Portuguese Influence

	KRISTANG / ENGLISH		MODERN EUROPEAN PORTUGUESE / ENGLISH	
1	*teng bong! / klai!*	hello	*olá!*	hello
2	*gradesidu, mutu mersé*	thank you	*obrigado*	thank you
3	*kifoi* [kifói]	what happened?	*que foi?* [kə fój]; [kᵓ fój]	what happened?
4	*mutu*	very		
	mutu tantu	many, a lot	*muito* ["mw̃ĩtᵘ]	very; many, a lot
5	*festa* [fésta]	festival	*festa* [féštɐ]	festival, party
6	*misturá* [misturá]	to mix	*misturar* [mišturár]	to mix

Items 1 and 2 in Table 5.5 represent novel introductions, and items 3 and 4 represent both a semantic and phonological change, whereas items 5 and 6 demonstrate only the influence of European Portuguese pronunciation on Kristang words. In the latter respect, the introduction of the palatal voiceless fricative [š] in syllable-final position is novel, as the Kristang phonology derives from varieties of pre-nineteenth century Portuguese that did not palatalize /s/ in this position. Malay phonology has reinforced this non-palatalized quality. Similarly, item 3 displays the introduction of unstressed [ə] and syllable reduction, again a sound that the varieties of pre-nineteenth century Portuguese from which Kristang derives, did not have in this particular case.

The Name of the Language: Kristang → Portuguese?

In the last three years, the name of the language has also shown signs of change under external influence. Some prominent community members avoid, or even openly criticize, the use of the term "Kristang" as their language's name, promoting instead the use of the term "Portuguese". There have even been uninformed suggestions that the term "Kristang" has been touted by researchers!

Of course, over the years, the language has had many names, and the British administration referred to the language as local Portuguese, Malacca Portuguese or even just Portuguese. The current change may be rooted in several factors: wider Malaysian recognition of the Malayo-Portuguese culture; the tourism discourse; the influence from the presence of European Portuguese tourists and others; and a growing self-identity within these contexts (and perhaps an unconscious response to the partial *bumiputera* status[68]). These are, of course, perfectly natural social factors promoting equally natural processes of linguistic change.

PROSPECTS FOR MAINTENANCE AND STRENGTHENING

What are the prospects for maintaining the language? In this section, I will briefly summarize some suggestions from my 2005 work.[69] Several of these issues are now being addressed in the Portuguese Settlement.

A revitalization and maintenance programme is feasible and there are a number of factors in its favour. These are:

1. *Speaker numbers*. In spite of the radical shrinkage of the last decades, the language still has a reasonable number of speakers, yet probably only in the vicinity of 750 fluent functional speakers.

2. *Documentation*. There has been extensive linguistic documentation of the language, both by professional linguists and by members of the Portuguese-Eurasian community. Among this material there is linguistic and sociolinguistic description,[70] including an extensive descriptive grammar (Baxter 1988), four dictionaries (Baxter and da Silva 2004; Marbeck 1995 and 2004; and Scully and Zuzarte 2004), and some language and culture educational material (Marbeck 2004).[71] Furthermore, Tomás's 2004 study provides a detailed insight into shrinkage within the grammar and lexicon of Kristang.[72] Additionally, there are also the various sociolinguistic surveys referred to in earlier sections of the current chapter. All this documentation can and should serve a language maintenance programme. It is also feasible

to produce didactic materials, and to produce a range of bilingual community information materials.

3. *Community self-regard.* Kristang self-regard is changing, in part because the larger community now values their culture, and the core Kristang community is now more prosperous. In 1998, Dorian noted how such factors can aid a community to resist abandonment of an ancestral language.[73] Furthermore, national legislation now grants the language a special status, a prestige that it has not had previously. Most important, both Nunes's 1996 and Sudesh's 2000 studies registered positive respondent attitudes towards Kristang and regarding its possible promotion within Padri sa Chang.[74]

4. *Community recognition of endangerment.* A community must determine whether it has the motivation to preserve and maintain the language. This starts with recognition of the problem. In the literature, this has variously been referred to as "prior clarification"[75] or "goal setting".[76] The Kristang community appears to recognize the problem.

The professional literature on language maintenance and revitalization programmes outlines the following essential characteristics of a revitalization programme, if it is to have any chance of success:

1. *A community-based body exclusively devoted to language preservation*
   a. This body must involve community members actively competent in the endangered language.
   b. It should, ideally, involve community members who have worked on the language and oral traditions in some capacity.[77]
   c. It must have a wide representative base from different age groups.
   d. It should include community members who have skills useful to language revitalization, such as, for example, computing and pedagogical skills.
2. *Community involvement*
   a. A revitalization programme must be firmly in the hands of the community to obviate "avoidance strategies", whereby responsibility for the problem is handed to outsiders.[78]
3. *Sustainability*
   a. New members must be constantly involved, so as not to lose impetus.[79] In this sense, the committee needs to self perpetuate, training community members.
   b. The committee must be persistent, to overcome any negative attitudes on the part of the wider community, and indeed of the core community itself.
   c. It must be self-critical, assessing the effectiveness of its work.

4. *Associated professional consultants*
   a.   The revitalization and planning body must have recourse to outside professional consultants who have conducted research on the language and the community. This is of extreme importance where the mechanics of language planning are concerned (for example: advice about the spelling of a language, if it is to be written).
5. *Financial base*
   a.   Such a project is best sustained if it has a stable financial support base, preferably from the community itself, but also from larger recognized bodies (such as cultural foundations).
6. *School support: Language classes within the official school system*
   a.   Additionally, such a committee might envisage the introduction of the endangered language into a school system, say at an early level.[80]

Some of the above points have been partly achieved in recent times. There is now a project in place in the Portuguese Settlement involving committed people from the community who have initiated classes with young children to reinforce the language and create a greater awareness of its significance. The project has also spawned a newsletter in which Kristang is now being written.

Nevertheless, it is still important to stress the points I have outlined which have been identified by language professionals as being fundamental in successful linguistic revitalization projects internationally. In this way, existing projects might be fine-tuned in order give the Kristang language the very best chances of success in a revitalization programme.

In the next section, I will draw attention to certain issues that require a good deal of care in externally supported linguistic and cultural revival projects in Luso-Asian communities in South, Southeast and East Asia.

ON EXTERNAL SUPPORT FOR CULTURAL PRESERVATION

While bearing in mind that successful preservation programmes must be grounded in community-internal dynamics and initiative, it must be stressed that external aid and consultancy are very important factors in cultural preservation. However, at the same time, it is important to remember that it is not sufficient for an external intervention in the name of cultural preservation to be merely well intentioned. Such an intervention must first and foremost be well informed, and the receiving community must also be well informed. This means well informed in terms of the language and the culture, and well informed in terms of the possibilities of linguistic and cultural preservation and of how to achieve it. Unfortunately, often both parties, the external intervening party and the community itself, act without being well informed.

In Asia, minority Creole Portuguese communities have traditionally viewed themselves, and have been viewed by others, in terms of certain misconceptions that would be considered entirely unacceptable in the context of the Portuguese Creole speaking nations of Africa: Cape Verde, Guinea-Bissau, and São Tomé and Príncipe.

In the case of Malacca, there are enduring myths, seemingly harmless, that most outsiders and intervening bodies fail to deal with, and of which the community itself continues to be unaware. Unfortunately, they are myths that can open the door to a discourse and practices with potentially very negative consequences for the language and the culture.

One such myth is that the language of the Malacca Portuguese Eurasians is sixteenth-century Portuguese that became isolated after the Dutch takeover of Malacca. Certainly the vocabulary of the language, and its pronunciation to some extent, has its roots in older varieties of Portuguese, extending from the sixteenth through to the nineteenth century. Indeed, some recent research suggests that they were not so isolated as has previously been claimed. But the grammar of the language is definitely very far removed from that of any varieties of Portuguese, archaic or modern. It is the grammar of a language in its own right, independent from Portuguese. Nevertheless, the myth is popular in travel books, in the minds of (especially Portuguese) tourists and in work by certain historians:

> [O]s descendentes de Portugueses, em Malaca, fecharam-se a qualquer influência exterior, mantendo a língua portuguesa do séc. XVI.

> ([T]he descendents of the Portuguese, in Malacca, shut themselves off from any outside influence, maintaining the Portuguese language of the sixteenth century.)[81]

The danger of the myth is that it gives rise to a subordinate relationship between the local language and Portuguese. True, there is an historical connection between these languages, but the myth that Malacca Creole Portuguese is <old Portuguese> establishes a far more direct relationship than is the case and leads to the mistaken idea that the language of the Malacca Portuguese is a dialect of Modern European Portuguese.

A further myth in relation to the language is that it is a "mis-learnt" or "broken" Portuguese. This too is a centuries-old myth which can be found in the observations of early foreign travellers in the East. It too evidences linguistic ignorance on the part of the observer, and it also places the local language in a weak position, as a language that, if broken, could somehow be fixed. In this context, it is interesting to note that early British administrators and missionaries to Malacca in the nineteenth century did not hold this view; rather, they recognized the language for what it was: a variety of Indo-Portuguese Creole.

In stark contrast, however, we find that certain Portuguese missionaries saw it their personal crusade to stamp it out. Such was the case, reported by the late nineteenth-century Portuguese philologist, Adolpho Coelho, who referred to a certain Friar Santana, a priest at the Singaporean Mission in the second half of the nineteenth century, who endeavored to teach the most standard Portuguese that his studies of classical Portuguese writing would permit, and who was flabbergasted when Coelho suggested that the *português corrompido* "corrupt Portuguese" that he so earnestly tried to suppress was a worthy language in its own right![82]

The fate of Macao Creole Portuguese is an interesting case in point. Macao Creole was subjected to two centuries of stigmatization by a society in which Portuguese was the prestige language, the language that got one a job, the language taught in the schools by teachers who too considered the creole merely broken Portuguese. As a result, Macao Creole is now in the final throes of extinction. In 1942, Father António da Silva Rêgo wrote regarding Macao CP that

> desaparece diante do português escolar. As crianças, que em Macau frequentam as escolas, riem-se do crioulo falado por suas mães e avós.
>
> (it is disappearing in the face of the Portuguese of the schools. Children, who in Macao attend school, laugh at the creole spoken by their mothers and grandparents.)[83]

These two myths regarding Malacca Creole Portuguese — of it being an "isolated, Old Portuguese", or a "broken Portuguese" — can contribute to a discourse and a behaviour that have the potential to be detrimental to the language, if not appropriately handled. At another level, both myths can be applied in outsiders' readings of other aspects of the culture.

An interesting case of innocent, yet uninformed, cultural intervention which has had a lasting effect on the traditions of the MCP community is that of the introduction of European Portuguese regional folkdances in the early 1950s. Father António da Silva Rêgo writes of this phenomenon:

> Fundou-o (= o rancho popular português) em 1951 o Pᵉ Manuel Joaquim Pintado, superior das Missões de Malaca. Nesse ano passou pela cidade o Eng° Ruy Cinatti ... . O Pᵉ Pintado ... pediu-lhe que ensinasse algumas canções portuguesas, entrando-se assim na realização de um velho sonho

por ele tanto tempo alimentado. Canções e danças foram rapidamente assimiladas.

Mercê das canções que o Grupo Folclórico apresenta ... as cantigas de Malaca vão necessariamente sofrer influência benéfica. Estas canções entrarão, sem dúvida, no folclore local, passarão a ser contadas por todos com melhor pronúncia, corrigindo-se assim erros antigos.

([The Portuguese folkdance group] was founded in 1951 by Fr Manuel Joaquim Pintado. In that year, the engineer Ruy Cinatti passed through [Malacca, and] Fr Pintado asked him to teach some Portuguese songs ... realizing thus a long-held dream .... Songs and dances were quickly assimilated.

Thanks to the songs ... the Malacca traditional songs will undergo beneficial influence [they will] no doubt become part of the local folklore, will be sung by everybody with a better pronunciation, and former errors will thus be corrected.)[84]

These comments reveal a trace of the subordinating attitudes mentioned earlier. In reality, what occurred was that these dances and songs, through various forms of promotion, extinguished a long tradition of a rich creole music and dance repertoire that linked the community to its Indo-Portuguese roots. I was able to record some of this music in 1980–81, with elderly musicians, but it is now long gone. And it has disappeared in good part because it was not valued in the face of the newly introduced Portuguese dances and music that, in reality, have only a late twentieth-century connection with the community.

During my three decades of research in the Malacca CP community, in observing the nature of contacts with the community involving external elements, and in particular Portuguese elements, I have sometimes had the odd feeling that a lack of informedness on the part of external elements conspires to keep the Malacca Portuguese ignorant of certain very significant cultural realities. An effect of paternalism perhaps, that they must adhere to a Modern European Portuguese cultural path. In this sense, it seems curious that they should be constantly made aware of Portugal, often in the form of popular cultural icons (Bemfica or Porto football team paraphernalia, Portuguese regional cultural artefacts and fado music, for example) that in reality are completely extraneous to their traditions. Yet, the Malacca Creole Portuguese people are never made aware of the cultural and linguistic reality of other Creole Portuguese communities, such as, for example, of Cape Verde! Nor are they made aware of the reality of Creole Portuguese communities similar to their own, in India at Diu, Daman or Chaul. Surely this "bring them back into the Portuguese fold" approach holds echoes of the political cultural matrix of the colonial Portuguese era. The impact of contact between European Portuguese language and culture and the Creole language in a populous creole community such as that of Cape Verde, where the creole has very strong community roots, including roots in an educated middle class, is unlikely to have serious negative consequences for the creole. However, in a tiny minority which is yet to properly understand the nature of its traditional language, the presence of Modern Portuguese and its relation to the creole needs to be handled with great care.

A fundamental factor in linguistic or cultural preservation projects is the need for all parties to be well informed about the local language and culture, and for the assisting intervening parties not to impose external agendas. Nevertheless a creole community will do with its culture what it chooses to do. If it chooses to decreolize linguistically and culturally, or if it chooses to acquire some degree of bilingualism in the former colonial language, that is its own business. However, any minority linguistic community must be aware of what it stands to lose if its traditional language and culture are not valued. The case of the Macao CP community is an interesting point: having lost their traditional creole language, they are now desperate to somehow revive it. Other than in a simple symbolic way, this revival is pretty much impossible.

THE ROLE OF PORTUGUESE-BASED FOUNDATIONS

Over many years, the Gulbenkian Foundation has funded a number of successful initiatives in Malacca. These projects have included publications such as the didactic materials in Malacca Creole Portuguese prepared by Joan Marbeck, a retired teacher. Very significant, however, was the creation of the Portuguese Square in the Settlement, an initiative that in the long term must be seen as the start of a shift in employment from part-time fishing and work in factories towards restauranting on the basis of the Kristang traditional cuisine. Indeed, the long term outcome of this project has had a positive effect on language preservation and strengthening of the Kristang cultural self-esteem.

On the other hand, the role of Portuguese-based bodies promoting the Portuguese language has been rather marginal until recent times. While teaching Modern European Portuguese in Malaysia, bodies such as the Instituto Camões have not voiced an opinion on the question of the Creole language.[85] This is logical, as their brief is to teach Modern European Portuguese. However, Creole Portuguese communities do constitute a very significant cultural and linguistic component of the Lusophone world. In this respect, it is interesting to note that the presence in Malacca of a project funded by the Instituto Camões has inspired a recent language revitalization programme run by community members.

CONCLUSION

The Malacca Creole Portuguese community is shifting strongly towards English; meanwhile, transmission of the creole language to younger generations is severely weakened and the language system itself is showing strong signs of attrition.

A language revitalization programme has now begun and there are many positive factors that should lead to its success. Kristang might still be saved for future generations. However, a great deal of attention and care needs to be exercised with respect to the actual Kristang component of the revitalization process. A most essential part of this process is to educate the community about the genuine nature of its language and culture, and to foster a fundamental respect for these. At the same time, it is essential to fully explain the relationship of the local language and culture to those of other creole Portuguese communities, and historically to those of Portugal. Let us all work together to ensure the success of such revitalization programmes!

ABBREVIATIONS

1s:	first person singular
3pl:	third person plural
3s:	third person singular
ACC:	accusative relator
EMPH:	emphasis
FUT:	future marker
GEN:	genitive relator
LOC:	locative relator
NEG:	negation
PF:	perfective aspect marker
S:	source relator

Notes

1   The present study builds on earlier work on the survival of this language, Alan N. Baxter, "Kristang (Malacca Creole Portuguese): A Long-Time Survivor Seriously Endangered", *Estudios de Sociolingüística* 6, no. 1 (2005): 1–37, and is part of

project RG-UL/07-08S/Y1/BA01/FSH supported by the Research Committee of the Universidade de Macau.

2 John Holm, *Pidgins and Creoles*, vol. 2, *Reference Survey* (Cambridge: Cambridge University Press, 1989).

3 The language has been referred to by many names over the years. For example, in English it has been called *Portuguese, local Portuguese*, or *Malacca Portuguese*. In Malay it has been referred to as *(bahasa) serani* "Catholic (Eurasian) language" or *bahasa geragau* "shrimp language". On the other hand, Portuguese writers have termed it *Malaquero, Malaquense, Malaquês, Malaquenho*, and even *dialecto português de Malaca* "Portuguese dialect of Malacca", the latter term being quite inappropriate as, technically, it is a language in its own right, derived from Portuguese, but not a dialect thereof. Henceforth, I will use the term "Kristang" to refer to Malacca Creole Portuguese.

4 I use the term Kristang to refer to Malacca Creole Portuguese throughout this period.

5 The respective periods are: Portuguese, 1511–1641; Dutch, 1642–1795 and 1818–23; British, 1795–1818 and 1823–1957; and Malaysia, 1957 to the present.

6 Nancy Dorian, "Western Language Ideologies and Small-Language Prospects", in *Endangered Languages: Current Issues and Future Prospects*, edited by Lenore A. Grenoble and Lindsay J. Whaley (Cambridge: Cambridge University Press, 1998), p. 16.

7 Manuel Teixeira, "Batávia", in *Macau e a sua Diocese*, vol. 6, *A Missão Portuguesa de Malaca* (Lisbon: Agência Geral do Ultramar, 1963).

8 António da Silva Rêgo and Alan N. Baxter, *Dialecto Português de Malaca e Outros Escritos* (Lisbon: Comissão Nacional para os Descobrimentos Portugueses, Imprensa Nacional, 1998). Within the Catholic Church's domain in the nineteenth century there may have been some degree of "diglossia" in the Creole community, as the records of the governing body of the Saint Peter's Church for the nineteenth century are written almost exclusively in Portuguese. See Alan N. Baxter, *A Grammar of Kristang* (Canberra: Pacific Linguistics, 1988), p. 12, a re-edition of António da Silva Rêgo, *Dialecto Português de Malaca* (Lisbon: Agência Geral das Colónias, 1942), including the re-edition of some of the author's articles.

9 "Correio das missões: Malaca", *Boletim do Governo Eclesiástico da Diocese de Macau* 86 (1911): 250.

10 Baxter, *A Grammar of Kristang*, p. 9. It is unclear from available documentation whether schools were run by the Portuguese Mission during the eighteenth century.

11 Baxter, *A Grammar of Kristang*, p. 12; and Alan N. Baxter, "Portuguese and Creole Portuguese in the Pacific and Western Pacific Rim", in *Atlas of Languages of Intercultural Communication in the Pacific, Asia, and the Americas*, edited by Stephen A. Wurm, Peter Mühlhäusler and Darrell T. Tryon (Berlin: Mouton de Gruyter, 1996), p. 308.

12   *The Eleventh Report of the Anglo-Chinese College: For the Year 1835* (Malacca: Mission Press, 1836).

13   Indo-Portuguese is the blanket term used by the missionaries to refer to "Creole Portuguese" in South and Southeast Asia.

14   Baxter, "Portuguese and Creole Portuguese", p. 308.

15   Alan N. Baxter, "Vestiges of Etymological Gender in Malacca Creole Portuguese", *Journal of Pidgin and Creole Languages* 25, no. 1 (2010): 120–54.

16   "Letter from Mrs. Garling, dated March 28, 1830", Malacca, Incoming Letters, box 3, Correspondence of the London Missionary Society, Council for World Mission Archives (formerly London Missionary Society), Library of the School of Oriental and African Studies, University of London, apud Baxter, "Portuguese and Creole Portuguese", p. 308.

17   It is likely that these schools were in operation from the beginning of the nineteenth century. Unfortunately, documentation of the mission schools for the period is incomplete.

18   Baxter, *A Grammar of Kristang*, p. 12.

19   Ibid., pp. 12–13.

20   Baxter, "Vestiges".

21   Baxter, *A Grammar of Kristang*, pp. 6–7.

22   Baxter, "Vestiges"; and Radin Fernando, "Metamorphosis of the Luso-Asian Diaspora in the Malay Archipelago, 1640–1795", in *Iberians in the Singapore-Melaka Area (16th to 18th Century)*, edited by Peter Borschberg (Wiesbaden: Harrassowitz; and Lisbon: Fundação Oriente, 2004), pp. 161–84.

23   The bond between religion and language, and the cultural intermediary status of the creoles in colonial society, traditionally facilitated a strong assimilation dynamic through intermarriage. Thus, the creoles have assimilated Eurasians of Dutch and English origins as well as Chinese, Indian, and even occasional Malay elements.

24   British Administration Census, 1827, apud A.H. Dickinson, "The History of the Creation of the Malacca Police", *Journal of the Malayan Branch of the Royal Asiatic Society* 19, no. 2 (1941): 260–61.

25   Recent research in the Dutch and British archives of Malacca suggests that there was another, albeit smaller component of the Malacca Portuguese community that was better off, and which had a knowledge of a variety of Portuguese resembling the metropolitan variety (see Baxter, "Vestiges"). It has also been found that throughout the Dutch period, certain elements of the Malacca Portuguese traded frequently with Indo-Portuguese ports and Macao. Evidently, it is not necessarily the case that the Malacca Portuguese were as isolated as some writers suggest.

26   The name reflects the fact that it was a priest who organized the resettlement project.

27   Chan Kok Eng, "A Study in the Social Geography of the Malacca Portuguese Eurasians", master's thesis, Universiti Malaya, 1969.

28   Baxter, *A Grammar of Kristang*, p. 12.

29 Bernard Sta Maria, *My People, My Country: The Story of the Malacca Portuguese Community* (Malacca: Malacca Portuguese Development Centre, 1982).

30 The venture was funded by the Portuguese-based Calouste Gulbenkian Foundation, through the intervention of the superior of the Portuguese Mission, community leaders, local and national politicians, and the Portuguese Embassy in Thailand.

31 Gerard Fernandis, "*Papia, Relijang e Tradisang*: The Portuguese Eurasians in Malaysia: *Bumiquest*, A Search for Self Identity", *Lusotopie* (2000): 263.

32 A panel of historians was constituted by the State to determine whether the Portuguese community could be accorded *bumiputera* status. A decision has not been announced, yet the attitude of some prominent Malay figures has been positive. See Fernandis, "*Papia, Relijang e Tradisang*", p. 264.

33 The inclusion of the language factor was the initiative of community elder Patrick de Silva.

34 Fieldwork in preparation for Baxter, *A Grammar of Kristang*.

35 Baxter, "Kristang (Malacca Creole Portuguese)", p. 19.

36 Hyacinth Gaudart, "A Typology of Bilingual Education in Malaysia", *Journal of Multilingual and Multicultural Development* 8, no. 6 (1987): 533.

37 Mário P. Nunes, "By How Many Speakers, by Whom, with Whom, and for What Purposes, Is Kristang Still Used in the Portuguese Settlement of Malacca?", paper presented at the 8e Colloque International d'Études Créoles, Guadeloupe, May 1996; Maya Khemlani David and Faridah Noor Mohd Noor, "Language Maintenance or Language Shift in the Portuguese Settlement of Malacca in Malaysia?" *Migracijske teme* 15 (1999): 417–549; Nicholas Sudesh, "Language Maintenance and Shift among the Portuguese-Eurasians in the Portuguese Settlement", master's thesis, Universiti Malaya, 2000; and Eileen Lee, "Language Shift and Revitalization in the Kristang Community, Portuguese Settlement, Malacca", Ph.D. dissertation, University of Sheffield, 2004. Nunes surveyed 225 residents of Padri sa Chang in six age-groups: <15, 16–20, 21–30, 31–40, 41–50 and >50. David and Noor surveyed sixty-two respondents (one each from sixty-two households) in five age-groups: 10–19, 20–29, 30–39, 40–59, and 60–89. Sudesh worked with sixty-four respondents in four age-groups. Lee surveyed informants in eighty-five households.

38 Nunes, "By How Many Speakers".

39 Lee, "Language Shift".

40 David and Noor, "Language Maintenance".

41 Ibid., and Sudesh, "Language Maintenance and Shift".

42 Ibid.

43 Sudesh, "Language Maintenance and Shift".

44 David and Noor, "Language Maintenance".

45 Sudesh, "Language Maintenance and Shift".

46 Ibid., pp. 139–40.

47 Chan, "A Study in the Social Geography"; Baxter, *A Grammar of Kristang*; and Sudesh, "Language Maintenance and Shift".

48 David and Noor, "Language Maintenance"; and Lee, "Language Shift".
49 Lee, "Language Shift".
50 Data collected for grammatical description of the language of Kristang-dominant speakers.
51 Data collected for the preparation of Baxter and de Silva (2004). Alan N. Baxter and Patrick de Silva, *A Dictionary of Kristang (Malacca Creole Portuguese): English* (Canberra: Pacific Linguistics, 2004).
52 The discussion in this and the following two sections revises and develops topics in Baxter, "Kristang (Malacca Creole Portuguese)".
53 Rêgo and Baxter, *Dialecto Português* (1998). Additionally, Rêgo listed a large number of phrasal expressions.
54 Baxter and de Silva, *A Dictionary of Kristang*.
55 Ian F. Hancock, "Malacca Creole Portuguese: A Brief Transformational Account", *Te Reo* 16 (1973): 23–44, with the list in Baxter and de Silva, *A Dictionary of Kristang*.
56 The latter number excludes 574 variants of head words and a huge number of lexical phrases listed under the head words. In reality, the total number of "lexical concepts" (that is, those represented by single lexical items or by lexical phrases) appears to lie in the vicinity of 4,500, since the English-to-Kristang entries total 4,350.
57 Rêgo and Baxter, *Dialecto Português* (1998).
58 Gloves were formerly used by brides during the traditional Kristang bridal ceremony.
59 In comparing data from different periods, it is evident that extensive comparisons cannot be made because sample sizes are different and the nature of the informants is not fully clear.
60 Rêgo and Baxter, *Dialecto Português* (1998); Hancock, "Malacca Creole Portuguese"; and Baxter and de Silva, *A Dictionary of Kristang*.
61 The absence of a word in Rêgo's list could indicate that the word was either not a notable variant, or not a variant at all. As Rêgo's field experience was extensive, involving contact with a wide range of speakers of Kristang, and in his 1942 study he shows a keen awareness of Malay items, it seems reasonable to assume that his work presents a good level of observational accuracy. Hancock had considerable contact directly and indirectly with younger speakers, so the same assumption seems valid.
62 Exerpt from an interview recorded in 2009.
63 Ibid.
64 Baxter, "Kristang (Malacca Creole Portuguese)". The presence of English and Malay words depends on diverse linguistic and non-linguistic factors. An extensive study of this conditioning is beyond the scope of this work.
65 The counting excludes intersentential switching and includes only the first instance of an English or Malay item.
66 This was a pilot study conducted during fieldwork in 1981. The interviews

were of 1.5 hours duration, followed a Labovian format, and were conducted in Kristang.

67 A pilot study conducted in 1980.

68 Some community members may be playing down the Kristang word because of the obvious association with the Catholic religion. At the same time, they may be capitalizing on a wider community recognition of their Portuguese origins.

69 Baxter, "Kristang (Malacca Creole Portuguese)".

70 Ian F. Hancock, "The Malacca Creoles and Their Language", *Afrasian* 3 (1969): 38–45; Ian F. Hancock, "Some Dutch-Derived Items in Papia Kristang", *Bijdragen tot de Taal-, Land-, en Volkenkunde* 136, no. 3 (1970): 352–56; Hancock, "Malacca Creole Portuguese"; Ian F. Hancock, "Malacca Creole Portuguese: Asian, African or European?", *Anthropological Linguistics* 17, no. 5 (May 1975): 211–36; Alan N. Baxter, "Some Observations on Verb Serialization in Malacca Creole Portuguese", *Boletim de Filologia* (Lisbon) 31 (1990): 161–84; Baxter, "Portuguese and Creole Portuguese"; Baxter, "Kristang (Malacca Creole Portuguese)"; Alan N. Baxter, "Causative and Facilitative Serial Verbs in Asian Ibero-Romance Creoles: A Convergence of Substrate and Superstrate Systems?", *Journal of Portuguese Linguistics* 8, no. 2 (2009): 65–90; Baxter, "Vestiges"; Pierre F.G. Guisan, "Línguas em contato no Sudeste Asiático: O caso do *'Kristang'*", master's thesis, Universidade Federal do Rio de Janeiro, 1992; Mário P. Nunes, "Concepção de tempo e espaço no kristang e no malaio", *Papia* 3, no. 2 (1994): 116–26; Elzbieta Thurgood and Graham Thurgood, "Aspect, Tense, or Aktionsart? The Particle *Ja* in Kristang (Malacca Creole Portuguese)", *Journal of Pidgin and Creole Languages* 11, no. 1 (1996): 45–70; and Maria Isabel Gonçalves Tomás, "O *Kristang* de Malaca: Processos linguísticos e contextos sociais na obsolescência das línguas", Ph.D. dissertation, Universidade Nova de Lisboa, 2004.

71 Baxter, *A Grammar of Kristang*; Baxter and de Silva, *A Dictionary of Kristang*; Joan Marbeck, *Ungua Adanza: An Inheritance* (Malacca: Loh Printing Press, 1995); Joan Marbeck, *Kristang Phrasebook* (Lisbon: Calouste Gulbenkian, 2004); Valerie Scully and Catherine Zuzarte, *Eurasian Heritage Dictionary* (Singapore: SNP International, 2004); and Joan Marbeck, *Linngu Mai: Mother-Tongue of the Malacca Portuguese* (Lisbon: Calouste Gulbenkian, 2004).

72 Tomás, "O *Kristang* de Malaca".

73 Dorian, "Western Language Ideologies", p. 12.

74 Nunes, "By How Many Speakers"; and Sudesh, "Language Maintenance and Shift".

75 Nora Marks Dauenhauer and Richard Dauenhauer, "Technical, Emotional, and Ideological Issues in Reversing Language Shift: Examples from Southeast Alaska", in *Endangered Languages: Current Issues and Future Prospects*, edited by Lenore A. Grenoble and Lindsay J. Whaley (Cambridge: Cambridge University Press, 1998), pp. 61–62.

76 Leanne Hinton, "Language Planning", in *The Green Book of Language*

Revitalization in Practice, edited by Leanne Hinton and Ken Hale (New York: Academic Press, 2001), p. 53.

77   *Cf.* Leanne Hinton, "Language Revitalization: An Overview", in *The Green Book*, edited by Hinton and Hale, p. 17; and Hinton, "Language Planning", pp. 51–55.

78   Dauenhauer and Dauenhauer, "Technical, Emotional, and Ideological Issues", pp. 68–71.

79   Hinton, "Language Revitalization", p. 17.

80   In the case of Kristang, this could be in the pre-school and primary school programmes, under the umbrella of Malaysian government legislation regarding the teaching of minority languages. An Education Act of 1961 provided that instruction can be given in a student's mother tongue if the parents of at least fifteen pupils request it, and provided an appropriate teacher can be found (Rita Lasimbang, Carolyn Miller and Francis Otigil, "Language Competence and Use among Coastal Kadazan Children: A Survey Report", in *Maintenance and Loss of Minority Languages*, edited by William Fase, Koen Jaspaert and Sjaak Kroon [Amsterdam: John Benjamins, 1992], p. 335). The fact that Nunes, "By How Many Speakers", found that 77 per cent of his respondents were in favour of Kristang being taught suggests that an education programme would be well received.

81   Beatriz Basto da Silva, *Em Malaca: Redescobrir Portugal* (Macao: Direcção dos Serviços de Educação de Macau, 1989), p. 27.

82   Francisco Adolfo Coelho, "Os dialectos românicos ou neo-latinos na África, Ásia e América: Novas notas suplementares", in *Estudos Linguísticos Crioulos: Reedição de Artigos Publicados no Boletim da Sociedade de Geografia de Lisboa*, edited by Jorge Morais-Barbosa (Lisbon: Academia Internacional da Cultura Portuguesa, 1967 [1886]), p. 175.

83   Rêgo and Baxter, *Dialecto Português* (1998), p. 272.

84   Ibid., p. 280.

85   Baxter, "Kristang (Malacca Creole Portuguese)".

6

ORAL TRADITIONS OF THE LUSO-ASIAN COMMUNITIES: LOCAL, REGIONAL AND CONTINENTAL[1]

Hugo C. Cardoso

To this day, instrumental music and singing still play a prominent role in social events among the Luso-Asian communities, be it at religious services, processions and feasts, weddings, receptions, or whenever the occasion calls for a display of the community's cultural heritage. This is also true of the Indo-Portuguese communities, for which we have considerably numerous records of oral traditions, including songs, riddles, prayers, stories, sayings and the like. Among the various such collections, the richest concern the communities of Sri Lanka, a body of literature studied in-depth by Jackson[2] and Jayasurya.[3] In this chapter, the point of departure will be an analysis of the relatively understudied song repertoire of the Indo-Portuguese communities of the former Província do Norte (comprising the cities of Bassein, Bombay, Chaul, Daman, and Diu). My aim is to characterize this corpus in formal terms, in the light of our present knowledge of the languages spoken by the Norteiros, and uncover some thematic links it establishes with other repertoires collected elsewhere.

The oldest records of Norteiro songs we have access to are found in the late nineteenth-century writings of Schuchardt.[4] Later published sources include Dalgado,[5] Quadros,[6] Moniz,[7] and scattered contributions to periodicals such as the bulletin *O Oriente Português*, *Revista da Academia da Língua e*

Cultura Portuguesa or *Ta-Ssi-Yang-Kuo*. Recent fieldwork data, collected by members of the communities and researchers alike in Diu, Daman and Korlai, also complements whatever material can be gathered from these written sources.

Issues of a linguistic nature are particularly important due to the fact that Portuguese-lexified creole languages formed among all of the Norteiro communities (see the second section of this chapter, "The Norteiros and Their Language"), as they did in many other Luso-Asian communities across the continent. Yet, to be precise, our corpus does not constitute a "creole song repertoire". It is, as a matter of fact, linguistically very heterogeneous, with registers spanning from the most basilectal creole to the most metropolitan Portuguese. Linguistic matters will be tackled in the third section, "Brief Linguistic Profile", and the corpus's formal heterogeneity will be addressed in the fourth section. The fifth section, "Geographical Dispersion", will provide an analysis of the observed themes and their circulation across Asia.

Samples of songs and oral traditions, both from the Província do Norte and elsewhere in Asia, are transcribed according to the orthography used by their various collectors, which results in significant formal variation. Many of the songs in the corpus are rather long; in the interest of brevity, I have selected only representative excerpts.[8]

THE NORTEIROS AND THEIR LANGUAGE

"Norteiro" was, during colonial times, an accepted designation for a member of the Catholic and creolophone Indo-Portuguese communities of the territory known as Província do Norte, or "Province of the North". In the seventeenth century, when the territory was at its largest, the Província do Norte comprised the Portuguese domains along the northwestern coast of India from Daman to Chaul, including the regions around Bombay and Bassein, its largest settlement. Though physically discrete, the territory of Diu was also seen as an integral part of the Província, on account of its cultural and geographical proximity. Dalgado is very explicit with respect to this when, having clarified the geographical extent covered by the term "Norte", he says[9]

> Mas o termo *Norteiro*, como é ao presente entendido, tem sentido muito mais circunscrito. Não compreende todos os habitantes do *Norte* indistintamente, mas tão-somente os que adoptaram a religião e a língua dos dominadores, isto é, os que são cristãos e falam português, embora não sejam, como não são na sua maioria, descendentes de portugueses.[10]
>
> (But the term *Norteiro*, as it is presently understood, has a much narrower meaning. It does not include all inhabitants of the *Norte* indiscriminately,

but only those who have adopted the religion and language of the overlords, that is, those who are Christians and speak Portuguese, although they are not, as in the case of the majority, descendents of Portuguese.)

Established as an ethnonym, the term could then be applied as a glottonym. In the writings of some early scholars, Norteiro Creole referred to the various Indo-Portuguese Creoles of the region. Notice, for instance, the following passage in one of Dalgado's articles:[11]

> O dialecto de Damão, junto com o de Diu, de que muito se aproxima, pode bem ser considerado como um dos subdialectos do crioulo *norteiro* ou, como é denominado na Índia, português dos norteiros, que os tem muitos, com variantes de maior ou menor importância, na presidência de Bombaim.[12]

> (The Daman dialect, together with the one from Diu, to which it is very similar, can properly be considered one of the subdialects of the Norteiro creole or, as it is known in India, Portuguese of the Norteiros, of which there are many, with more or less important variants, in the Bombay presidency.)

In this region, Portuguese-based creoles were documented or identified in Chaul and neighbouring Korlai, the city of Bombay and surroundings (Mahim, Bandra, Thane, Chevai, Tecelaria and so forth), Bassein, Daman and Diu. According to Dalgado's calculations,[13] the largest of these communities in the early twentieth century was to be found in the Bombay region, but that is precisely where the creole first became extinct. At present, varieties of what was known as Norteiro Creole are spoken in Diu, Daman and Korlai. Of these, the one with the largest body of speakers is that of Daman, where the local creole is estimated to be the native language of about 4,000 people,[14] and the smallest is that of Diu, with around 180 native speakers.[15] The survival of Korlai Creole is interesting, if one considers that Portuguese domination of the area ended in 1740 with the Maratha conquest of Chaul. Part of the city's then-established Catholic population relocated across the Kundalika River to Korlai, which has remained homogeneously Catholic and creolophone to this day. The number of speakers nowadays ascends to around 760 people.[16] Even though these languages are still transmitted to the younger generations, they remain under considerable threat, whether from the pressure of the regional languages (Marathi in Korlai, Gujarati in Daman and Diu) or English in various domains, from lack of official recognition and support, or from die-hard colonial-era attitudes that regard the creoles as "broken Portuguese".

BRIEF LINGUISTIC PROFILE

It is not the purpose of this chapter to provide an exhaustive description of the Norteiro creoles. However, since one of the challenges to the study of the local oral traditions is to make sense of the linguistic variation encountered, I will simply point out some basic and conspicuous differences between these languages and Portuguese.

One feature that is common to the various Norteiro Creoles has to do with word endings. These languages have a clear preference for word-final stress: for example, Ptg. *arroz* "rice" (stress on the last syllable) > Bombay *arôs*, Diu *aros*, Korlai *haro* "rice" (stress on the last syllable). This is, however, not the case in Portuguese. In the transition into the creole lexicon, words of Portuguese origin inevitably lost all post-stress syllables, of which only some consonantal segments were retained in syllable codas; the last vocalic segment retained was the one bearing the stress in the etymon:[17] for example, Ptg. *roupa* "clothing" (stress on the penultimate syllable) > Bombay *rôp*, Daman *rrop*, Diu *rop*, Korlai *rhop* "clothing" (monosyllable); Ptg. *búfalo* "buffalo" (stress on the antepenultimate syllable) > Daman *bufl*, Diu and Korlai *buf* "buffalo"[18] (monosyllable).

Another characteristic, partly related to the previous one, is the absence of gender and number inflection in nouns and adjectives. Let us take a look at some examples from Creole Diu: *ū pork* "one pig (male or female)", *bastāt pork* "many pigs (male or female)". In Portuguese, on the other hand, morphology is employed to indicate gender (typically, but not only, *-o* for masculine and *-a* for feminine) and plural reference (typically *-s*): for example, *porc-o* "pig (masculine)", *porc-a* "pig (feminine)", *porc-o-s* "pigs (masculine)", *porc-a-s* "pigs (feminine)".

There are also considerable differences with respect to verbal categories, given that, unlike in Portuguese, verb forms in the creoles do not inflect for person and number. In Portuguese, for example, the present tense paradigm of the verb *brincar* "to play" constructs different forms for different person-number combinations (*eu brinco* "I play", *nós brincamos* "we play", *vocês brincam* "you [plural] play", and so forth). By contrast, the Creole of Diu, for instance, only contains one invariant non-past finite form (*yo / use / el / nɔs ... brīk* "I/you/he/we ... play").

The categories of tense and aspect, on the other hand, are expressed in these languages through a combination of morphological marking (verbal inflection) and a number of independent pre-verbal markers. In the following excerpt of a tale in the extinct Creole of Bombay,[19] notice the use of the particle *had* to indicate future tense, in combination with an infinitive form of the main verb (*tucá* and *fazê*), and notice also the use of the particle *já* as a past marker next to a past finite verbal form *trouxe*:

Falá ...	dond	ocê	já	trouxe	tud	est	dinheir,	senão
speak	from.where	you	PST	bring[PST]	all	this	money	otherwise

eu had	tucá	e	had	fazê	por'cê	pum
I FUT	play[INF]	and	FUT	make[INF]	to.you	to

dansá	e	pum	ôtre	pum	marivilhá
dance	and	to	other	to	wonder

(Tell [us] where you brought all this money from, or else I will play and [I] will make you dance and the others wonder.)

The various Norteiro Creoles diverge with regard to certain characteristics of the verbal forms as well as the pre-verbal particles and auxiliaries employed. Let us take the future tense marker as an example: whereas in Daman, Diu, and Bombay it takes the form *a / ad / had* (from Ptg. *há-de* "shall"; see the Bombay example above), the variety of Korlai uses the particle *lə* (from Ptg. *logo*), a particle shared with the Portuguese-based creoles of southern India, Sri Lanka, Malacca and Macao.

The differences between the various Norteiro Creoles (in linguistic terms and with respect to their longevity) reveal social and historical differences among them. It is important to recall that Portuguese domination of the various territories had strikingly different chronologies: Diu was under colonial rule for 426 years (1535–1961) and Daman for 403 years (1558–1961), whereas part of the Bombay region was ceded to the British crown in 1661 and the remainder of the Província do Norte (including Bassein and Chaul) was annexed by Maratha forces between 1739 and 1740. It is no surprise, therefore, that the normative pressure of Portuguese is felt more strongly in Daman and Diu. However, one should not assume that the end of colonial rule abruptly severed contact with Portuguese in other regions. Under the auspices of the Padroado, missionary activity and associated educational institutions were, without a doubt, significant and long-lasting vehicles of linguistic propagation in former colonies. Consider, for instance, Dalgado's comment concerning the creolophone community of Bombay:[20]

As classes ilustradas manifestam desamor à sua língua maternal, pela consciência e pejo que têm da sua corrupção, e procuram descartar-se dela, servindo-se ou do português legítimo ou do inglês, língua oficial, principalmente em Bombaim e nos subúrbios.[21]

(The educated classes reveal a lack of love for their mother tongue, because of their conscience of its corruption and their disdain for it, and they attempt to distance themselves from it, using instead either legitimate Portuguese or English, the official language, particularly in Bombay and its suburbs.)

Across the world, colonial-era attitudes render the coexistence of creoles and their lexifiers uneasy. As described in the following section, this tension is partly responsible for the formal heterogeneity one encounters in records of Norteiro oral traditions.

FORMAL HETEROGENEITY

The early corpus of Norteiro oral traditions was compiled by several collaborators of Schuchardt's and Dalgado's, who, despite being two of the most prolific scholars of the Norteiro creoles, were unable to collect their own data. Their corpora, however small, are therefore highly heterogeneous from an orthographic point of view. On the one hand, the writers often reveal some attention to the representation of dialectal peculiarities, but we may also expect the effect of various types of constraints on the output of both informants and collectors. As an example, let us consider the following verses from Bombay as transcribed by Dalgado:[22]

Ai! Já açandeu a candeia, Senhor,	(Ah, the lamp was lit, Lord,
Com azeite margosa;	With bitter oil;
Ai! Noivo com noivinho, Senhor,	Ah, the bridegroom and bride, Lord,
Na cama mimosa.	In the delicate bed.)

There is a clear tendency to approximate these verses to Portuguese orthography. Nonetheless, anyone approaching them from a Portuguese standpoint will immediately notice the violation of gender agreement between *azeite* "lit. olive oil" (used in India with the generic meaning "oil"), a masculine noun, and (*a*)*margosa* "bitter", a feminine adjective. Clearly, the vowel -*a* has been added paragogically to the adjective so that it would rhyme with *mimosa* "delicate" below, whether by the initiative of the informant or the transcriber. If one recalls what was said about the creoles' preference for word-final stress, however, we may expect the original forms to have been *margos* and *mimos*, therefore resulting in a successful rhyme. One further comment concerns the expression *noivo com noivinho*, which in Portuguese would literally mean "the bridegroom and the little bridegroom". Once again, paragogic -*o* (the typical masculine suffix in Portuguese) has been added to both words, where one would expect *noiv com noivinh*. As it turns out, this transcription fails to apprehend the fact that, in the Norteiro creoles, the Portuguese diminutive suffix -*inh*- was reinterpreted, in certain cases, as a feminine affix.[23] The correct interpretation of the creole expression *noiv com noivinh* is, therefore, "the bridegroom and the bride".

More recent documentation efforts, relatively isolated with the exception of Kenneth David Jackson's work, add yet another layer of formal variation and show different degrees of attention to detail. One must therefore approach the entire corpus critically, in order to interpret the transcribers' options, read between the lines of grammatical variation, and recognize the interference of typical (post-)colonial attitudes and values.

Despite these caveats, it is clear that not all linguistic variation in the corpus is the result of editorial options. Let us consider two extreme examples collected in Diu, as they are transcribed in a recent anonymous and unpublished collection of local songs, the photocopies of which circulate among the creolophone communities in Diu and Daman:

Burro de mainate,	(The washerman's donkey,
burro de mainate	The washerman's donkey
Já quibrô mão, já quibrô pé	Broke its hand, broke its foot
Marrô um pau, já fêz empê[24]	A stick was bound [to it], it was made to stand
– ó jumbecê	– ó jumbecê)[25]
Burro de mainate,	(The washerman's donkey,
burro de mainate	The washerman's donkey
Já rachô cóss, ficô lulá	Broke its back, started limping
Marrô patá, já fêz andá	A bandage was tied, it was made to walk
– ó jumbecê	– ó jumbecê)
Burro de mainate,	(The washerman's donkey,
burro de mainate	The washerman's donkey
Quimô fucinho, butô azêt	Burnt its face, oil was applied
Sentiu frescúr e marrô na carrêt	It felt freshness, it was tied to the cart
– ó jumbecê	– ó jumbecê)

The linguistic register of this song is very close to that of modern-day Diu Creole. Despite some orthographic inconsistencies, this transcription represents the language's final-stress rule, in words such as *cóss* "back" (from Ptg. *costas* "back"), *azêt* "oil" (from Ptg. *azeite* "olive oil"), *fréscur* "freshness" (from Ptg. *frescura* "freshness") and *carrêt* "cart" (from Ptg. *carreta* "cart"). Notice also the frequent use of *já* as a pre-verbal past tense marker (which was used in earlier stages of Diu Creole, as evidenced in Schuchardt's corpus,[26] but not nowadays) as well as some Indic lexemes such as *patá* — possibly derived from Malayalam *patta*, which Dalgado[27] translates as "sash".

This song, therefore, has every indication of being a true creole song. Let us now compare it with the "Marcha de Diu", transcribed in the same collection:

Esta marcha vai em Diu a passar	(This march is passing through Diu
Como é muito alegre, toda a	Since it is very happy, everyone
gente vem	comes
P'ra ouvir cantar	To hear the singing
Vamos raparigas	Come on, girls
Que as nossas cantigas estão a agradar	Because our songs are pleasing
Toda a gente canta	Everyone sings
E a todos encanta	And everyone is enchanted
Porque é popular	Because it is popular
....	....
Tanto no bairro cristão	Whether in the Christian quarter
Como na rua de cima	Or the high street
Toda a gente se conhece	Everyone knows one another
Toda a gente se estima	Everyone likes one another
Mouros, hindús e cristãos	Muslims, Hindus and Christians
São amigos de verdade!	Are true friends!
Viva pois a animação (Bis)	So long live the cheerful spirit
Da gente desta cidade.	Of the people in this town.)

Both the topic and melody recall the traditional Portuguese June parades (*marchas populares*), and it is obvious that this song has none of the distinctively creole linguistic signposts: verbs have standard Portuguese tense, person and number inflection, nouns inflect for number and their modifiers for number and gender, and much more. The transcriber credits "Ten. [lieutenant] Marques d'Abreu" as the author of the lyrics, perhaps a Portuguese soldier on duty in Diu, but the song is presently known and performed by members of the local community.

This comparison shows that, although both songs are unmistakably Diuese and deserve a place in the local song repertoire, they have a distinct sociocultural provenance, and this is reflected in their linguistic profile.

Somewhere in between these two extremes, the corpus contains a few songs whose register (as collected) does not seem to correspond fully either to the creoles as we know them or to standard Portuguese. Consider the following refrain of a song collected in 2007 in the village of Korlai:[28]

noytə diə, də Mariə	(Night and day, of Mary
a bəlêzə êdi kanta	The beauty I shall sing)

Fortunately, Korlai Creole has been well described,[29] which allows for a solid linguistic interpretation of these verses. Interestingly, we see here various elements which diverge from Korlai Creole and resemble Portuguese, such as, for instance, the structure of the possessive construction (which, in the local creole, is usually "Possessor" + *su* + "Possessee"), the occurrence of non-final-stress words (for example, *diə* "day", *bəlêzə* "beauty"), the presence of a Portuguese definite article *a* (in *a bəlêzə* "the beauty") and the future marker *êdi* (instead of the particle *lə*, which is typical of Korlai Creole). Such inconsistencies may reflect an ongoing process of adaptation, or they may be due to sociolinguistic pressures of various kinds. In this particular case, the singer appears to be repeating a song in a language of which he is not a native speaker; notice that the paragogic vowel -*ə* indistinctly occurs where modern Portuguese would have [ə] (*noytə*) or [ɐ] (*diə*, *Mariə*, and *bəlêzə*).

GEOGRAPHICAL DISPERSION

There are various linguistic similarities among the Luso-Asian Creoles suggesting that the different varieties did not develop in isolation.[30] With regard to the Norteiro song repertoire, one striking observation is that it partly repeats, adapts and recombines elements also encountered in far-flung territories of Asia. Geographical proximity is expected to result in more shared cultural elements, which is borne out by a study of the oral traditions of the Norteiros. Consider the following song, heard and transcribed in Diu:[31]

Amor de soldad, Bastiana,	(The love of a soldier, Bastiana,
Amor é de um ór[32]	[Is] love of an hour
Ouviu rufar caix, Bastiana,	[He] heard the drums, Bastiana,
Largá, vae cimbór.[33]	[He] leaves and goes away.)

Contrast it now with the following, from Daman:[34]

Amor de soldado	(The love of a soldier
Amor de uma hora,	[Is] love of an hour,

Ouviu rufar caixa,   [He] heard the drums,
Larga, vae-se embora.   [He] leaves, and goes away.)

Another theme that is repeated in the Norteiro corpus is that of the "groom and bride", an example of which was already transcribed in the previous section. Notice now the following song from Diu:[35]

Noibo com noibinh,   (A groom and bride,[36]
Galinh com pentinh   A chicken and chick
Baix de janell   Under the window
Já trucá anell.   [They] exchanged rings.)

Now, contrast it with the following stanza collected in Bombay:[37]

Já nasceu luar, Dopina,   (The moon has risen, Dopina,
Fronte de janella, Dopina;   In front of the window, Dopina;
Noivo com noivinho, Dopina,   The groom and bride, Dopina,
Já trocou anela, Dopina.   Exchanged rings, Dopina.)

Repetitions of this kind make it difficult to establish with any degree of certainty the place of origin of a song. However, it is not uncommon to come across explicit references to particular environments, most often in the form of toponyms. The following refrain is a good example:[38]

Barra de Damão   (The harbour of Daman
Estreito e comprido   [Is] narrow and long
Alegre na entrada   Happy at the entrance
Triste na sahida   Sad at the exit)

Another is the following song (from the anonymous collection mentioned earlier), in which reference is made to Simbor, a fortified island not far from Diu where Portuguese soldiers were stationed:

A respêt de vós, Marú   (Because of you, Maru
Foi comprá cinôr, Marú   [I] went to buy carrots, Maru
Panhô grand castig, Marú   Panhô received great punishment, Maru
Foi pará no Simbôr, Marú   Ended up in Simbor, Maru)

The song below, from the same collection, remains very vital in Diu:

Ó diwan de Mogará   (Oh diwan[39] of Mogará
Parmim já mandô chamá   Sent for me

Sem razão, sem porquê   With no reason, no explanation
Minha vida querê tirá   [He] wants to take away my life)

Soltá parmim, largá   (Let go of me, let me go
Solta [*sic*] parmim, largá   Let go of me, let me go
Dixá iô ir morrê   Let me go and die
Na praia de Gogolá   On the beach of Goghla)

....

Dixá iô ir morrê   (Let me go and die
Na praia de Nagoá   On the beach of Nagoa)

....

Dixá iô ir morrê   (Let me go and die
Na praia de Brancavará   On the beach of Vanakbara)

The toponyms Gogolá, Nagoá and Brancavará make doubtless reference to three villages in the territory of Diu, and therefore suggest this to be a locally born song. The first of these toponyms reappears in another song, from the same anonymous collection:

Olá, olá, marinhêr de Gogolá (Hello, hello, Goghla sailor
Olá, olá, marinhêr de Gogolá Hello, hello, Goghla sailor)

Ai Maria butô red, ó mãi (Ah, Maria threw the net, oh mother
Sú pai já pescô pambirá Her father caught a pambirá)[40]

Filha de pescador, ó mãi (The daughter of the fisherman, oh mother
Sempre foi patratêr   Was always a loud-mouth)

....

Mar foi tint, ó mãi!   (The sea was ink, oh mother
Pêx foi escrivão   A fish was the scribe)

....

Só p'ra escrevê, ó mãi (Only to write, oh mother
Mal de coração   Ailments of the heart)

....

In this case, despite the clear local toponym, one cannot safely defend the Diuese source hypothesis for the entire song. In fact, notice the reappearance of some verses in the last stanza of a song as often performed in Daman:

No inverno rigoroso surumbai (In the harsh winter, surumbai[41]
Nasceu florinhas no chão Little flowers grew on the ground
E assim nasceu o amor surumbai And thus was love born, surumbai
Dentro do meu coração Inside my heart)

....

Mar foi a tinta surumbai   (The sea was ink, surumbai
Peixe foi escrivão   A fish was the scribe
Só para escrever surumbai   Only to write, surumbai
Mal do meu coração.   Ailments of my heart)

The contexts in which the same verses appear in the two songs are starkly different. This highlights the composite nature of many songs in the corpus, which recombine popular verses and themes in novel and creative ways. Let us exemplify this with a recurrent theme studied by Jackson[42] in connection with Sri Lanka, which will simultaneously show how the circulation of poetic material transcends local boundaries to reach across South Asia. This is the topic of the "golden ring", or "ring with seven stones", often accompanied by reference to a well. Jackson traces this theme back to the medieval Portuguese *romance* (novel) *Bela Infanta*. These items feature in various combinations in love songs across South Asia. Let us look at some extracts from Sri Lanka:[43]

Analla de oroe   (Golden ring
Ja kai ne posoo   Fell into the well
Tira vossa lanso   Take out your handkerchief
Sakka minhe rostoe   Dry off my face)
………   ………
Analla de oroe   (Golden ring
Sathi pedra Joontho   With seven stones
Sie kerra analla   If you want the ring
Kasa minhe Juntho   Marry me)
………   ………
Analla de oroe   (Golden ring
Nucca justa dadoe   Does not fit on the finger
Eau kerra analla   I want a ring
De vossa cavaloe   From your hair)

In Cannanore/Mahé, it occurs thus:[44]

Anela de or, jambalon   (Golden ring, jambalon[45]
Sete pedra junto   With seven stones
Quem quer esta anela, jambalon   Whoever wants this ring, jambalon
Caza minha junto.   Shall marry me.)

Anela de or, jambalon   (Golden ring, jambalon
Ja cahi no poço   Fell into the well

| Eu naõ tem fortuna, jambalon | I do not have the good fortune, jambalon |
| Olhar vosso rosto. | Of looking at your face.) |

And thus in Nagappatinam:[46]

Anela de ourú	(Golden ring
Núcu cavá dedú	Does not fit on the finger
Ló mandá um anela eu	I will send a ring
De minha cavelhú	From my hair)

The following is from Vypeen island, in Cochin:[47]

Analu do oru, Anatha	(Golden ring, Anita
Saethi padra junthe, Anatha	With seven stones, Anita
Kaim kara isse anala, Anatha	Whoever wants this ring, Anita
Casa mainja junthe, Anatha.	Come marry me, Anita.)

And this one was collected in Mangalore:[48]

Annel de our,	Golden ring,
Quem ja da para Boz?	Who gave [it to] you?
Ja da minha amor	My love gave it
Por anda brios.	For its dedication.)

To return to the Norteiro repertoire, we find the theme in a Bombay song, creatively modified into a satirical stanza:[49]

Anel de oiro, Dopina,	(Golden ring, Dopina,
Já caiu na escada, Dopina;	Fell down the stairs, Dopina;
Si quer anela, Dopina,	If you want the ring, Dopina,
Coxo e bofetada, Dopina.	Kicks and slaps, Dopina.)

A less humouristic treatment is found in yet another song from Bombay:[50]

Anel do oiro, bai Monquim,	(Golden ring, Miss Monquim,
Sete pedra junta;	With seven stones;
Si quer anel, bai Monquim,	If you want the ring, Miss Monquim,
Casae minha junta	Marry me)
....	....
Ai! Anel de oiro, Senhor,	(Ah! Golden ring, Sir,
Todos falá cobre;	Everyone says it's copper;

Ai! Todo mundo sabe, Senhor,   Ah! Everybody knows, Sir,
Eu sou filha de pobre.   I am the daughter of a poor family.)

Now contrast the last stanza with another one from Mangalore, noticing, in particular, the repetition of verses 2 and 4:[51]

Ai anel de our, Margarita,   (Ah golden ring, Margarita,
Tud falla cobre,   Everyone says it's copper,
Ai tud mundo sabé, Margarita,   Ah everybody knows, Margarita,
Eu hum filha pobre.   I am a poor girl.)

As we can see, the poetic material that circulated among the Luso-Asian communities was subject to creative manipulation, recombination and adaptation to different realities. And, as the previous examples also show, not all recurrent themes show the same pattern of geographical dispersion. Within the realm of religiously themed songs, of which there are many in the Norteiro corpus, the repetition of the verse "midnight, the child is born" with the same rhyme pattern in various locations of India suggests that a Christmas song travelled widely in the region. The first attestation of this verse is found in Schuchardt's study of Diu:[52]

Sam Paulo, já bate cino,   (Saint Paul's, the bell has struck,
Meia noite, já nacê minino,   Midnight, the child is born,
Meia noite, já nacê minino.   Midnight, the child is born.)

Here, *Saint Paul's* refers to the main church in Diu Town, and Schuchardt attributes this song to the "black" section of the city's Catholics, that is, the African slaves and their descendants.[53] The following is from Mangalore:[54]

Pai Jose ja mata cavallo,   (Father Joseph killed a horse
Secco secco manda bata sal,   Very dry, has salt added [to it],
Cafrinha, ja repica sino   The black [man] struck the bell
Meia noite, ja nasce menino.   Midnight, the child is born.)

Here, the verse is coupled with reference to a *cafre*, as people of African descent were known in colonial India, which reminds us of Schuchardt's remarks on the Diuese version. This verse may have been associated with an iconic "black" Christmas song. In this respect, it is interesting to note that the final record of this verse appears within the context of a Goan song which Dalgado offers as proof that a *cafreal* creole was once current among the African slaves there:[55] "Já tocá xinu Xanta Dominga; mea noiti já naxê Minino"

(The bell struck at Saint Dominic's; midnight, the child was born). Reference is made here to Saint Dominic's convent, in Goa, which once again bears witness to the adaptive nature of poetic material circulating across Asia.

For a different South Asian theme, contrast the following two songs. The first one is included in the anonymous Diuese collection mentioned earlier, but deemed by some local residents to be of Damanese origin:

Terra de Bengal, baí-mim	(The land of Bengal, my girl
Terra muita quent	Is a very hot land
Se marid tê dinhêr, baí-mim	If the husband has money, my girl
Muér tê content	The wife is content)

The second comes from Mangalore:[56]

Ai terra Talicheira, Margarita,	(Ah, the land of Tellicherry, Margarita,
Terra muito quente,	Is a very hot land,
Ai marido tem dinheiro,	Ah, the husband has money,
Margarita,	Margarita,
Mulher tem contente.	The wife is content.)

Tellicherry is relatively close to Mangalore, in South India, and therefore it is hardly surprising that this version should have circulated in the region. Despite the toponymic difference, the two songs are otherwise perfectly equivalent, which only goes to show that the insertion of local toponyms must have been, in some cases, part of the process of adapting poetic material received from elsewhere.

Other themes identified in the Norteiro corpus extend beyond the South Asian (India and Sri Lanka) sphere, spreading wide across Asia. As an illustration, let us recuperate a few verses noted earlier in a Diuese song: "Mar foi a tinta / Peixe foi escrivão" (The sea was ink / A fish was the scribe). Reference to ink is recurrent in songs from all over Asia, in many of which the poetic treatment involves an identification with blood. The following excerpt is from a Malaccan song:[57]

Passá nona sa porta,	(Passing by the maiden's door,
Oubí tá matá gansa;	I heard they were killing a goose;
Sa sangue fazê tinta,	Its blood will make ink,
Sa pena fazê lembrança.	Its quill[s] will make mementos.)
....	....
Passá nona sa porta,	(Passing by the maiden's door,
Oubí tá matá galinha;	I heard they were killing a chicken;

Sa sangue fazê tinta,	Its blood will make ink,
Sa letra di rainha.	[For] her queenly handwriting.)

Passá nona sa porta,	(Passing by the maiden's door,
Oubí tá matá ádi;	I heard they were killing a duck;
Sa sangue fazê tinta,	Its blood will make ink,
Sa pena di saudade.	Its quill[s] of longing.)

In another song from Malacca, we find the following stanza:[58]

Pena mudá pena,	(Feather change feather,
Sua pena di ádi;	The feather of a duck;
Sa sangue faze tinta,	Its blood will make ink,
Sa letra di bondade.	Its writing is of kindness.)

The following was recorded in Mahé/Cannanore:[59]

A là outra vonda	(Over the other side
Já matá duas robas	[I] killed two doves[?]
Sangue faze tinta	I will turn their blood into ink
Carne faze assado.	And roast their meat.)

The theme of the feather is commonly articulated with ink and blood, as seen here, and often also with reference to a scribe/writer (as seen above in the Diuese song). Notice one more example from Malacca:[60]

Quando querê casá,	(Whenever you want to marry,
Casá com scribão;	Marry a scribe;
Más qui num tem nada,	Even if he has nothing,
Pena tinta tem na mão.	He has a quill and ink in his hand.)

And yet another:[61]

Pescador, mia pescador,	(Fisherman, my fisherman,
Pescador, muito fedê;	Fisherman, so smelly;
Pena tinta tem na mão,	If you had a quill and ink in your hand,
Todo nona logo querê.	All the young ladies would want you.)

The idea transmitted here is that those who are able to write — that is, white-collar workers — were more desirable husbands than blue-collar workers, as they could easily find work. The following version comes from Mahé/Cannanore:[62]

Se quer tomar amor	(If you want to fall in love
Tom com escrivão	Do so with a scribe
Olha sua pena	Take a look at his feather
Rende coração	Surrender your heart)

Another theme recorded across the continent refers to the *mogarim* (jasmine) flower. In the Província do Norte repertoire, it appears in a Bombay song:[63]

Já foi passeio, bai Monquim,	(I went to visit, Miss Monquim,
Bazar Canería;	The Canara market;
Já foi comprar, bai Monquim,	I went to buy, Miss Monquim.
Fula de mogaría.	Jasmine flowers.)

Fula de mogaría, bai Monquim,	(Jasmine flowers, Miss Monquim,
Espalhá na mesa,	Scattered them on the table,
Sinhora d'esta casa, bai Monquim,	The lady of this house, Miss Monquim
Já ganhou um fortaleza.	Gained some strength.)

In the anonymous collection circulating in Daman and Diu, we find the theme in two different songs. I will transcribe a representative stanza from the first one, claimed to be of Damanese origin:[64]

....	....
Ful de mogarinh, baí-mim	(A jasmine flower, my girl
Fiad numa linh	Strung in thread
Assim fiarei, baí-mim	Thus will I string, my girl
Vóss amor em mim	Your love in me)

Reference to the jasmine flower is also recorded in a song from Batavia/Tugu, in Java:[65]

Kopa di oroe ki ja kebra	(The golden cup which was broken
Noenteng jeenti per konsrta	There is no one to repair [it]
Voela moegrie ja ispela	The jasmine flower which was scattered
Noenteng jeenti perpanja.	There is no one to pick [it].)

A version of the well-travelled "Jinkly Nona" song recorded in Malacca in 1991[66] includes the following stanza:

Da lisensia Siara mai	(Allow me, madam
Yo rinta bos sa jarding	To enter your garden

Rafinadu sua cheru   Your refined smell
Chuma rosa menggaring   Is like the jasmine)

In Macao, a popular traditional song also recuperates the theme:

Nhonha na jinela   (Lady in the window
Cô fula mogarim   With a jasmine flower
Sua mâe tancarera   Her mother is a Tanka[67]
Seu pai canarim   Her father is an Indian)

Another striking proof of combinatory flexibility and wide range of circulation of poetic elements is the treatment of the green parrot theme, also studied extensively by Jackson.[68] In the Norteiro corpus, this reference was documented as follows in Bombay:[69]

Papagaio verde, bai Monquim,   (Green parrot, Miss Monquim,
Biquinho de chumbo,   With a leaden beak,
Levae esta carta, bai Monquim,   Take this letter, Miss Monquim,
E pinchae no mar fundo.   And throw it in the deep sea.)

And thus in Daman:[70]

Papagaio verde   (Green parrot
Cima da cidáda   On top of the city
Batê, batê azas   Flap, flap your wings
Chama mulher de soldada.   Call the soldier's wife.)

And Schuchardt also records its occurrence in Diu:[71]

Papágai verd   (Green parrot
Com bicc du lacre,   With a beak of sealing-wax,
Levai est cart   Take this letter
Aquell ingrat.   To that ungrateful [one].)

Beyond the Província do Norte, one finds the theme in Mangalore:[72]

Ai papagayo verde, Margarita,   (Ah, green parrot, Margarita,
Sube riba sebe   Perches on the hedge
Ai bate bate aza, Margarita   Ah, it flaps, flaps its wings, Margarita
Panha manga verde.   [And] catches a green mango.)

Jackson also records the following in Vypeen, outside the city of Cochin:[73]

Papa gaya vade	(Green parrot
Santhad en tha save	Sitting on the hedge
Batha Bath Agu	It flaps, flaps its wings
Panja manga vede;	Catches a green mango;)

There are plenty of similar records from Sri Lanka, but the following stanza has a similar context to the ones from Mangalore and Vypeen:[74]

Papugachi vardi	(Green parrot
Riva aka Savie	On top of the hedge
Panya manga vardie	It catches a green mango
Da per nona Mary	Gives [it] to madam Mary)

Further afield, similar verses were also collected in Malacca:[75]

Pastorinho berde,	(Little green bird,
Más bêrde di rico flor;	Greener than the richest flower;
Bai lebá êste chito,	Go take this note,
Dá com eu sa amor.	Give it to my love.)
………	………
Pastorinho berde,	(Little green bird,
Ramo seco já santá;	Sat on the dry branch;
Santá na ramo seco,	[If you] sit on the dry branch,
Qui repairo logo achá?	What fortune will you receive?)[76]
Pastorinho berde,	(Little green birds,
Um ramo santá dôs dôs;	Sit on a branch in pairs;
Eu nádi morrê lonzi,	I will not die far away,
Eu logo more perto bôs.	I will die next to you.)

For a comprehensive account of the circulation of the "green parrot" or "green bird" theme across Asia, see K. David Jackson's contribution in volume 1 of this work.

CONCLUSION

Many more instances of shared themes and verses could be adduced to this discussion, but the ones we have explored already give an impression of the extent to which the oral traditions of Luso-Asian communities are interconnected. We have also seen how far some of this material was nativized through linguistic adaptation, thematic recombination and the addition of local referents. As Dalgado[77] correctly pointed out,

> [t]ambém as poesias intentadas para canto popular emigram facilmente duma região para outra, onde se tenta, às vezes, dar-lhes cor local, com troca de algumas palavras e formas.
>
> (The poetry intended for popular singing also migrates easily from one region to another, where one sometimes tries to lend it local colour through the exchange of some words and forms.)

These formal and thematic links have important implications for the history of the former Portuguese empire in Asia and that of the Luso-Asian communities. The exchange of poetic material hints at a considerable flow of population between the various territories, which Dalgado earlier assumed when he articulated his "recíproca transfusão parcial" (partial reciprocal transfusion) hypothesis,[78] according to which the various creoles of Asia would have had ample opportunity to cross-pollinate. The view that, throughout their history, the discrete Asian territories under Portuguese domination kept closer ties than often assumed is gaining increasing historical support[79] and, therefore, so are the cultural and linguistic links which have already been established among the various Luso-Asian communities.

Notes

[1]   The present work revisits and expands on some topics treated in my Portuguese-language article in press: Hugo Cardoso, "O cancioneiro das comunidades norteiras: Língua, fontes e tradição", *Camões: Revista de Letras e Culturas Lusófonas* 20 (2010): 105–23. I am indebted to Alan Baxter and K. David Jackson for precious insights into the topic. All possible shortcomings, nonetheless, remain my own responsibility.

[2]   Kenneth David Jackson, "Canta sen Vargonya: Portuguese Creole Verse in Sri Lanka", *Journal of Pidgin and Creole Languages* 2, no. 1 (1987): 31–48; *Sing without Shame: Oral Traditions in Indo-Portuguese Creole Verse* (Amsterdam: John Benjamins; Macao: Instituto Cultural de Macau, 1990); "The Indo-Portuguese Folklore Text", *Boletim do Instituto Menezes Braganza* 168 (1993); and *De Chaul a Batticaloa: As Marcas do Império Marítimo Português na Índia e no Sri Lanka* (Ericeira, Portugal: Editora Mar de Letras, 2005).

[3]   Shihan de Silva Jayasuriya, "Indo-Portuguese Songs of Sri Lanka: The Nevill Manuscript", *Bulletin of the School of Oriental and African Studies* 59, no. 2 (June 1996): 253–67.

4   Hugo Schuchardt, "Kreolische Studien III: Über das Indoportugiesische von Diu", *Sitzungsberichte der Kaiserlichen Akademie der Wissenschaften zu Wien (philosophisch-historische Klasse)* 103 (1883): 3–18.

5   Sebastião Rodolfo Dalgado, "Dialecto indo-português de Damão", *Ta-Ssi-Yang-Kuo* 3 (1902): 359–67; 4 (1903): 515–23; and "Dialecto indo-português do Norte", *Revista Lusitana* 9 (1906): 142–66 and 193–228.

6   Jeronymo Quadros, *Cartas de Diu*, 1st ser. (1902–05) (Nova Goa: Tipographia Fontainhas, 1907).

7   António Francisco Moniz, *Notícias e Documentos para a História de Damão: Antiga Província do Norte*, vol. 1. (Bastorá: Tipografia Rangel, 1923); and "The Negroes and St. Benedict's Feast", in *The Mission Field: The Diocese of Damaun* (Bombay: S.R. Santos, 1925), pp. 570–72.

8   For a detailed list of sources, see Maria Isabel Tomás, *Os Crioulos Portugueses do Oriente: Uma Bibliografia* (Macao: Instituto Cultural de Macau, 1992).

9   Dalgado, "Dialecto indo-português do Norte".

10   Dalgado, "Dialecto indo-português de Damão".

11   Ibid.

12   Dalgado, "Dialecto indo-português do Norte".

13   Ibid.

14   See Joseph Clancy Clements, "The Indo-Portuguese Creoles: Languages in Transition", *Hispania* 74, no. 3 (September 1991): 637–46.

15   See Hugo C. Cardoso, *The Indo-Portuguese Language of Diu* (Utrecht: LOT, 2009).

16   See J. Clancy Clements, *The Genesis of a Language: The Formation and Development of Korlai Portuguese* (Amsterdam: John Benjamins, 1996).

17   Sources of examples in this section are from Dalgado, "Dialecto indo-português do Norte" (Bombay); Dalgado, "Dialecto indo-português de Damão" (Daman); Clements, personal communication (Daman); fieldwork by the author (Diu); and Clements, *The Genesis of a Language* (Korlai).

18   Korlai Creole makes a distinction between *buf* "female buffalo" and *ʈatya*, *tɔnga* "male buffalo" (see Clements, *The Genesis of a Language*, p. 262).

19   Dalgado, "Dialecto indo-português do Norte".

20   Ibid.

21   Ibid.

22   Dalgado, "Dialecto indo-português do Norte".

23   See Cardoso, *The Indo-Portuguese Language of Diu*, pp. 254–55 and 270.

24   According to my own observation in the field, the most current form of this verse is "Já marrô pau, já fêz empê".

25   The meaning of this verse is not clear; it could be a meaningless refrain.

26   Schuchardt, "Über das Indoportugiesische von Diu".

27   Sebastião Rodolfo Dalgado, *Glossário Luso-Asiático* (Coimbra: Imprensa da Universidade, 1919).

28   This song was transcribed from the sound file by myself. The transcription is impressionistic, loosely based on Portuguese orthography. It is important to

clarify, however, that "ə" is a standard symbol in the International Phonetic Alphabet corresponding to a relaxed vowel such as that graphed <e> in Ptg. *que* or *lhe*.

29 Clements, *The Genesis of a Language*.

30 For a pioneer account of the issue, see Luis Ivens Ferraz, "Portuguese Creoles of West Africa and Asia", in *Pidgin and Creole Languages*, edited by Glenn G. Gilbert (Honolulu: University of Hawai'i Press, 1987).

31 Quadros, *Cartas de Diu*.

32 Incidentally, in Cardoso, "O cancioneiro das comunidades norteiras" (in press), I make the point that the theme of the one-hour love that unifies the two songs can probably be traced back to Portuguese oral traditions, where the topic is explored in similar fashion in local traditional verses. The following were collected in Coimbra and are found in J. Leite de Vasconcellos, comp., *Cancioneiro Popular Português*, vol. 1, edited by Maria Arminda Zaluar Nunes (Coimbra: Imprensa da Universidade, 1975):

> O amor do estudante   (The love of a student
> Não dura mais que uma hora: Lasts no more than an hour:
> Toca o sino, vai p'rá aula,   The bell tolls, he goes to class,
> Vêm as férias, vai-se embora. The holiday comes, he goes away.)

33 In the Diuese context, as pointed out by K. David Jackson (personal communication), "vae cimbór" may logically be interpreted as "goes to Simbor". I have opted for the translation "goes away" in view of the fact that the verse occurs in other locations where Simbor would be a less obvious reference, but also because of the Portuguese antecedent I proposed in the previous note. It is also interesting to note that, in the anonymous collection circulating in Diu, this verse is transcribed "Largô, foi imbór, Manavela", or "Left and went away, Manavela [Manuela]".

34 Moniz, *Notícias e Documentos para a História de Damão*.

35 Schuchardt, "Über das Indoportugiesische von Diu".

36 See the section "Formal Heterogeneity" for an interpretation of this verse.

37 Dalgado, "Dialecto indo-português do Norte".

38 Moniz, *Notícias e Documentos para a História de Damão*.

39 Perso-Arabic word ("collector", the name of various public posts in Muslim societies), used among the Indo-Portuguese communities with the meaning "minister of state" (see Dalgado, *Glossário Luso-Asiático*).

40 A small fish very common in Diuese waters.

41 One could speculate that this form consists of the combination of *bai* as "sister, young woman" (a vocative still current in the Norteiro creoles and Goan Portuguese) with *surum*, perhaps a proper name.

42 Jackson, *Sing without Shame*.

43 Ibid.

44 Hugo Schuchardt, "Beiträge zur Kenntnis des kreolischen Romanisch: VI. Zum Indoportugiesischen von Mahé und Cannanore", *Zeitschrift für Romanische Philologie* 13 (1889): 516–24.

[45] Once again, "jambalon" may be simply a meaningless refrain, but it is reminiscent of the local name for the jamun fruit, which in the creoles takes a form close to "jambláw".

[46] Sebastião Rodolfo Dalgado, "Dialecto indo-português de Negapatão", *Revista Lusitana* 20 (1917): 40–53.

[47] Jackson, *Sing without Shame.*

[48] Hugo Schuchardt, "Kreolische Studien VI: Über das Indoportugiesische von Mangalore", *Sitzungsberichte der Kaiserlichen Akademie der Wissenschaften zu Wien (philosophisch-historische Klasse)* 105, no. 3 (1883b): 882–904.

[49] Dalgado, "Dialecto indo-português do Norte".

[50] Ibid.

[51] Schuchardt, "Über das Indoportugiesische von Mangalore".

[52] Schuchardt, "Über das Indoportugiesische von Diu".

[53] See Hugo Cardoso, "The African Slave Population of Portuguese India: Demographics and Impact on Indo-Portuguese", *Journal of Pidgin and Creole Languages* 25, no. 1 (2010): 95–119.

[54] Schuchardt, "Über das Indoportugiesische von Mangalore".

[55] Sebastião Rodolfo Dalgado, *Berço de uma Cantiga em Indo-Português (à Memória de Ismael Gracias)* (Porto: Tip. Sequeira, 1921 [separate da *Revista Lusitana*, vol. 22]).

[56] Schuchardt, "Über das Indoportugiesische von Mangalore".

[57] António da Silva Rêgo, *Dialecto Português de Malaca: Apontamentos para o seu Estudo* (Lisbon: Agência Geral das Colónias, 1942).

[58] Ibid.

[59] Schuchardt, "Zum Indoportugiesischen von Mahé und Cannanore".

[60] Rêgo, *Dialecto Português de Malaca.*

[61] Ibid.

[62] Schuchardt, "Zum Indoportugiesischen von Mahé und Cannanore".

[63] Dalgado, "Dialecto indo-português do Norte".

[64] Stanzas reminiscent of this and the ones in the previous song from Bombay feature in a long Damanese song transcribed in Moniz, *Notícias e Documentos para a História de Damão*, eloquent proof of the geographical dispersion and frequent recombination of poetic material.

[65] Hugo Schuchardt, "Kreolische Studien IX: Über das Malaioportugiesiche von Batavia und Tugu", *Sitzungsberichte der Kaiserüchen Akademie der Wissenschaft zu Wien (philosophisch-historische Klasse)* 122 (1890): 1–255.

[66] Collected by Margaret Sarkissian and transcribed in the booklet accompanying *Kantiga di Padri sa Chang: Malaca*, compact disc (Vila Verde, Portugal: Tradisom, 1998), part of the collection *A Viagem dos Sons.*

[67] The Tankas are traditionally boat dwellers in coastal areas of southern China, including Macao.

[68] Jackson, *Sing without Shame.*

[69] Dalgado, "Dialecto indo-português do Norte".

[70] Moniz, *Notícias e Documentos para a História de Damão.*

71   Schuchardt, "Über das Indoportugiesische von Diu".
72   Schuchardt. "Über das Indoportugiesische von Mangalore".
73   Jackson, *Sing without Shame.*
74   Ibid.
75   Rêgo, *Dialecto Português de Malaca.*
76   Ibid. The interpretation of this stanza follows Rêgo's proposal.
77   Dalgado, "Berço de uma cantiga em Indo-Português".
78   Dalgado, "Dialecto Indo-Português de Negapatão".
79   See, for example, Maria Isabel Tomás, "The Role of Women in the Crosspollination
     Process in the Asian-Portuguese Varieties", *Journal of Portuguese Linguistics* 8,
     no. 2 (2009): 49–64; and Alan N. Baxter, "Vestiges of Etymological Gender in
     Malacca Creole Portuguese", *Journal of Pidgin and Creole Languages* 25, no. 1
     (2010): 120–54.

7

VERB MARKINGS IN MAKISTA: CONTINUITY/DISCONTINUITY AND ACCOMMODATION

Mário Pinharanda-Nunes

Makista (PCMac), the Portuguese-based Creole of Macao, came into existence in the wake of the settlement of the Portuguese in Macao in the mid-sixteenth century. As is common to Creole languages created in the sequence of the European maritime expansion, the *raison d'être* behind their formation lies in the sudden and often forced confluence and coexistence of speakers from diverse linguistic and ethnic backgrounds and, thus, the need for a common linguistic code. Given certain demographic, linguistic and historical constraints, such languages share in common the co-existence of lexical, morphologic and syntactic traits from the different contributing languages (specific to each Creole), in varying degrees. From the time Macao was occupied on a permanent basis by the Portuguese from 1557 onwards, the main linguistic contributor to the formation of Makista was Kristang (PCMal), the Portuguese-based Creole of Malacca, and thus considered this Creole's substrate. Besides Luso-Malay families, we find references to Malays in Macao by 1565 who would have spoken Kristang.[1]

In the case of the formation of Creoles, the co-existence of several variants, from the different languages in contact for a common linguistic function, has been described as a "feature pool".[2] From this pool of joint features, some variants will be dropped and others selected, and many times modified by the speakers of the emerging language. In the case of PCMac, PCMal, as well as other Asian varieties of Portuguese-based pidgins and non-standard

Portuguese, standard Portuguese, Cantonese and Hokkien[3] came together in Macao[4] and formed the "feature pool" of this Creole. The linguistic items ultimately selected and transposed to the emerging Creole may either retain their exact original functions, narrow or widen them.

This chapter takes a comparative look at the frequent aspectual marker in PCMac, *ja*. A marker shared in common with PCMal, albeit in the latter, as with the other two verbal markers they share in common (*ta*, *logu*), the use is much more restrictive.[5] As our analysis shall reveal, apart from a much loser, non-obligatory use of *ja* in PCMac for the tense-aspect context it is associated with, its range of functions have been comparatively widened relative to its substrate font. Our research hypothesis is that these similarities and differences in Makista compared to Kristang are evidence of (a) continuities and discontinuities of those features, resulting from the accommodation of speakers[6] of the various languages who came in contact with one another in early Macao; and (b) the competition/selection process of the features' effect.

For PCMac, analysis is based on an oral corpus, namely, recordings of eighteen elderly speakers made between 1984 and 2007. As for Kristang, we base our references on Baxter's 1988 work.[7]

THE SOCIO-HISTORIC BACKGROUND TO THE FORMATION OF MAKISTA

For a better understanding of the formation and functioning of PCMac's TMA (tense, mood and aspect) system, one has to look at this Creole's origins and the socio-historic dimensions which shaped Macao's society as a whole and this Creole's speaking community in particular from its onset until the twentieth century.

The permanent settlement of the Portuguese in Macao took place from 1556–57 onwards.[8] However, Portuguese merchant ships had anchored seasonally at this fishing port since about 1553 for trading purposes at the port of Canton, further up the Pearl River Delta. The establishment of Macao as a Portuguese port was yet another milestone in the succession of territorial occupations in Asia by the Portuguese, ranging from the west coast of India, through Sri Lanka, Malacca, and the present-day Indonesian Archipelago and East Timor. Considering this reality, we cannot envisage that PCMac would have had its origins solely from linguistic contact between European Portuguese and the local Chinese community.

We all know of the famous official interracial marriage policy encouraged by the Portuguese crown as a way of overcoming the unbalanced population numbers between the Portuguese and native peoples in all the Asian ports under Portuguese rule, which was largely to the disfavour of the occupying force. This policy was directly responsible for the rapid formation of a mixed racial group which ethnically and socially identified itself with the Portuguese occupying force, but which simultaneously was culturally and linguistically integrated into the various locales in South and Southeast Asia from which they originated. Further, they adapted easily to other Asian ports under Portuguese rule to which they either migrated voluntarily or were transferred.

Thus, key figures in the formation of Portuguese-based pidgins and Creoles, as well as other less radical varieties of Asian Portuguese, would have included both of these groups, the native populations at the service of the Portuguese (whether voluntarily, as in the case of soldiers and seamen, or involuntarily, as in the case of slaves), and merchants and other people related to the maritime trade between the Far East and South and Southeast Asia. A few of these pidgins and Creoles have survived until today, albeit in dire conditions in most cases. Such varieties, and especially Kristang from Malacca and its varieties at other ports of Southeast Asia (Tugu, Ternate, Flores), formed a lingua franca widely used at the time the Portuguese settled in Macao. This means that even before Macao came under Portuguese rule, local merchants would have had some sort of contact with Southeast Asian sea merchants — speakers of that lingua franca. This scenario for the eve of the formation of Makista and the very probable contribution of those Portuguese-based Asian Creoles (PC) and even Malay towards this Creole of Macao seems very similar to what Baxter has pointed out for Kristang:

> The setting for the development of MCP was highly complex.... It would have involved the importation of both foreigner talk and pidgin models from India and beyond, a local genesis, and the eventual introduction of Creole models from India. (Baxter 1988, Holm 1989). Subsequently, there may have been further influence on the creole through continuity of trade with Asian ports where Portuguese and Creole Portuguese communities existed.[9]

There was, however, one striking difference in relation to PCMal. While the Malacca Creole was formed in the above-mentioned multilinguistic context of the varying presence of several PCs from South Asia, it had as its substrate the local language, Malay, and possibly to a large extent Hokkien as its adstrate (a language of close and intense contact), given the large numbers of speakers of this Chinese language settled there. In the case of PCMac, the socio-historic data indicate that intense contact with the local Chinese community did not take place until much later after the establishment of Macao. The socio-historic data are evidence of a distant relation between the Chinese community and the newly arrived Luso-Asians and others. This leads us to propose that at the initial stages of the formation of PCMac, Cantonese did not play as crucial a role as did the local languages found at the other South and Southeast Asian ports where Portuguese-based Creoles were formed. For PCMac, the local language was not its substrate; instead, this role was taken over by PCMal, a Creole well into its second generation of native speakers by then, considering the forty-five-year span between the occupation of Malacca (1511) and of Macao (1556). For this reason, PCMac must have had as its substrate not Cantonese or Hokkien (also widely spoken in Macao at the time), but PCMal. Other varieties of Portuguese-based Creoles and Malay would have been its primary adstrates and, to a lesser extent in the initial stages, Cantonese.

In Wekker we find a straightforward description of such a multilinguistic context in the formation of Creoles: "Creolization is best described as a gradual process of language formation, involving a period of bilingualism in which substrate features will be transmitted."[10]

Adding to all these linguistic influences and sources of PCMac, one cannot discount the role of the constant presence of speakers of standard Portuguese, given that this lexifier was the language of social prestige, as is normally the case in Creole-speaking communities. Nonetheless, the contact the PCMac-speaking community had with the Portuguese one was always restricted, given the typical colonial sociopolitical structure. Such a situation would only gradually begin to change at the turn of the nineteenth to the twentieth century, with reforms in public education which led to the opening of public schools and a policy of compulsory education, mostly in Portuguese. This in turn gave way to an increasing number of members of the PCMac-speaking community taking up jobs as administrative clerks, resulting in an ever-greater exposure to and use of standard Portuguese, along with the consequent decrease in the use of PCMac.

THEORETICAL FRAMEWORK

Given the socio-historic setting of the formation of Macao, a study of a feature of PCMac's TMA system calls for a theoretical framework that accounts for the subsequent emergence of this Creole in such a context. We shall briefly present the main linguistic theoretical concepts developed for the study of Creole languages that we see as applicable to the case of the PCMac TA (tense and aspect) system. A common tie between the concepts taken into consideration is the notion that the substrate language plays a key role in the formation of a Creole language. This basically means that some features of the substrate language will be retained in the emergent Creole, rather than it resulting solely from a process of relexification of lexical and functional items of the European lexifier language. The concepts in question are interrelated and part of a whole process. We shall be looking at: (1) the "feature pool" phenomenon; (2) transfer; (3) levelling; and (4) congruency.

1. *Feature pool.* In the field of linguistics, and in particular in contact linguistics, "feature pool" is equivalent to what in genetics is referred to as a "common gene pool".[11] In other words, it is the set of linguistic material or features available for selection at any given moment to a community of speakers. In the case of Creole language formation, this pool is made up of features from all of the various source languages involved in the contact situation. After a process of selection, some features will be dropped while others are transferred and retained.

2. *Transfer.* In a scenario where a Creole may be considered a type of L2 (second language) gradual acquisition by adults, the prolonged presence of such adult speakers implies a process of transfer of elements from their L1 (first language). As Mather states, "transfer from substrate languages probably occurred during a long period ... as long as there were substrate speakers left or being brought in."[12] Other terms have been used for the same phenomenon such as, "calquing"[13] and "retention of the substrate".[14]

The transfer of L1 elements into the emerging L2 requires a selection process on the part of the speakers. This is termed as "levelling".

3. *Levelling.* Siegel proposes that this process takes place during the passing of L1 elements to the contact variety, and that it consists of the elimination of some idiolectal or sociolectal variants.[15] This in turn results in the stabilization of retained forms used by the community.

Among the several factors that promote the transfer of linguistic features from L1 to L2, the use of *ja* in PCMac and PCMal calls for our attention to "perceptive salience" and "congruence".

4. *Congruency.* "Congruency" relates to the formal similarities between certain corresponding elements in various languages in contact, perceived by the speakers of an emerging language. Heine and Kuteva refer to it as "equivalence": "situations where a use pattern or category in one language is conceived or described as being the same as a corresponding use pattern or category in another language."[16] According to this concept, whenever there is a formal similarity between morphemes or categories of the languages involved, we may expect a higher probability of transfer. In Siegel's terms,[17]

what counts in establishing congruence is the functional similarity; hence, he prefers the term "functional transfer".[18]

THE VERBAL MARKER *JA*: A COMMON CONSTITUENT OF THE TMA SYSTEMS OF PCMAC AND PCMAL

Both Creoles under comparison present the same verbal aspect markers: *ja, ta, logo(gu)*[19] / *lo*.[20] They result from the grammaticalization of Portuguese lexical elements in PCMal, later transferred into PCMac. In that sense, (1) *ta* was grammaticalized from the Portuguese auxiliary verb *estar* ("to be", for temporality) and came to function in both Creoles as an imperfective marker with certain fine grain functional differences in PCMac compared to PCMal; (2) *logo* is the grammaticalization of the Portuguese adverb "logo" ("later") and is the common marker in both Creoles for the future mode (*irealis*); (3) *ja* was grammaticalized from the Portuguese adverb *já* ("already", immediately), and functions in PCMal, as well as in PCMac, as a perfective *aktionsart* (kind of action) marker.[21]

We shall look at the functions and restrictions of *ja*, the most frequent of these three markers in PCMac, with two goals in mind: (a) to understand which of its features were transferred from PCMal into PCMac and which were not; and (b) to understand how the latter has expanded its functions in PCMac compared to PCMal. Such differences are presented as a possible effect of the particular "feature pool" from which PCMac emerged, as well as this Creole's continuum. All references to *ja* in PCMal are based on Baxter 1988.

The Perfective Marker *Ja* in PCMac and PCMal

We shall proceed with our description of the characteristics of the verbal marker *ja* in PCMac first by looking at what it has in common with its use in PCMal, followed by the differences. All examples pertaining to the use of *ja* provided hereafter refer exclusively to PCMac.[22]

In PCMal, the preverbal marker *ja* is only used in contexts of perfective aspect. In such contexts, this marker shares the following common traits in PCMal and PCMac:

A. Its syntactic positioning is mainly preverbal:
    [1] *Eu   sa   māe   ja   vem   recolhê   ela.*
        I   POSS   mother   PRF   come   get   she.
        (My mother came to get her.)

B. It mainly marks the perfective aspect (1) with active and semi-stative verbs.
C. It can also mark anterior aspect:
    [2] *Quelora   eu   vai   América,   filho   ja   nacê.*
        That time   I   go   América,   son   ANT   born.
        (When I went to America, my son had already been born.)
D. It is restricted by the presence of negation adverbs:
    [3] *Acunga   noite   eu   nunca   vai.*
        That   night   I   NEG   go.
        (That night I did not go.)
E. It is restricted by the presence of modal verbs and existencial "teng" (there is/are).
F. It may be used as an adjunct of an adjectival clause:
    [4] *Eu   sa   filho   ja   perigo.*
        I   POSS   child   PRT   danger.
        (My son was in danger.)

As for the differences between the use of *logo* in PCMac and *logu* in PCMal, we observed that:

A. In PCMac the use of *ja* for both functions that it has in common with PCMal (that is, marking of the perfective aspect and of the incoative anterior aspect) is much more facultative than in PCMal, where it generally cannot be omitted for the mentioned contexts. The non-obligatory characteristic of this marker in perfective contexts in PCMac becomes very clear when we look at the results of the quantative distribution of the sequence [*ja*+ V] in such aspectual contexts comparatively to the marking [Ø + V] in the oral corpus of this Creole (see Table 7.1).

TABLE 7.1
The Distribution of *Ja* in Perfective Aspectual Contexts in the PCMac Oral Corpus

PAST (Perfective)		*Ja* + V	Ø + V
	N	420	1941
	%	17.8	82.2
Total	N	2361	
		41.5	

B. In PCMal the marking of the anterior aspect is obtained by placing *ja* post-verbally, whereas in Makista this condition is not required.

C. In PCMal *ja* may precede the anterior marker *kaba,* whereas in PCMac this is not possible, as *kaba* functions as an adverbial marker of narrative sequence and not as an anterior marker:

[5] **Cava** *misa* *galo* *vai* *casa* *rufa.*
    Finish   mass   rooster   go   home   celebrate.
    (After midnight mass, we would go home and celebrate.)

D. In PCMac the incoative anterior marking is not restricted by verb class as it is in PCMal, where it is used merely with a small number of stative verbs.

E. As far as its adverbial value in perfective contexts, in PCMal *ja* marks the prior completive notion as in (already), whereas in PCMac, it comprises both this value, [6], [7], [8], as well as the notion of immediateness [9] of an action or a change of state.

F. In PCMal the use of *ja is* restricted to the perfective aspect (and thus past tense contextual references), whereas in Makista *ja* may also occur in continuous [6] and [7], and habitual [8] aspectual contexts, both in the present as well as in the past. In such cases *ja* takes on the adverbial function equivalent to "already" [6], [7] and [8], as well as the notion of immediateness [9]. Both functions are part of the use of *ja* in PCMac's superstrate (that is, standard Portuguese):

[6] *Ja*   *nang*   *há*   *mais*
    ADV   NEG   there is   more
    (There is no more [already].)

[7] *Ieu* *vai* *ixcola* ... *pixoti,* *ieu* *djá* *sabe*
    I   go   school ...   small   I   ADV   know
    (When I was small and went to school, I already knew.)

[8] *Agora* *você* *ja* *visti* *preto*
    Now   you   ADV   wear   black
    (Now you already wear black.)

[9] *Vezis*   *tem*   *"function".*   *"Ah*   *eu*   *faz*   *estunga".*
    Sometimes   have   function.   I   make   this.
    Já   *vai*   *eu*   *sprimentá*   *pa*   *tudo.*
    ADV   go   I   taste   ACC   all.
    (Sometimes there are functions. "Oh, I did this [dish]. I will go immediately to taste all.)

G. In Makista, *ja* may also present a non-adverbial function when in past contexts of habitual aspect, where it becomes a general marker of the past tense:

[10] *Eu*   *sa*   *mama*   *dja*   *vai*   *praça.*
    I   POSS   mother   MRK   go   market.
(My mother would go to the market.)

The above brief description of the preverbal marker *ja* in both PCMal and PCMac shows how it is used in more aspectual contexts and with a wider scope of functions in the latter Creole, compared to the former. The use of *ja* in aspectual contexts other than the perfective, and especially with the present tense, reveals adverbial functions similar to those innate to *ja* in standard Portuguese, PCMac's superstrate and lexifier. Given the sociolinguistic context in which PCMac was formed and evolved, we should also take into consideration possible convergences with the Cantonese markers for the perfective aspect. The following section looks briefly at these.

The Cantonese Verbal Markers *Jó* and *Gwó* and the Possible Correlations with *Ja*

The words *jó* and *gwó* are the two verbal markers in Cantonese related to the perfective aspect.[23] In the case of *jó*, within its range of perfective marker, it carried the following semantic values: (a) marks a result; (b) refers to situations without a result; and (c) refers to a time span extending until and including the present.[24]

As for *gwó*, it has the particularity of expressing an experience lived in an indefinite past. Contrary to *jó* it does not express the idea of endurance but marks only an experience lived at least once.

We may find examples in the oral corpus of PCMac, where the use of *ja* corresponds to the functions listed for the Cantonese markers *jó* and *gwó*. As for the first, we observe the following possible congruencies:

A. Marking a result (similarly to the first function listed for *jó*):

[11] *Oh,*   *mesa*   **ja**   **vai.**   *Ja*   **vai**   *cu*   *vento.*
          table   PRF   go   PRF   go   with   wind.
(Oh, the table fell over. It fell over with the wind.)

B. Marking an event without a result:

[12] *Titi*   *Chai*   ...   *corê*   *vai*   *cozinha*   *olá*
                      run   go   kitchen   look

> cuza   ja   sucedê.
> thing   ANT   happen.
> (Titi Chai ran to the kitchen to see what had happened.)

Regarding marking of an experience by *gwó*, we quote the following examples from the PCMac oral corpus as evidence for a possible correlation between *ja* and the Cantonese marker:

[13] *Venánco* ***já***   ***panhá***   *co*   *pau.*
         PRF   catch   with   stick.
      (Venâncio was hit with a stick.)

[14] *Esses*   *doci* ....   *Ja*   *xêgá*   *comê?*
       Those   sweets ....   ADV   arrive   eat?
      (Those sweets .... Have you already gotten to eat them?)

The use of *ja* **with** semi-stative and active verbs in perfective contexts suggests that this marker, apart from marking the perfective aspect on those verbs, may carry the function of stressing changes of state in the past with a result stretching up to the present. This establishes a correlation with the Cantonese *jó*, as well as with *gwó*. We should also note that the use of *ja* in [14] also corresponds to one of its uses in standard Portuguese, just as do those in [6], [7], [8] and [9].

CONCLUSION

The above discussion of the use of *ja* in PCMac, and the cross-reference with that of its substrate (PCMal), its superstrate (Portuguese), and with the corresponding markers in Cantonese (its adstrate), have provided us with evidence of situations of continuity of traits, as well as of discontinuity of data transferred into PCMac from the "feature pool" from which this Creole emerged. This evidence supports our initial hypothesis of the type of formation theorization that PCMac falls into, namely, a gradual formation, initiated by adult speakers in a multilingual context. In the case of PCMac, its "feature pool" throughout the continuum of this Creole mainly comprised elements from PCMal, Portuguese and Cantonese. The retention of some traits from PCMal with regard to the use of *ja* is evidence of the continuity of a prolonged contact between Macao and Malacca. On the other hand, the widening of scope of use of *ja* to the present tense — where it takes on an adverbial function similar to that performed by *já* in Portuguese (the adverb from which *ja* in PCMal and PCMac and other PC originally grammaticalized)

— provides evidence of the effect of a close contact and exposure of the PCMac speakers in Macao to standard Portuguese. The possible correlations between the use of *ja* and some of the functions of the Cantonese markers *jó* and *gwó* also fit concepts of congruency and levelling in the whole process of transfer and use of linguistic elements in a Creole continuum. Undoubtedly, the more facultative use of *ja* compared to PCMal is also testimony both to the increasing contact with Cantonese speakers (where the aspectual markers are highly optional), as well as with Portuguese where *já* only has an adverbial function, thus exerting pressure on PCMac speakers to drop its use as an aspectual and *aktionsart* marker.

ABBREVIATIONS

ACC: accusative relator
ADV: adverb
ANT: anterior marker
MRK: verbal marker
NEG: negation adverb
POSS: possessive
PRF: perfective marker

Notes

[1]   Custódio N.P.S. Cónim and Maria Fernanda Bragança Teixeira, *Macau e a sua População, 1500–2000: Aspectos Demográficos, Sociais e Económicos* (Macao: Direcção dos Serviços de Estatística e Censos, 1998), p. 90.

[2]   Salikoko Mufwene, *The Ecology of Language Evolution* (Cambridge: Cambridge University Press, 2001).

[3]   Mário Pinharanda Nunes, "Os demonstrativos em Maquista: Uma análise morfo-sintáctica constrativa", *Papia: Revista Brasileira de Crioulos e Similares* 18 (2008): 7–21.

[4]   Alan N. Baxter, "O português em Macau: Contato e assimilação", in *Português em Contato*, edited by Ana Maria Carvalho (Madrid: Iberoamericana; and Frankfurt: Editorial Vervuert, 2009).

[5]   Mário Rui Pinharanda Nunes and Alan N. Baxter, "Os marcadores pré-verbais no crioulo de base lexical portuguesa de Macau", *Papia: Revista Brasileira de Crioulos e Similares* 14 (2004): 31–46.

[6]   Howard Giles and Peter F. Powesland, *Speech Style and Social Evaluation* (London: Academic Press in cooperation with the European Association of Experimental Social Psychology, 1975).

[7]   Alan N. Baxter, *A Grammar of Kristang* (Canberra: Pacific Linguistics, 1988).

8   Luís Filipe Barreto, *Macau: Poder e Saber, Séculos XVI e XVII* (Lisbon: Editorial Presença, 2006).

9   Alan N. Baxter, "Vestiges of Etymological Gender in Malacca Creole Portuguese", *Journal of Pidgin and Creoles Languages* 25, no. 1 (2010): 120–54, esp. p. 122.

10 Herman Wekker, "Creolization and the Acquisition of English as a Second Language", in *Creole Languages and Language Acquisition*, edited by Herman Wekker (Berlin: Mouton de Gruyter, 1996), pp. 139–49.

11 Mufwene, *The Ecology of Language Evolution*.

12 Patrick-André Mather, "Second Language Acquisition and Creolization: Same (I-) Processes, Different (E-) Results", *Journal of Pidgin and Creole Langauges* 21 (2006): 231–74.

13 Roger M. Keesing, *Melanesian Pidgin and the Oceanic Substrate* (Stanford: Stanford University Press, 1988).

14 Bettina Migge, "Substrate Influence in Creole Formation: The Origin of Give-Type Serial Verb Constructions in the Surinamese Plantation Creole", *Journal of Pidgin and Creole Languages* 13 (1998): 215–65.

15 Jeff Siegel, "Mixing, Leveling and Pidgin/Creole Development", in *The Structure and Status of Pidgins and Creoles*, edited by Arthur K. Spears and Donald Winford (Amsterdam: Benjamins, 1997), pp. 111–49; Jeff Siegel, "Morphological Simplicity in Pidgins and Creoles", *Journal of Pidgin and Creole Languages* 19, no. 1 (2004): 139–62; Jeff Siegel, "Morphological Elaboration", *Journal of Pidgin and Creole Languages* 19, no. 2 (2004): 333–62; and Jeff Siegel, *The Emergence of Pidgin and Creole Languages* (Oxford: Oxford University Press, 2008).

16 Bernd Heine and Tania Kuteva, *Language Contact and Grammatical Change* (Cambridge: Cambridge University Press, 2008), p. 220.

17 Siegel, *The Emergence of Pidgin*, p. 164.

18 Ibid., p. 112.

19 The spelling *logo* is used according to that used in Pinharanda Nunes and Baxter (2004) for the marker in PCMac, whereas for PCMal the same marker is spelt by Baxter (1988) as *logu*.

20 The marker *logo / logu* may present itself in the abridged form *lo* — much more frequently in PCMal than in PCMac.

21 *Cf.* Elzbieta Thurgood and Graham Thurgood, "Aspect, Tense, or Aktionsart? The Particle *Ja* in Kristang (Malacca Creole Portuguese)", *Journal of Pidgin and Creole Languages* 11, no. 1 (1996): 45–70; and Pinharanda Nunes and Baxter, "Os marcadores pré-verbais".

22 All references and examples provided for *ja* in PCMac were taken from my research on verbal markings in PCMac, undertaken for my Ph.D. dissertation, submitted to the University of Macao in October 2010.

23 Stephen Matthews and Virginia Yip, *Cantonese: A Comprehensive Grammar* (London: Routledge, 1994).

24 Ibid., pp. 204–05.

8

FROM EUROPEAN-ASIAN CONFLICT TO CULTURAL HERITAGE: IDENTIFICATION OF PORTUGUESE AND SPANISH FORTS ON TERNATE AND TIDORE ISLANDS

Manuel Lobato

When one thinks about the Portuguese fortifications in the Malay Archipelago, what immediately come to mind are such images as Malacca's Famosa or Fort Vitoria on the island of Ambon. Given their prominance, it is not an easy task to present new materials concerning these two Portuguese fortresses. By contrast, several other forts in the region that were built up by the Portuguese and the Spaniards over the course of about a century are not sufficiently known, even to historians dealing with Southeast Asia in the modern age. Actually, the Iberian historical and cultural legacy in the Malay Archipelago includes a number of fortifications and remains of fortifications throughout the Northern Maluku islands, especially those on the islands of Ternate and Tidore. In these locations, the Portuguese forts date from between 1522 and 1603; those of Spanish origin date from 1606 onwards, when the Maluku islands, as part of the Portuguese empire in Asia, or the Estado da Índia, were incorporated into the Philippines. The Spanish abandoned Maluku in 1663, but there is no indication that they built any new fortifications after 1637. The forts and ruins of forts are scattered throughout the islands of Ternate, Tidore, Halmahera, Bacan, Seram and Ambon where more than twenty Iberian archaeological sites can be identified out of a total of ninety-six forts built in the region by local rulers, Europeans and Japanese.[1]

This heritage was virtually forgotten until recent times by both Portuguese and Spanish historiographies. In the late 1980s, Florentino Rodao, a Spanish historian, in an article illustrated by photos of forts on Ternate and a map displaying their location, made the first attempt to positively identify such forts and their ruins by direct observation and across literary materials.[2] During the nineteenth century, some Dutch historians and erudite colonial officers worked on this architectural patrimony based upon records and reports produced by representatives and administrators of the Vereenigde Oost-Indische Compagnie (VOC), or Dutch East India Company.[3]

In 1955, perhaps based on information gathered in the field, Professor Charles Boxer released a photo of Fort Toluku on the island of Ternate, which he supposed to have been erected by the Portuguese.[4] In fact, this fort was built in 1607 by Spaniards coming from the Philippines.[5]

Among all fortifications built by the Portuguese in the Malayan Archipelago during the sixteenth century, only three of them — Malacca (1513), Pasai (1521) and Ternate (1522) — were directly ordered by the Portuguese crown. The construction of the first Portuguese fort on Ternate was undertaken at the express order of Portugal's king, Dom Manuel I (ruled 1495–1521), although it was constructed after his death. For this reason and also due to their architectural features, these three fortresses can all be considered "Manueline" in style, belonging to the late medieval era.[6]

Other fortifications, however, were due to the initiative of individual Portuguese crown representatives, as well as to merchants, missionaries, *casados* (literally, "married men") and mestizo leaders. Thus, even the forts of Nossa Senhora da Anunciada on the island of Ambon, and Reis Magos on the island of Tidore (the only ones, apart from the one on Ternate, that the Portuguese officially owned across Maluku) were both built under the initiative of the captain of Ambon, Sancho de Vasconcelos, in 1576 and 1578, respectively.

Finally, a number of other small forts and fortified trading posts, ephemeral and functionally limited, were mostly built with perishable materials such as wood or mud, and only more rarely in stone. These fortifications were due to the initiative of captains of the main forts, ships' commanders and missionaries, along with support from local populations. Actually, the defensive system was often reduced to a fence built up to protect a pre-existing indigenous village, like the one the Jesuit priest Diogo de Magalhães erected in Nusanive, on the island of Ambon, in 1562.[7]

THE FORTRESS OF SÃO JOÃO BAPTISTA ON TERNATE

In June 1522, four months after the ships *Victoria* and *Trinidad* from the fleet of Ferdinand Magellan had left the island of Tidore, António de Brito, the first Portuguese captain of Maluku (1522–26), founded the fortress of São João Baptista on the island of Ternate. This was a response by Dom Manuel I to the appeal from Abu Lais (ruled ca. 1501–21), sultan of Ternate, who asked the Portuguese for support in order to enhance his ascendance over the rulers of Maluku. However, Dom Manuel's main reason for ordering the construction of a fortress in Maluku — and another one at the Sunda Strait, which would never be built — was to prevent the Spaniards from settling in this vast region, of which they had knowledge through hearsay from Portuguese sailors. Since 1516, the Spanish crown had been claiming possession of the area under the 1494 Treaty of Tordesillas, by virtue of which the pope had divided the world into two separate areas of influence, one by Portugal and the other by Spain.[8]

The exact location and the architectural features of the first Portuguese fortress in Maluku are well known to us from a multitude of testimonies and literary references, iconography and archaeological remains of the main building, now extremely ruined. The site for the fort was originally chosen by Tristão de Meneses, commander of the third Portuguese expedition sent from Malacca to Maluku, in May 1518, at the initiative of the governor of the Estado da Índia, Lopo Soares de Albergaria (1515–18), and the support of the captain-general of the Sea of Malacca, Aleixo de Meneses (1518),[9] who provided one ship and fifty men, foodstuffs and trading goods, at the expense of both the royal treasury and some Asian merchants from Malacca, owners of two junks that joined the fleet.[10]

Tristão de Meneses was commissioned to build up a fortress in Maluku, possibly on the island of Makian, whose territory was shared by the kings of Ternate and Tidore. These kings and Ala-ud-Din, king of Bacan, all wanted the fort to be built on their own land. Fearful of being the cause for a major conflict among these kings, which, in his view, would be detrimental to Portuguese commercial interests, Tristão de Meneses gave up construction of the fortress, announcing his intention of merely collecting information about the place where the future fortification was to be built.[11] He then chose a place one league distant from Talangame, a deepwater port on the island of Ternate, free of reefs, where Malay junks from Malacca used to anchor. This port had also been used since 1516 by Portuguese ships coming from Malacca to load cloves provided by Francisco Serrão, the first Portuguese to settle in Maluku, where he shipwrecked in 1512, along with ten other companions.[12]

On the southeast coast of the island, the fort was built near the sultan's court,[13] which João de Barros called the "city of Ternate".[14] António Galvão, seventh Portuguese captain of Ternate (1536–39), pointed out the inconvenience of that choice, by virtue of the great distance that separated the fortress from the port of Talangame, and especially given the exposure of the ship traffic to action by the fleets belonging to the king of the neighbouring island of Tidore.[15] Ternate had another deep-water port sufficient to receive large ships and galleons, which stood near the previously mentioned village of Toluku, one league to the northeast of Talangame, that is, two leagues from the Portuguese fortress.[16]

Initially, the command of the fleet, which sailed from Lisbon in April 1521 to construct the fort in Maluku, was assigned to Jorge de Brito, appointed to succeed Jorge de Albuquerque, captain of Malacca (1514–1515 and 1521–25).[17] Jorge de Brito, however, after calling at Goa, died in a skirmish in Sumatra. According to royal instructions, his brother, António de Brito, succeed him in the command of the fleet. Due to delays in Sumatra, Malacca[18] and Banda, the fleet of António de Brito was anchored at Ternate by May 1522, too late to intercept the Spanish ships *Victoria* and *Trinidad,* which had left Tidore four months earlier.[19]

By ordinance, António de Brito took up the task of building a fortress and a trading post (*feitoria*),[20] two different entities, perhaps designed to operate separately in different buildings, as it would happen.[21] Brito brought some stonemasons and a master mason from Portugal, as well as ornaments for the church that was to be built inside the fortress.[22] Nevertheless, the shortage of manpower did not allow the works to progress at the desired pace. The "queen-mother" Niachil Boki Raga, widow of the late Sultan Abu Lais (alias Bayan Sirrullah; ruled ca. 1501–21), and his brother, Cachil Daroes (Darwis), regents of the sultanate during the childhood of Sultan Abu Hayat (ruled 1521–29), suspended the previous policy of the deceased sultan and his promises of supporting the Portuguese,[23] who experienced great trouble in erecting the section of the wall facing the sea and the first floor (*sobrado*) of the tower (*torre de menagem*), now in ruins (see Figure 8.1).[24]

In the early decades, the fort consisted of only a two-floor tower inside a walled trapezoidal perimeter of twenty-seven to twenty-four fathoms in length by twelve in height at the seaside and eight in height at the top, facing the

FIGURE 8.1
Fortress of São João Baptista, Ternate

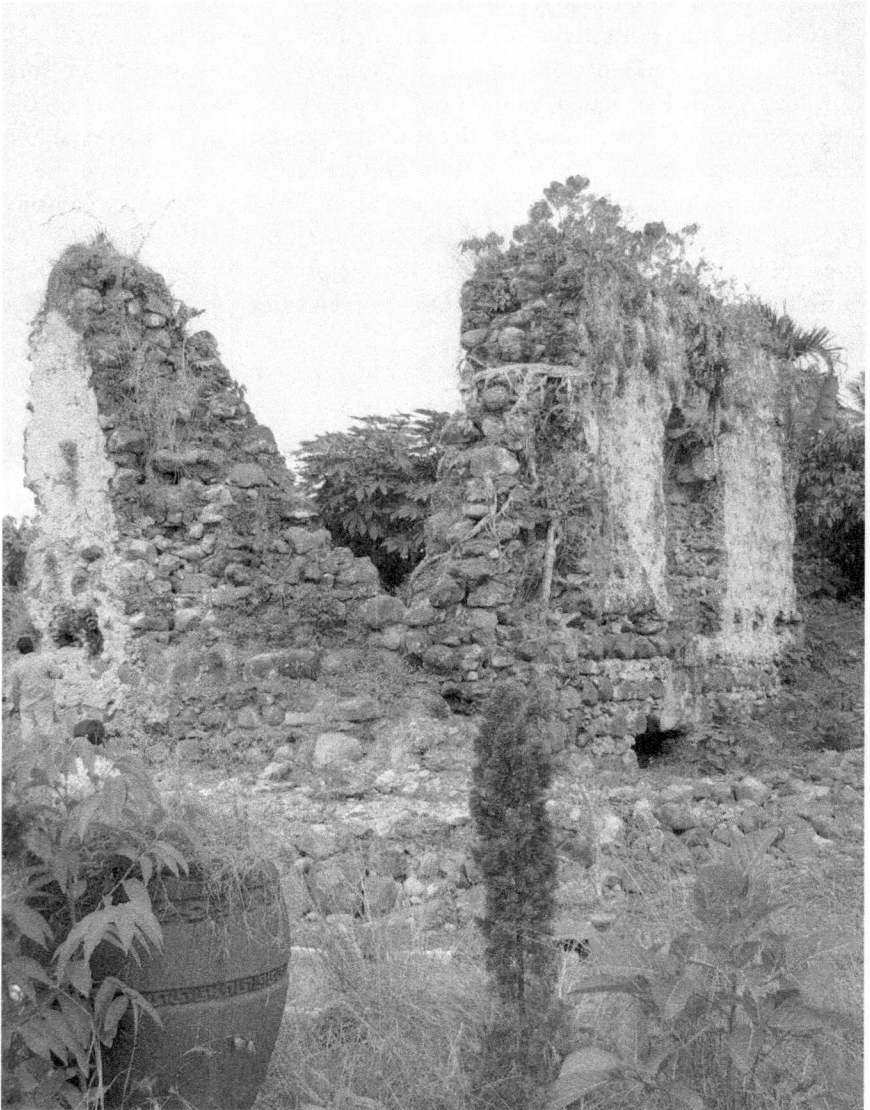

Source: Photo taken by the author.

volcano. The walls offered a weak defence because they were made of mud and set out with moisture, the reason for not having niches, and were also too low on the seaside[25] and the side facing the island's interior, although, at some twenty-five feet, it exceeded the heighth of the walls of the Malacca fort.[26]

The fortress was poorly effective, not only for military purposes, but for administrative functions and the factory's trading in cloves, too. The barracks and warehouses located within the walled area were covered with palm fibre. The bad design and features were denounced by many testimonies dating back into the mid-sixteenth century. In fact, the fort — or "the stone and lime castle, square, and no less strong than hives' enclosure",[27] in the ironic words of the chronicler Gabriel Rebelo — was built to resist an eventual assault from the Spanish navy and its regional allies. Special care was taken to site the fort where it could not be reached by artillery fired from aboard, which contrasts notably with the neglect shown for the possibility of a siege by local Ternatese forces. As these neighbours were known to be averse to the construction of the fortress on their island, some 120 Portuguese soldiers worked hard for several months to erect it.

The Portuguese fortress on Ternate received successive improvements. Captain Gonçalo Pereira (1530–31) began to construct two bulwarks in what had been a "rough wall".[28] According to João de Barros, Captain António Galvão (1536–39) "built the necessary buildings and working areas using stone and lime, as previously the fortress was built in weak materials in the local manner and the compound surrounded by a wall".[29] To enhance its seaside defences, new bastions were built up in the angles facing the ocean. Fernão de Sousa, a military engineer and superintendent of the works of the Portuguese fortifications in Asia, who visited Maluku during the captaincy of Jorge de Castro (1539-44), was responsible for the first of these two bastions.[30] Castro mentioned that Sousa built it to replace an older one made partially of wood, with the cooperation, this time, of the kings of Ternate and Tidore.[31]

However, despite all these improvements, Baltasar Veloso, a *casado* resident of Ternate, writing to the king of Portugal in 1547, affirms that the fort was merely "an enclosure for goats".[32] Indeed, five years later it was found to be partially damaged, having lost almost all buildings inside it.[33] One bulwark had collapsed as well, being rebuilt by Captain Duarte d'Eça (1555–58), with help from Sultan Hairun (ruled 1536–45 and 1546–70). Both bulwarks would end up totally ruined during the long-term siege imposed by Sultan Baab Ullah (1570–83), who repaired them after the eviction of the Portuguese from Ternate in 1575.

Chronicler Gabriel Rebelo, another casado resident of Ternate, where he occupied a few royal posts, has left the best description of this fort.[34] Located next to the "city of the Moors", the village serving as a capital to the sultan, the fortress was implanted on a high reef overlooking the *poço* (literally, "well"), also known as the *calheta*, or little harbour,[35] where small ships, such as caravels, could find safe anchorage at high tide,[36] less than a quarter of a mile (200 fathoms) distant from the fortress. António Galvão, assisted by the vicar, Fernão Vinagre, and some native workers, who had gathered on the occasion of constructing a mosque, committed himself to disengaging the reefs inside this anchorage that made it dangerous at low tide.[37] Along this small anchorage, he stood up the chapel or hermitage of Nossa Senhora da Barra, which has long since disappeared.[38] In a prominent spot overlooking the seacoast, the fortress was open to the winds, which made it healthy and prevented it from being damaged by cannons shooting from ships. In 1552, there was not "any roofed building inside it",[39] which compelled the king of Jeilolo to pay three thousand *olas* of tribute (*páreas*) each year to cover the barracks and warehouses with palm fibre, a requirement mentioned in the fortress ordinance (*regimento*) with which he rarely complied.[40]

The Portuguese settlement near the fortress walls was encircled by a wooden fence. Having burned several times, António Galvão rebuilt it in mud, he says, with fighting pits and bulwarks,[41] similar to the fortification in Malacca, where the local stockade was gradually replaced by a wall in masonry and mud. Galvão forced the Portuguese to build their houses of stone and lime with Portuguese-styled chimneys.[42] He also protected the factory house with a wall of mud and built several *bangsal* or warehouses for cloves inside it.[43] Thus, by reconstructing the Portuguese settlement on Ternate and in addition to the new buildings made of stone and mortar, António Galvão introduced a new urban type by plotting out streets according to a pattern typically used in Portugal. This model was soon locally reproduced by the sultan, who also rebuilt his capital, which, together with the Portuguese settlement, formed a single urban core where the use of perishable materials from the local architectural tradition was partially abandoned.[44] Leaning against the walls of the fortress were the houses built by the Jesuits missionaries to serve as the residences and headquarters of the Maluku mission.[45]

The Residences of the Sultan of Ternate: Gamalama and Toluku

The fortress of São João Baptista fell into the hands of Sultan Baab Ullah (ruled 1570–83) of Ternate in 1575 after five long years of siege, a fact enshrined in a monument on the spot, erected there on the occasion of the fourth centenary of this event. During the assault, both bastions collapsed, as mentioned before. The Ternatese, militarily assisted by Javanese warriors, profoundly altered the outlines of the fortification, transforming it into a military compound with remarkably local features, surrounded by a digging hole in the ground and a stone wall around the perimeter that incorporated the previous Portuguese and Muslim settlements, both converted into a single and almost invulnerable citadel.

Within this complex remained the fortress itself, considered by the governor of the Philippines, Pedro de Acuña (1602–06), who would capture it in 1606, to be too small to host soldiers and to install the arsenal required to defend it against the Dutch and the Ternatese. However, the description of this fortress — written by Juan de Esquivel, the first Spanish governor of Maluku, who served under Pedro de Acuña and took part in its achievement — reveals that, under Sultan Said al-din Berkat Syah (ruled 1583–1606), the fortress became the house of the royal family and suffered extensive reconstruction with marks of the Austronesian building tradition. The bulwark system inherited from the Portuguese was maintained, but the ramparts received new names, like Cachil Tulo, derived, perhaps, from the name of the person in charge of its defence.[46] The characteristics recorded by Esquivel are similar to those we observe today at Fort Toluku, built after 1612, under Sultan Muzaffar (ruled 1606–27), son and successor of Sultan Said Berkat, to replace the old Portuguese fort that had fallen into the hands of the Spaniards. These characteristics are mentioned in this excerpt from a letter by Juan de Esquivel to Pedro de Acuña:

> The stronghold that Your Majesty had in this place is a walled house without any resistance to artillery ... so that it did not serve the enemy more than to be the house where he lived ... [its] defence was a wall at the entrance to the place with two ... round bastions and the same in the opposed side and as the place is stretched along the beach should be more than two miles from one wall to another.[47]

In fact, Toluku fort is not originally indigenous, but Spanish. Indeed, Captain Fernando de Ayala, commander of five companies of soldiers, was commissioned by the governor of the Philippines, Juan de Silva, to construct it; as he himself says: "I made a fort called San Juan de Toloco that is a shot of cannon from the Melayu fort."[48] Its construction probably dates from 1606 or 1607, having been abandoned by the Spaniards between 1609 and 1613.[49]

Ciudad del Rosario

The governor of the Philippines, Pedro de Acuña, at the request of the Dominican friars who accompanied him on the journey to Ternate, renamed the fort and the small town environment, respectively, fortress of Nuestra Señora del Rosario and Ciudad del Rosario. Thus, the origin of this city's name is not Portuguese, contrary to the opinion of the Dutch scholar François Valentijn (1666–1727) in his *Oud en Nieuw Oost-Indien* (*Old and New East India*), published in 1724. The Spaniards also sometimes refer to it as a stationary garrison (*presidio*), a fortress, or the town of Ternate, while the native people preferred and continue to prefer the names of Gamalama (literally, the "Great Place" or "big town", a term which is assigned to various sites scattered around the island that once served as the residence of the sultans), and the term Kastela, a corruption of *castelo* (castle), a term that the aforementioned chronicler Gabriel Rebelo recorded in his mid-sixteenth century writings and thereby certainly confirming its common use.[50]

In reconstructing the defensive Ternatese compound described in the previous section, the Spaniards converted it into a new compound made in the image of Manila, the capital of the Philippines. The former Portuguese fortress continued to be the core of the new Ciudad de Nuestra Señora del Rosario, which the Spaniards designed as the "cube", occupied by administrative buildings (*casas reales*), the governor's residence, the royal warehouses, and the parish church.

This core was surrounded by two walls, the most extensive one with six bastions, each of them firing twenty cannons. Inside — that is, in the space between the two-walled perimeter — was located the Spanish city itself, which had two convents (San Francisco and San Augustín), the Jesuit college, and the hospital. Outside the fortified perimeter and leaning against the external wall laid the city of the *mardika* or free men (mostly Portuguese-Asian Christian mestizos), the Chinese quarter, the houses of the Spanish infantry, and the Filipino Pampanga militia companies.[51] This new arrangement was completed by 1619[52] when some two thousand souls lived in the town, and it lasted until 1663, when Manila decided to abandon Maluku.

Apart from a few stretches of ruined walls and the foundations of the hospital, only the old Portuguese tower remains, in ruins, up to the first floor. It once had three floors, easily recognizable by its plan, wall thickness and strong foundations (partially uncovered), all of which are typical of the Manueline-styled towers built in different parts of the Portuguese empire in Africa and Asia, sometimes using pre-carved stone and other materials brought from Portugal.

The state of disrepair of the old Portuguese fortress is partially due to the demolition of the fortified compound site in 1663 by the last Spanish governor of Maluku, Francisco de Atienza (1659–60 and 1663), who was following orders of the governor of the Philippines, Manrique de Lara (1653–63).[53] However, despite the Spanish references to the Dutch dismantlement of the remains of all Spanish fortifications in Maluku, reusing the materials in their own buildings, such reports are partly denied by the Dutch records and by the standing physical remains. On this subject, the authoritative Father Hubert Jacobs stated, with his well-known accuracy:

> In the Spanish reports the levelling of the Maluku forts appears always more thorough than in the Dutch accounts. The *Daghregister 1663* reports that the destroyed Gamulamo "could soon be put into a state of defence" (531–532). It even states that the VOC stationed a small garrison there. Ruins of this fortress are to be seen up to the present day: pieces of the ramparts, some loop-holes, a square central building once the Portuguese *torre de menagem*, a still intact breakwater, and outside the fort the walls of the hospital, the foundation of the church, and an intact walled-in pond.[54]

OTHER SPANISH FORTIFICATIONS IN TERNATE

The Spaniards considered the old Portuguese fortress at Ternate badly located and extremely vulnerable, so they decided to build a new fort nearby. Juan de Esquivel pointed out in his letter to King Philip III that

> nearby the old fortress exists a high place in a part where a large ravine girds it from the back, a place where D. Pedro de Acuña, with the advice of all men, ordered a fort to be built that should have 600 feet in centre with three bastions, although it is square, as shown in the plan that with this letter I am sending to Your Majesty.[55]

The plan mentioned by Esquivel, that he allegedly sent to the king, is kept in the Archivo de Indias and was published a century ago by Father Pablo Pastells in his edition of the work of Father Francisco Colín.[56] In fact, a Dutch engraving shows, at the exact spot indicated in the excerpt of the letter by Esquivel to the Spanish king reproduced above (that is, "over the fortress" and in its "back") a small pentagonal fort with a surveillance turret in a top corner and a one-story building inside,[57] very different, thus, from the plan he sent to the king. However, nowadays no such remains of a fort built near the old Portuguese fortress exist any longer. At present, the nearest fort to the old Portuguese fortress is seven kilometres distant from Gamalama, following the coastline to the northeast. It is of Spanish origin and is called San Pedro y San Pablo (see Figure 8.2), with three bastions and situated on a promontory over the shore. These characteristics correspond to Esquivel's

FIGURE 8.2
Fort San Pedro y San Pablo (Fort Don Gil)

Source: Photo taken by the author.

report and plan in size, which is essentially the six hundred feet (or about 180 metres) indicated in the letter. However, the plan mentioned by Esquivel has greater similarities to Fort Kalamata (see Figure 8.3) than with Fort San Pedro y San Pablo.

Fort San Pedro y San Pablo (Fort Don Gil)

As noted above, this fort, in the vicinity of Lake Laguna[58] ("laguna" is Spanish for "lake"), is located midway between Kastela and the Dutch fort of Orange (Melayu), and hence a reason to be considered "the frontier of Melayu".[59] Also known as Fort Don Gil (Donjil) or Kota Janji, it is a small fort with three bulwarks for four to six cannons whose function was to control the channel between the islands of Ternate and Tidore. Although some Spanish sources assign it a Portuguese origin,[60] and even though its foundation was allegedly due to its location overlooking a contiguous anchorage, its strategic importance derives from the Dutch settlement at Fort Orange or Melayu and from the control it exerts over the food supply lines linking Tidore to Rosario. The garrison was nominally fixed with sixty soldiers, but their numbers were usually reduced to a dozen.

Kalamata

The fort of Kalamata, also referred to as Fort Santana, San Francisco and Santa Lucia de Calomata, is located on the beach at Kayu Merah. Of Dutch origin,[61] it was captured by the Spaniards, who held it until 1663 when they abandoned the positions they owned in the Maluku archipelago. Being a key position for the Spaniards on Ternate, it is in fairly good condition after a major restoration in 1994, which an inscription at the entrance proclaims.

The English Fort

To the north of the present city of Ternate lay some ruins of a fortification or architectural structure surrounding an inner courtyard. Oral tradition attributes its construction to the Portuguese, although it is known and officially labelled as the "English fort".[62] By 1575, in that very same area, an uncle of Sultan Baab Ullah (ruled 1570–83), Cachil Tulo, erected a fortification in order to prevent the Portuguese from disembarking, thus providing its name.[63] It cannot be determined if the structure at this site is the same fort.

FIGURE 8.3
Fort Kalamata

Source: Photo taken by the author.

Fort Orange (Melayu) in Ternate

Pedro Sarmiento, commander of the first Spanish expedition sent from Manila to recover the ancient Portuguese fortress, reported in 1584 that "the king has in the same island of Ternate half a league towards the East side another port called Melayu surrounded by walls with many bastions and pieces of artillery of small and medium calibre; in this fort there are five hundred warriors."[64] Hence, the native origins of Fort Orange are well established, contrary to the historiography that has repeatedly attributed it to the Dutch, although the present design, Italian-styled, was due to Cornelius Matelieff, who started its reconstruction in 1605[65] and completed it within two years.

THE REIS MAGOS FORTRESS IN TIDORE

The construction of the Portuguese fort of Reis Magos on the island of Tidore was initiated in January 1578 by Sancho de Vasconcelos, captain of the fortress of Ambon (1572–91), and forty Portuguese who accompanied him expressly for that purpose, corresponding to a request from the local sultan three years after the eviction of the Portuguese from their fort on Ternate (see Figure 8.4).[66]

Concerning the new fortress on Tidore, the Jesuit chronicler Francisco de Sousa states:

> Also coming from Ambon, Sancho de Vasconcelos began the new fort, dedicated to the Magi in 1557 [sic]. Diogo de Azambuja, sailing from India as Captain of Maluku, finished it. And to know how little care, or too much neglect, the Portuguese at that time used to fortified themselves, the fort was loose stone, square, thirty fathoms per side, with two bastions at two corners, a much weaker work, which could easily be conquered. Similar was that of Ternate, while the one in Ambon was made up of wood. So the Portuguese are exceeding in value to conquer land and not lacking of passion for enjoying it, but their hands are too scarce to spend the necessary [resources] to secure their conquests.[67]

This fort was located on the eastern shore of Tidore, half a mile north of Soasio,[68] the sultan's court, and at the distance of "two gunshots" from the Socanora cape.[69] Once destroyed by a gunpowder keg explosion in May 1605, during the Dutch siege, its defenders, under Captain Pedro Álvares de Abreu (1602–05), were forced to surrender. The Portuguese settlement was sacked and the houses, entirely made of perishable material, burned, while about four hundred inhabitants were allowed to leave.[70]

FIGURE 8.4
Map of Fort Locations on the Islands of Ternate and Tidore

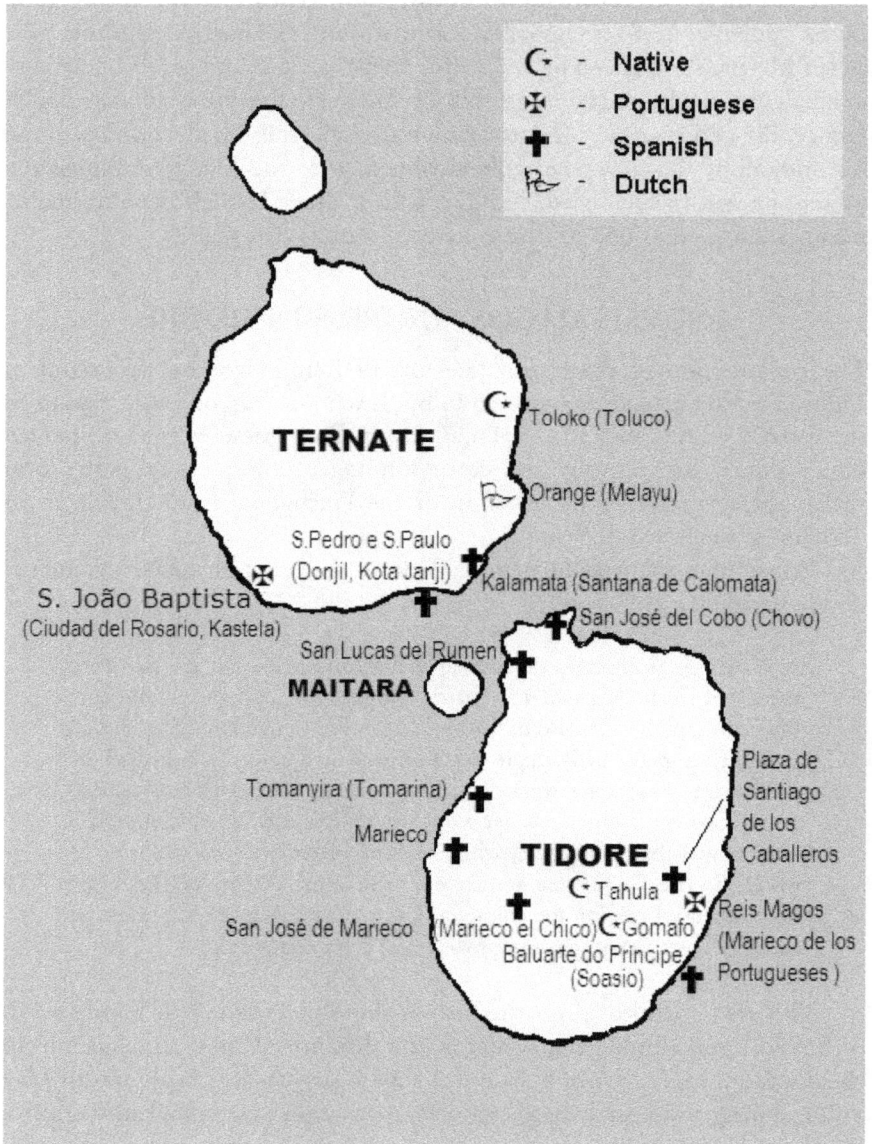

Recovered by the Spaniards in 1606, the fort suffered repeated attacks by the fleets of Cornelius Matelieff de Jonge, in May 1607, and Paulus van Caerden, in June 1608. The Spaniards began to rebuild it in 1609, under the second governor of Maluku, Lucas de Vergara Gabiria (1609–10).[71] They called it the "Portuguese fortress" and, it seems, Marieco de los Portugueses, a name that should not be confused with Marieku itself, or Marieco el Grande, on the west coast of Tidore, both of which were to be taken by the Dutch in 1613.

Meanwhile, the reconstruction of the former Portuguese fortress on Tidore carried out by the Spaniards progressed very slowly. In 1610, the third governor of Maluku, Cristóbal de Azcueta Menchaca (1610–12), reported that it was still in ruins, having then decided to accelerate its reconstruction by being situated in the best port of Tidore.[72] He garrisoned it with sixteen soldiers and three cannons.[73] It was probably badly damaged during several attacks it suffered, since the sultan of Tidore, Cachil Mole (ruled 1599–1627), advised the new Spanish governor, Jerónimo de Silva (1611–17), to dismantle its ruins in order to prevent the Dutch from conquering it.[74] As expected, this soon came to pass. John Saris, the British navigator who anchored in front of the old Portuguese fort in April 1613, described it as a mere battery with eight cannons.[75] Silva assigned to the fort, or its remains, a garrison of fifty soldiers chosen from among the best, who were killed when eight hundred Dutch and twelve vessels from the fleet of Admiral Pieter Botha assaulted it on 9 July 1613.[76] Conquered by the Dutch, the old Portuguese fort was dismantled and abandoned.[77] However, according to an anonymous Portuguese description from 1617, it appears that the Dutch renovated it subsequently.[78]

EARLY SPANISH BULWARKS ON TIDORE

In January 1527, the Spanish fleet of García Jofre de Loaysa, captained after his death by Martín Iñiguez of Carquizano, built a sort of pier or breakwater with two bastions and abundant artillery on the island of Tidore. This structure was near Soasio, the court of the local king, Raja Mir (Amir ud-din, ruled 1526–ca. 1551), and was constructed under his patronage. Located over the anchorage, it had walls that were two fathoms high and six feet thick that defended the entrance to the Portuguese and Ternatese vessels.[79] This fortification had a chapel or church invoking Nuestra Señora del Rosario. It was captured in 1529 by Vicente da Fonseca, who demolished it, following orders from the captain of Ternate, Jorge de Meneses (1527–30). However, in 1528, Hernando de la Torre and a few survivors of the Spanish expeditions to the Pacific had built a fort made up of "stone and mud" on the seashore near the same spot, a little further north.[80]

Back to Maluku, the Spaniards from Ruy Lopez de Villalobos's expedition chose not to build fortifications of their own but encouraged the local kings to do it. Thus, in August 1545, the sultan of Tidore, Raja Mir, fearing the Portuguese, built a fort of loose rock in a high place on this island,[81] in the same cliff where, in about 1532, he had raise another fort, destroyed in 1536 by António Galvão, the Portuguese captain of Ternate (1536–39). The new fort, constructed with the assistance of the Spanish soldiers, was also demolished by Bernardim de Sousa, the Portuguese captain of Ternate (1546–49 and 1550–52) in 1551. Another sultan, probably Gapibaguna (ruled ca. 1571–99), rebuilt it again later on. Women and children took refuge there, escaping from the Reis Magos fort and from the Portuguese settlement on Tidore when they were seized by the Dutch in 1605, as mentioned above.

The panorama of the Spanish fortifications on Tidore is quite confusing since each building appears to be named in different ways. Also, the term "fuerza" was used interchangeably to refer to a fortress, a bulwark or even a simple vault.[82] Despite these difficulties, I will try to identify and locate each one of these fortifications.

Marieco el Grande

On the west coast of Tidore, the Spaniards, by order of the governor of Maluku, Lucas de Vergara Gabiria (1609–10), erected a small fortification on the beach that they called Marieco, with a garrison of fourteen soldiers.[83] The original project, from 1609, was described as follows:

> The fort of Tidore is planned for a prominent site overlooking the sea, of which both sides are girded by two large ravines, the volcano laying at its back; under its cannons may anchor two or three galleons, near the King's place, some quarter of a mile from where the former one, which was blown up, was located and in the same spot where, some say, André Furtado de Mendonça wanted to build it when he was here.[84]

In its original design, Marieco el Grande consisted of a fence and two bastions of stone, although this fort is also said to have been constructed totally of wood.[85] It was visible from the Spanish forts of Gamalama (Rosario) and Don Gil on Ternate, which were of no help when the Dutch devastated and seized it on 8 February 1613. Taking advantage of its location and the existing structures, Admiral Pieter Botha rebuilt and expanded it according to a different square plan, with bulwarks at the angles,[86] which the Spaniards called Marieco el Grande to distinguish it from a new fortress they built nearby. According to the Jesuit priest João Baptista, Marieco el Grande was "a little fort" while it was controlled by the Spaniards,[87] the first one that they built on Tidore since Maluku begun to be ruled from Manila. It was also the only one they had there from 1606 to 1613, not considering the ruins of the old Portuguese fortress of Reis Magos. Its function was to protect Soasio, the court of the sultan of Tidore, in connection with the Spanish forts on Ternate, which were supplied via Tidore. In 1621, after an eight-year occupation, the Dutch abandoned that position, having razed the fort to the ground.[88]

After the seizure of Marieco el Grande by the Dutch, in 1613, the Spaniards built a small new fort nearby, as mentioned above, which they named La Plaza de Santiago de los Caballeros, *caballero* (literally, "knight") being the Spanish term to designate a bulwark or small fort. Actually, the Spanish literature on Maluku refers to at least one other bulwark in the surrounding area.

The Prince's Bulwark

Below the previous fort and next to the beach, there was a bastion, part of the system implemented by the Spaniards to protect Soasio, the capital of Tidore, also called the "Great Place" (Lugar Grande) of Tidore's king. Natives and Spaniards worked together on its construction during 1613, when they abandoned this task to concentrate instead on a major fort at Tahula, considered to be more urgent.[89]

The San Lucas del Rumen Fort

There are traces of a fortification in Rum, in northwestern Tidore, opposite the islet of Maitara, over the modern anchorage, which the local oral tradition wrongly considers to be the remnants of an old Portuguese fortress. Indeed, the fort of San Lucas del Rumen or Rum dates back to the period of Spanish rule over Tidore. It was partially built of stone and lime in 1618, during the second government of Lucas de Vergara Gabiria (1617–20), who chose its patron saint. It was probably a structure too weak to defend the port, a mere "platform" for shooting artillery, according to a contemporary description. In the 1650s, Governor Francisco de Esteibar (1652–56 and 1658–59) restored it, and, it seems, enlarged the old wooden structure that was spoiled.[90] Its location made it possible to control the shortest route linking Ternate to Tidore.[91] Since the Spaniards often used the harbour of Rum to connect both islands, it was also almost a mandatory port-of-call for ships sailing from the Philippines to the city of Rosario on Ternate.[92]

Nowadays, due to a large degree of destruction, only part of a bulwark platform still exists. The main gate would have been razed some years ago, during the construction of the road giving access to the port of Rum.

San José del Cobo (or Chovo)

To control the channel between the islands of Tidore and Ternate, the Spaniards built up the fort of Cobo or Chovo by 1612 or 1613, at the northernmost part of Tidore, opposite the San Pedro y San Pablo fort on Ternate. Its port was preferred to the one in Rum during the monsoon of south and south-westerlies.[93] Even though it is said that the Spaniards dismantled it in 1663, it continued in the possession of the Dutch, being mentioned as militarily functional until the late eighteenth century.[94]

The Tahula (or Tohula) Fort

The construction of the Tahula fort, on the eastern coast of Tidore, reasonably preserved still today, began in 1610 by order of the governor, Cristóbal de Azcueta Menchaca (1610–12), and concluded in 1613 under the government of Jerónimo de Silva (1611–17), to whom it is often assigned.[95] Located on a hill to the west of Soasio, the sultan's court, its construction was due to the need of protecting it, a function that the old Portuguese fortress, too far away and in ruins, could not secure,[96] even before its capture by the Dutch in 1613. Governor Jerónimo de Silva (1611–17) decided to concentrate efforts to complete Tahula expeditiously, as mentioned in a previous section. It proved to be a prudent decision when, in June 1614, the Dutch suffered a serious setback while attacking it.

Partially demolished and abandoned by the Spaniards in 1663, the fortress of Tahula, rehabilitated by the Dutch, served as a regular fort until the late eighteenth century.[97] Indeed, Tahula was considered a "strong and invincible" fort, which "cannot be seized except [if] the natives want to capture it by siege".[98]

San José de Marieco or Marieco el Chico

The fort of San José de Marieco is more commonly referred to as Marieco el Chico because it was built by a military expedition sent for that purpose in 1618[99] to replace an old one on the west shore of Tidore, known as Marieco el Grande, which had been seized by the Dutch in 1613. Some scholars believe that Marieco el Chico and the Tomanyira fort, or even the Tahula fort, are one and the same. This confusion derives from the fact that, on the one hand, Marieco el Chico obviously stood near Marieko, the Tidorese ancient capital, where the raja had its seat in the first quarter of the sixteenth century; on the other hand, it was also fairly close to Tomanyira, on the western face of the volcano Kiematabu.[100] In my opinion, there were two different fortifications, not one, since Tomanira is said to be a fort monitoring and supporting the coastal navigation (see below), while Marieco el Chico was located some distance inland and thus not positioned to fulfil that obligation.

The Sokonora (or Bokonora) Fort

The fort at Sokonora was a small Spanish fort reportedly built in 1613.[101] Located by the sea on a "naturally fortified hill" to the south of the Tahula fort, the Dutch tried to capture it from the Tidorese in June 1613.[102] By 1617–18, it was renovated under Governor Lucas de Vergara Gabiria, who made it an essential piece of the Spanish defensive system, being considered a fort of some size and importance.[103]

The Tomanyira (or Tomanira, or Tomarina) Fort

Initially this was a small fort on Tidore's shore, usually considered to be "the border of Marieko",[104] because the Dutch fort was located to the south. The Tomanyira fort was built for the purpose of controlling the channel that separates Tidore from Ternate, together with the forts of Marieco and Don Gil (on Ternate).[105] After the fall of Marieco to the Dutch, the fort at Tomanyira became a key position in the Spanish defensive system from 1618 onwards.[106]

Gomafo

On the hillside overlooking Soasio, the capital of Tidore, there was a bastion, the so-called Gomafo fort, built by the Tidorese sultan Cachil Mole Majimu (ruled 1599–1627). Some Spanish soldiers cooperated in repairing and renovating it. Afterwards, a small Spanish garrison moved into Gomafo.[107]

CONCLUSION

On a 1996 visit to Ternate, I was left with the impression that there were almost no truly Portuguese remains worthy of mention there, an impression reinforced by certain photos of Spanish and Dutch fortifications on the island. The feeling that there would not be much to say about the subject vanished during a second visit, in 2007, around several of the Maluku islands, leading me to formulate a new working hypothesis.

Spanish historians who visited Northern Maluku in the late 1980s did not succeed in identifying most of the existing fortifications. Instead, positive identification was made possible only by crossing field data with a vast body of literary and archival materials I had collected previously. This step made it possible to create a solid and referential framework that Spanish historians, who had not paid careful attention to the European historiography about the region, failed to establish. In particular, the works by Hubert Jacobs and the much more recent study by Marco Ramerini on the Spanish fortifications on Tidore provided major insights. However, positive identification of some of these sites in light of historical evidence proved to be difficult, as most narrative and archival sources are only marginally informative and oral traditions are often inaccurate.

These fortifications lack the magnitude of other Portuguese or Spanish military architecture that is often embedded in larger and richer patrimonial contexts. Nevertheless, despite the destruction and remodelling suffered over the centuries, they form a unique and interesting set of structures, highly valuable to local populations in terms of their contributions to collective memories, and also a vehicle to affirm their identity. This is the way in which the early European architecture and artefacts are appreciated by the Muslim peoples of most of the Northern Maluku islands, such as Ternate and Tidore. It also presents a tourism possibility for this economically depressed area, in contrast to its wealthier and more prestigious past.

To some extent, this study aims to fill major lacunae in our knowledge of the Iberian architectural heritage in the Northern Maluku islands. It begins to answer some of the questions posed by the authorities and experts involved in the restoration that has taken place, which aroused some controversy on Ternate. Local observers have expressed their concern about the preservation of several forts and ruins, especially on the archaeological site of Kastela-Rosario, the early Portuguese fortress on Ternate, noting that little care has been taken in the choice of techniques and materials used.

Finally, this research did not address the existence of verifiable ruins of Spanish or Portuguese origin on the islands of Halmahera and Makian, where a tentative survey of sites mentioned in archival sources was undertaken. The survey was not always successful, given difficulties in obtaining reliable maps and plans, as well as the low level of credibility of my informants, whose statements rarely withstood further investigation. Accordingly, and for purposes of concision, this topic will be discussed in a forthcoming study.

Notes

1   See "Appendix E" in Pusat Dokumentasi Arkitektur, *Inventory and Identification of Forts in Indonesia* (Jakarta: Pusat Dokumentasi Arkitektur, 2006).

2   Florentino Rodao, "Restos de la presencia ibérica en las islas Molucas", in *España y el Pacífico*, edited by F. Rodao and Leoncio Cabrero (Madrid: AECI-AEEP, 1989), pp. 243–54.

3   F.S.A. de Clercq, *Ternate: The Residency and Its Sultanate*, edited and translated by P.M. Taylor and M.N. Richards, digital ed. (Washington, D.C.: Smithsonian Institution Libraries, 1999), <http://www.sil.si.edu/digitalcollections/ anthropology/ternate/ternate.pdf> (accessed 26 March 2007). Originally published as *Bijdragen tot de kennis der Residentie Ternate* (Leiden: Brill, 1890).

4   Charles Boxer and Frazão de Vasconcelos, *André Furtado de Mendonça* (Lisbon: Agência Geral do Ultramar, 1955; repr., Lisbon: Fundação Oriente; and Macao: Museu e Centro de Estudos Marítimos, 1989), photo between pp. 70–71.

5   Méritos y servicios Fernando de Ayala, 23 July 1622, *Patronato* 53, ramo 25, Archivo General de Indias (hereafter cited as AGI), Seville, apud Marco Ramerini, *Le fortezze spagnole nell'isola di Tidore*, <http:// www.colonialvoyage. com/molucche/4_fortispagnoli.html> (accessed 24 April 2008). This work is no longer freely available on-line, having been converted into an e-book, for sale at <http://ilmiolibro.kataweb.it/schedalibro.asp?id=18032>.

6   The Portuguese fortress in Pasai was just a "little fort" defended by sixty cannons. It was captured by the Sultan of Aceh in 1523. See "Lembranças de cousas da Índia em 1525", in *Subsídios para a Historia da India Portugueza*, edited by Rodrigo José de Lima Felner (Lisbon: A.R.S., 1868), p. 16; Jorge M. dos Santos Alves, "Une ville inquiète et un sultan barricadé: Aceh vers 1588 d'aprés le *Roteiro das Cousas do Achém* de l'Evêque de Malaka", *Archipel* 39 (1990): 94. About the military "Manueline" architecture in Asia, see the recent study by André Teixeira, *Fortalezas: Estado Português da Índia; A Arquitectura Militar na Construção do Império de D. Manuel I* (Lisbon: Tribuna da História, 2008).

7   Father Baltazar de Araújo to his brothers, Maluku, 24 February 1563, in *Documentação para a História das Missões do Padroado Português do Oriente: Insulíndia*, vol. 3, *1563–1567*, edited by A. Basílio de Sá (Lisbon: Agência Geral do Ultramar, 1955), p. 34.

8   For political details on the foundation of this fortress and the troubled process of its construction, as well as its architectural features, see Manuel Lobato, "Fortalezas do Estado da Índia: Do centro à periferia", in *A Arquitectura Militar na Expansão Portuguesa*, edited by Rafael Moreira (Porto: Comissão Nacional

para as Comemorações dos Descobrimentos Portugueses, 1994), pp. 43–55. See also *Política e Comércio dos Portugueses na Insulíndia: Malaca e as Molucas de 1575 a 1605* (Macao: Instituto Português do Oriente, 1999), pp. 102–04.

9   King of Ternate to Garcia de Sá, captain of Malacca, 1520, in Sá, *Documentação*, vol. 1, *1506–1549* (Lisbon: Agência Geral do Ultramar, 1954), p. 118.

10 Gaspar Correia, *Lendas da Índia*, vol. 2, edited by R.J. de Lima Felner (Lisbon: Typographia da Academia Real das Sciencias de Lisboa, 1856), p. 711; and João de Barros, *Décadas da Ásia de João de Barros: Década Terceira* [1563], CD-ROM (Lisbon: Comissão Nacional para as Comemorações dos Descobrimentos Portugueses, 1998), bk. 5, chap. 6, pp. 272–73.

11 Barros, *Ásia, Década Terceira*, bk. 5, chap. 6, pp. 272–73.

12 Manuel Lobato, "A Man in the Shadow of Magellan: Francisco Serrão, the 'Discoverer' of the Maluku Islands (1511–1521)", paper presented at the international seminar "Indonesia and Portugal: Past, Present and Future: In Commemoration of Ten Years of the Reestablishment of Diplomatic Relations", Museu do Oriente, Lisbon, 16–17 November 2009.

13 Diogo do Couto, *Década Quarta da Ásia*, vol. 1, edited by M.A. Lima Cruz (Lisbon: Comissão Nacional para as Comemorações dos Descobrimentos Portugueses, Fundação Oriente, and Imprensa Nacional - Casa da Moeda, 1999), bk. 7, chap. 7, p. 393.

14 Barros, *Ásia, Década Terceira*, bk. 5, chap. 6, p. 274.

15 António Galvão, *A Treatise on the Moluccas (c. 1544): Probably the Preliminary Version of António Galvão's Lost* Historia das Molucas, edited by Hubert Jacobs (Rome: Jesuit Historical Institute; and St. Louis: St. Louis University, 1971), p. 234.

16 Gabriel Rebelo, "Informação sobre as Molucas", text 1, in Sá, *Documentação*, 3:239, and similar in text 2, 3:380.

17 Luís Filipe Thomaz, "O malogrado estabelecimento oficial dos portugueses em Sunda e a islamização de Java", in *Aquém e Além da Taprobana: Estudos Luso-Orientais à Memória de Jean Aubin e Denys Lombard*, edited by L.F. Thomaz (Lisbon: Centro de História de Além-Mar, 2002), 429n196 and 520n478.

18 Details on the activities of this fleet in the Malacca Strait can be found in a letter from António de Brito to Jorge de Albuquerque, in Sá, *Documentação*, 1:129; "Noticia preliminar", in Felner, *Subsidios*, p. xxxi; Correia, *Lendas da Índia*, 2:713; Caderno de Recibos do Almoxarife dos Mantimentos de Malaca, Corpo Cronológico, pt. 2, ms. 98, doc. 62, Arquivo Nacional da Torre do Tombo (hereafter cited as ANTT), Lisbon, apud Luís Filipe Thomaz, "As cartas malaias de Abu Hayat, sultão de Ternate, a el-rei de Portugal e os primórdios da presença portuguesa em Maluco", *Anais de História de Além-Mar* 4 (2003): 430n159; Barros, *Ásia, Década Terceira*, bk. 5, chap. 7, p. 276, and reproduced by Manuel de Faria e Sousa, *Asia Portuguesa*, vol. 2, translated by M.V.G. Santos Ferreira (Porto: Livraria Civilização, 1947), pt. 3, chap. 5, p. 56. About the insufficient supplying of this fleet by Jorge de Albuquerque, captain of Malacca (1521–25),

see "Sumário de uma carta de Simão de Abreu para el-rei", Malacca, 11 January 1524, Núcleo Antigo, no. 75, fol. 28, ANTT.

[19] Rui Gago to the king, Maluku [Ternate], 15 February 1523, in Sá, *Documentação*, 1:161; and Correia, *Lendas da Índia*, 2:713.

[20] Testimony by Jorge Botelho, in *As Gavetas da Torre do Tombo*, vol. 3, edited by António da Silva Rego (Lisbon: Centro de Estudos Históricos Ultramarinos, 1963), p. 27.

[21] Galvão, *A Treatise on the Moluccas*, p. 294.

[22] António da Silva Rego, "As Molucas em princípios do século XVI", in *A Viagem de Fernão de Magalhães e a Questão das Molucas*, edited by A. Teixeira da Mota (Lisbon: Junta de Investigações Científicas, 1975), p. 82.

[23] Fernão Lopes de Castanheda, *História do Descobrimento e Conquista da India pelos Portugueses*, vol. 2, edited by M. Lopes de Almeida (Porto: Lello & Irmão, 1979), bk. 6, chap. 41, p. 218.

[24] Gago to the king, in Sá, *Documentação*, 1:172.

[25] Vicente da Fonseca to the king, Maluku [Ternate], 8 December 1531, in Sá, *Documentação*, 1:237.

[26] António de Brito to the king, Ternate, 28 February 1525, in Sá, *Documentação*, 1:194. The information disclosed by Brito is not as clear as it seems since, according to Galvão, the wall would have been only eight feet high in the sections where the ground was higher, and twelve feet where it was lower. See Galvão, *A Treatise on the Moluccas*, p. 210.

[27] "Informação das Molucas", text 3, in Sá, *Documentação*, vol. 6, *1595–1599* (Lisbon: Centro de Estudos de História e Cartografia Antiga, Instituto de Investigação Científica Tropical, 1988), p. 196.

[28] Couto, *Década Quarta da Ásia*, bk. 7, chap. 7, 1:382.

[29] João de Barros, *Décadas da Ásia de João de Barros: Década Quarta* [1615] CD-ROM (Lisbon: Comissão Nacional para as Comemorações dos Descobrimentos Portugueses, 1998 [1778–88]), bk. 9, chap. 22, p. 632. Barros's unclear words suggest that Galvão would have added the wall to the fortress, which previously would not yet be complete, or that he would have included within it parts of the Portuguese village previously located outside the city walls.

[30] Fernão de Sousa to the king, Bassein, 24 November 1547, in *Diccionario Historico e Documental dos Architectos, Engenheiros e Constructores Portuguezes*, vol. 2, edited by Sousa Viterbo (Lisbon: Imprensa Nacional, 1904), p. 302; Sá, *Documentação*, 3:304; and Sá, *Documentação*, vol. 4, *1568–1579* (Lisbon: Instituto de Investigação Científica Tropical, 1956), p. 468.

[31] Jorge de Castro to the king, Maluku [Ternate], 10 February 1544, in Sá, *Documentação*, 1:388–89. See also Rebelo, "Informação", text 2, 3:198; and Jerónimo Pires Cotão, factor of Maluku, to the king, Ternate, 20 February 1544, in Sá, *Documentação*, 3:405.

[32] Baltazar Veloso to the king, Maluku, 20 March 1547, in *As Gavetas da Torre do Tombo*, vol. 1, edited by António da Silva Rego (Lisbon: Centro de Estudos Históricos Ultramarinos, 1960), p. 520.

33 Rebelo, "Informação", text 2, Sá, *Documentação*, 3:491.

34 Ibid., text 1, 3:304–05, and 4:468.

35 Father Francisco Vieira to his Jesuit brothers in Portugal, Ternate, 9 March 1559, in *Documenta Malucensia*, vol. 1, *1542–1577*, edited by Hubert Jacobs (Rome: Institutum Historicum Societatis Iesu, 1974), p. 278.

36 Bartolomé Leonardo de Argensola, *Conquista de las Islas Malucas* (1609; Madrid: Miraguano-Polifemo, 1992), p. 60, and similar in Pedro Fernández del Pulgar, *Descripción de las Philippinas y de las Malucas e Historia del Archipiélago Maluco, desde su Descubrimiento al Tiempo Presente*, ms. 3002, bk. 2, chap. 1, Biblioteca Nacional de Madrid, apud Maria Bellén Bañas Llanos, *Islas de las Espécies: Fuentes Etnohistóricas sobre las Islas Molucas, s. XIV–XX* (Cáceres: Universidad de Extremadura, 2000), p. 133.

37 Galvão, *A Treatise on the Moluccas*, p. 190.

38 Castanheda, *História do Descobrimento*, bk. 7, chap. 163, 2:833.

39 Rebelo, "Informação", text 2, Sá, *Documentação*, 3:491.

40 Regimento pera a fortaleza de maluquo, in Diogo Velho, *Regimento da Ordem … no Receber e Despender*, Lisbon, 14 March 1578, Arquivo Histórico Ultramarino (Lisbon), *Conselho Ultramarino*, cod. 217, fol. 131.

41 Galvão, *A Treatise on the Moluccas*, p. 292.

42 Barros, *Ásia*, bk. 9, chap. 22, p. 632.

43 Galvão, *A Treatise on the Moluccas*, p. 294.

44 Scattered and fragmentary references to urban planning and its subsequent development do not allow reaching any solid conclusions. Apparently, this development took place at an early stage, since non-perishable materials for non-military purposes just started to be used in Malacca by the hand of local *casados*, although this Portuguese stronghold was much more important and larger than Ternate. See Luís Filipe Ferreira Reis Thomaz, "Os Portugueses em Malaca: 1511–1580", vol. 1 (Licenciatura thesis, Universidade de Lisboa, 1964), p. 169.

45 João de Lucena, *História da Vida do Padre Francisco Xavier*, vol. 2, edited by Luís de Albuquerque and M.G. Pericão (Lisbon: Alfa, 1989), bk. 4, chap. 14, p. 65.

46 See the letters from Juan de Esquivel to King Philip III, Ternate, 9 April and 2 May 1606, Patronato 47, ramo 3, 2, 1/14, and ramo 21, 1, 1–32, AGI, partially published by Francisco Colín and Pedro Chirino, *Labor Evangélica*, vol. 2, edited by Pablo Pastells, new ed. (Barcelona: Henrich, 1904 [1900–02]), pp. 48 and 56 (original ed.: Madrid, 1663).

47 Colín and Chirino, *Labor Evangélica*, 2:56n.

48 See note 5 above.

49 Actually, the Spanish fort at Toluku, named San Juan de Toluco, was built in 1611, under Captain-General Juan de Silva, a "cannon shot" (about half a mile) in distance to the north of the Melayu fort, which the Dutch baptized Fort Orange. Given the difficulty of the enterprise, the Spaniards organized an expeditionary force, led by Sergeant-Major Fernando de Ayala, to build up

Fort Toluku (Méritos de Fernando de Ayala, 27 July 1643, Indiferente, 112, no. 47, AGI). It comprised five companies under the command of Fernando Centeno Maldonado, Andrés Hinete and Pedro Zapata (Informaciones de Fernando Centeno Maldonado, 1615, Filipinas 60, no. 18; Méritos y servicios de Fernando de Ayala, 23 July 1622, Patronato 53, ramo 25, AGI). Abandoned by the Spaniards soon after its construction, Fort Toluku was occupied by the Dutch, who renamed it Fort Hollandia. See note 5 above.

50 Gabriel Rebelo, "Informação das Molucas", text 3, in Sá, *Documentação*, 6:196.

51 Auxiliary troops from the Philippine province of Pampanga, north of Manila, on Luzon Island. *Cf. Documenta Malucensia*, vol. 3, *1606–1682*, edited by Hubert Jacobs (Rome: Institutum Historicum Societatis Iesu, 1984), pp. 602 and 602n3. They assisted the Spaniards militarily while preserving their traditional leaders and ethnic identity, as shown in the treatment of *don* given to their captains; see Gary William Bohigian, "Life on the Rim of Spain's Pacific-American Empire: Presidio Society in the Molucca Islands, 1606–1663", master's thesis, University of California, Los Angeles, 1994, pp. 93 and 330.

52 Anonymous, "Relação breve da ilha de Ternate Tidore e mais ilhas Malucas, aonde temos fortaleza e presidios, e das forças, naos e fortalezas que o enemigo olandes tem por aquellas partes", in *Documentação Ultramarina Portuguesa*, vol. 1, edited by António da Silva Rego (Lisbon: Centro de Estudos Históricos Ultramarinos, 1960), pp. 163–70, and repeated in vol. 2 (1962), pp. 49–56. About the city of Rosario on Ternate, see 1:165 and 2:50.

53 There are good reasons to think that Governor Atienza failed to demolish the Spanish fortifications in Maluku since this had not yet been accomplished as late as 1666. See Leonard Y. Andaya, *The World of Maluku: Eastern Indonesia in the Early Modern Period* (Honolulu: University of Hawai'i Press, 1993), pp. 155–56.

54 *Documenta Malucensia*, 3:659 and 3:659n3.

55 Colín and Chirino, *Labor Evangélica*, 2:56.

56 Ibid., p. 73.

57 This engraving displays the inscription "De Stadt van Gamalama in't Eylant Ternate, by de Spaensche beseten", inserted by Isaac Commelin in his *Begin ende van de Voortgangh Vereenighde Geoctroyeerde Nederlandsche Oost-Indische Compagnie* (Amsterdam: Jan Jansz, 1646), representing the 1607 Dutch siege of the Spanish fortress of Gamalama.

58 Hubert Jacobs, "The *Discurso Politico del Gobierno Maluco* of Fr. Francisco Combés and Its Historical Impact", *Philippine Studies* 29 (1981): 312.

59 *Documenta Malucensia*, 3:347.

60 Rodao, "Restos de la presencia ibérica", p. 248.

61 Clercq, *Ternate*, 111n34.

62 Rodao, "Restos de la presencia ibérica", p. 249.

63 Argensola, *Conquista de las Islas Malucas*, pp. 158 and 186; Gaspar de San

Agustín, *Conquista de las Islas Filipinas, 1565–1615*, edited by Manuel Merino (Madrid: Consejo Superior de Investigaciones Científicas, Instituto Enrique Florez, 1975), bk. 2, chap. 38, p. 549.

64 Pedro Sarmiento, "Relación de la fuerza, poder y artilleria que tiene el Rey de Terrenate", Maluku [Tidore], 30 April 1584, Patronato 46, ramo 18, AGI, in Colín and Chirino, *Labor Evangélica*, 2:41.

65 "A discourse of the present state of the Moluccos, anexed to the former Journall [Voyage of George Spielbergen], extracted out of Apollonius Schot of Middleborough" [1617], in *Hakluytus Posthumus or Purchas His Pilgrimes*, vol. 2, edited by Samuel Purchas (Glasgow: MacLehose, 1905), p. 227.

66 Manuel Lobato, "Implementar a União Ibérica na Ásia: O relato da viagem de Francisco de Dueñas de Manila a Maluco em 1582", in *O Reino, as Ilhas e o Mar-Oceano: Estudos em Homenagem a Artur Teodoro de Matos*, vol. 2, edited by Avelino de Freitas de Meneses and João Paulo Oliveira e Costa (Ponta Delgada and Lisbon: Universidade dos Açores, Centro de História de Além-Mar, 2007), p. 803.

67 Francisco de Sousa, *Oriente Conquistado a Jesus Christo pelos Padres da Companhia de Jesus da Provincia de Goa*, edited by M. Lopes de Almeida (Porto: Lello & Irmão, 1978), p. 1102.

68 "Enformação da christandade de Maluco dada ao P.e Provincial, do P. Antonio Marta no anno 1588", in *Documenta Malucensia*, vol. 2, *1577–1606*, edited by Hubert Jacobs (Rome: Institutum Historicum Societatis Iesu, 1980), p. 268. Also in *Documentação para a História das Missões do Padroado Português do Oriente: Insulíndia*, vol. 5, *1580–1595*, edited by A. Basílio de Sá (Lisbon: Agência Geral do Ultramar, 1958), p. 116. Argensola, *Conquista de las Islas Malucas*, p. 95.

69 A. Botelho de Sousa, *Subsídios para a História Militar-Marítima da Índia* (*1585–1669*), vol. 1, *1585–1605* (Lisbon, 1930), p. 613.

70 Fernão Guerreiro, *Relação Anual das Coisas que Fizeram os Padres da Companhia de Jesus nas suas Missões … nos anos de 1600 a 1609*, vol. 2, edited by Artur Viegas (Coimbra: Imprensa da Universidade, 1931), p. 308.

71 Informaciones de Lucas de Vergara Gaviria, 1611, AGI, *Filipinas* 60, no. 12.

72 Cristóbal de Azcoeta to Juan de Silva, Governor of the Philippines, on the condition of the forces under his command, Ternate, 23 April 1610, in *Cartas del Virrey Luis de Velasco* 5, Mexico 28, no. 2, AGI, apud Ramerini, *Le fortezze spagnole*.

73 Actually the Dutch mentioned thirteen men and two guns. See *The Philippine Islands: 1493–1898*, vol. 15, edited by Emma Helen Blair and James Alexander Robertson (Cleveland: A.H. Clark Company, 1904), p. 325.

74 *Correspondencia de Don Gerónimo de Silva … sobre el Estado de las Islas Molucas*, edited by Marquis de Miraflores and Miguel Silva (Madrid, 1868), pp. 104–13 ("Documentos Inéditos para la Historia de España", p. 52).

75 "The Voyage of Captaine Saris in the Cloave, to the Ile of Japan, What Befell

in the Way: Observations of the Dutch and Spaniards in the Moluccas",
in *Hakluytus Posthumus or Purchas His Pilgrimes*, vol. 3, edited by Samuel Purchas
(Glasgow: MacLehose, 1905), p. 426.

[76] Father André Simi to the General of the Jesuits in Rome, Ternate, 17 June 1614,
in *Documenta Malucensia*, 3:268.

[77] "Tanto de carta que el gobernador don Gerónimo de Silva escribió á el rey de
Tidore", Ternate, 17 November 1613, in *Correspondencia de Don Gerónimo de
Silva*, pp. 178–79 ("Documentos Inéditos para la Historia de España", p. 52);
see also Ramerini, *Le fortezze spagnole*.

[78] Anonymous, "Relação breve da ilha de Ternate", 1:167, and repeated in 2:53.

[79] Pedro de Monte Mayor to the king, Cochin, 14 January 1533, in Sá,
Documentação, 1:266–67. See Castanheda, *História do Descobrimento* bk. 7,
chap. 42, 2:441, and bk. 7, chap. 6, 2:569; Gaspar Correia, *Lendas da Índia*,
vol. 3, edited by R.J. de Lima Felner (Lisbon: Typographia da Academia Real
das Sciencias de Lisboa, 1862), pp. 175 and 360; Rebelo, "Informação", text 2,
3:416; Couto, *Década Quarta da Ásia*, bk. 3, chap. 3, 1:144; and "Extracto de
la navegación que hizo el general Alvaro de Saavedra con la armada de tres naos
remitidas por Hernán Cortés desde las costas meridionales de Nueva España a
las Mollucas en los anos de 1527 y 1528", in *Obras de D. Martin Fernández de
Navarrete*, vol. 3, edited by Carlos Seco Serrano (Madrid: Atlas, 1964), p. 57.

[80] Vicente da Fonseca to king, Maluco [Ternate], 8 December 1531, in Sá,
Documentação, 1:245.

[81] Consuelo Varela, ed., *El Viaje de Don Ruy López de Villalobos a las Islas del
Poniente, 1542–1548* (Milan: Cisalpino-Goliardica, 1983), p. 144.

[82] See *Documenta Malucensia*, 3:450n3.

[83] "Memorial dado al rey ... por D. Juan Grau y Monfalcon" [1637], in *Colección
de Documentos Inéditos... de las Antiguas Posesiones Españolas de América y
Oceanía*, vol. 6, edited by Luiz Torres de Mendoza (Madrid, 1888), p. 399; in
translation in Emma Helen Blair, Edward Gaylord Bourne and James Alexander
Robertson, eds., *The Philippine Islands: 1493–1898*, vol. 27 (Cleveland: A.H.
Clark Company, 1905), p. 105.

[84] Juan de Esquível to Philip III, Ternate, 2 May 1606, Patronato 47, ramo 21, 1,
1–32, AGI, partially in Colín and Chirino, *Labor Evangélica*, 2:56.

[85] Bohigian, "Life on the Rim", p. 55.

[86] *Correspondencia de Don Gerónimo de Silva*, p. 297; "The Voyage of Captaine
Saris", 3:432; and Sousa, *Subsídios para a história militar-marítima*, 2:321.

[87] Father João Baptista to the General of the Jesuits in Rome, Ternate, 14 March
1613, in *Documenta Malucensia*, 3:246.

[88] Ramerini, *Le fortezze spagnole*.

[89] Ibid.

[90] Bohigian, "Life on the Rim", pp. 56 and 258.

[91] *Documenta Malucensia*, 3:617.

[92] Gregorio de San Esteban, "Historia de las islas Molucas", apud Lorenzo Perez,

"Historia de las misiones de los Franciscanos en las islas Malucas y Célebes", *Archivum Franciscanum Historicum* 7 (1914): 430n4.

[93]   Bohigian, "Life on the Rim", p. 54.

[94]   Andaya, *The World of Maluku*, p. 227.

[95]   *Documenta Malucensia*, p. 242n8.

[96]   Azcoeta to Silva, 23 April 1610. See note 72.

[97]   Andaya, *The World of Maluku*, p. 227.

[98]   Anonymous, "Relação breve da ilha de Ternate", 1:168, and repeated in 2:54.

[99]   Jacobs, "The *Discurso Politico del Gobierno Maluco*", p. 328n55.

[100] Bohigian believes that San José de Marieco can be Tomanyira, relying on the testimony of Francisco Ezquerra, commander of San José between 1615 and 1617. See Bohigian, "Life on the Rim", p. 55. Marco Ramerini, in the sections about Tomanira and Marieco El Chico, cross-reference each other, showing a map where both names appear in the same place; see Ramerini, *Le fortezze spagnole*. Earlier, Botelho de Sousa already indicated that Tahula was formerly called Marieco el Chico. See Sousa, *Subsídios para a história militar-marítima*, 2:322.

[101] *Documenta Malucensia*, p. 268n3.

[102] Father Manuel Barradas to the General of the Jesuits, Cochin, 10 December 1616, *Documenta Malucensia*, p. 315.

[103] Father Manuel Ribeiro to Fajardo de Tenza, governor of the Philippines, Cavite, 10 August 1618, *Documenta Malucensia*, p. 377.

[104] Certificate by Captain Diego de Quiñones y Arguelles, Tolo, 1 August 1613, in Colín and Chirino, *Labor Evangélica*, 2:571n.

[105] *Documenta Malucensia*, 3:347n4.

[106] Ribeiro to Fajardo de Tenza, 10 August 1618, p. 377.

[107] See, in the *Correspondencia de Don Gerónimo de Silva*, the letters from the king of Tidore (18 November 1615, p. 331) and from the governor and other Spanish officers to the governor of the Philippines, Juan de Silva (25 June 1616, pp. 374–75 and 378); see also the services record of Juan de Origuey, apud Ramerini, *Le fortezze spagnole*, including note 46.

9

THE INFLUENCE OF PORTUGUESE MUSICAL CULTURE IN SOUTHEAST ASIA IN THE SIXTEENTH AND SEVENTEENTH CENTURIES

Christian Storch

Portugal's encounter with the world has in many respects already been the subject of academic research. However, relatively little research has yet been done on Portugal's musical influence as a result of the development of, for instance, its Southeast Asian centres in Goa, Malacca, Macao and Timor. Until today, there have been only few studies of musical life in these centres in the sixteenth and seventeenth centuries. From the time of its first encounter with Portugal through Vasco da Gama's arrival in 1498, Southeast Asia faced a persistent European attempt to control, to dominate and to proselytize in the countries between India and the Philippines. Portuguese and other European cultural and musical influences necessarily accompanied the political and religious conquests from the very beginning.

This study is part of a post-doctoral project that seeks to summarize the hitherto existing research on this subject, prior to a comprehensive study of Portuguese musical culture in its Southeast Asian urban centres in the sixteenth and seventeenth centuries. The aim of this chapter is to examine how a musical culture was established, how it interacted with local music traditions, and how both Portuguese and local cultures influenced each other over the long term.

It will also try to show what kind of role music played at the intersection of missionary work, urban entertainment and imperial representation, being a means for both cultural exchange and political segregation.

"WE COME IN SEARCH OF CHRISTIANS AND SPICES": THE BEGINNINGS OF MUSICAL INFLUENCE IN CALICUT AND GOA, INDIA

Whether or not the quotation above represents the truth, it nonetheless defines what Vasco da Gama and his companions were looking to achieve when they entered Calicut on 20 May 1498: the spread of Christianity and trade. According to A.J.R. Russell-Wood, "the half century after Vasco da Gama's arrival in Calicut (May 1498) was characterised by trade and missionary activities rather than exploration *per se* in the East."[1] Right from the beginning the attempt to spread the Christian faith — and, of course, to find the Saint Thomas Christians — had been accompanied by the fight against Muslim culture and its representatives, who had already been trading with India for several centuries. The question reported to have been posed by some Arabs to the newcomers — "What the hell are you doing here?" — and the reply — "We come in search of Christians and spices" — marked the beginning of a cultural and musical conflict that was to continue for more than a century.

On their ships the Portuguese travellers brought not only presents from King Manuel I, along with weapons, but also missionaries and European musical instruments as a means of proselytization and to combat boredom among the sailors during the long journey by sea, respectively. After their arrival in Calicut, da Gama and some of his companions met the ruler of the area on 28 May 1498. Da Gama's diary reveals how the Portuguese used their instruments as a demonstration of power: "and we all went there very well dressed and took our weapons, trumpets and many flags with us".[2] According to the diary, the king of Calicut welcomed the Portuguese with "many drums, trumpets and shalms".[3] The first intercultural music parade between India and Portugal had taken place.

The first expedition of Pedro Álvares Cabral to India, with thirteen ships and seventeen clerics, arrived in Calicut on 13 September 1500. Among these clerics were eight diocesan priests, eight Franciscans, and one curate. Among the Franciscans were the famous Portuguese theologian Friar Henrique Soares de Coimbra and the organ player Friar Matteu, the latter of whom is said to have been able to play an organ on one of the ships.[4] Cabral, like his successors in the following years, used music to impress potential trade partners as well as to irritate enemies through the extensive and noisy use of trumpets, drums and other instruments. Several sources describe the use of musical instruments on specific occasions, such as the landing of Lopo Soares in Cannanore, which was accompanied by six "trombetas" (trumpets) and "com uns orgãos e um tangedor" (with an organ and a player) in 1504/05,[5] or the conquest of Goa in November 1510 by Afonso de Albuquerque, which was accompanied by the sound of "trombetas".[6]

THE FIRST CHURCHES AND THE MISSION OF MUSIC

The musicologists Victor Coelho and Antonio Alexandre Bispo mention documents from 1512 and 1514, respectively, which give evidence for the beginning of choral singing.[7] One of these documents is a letter of 17 December 1514 written by the Malacca-based curate Afonso Martins to Portugal's king, Dom Manuel I, in which he asks for chant books in order to use them for Sunday masses in Goa. Martins complains about the lack of chant in one of the churches he visited, most likely the first version of the church of Santa Catarina, the first and only church in Goa at that time. He also asks for books and bells for his own church in Malacca, mentioning that he had been looking for chant books all over the city without any success and that the bells for his church had not yet been sent.[8]

In his dissertation on church buildings in Old Goa, the architect António Manuel Nunes Pereira quotes a letter of 25 November 1514 from Friar Domingo de Sousa to the Portuguese king, in which he states that the construction of the main parish church, Santa Catarina, is about to begin: it is to have three naves, one crossing [sic], a massively vaulted chapel, a choir loft above the main entrance and a bell tower. This type of church was designed in the so-called "Manueline" style that was kept for the later churches of Espírito Santo and Nossa Senhora do Rosário.[9] We now have evidence that the church of Santa Catarina was designed for musical purposes, and Martins' letter reveals that its predecessor, built of loam and straw, had not been suitable for that. What is interesting here is that the church of Santa Catarina was located on the site previously held by the Muslim mosque — in fact, the mosque was occupied by the Portuguese and changed into a church, the first version of Santa Catarina.[10]

The first monastery in Goa was the São Francisco. In a letter of 27 October 1520 from the Franciscan Friar António to Dom Manuel I, he confirms the receipt of chant books for the monastery Santo António in Cochin. He further describes the laying of the foundation stone of the Goan monastery on 2 February 1520. After vespers, there was a procession to the place where the monastery was to be built; on the way back, the Te Deum was sung. As Bispo points out, at the time of Friar António, religious services were already being celebrated in Goa as they were in Portugal, due to the fact that more Franciscan clerics had arrived. According to him, the parish was then able to celebrate the inauguration of the first bishop of Goa with a ceremonial procession.[11]

AN ASSESSMENT OF SOURCE MATERIALS

As far as the sources mentioned by Bispo and other researchers such as Coelho reveal, no musical examples have survived in either Goa or Malacca, nor in Portuguese or Jesuit archives. At present, it seems that the archive situation is similar in Macao and Timor. Therefore, a study of the Portuguese musical influence in Southeast Asia in the sixteenth and seventeenth centuries must rely on other sources that give us hints about the subject. One of these sources is Portuguese musical culture itself, the study of which presents another obstacle, since many manuscripts from the period in question were lost after the earthquake in Lisbon in 1755.

One of these manuscripts was the music collection of Dom João IV. Fortunately, an index from 1649 that lists a part of this collection has survived. The musicologist Cristina Urchueguía has worked on this index for the Répértoire International des Sources Musicales (RISM). In her introduction, she argues that some of the compositions can be dated back to the first half of the sixteenth century and therefore would already have been present at court before João was crowned in 1640. Such compositions are worthy of our particular attention since they might be typical of musical culture at the time when Portugal began to expand its power in the direction of Southeast Asia, although we do not know for certain when such compositions reached the court of the Portuguese king.

At first glance, the collection contains music by three major groups of composers: Italians, Franco-Flemish and Portuguese/Spanish. Music by English and German composers can also be found. A closer look at the collection, however, reveals that there are some compositions from north of the Alps that need further explanation, namely works by Orlando di Lasso (Munich) and Hieronymus Praetorius (Hamburg). The presence of masses by a Protestant composer from Hamburg, unfortunately, cannot be explained here. However, Lasso's works might have found their way to Lisbon by any one of a number of routes. These include a possible Benedictine connection linking the composer Jacob Reiner with Portugal: his compositions also appear in the index, and he was one of Lasso's students. Reiner was master of chapel in the monastery of Weingarten near Stuttgart where he composed several masses, such as the *Missa Stephanus plenus gratiae* for eight voices, which was contained in the collection of Dom João IV. Another possible way by which music of northern European and other composers could have reached the Portuguese court was via the master of chapel in Madrid from 1580 onwards, George de la Hèle, who is said to have brought the music of Palestrina and Clemens non Papa, among others, to the Spanish/Portuguese court. Regardless of the exact route by which the music of northern European, Franco-Flemish or Italian composers found its way to the Portuguese court, by the mid-seventeenth century there must have been a sizeable collection of compositions both for secular and religious purposes.

It is reasonable to assume that musical life in the Southeast Asian Portuguese centres was influenced by developments in the mother country. The main cultural and musical centres in Portugal were the cities of Lisbon and Porto, as well as the monasteries and universities of Évora and Coimbra. Although Portuguese music of the time seems to have been a determining factor in sacred and profane musical life in the colonies, and therefore is of global importance, relatively little research has yet been done on the music "back home". The most recent overview of Portugal's musical history dates back to 1992 and is a book by the musicologist Manuel Carlos de Brito.[12] However, there are also case studies, books and articles dedicated to specific topics within the history of music in Portugal, some of which might be helpful for the present study.

The Portuguese musicologist Maria Augusta Barbosa mentions several Portuguese composers who played a particularly important role in the development of music in their time. These composers are Vicente Lusitano, Duarte Lobo, Manuel Cardoso, Filipe de Magalhães, Diogo Dias Melgás and João Lourenço Rebelo, some of whom also appear in the Lisbon index from 1649, along with music theorists like António Fernandes and João Álvares Frouvo.[13] Understanding what and how these composers wrote may help us understand the musical life of Portuguese immigrants in Southeast Asia, at least when they were among themselves.

Cristina Urchueguía's monograph on the polyphonic mass in the Golden Age, as well as her contribution to the RISM with listed chant book collections from Braga, Coimbra and Lisbon, among other locales, is also of importance to this research project. The fact that "one of the most eccentric musical characters that Portugal has ever produced",[14] the composer André de Escobar, spent several years in India, provides another clue as regards the export of Portuguese musical culture to the Estado da Índia. As far as we know, André de Escobar lived in Coimbra as a shalm player, and became quite successful there:

> He was appointed first musician of the cathedral of Evora; and afterwards he held the same appointment in the cathedral of Coimbra. When he played in public, the first professors of the art used to flock to hear him, and express their astonishment at the masterly manner in which he played the most difficult compositions; for they imagined it was impossible to produce such delightful harmony from an instrument heretofore thought incapable of arresting the attention of a polite audience, namely, the bag-pipes. He visited India, where he spent several years; and was admired by many of the native princes for his melodious tones. There is extant a treatise of his on the art of playing on the bag-pipes.[15]

Unfortunately, the treatise on playing bagpipes and shalms is lost. It may have contained information on instruments from India as described by Vasco da Gama at the beginning of the century.

A similar, but perhaps less striking problem appears with regard to another family of musical instruments, the keyboard. In an article entitled "A Portuguese Clavichord in Sixteenth-Century Japan?",[16] the Japanese musicologist Minoru Takahashi reflects on the history of Western and, in particular, Portuguese musical instruments in and on their way to Japan. The author traces the beginnings of the Portuguese-Japanese musical encounter to the first instrument that was brought to Japan by Francisco Xavier in 1551. According to a Japanese source to which Takahashi refers, the instrument was similar to a thirteen-string Japanese psaltery or *koto*, "on which can be played in 5 tunes [modes] or 12 modes [tunes] but it can be played without touching the strings [directly]".[17] Takahashi is not sure whether the correct English translation for the respective Japanese words is tunes or modes. His further explanations refer to the type of instrument that the Japanese source might have described. Many hints lead him to the conclusion that the instrument presented in 1551 was a "three and half octave clavichord made in Portugal",[18] most likely fretted and with the compass $E - a^2$.

Unfortunately, we do not have any more examples of clavichords made in Portugal during that time. However, worldwide at least five instruments from the sixteenth century have survived which all share common features. There is agreement among musicologists that sixteenth-century clavichords shared a similar design throughout Europe, except for some minor details. A painting inside the church of São João de Tarouca in Portugal shows an angel playing a clavichord that is elaborately ornamented.[19] The painting is from 1535/40. It is therefore likely that an instrument that was brought from Portugal and supposed to both impress and please a Japanese lord, who was in close contact with the emperor, boasted a similar design and ornamentation.

More interesting for the present study, however, is the fact that the clavichord must have had at least one stopover in Goa and perhaps two more in Malacca and Macao. Since the sailing route from Portugal to Japan went via Goa and led through the Straits of Malacca, we can assume that the introduction of such instruments to the cities by the Jesuits and other Portuguese had occurred previously, since Xavier used to live in Goa and Malacca. Takahashi himself mentions the third Jesuit mission that left Goa for Japan in 1554, bringing "one book for *canto llano* [plain chant] and one book for *canto de organo* [figured music] to Japan. As for the book for *canto de organo*, it was not only used for choral instruction, but also for instructing or practising keyboard instruments [and others]."[20] The Jesuit mission in Goa, and, most likely, in Malacca as well, must therefore already have had a kind of systematic music education with chant books and books for instrumental practice, on the model of the system that the Franciscans had introduced shortly after the Portuguese conquests: "By 1545, musical training and its attendant ceremony in Goa had become institutionalised as part of a pedagogical system for the parochial schools that all boys were required to attend."[21]

THE BRAZILIAN WAY? THE MISSIONARIES AND THEIR WAY OF UTILIZING MUSIC

The process of proselytization that accompanied the conquest not only of Southeast Asia faced problems that were in urgent need of solution. Such problems had largely to do with the different cultural backgrounds of the Portuguese and indigenous populations, an obstacle to missionary work that also applied to musical culture. The answer to such problems was either to use force against the indigenous culture and suppress it, or to try and reach a compromise. Recently discovered sources from Brazil demonstrate, for instance, how missionaries tried to approach the indigenous population by altering the musical patterns of their own sacred music in order to be more attractive to the locals.

One of the key figures in Jesuit missionary work in Brazil was Padre José de Anchieta, the father of Catholicism in the country, who co-founded the city of São Paulo in 1554. The sources mentioned are attributed to Anchieta and people around him in the middle and the second half of the sixteenth century, a time when the Jesuits had already discovered the advantages of using music in their proselytizing in which children and young native people were targeted.[22]

The success of the Franciscans in Goa, who from the beginning did not hesitate to utilize music for missionary purposes, became a model for the Jesuit missions, and Francisco Xavier, who lived in Goa from 1542 to 1545 before he moved to Malacca, is the key figure here. Padre Francisco Pérez mentions Xavier's influence, particularly as regards the musical behaviour of the young inhabitants of Goa, in a letter from 1548:

> The boys of the Portuguese and many girls, male and female slaves have a good command of the doctrine and are used to singing it at home in the evening; so that one who walks through the city in the evening after the Ave Maria has the pleasure of hearing from one house or another the doctrine and the declaration of articles just as our Father master Francisco had introduced them; and they are so happy to do so that they sing everywhere and anytime to praise the Lord.

> (Los hijos de los portugueses y muchas hijas, esclavos y esclavas seben ya toda esta doctrina, y tienen por costumbre de noche en casa de dizerla cantando, que, yendo de noche después del Ave Maria por la ciudad holgaran de oír en una casa y en otra dizer la doctrina a la declaración de los articolos de la fee la qual costunbre le dexó el nuestro Padre maestro Francisco; y andan tan encendidos en esto que por las [calles] y por onde van, van cantando y loando a Dios.)[23]

Xavier had obviously used music as a bridge to the indigenous population from the very beginning. The success that is mentioned in the letter quoted seems to have confirmed Xavier's approach, just as the scores found in Brazil reveal a musical life within the Jesuit community there. Such letters, and the reported export of musical instruments and chant books from Goa to further East Asian countries, lead to the assumption that, although musical manuscripts from Goa and Malacca are unlikely to have remained, there must have been a rich sacred musical life there. Xavier himself provided a report on the first Mass of Afonso de Castro on 19 June 1549, which was celebrated as a sung Mass.[24] Such a Jesuit-sung Mass must have sounded relatively similar to those celebrated in Portuguese and other European Jesuit parishes.

In a dissertation entitled "Jesuits and Music: The European Tradition, 1547–1622", the musicologist Thomas Frank Kennedy mentions the manner of singing adopted by the Jesuits in order to keep the music plain and the text understandable: the fauxbourdon (false bass).[25] Dating back to the first half of the fifteenth century and probably invented by the Franco-Flemish composer Guillaume Dufay, the fauxbourdon practice had already passed its peak, but still seemed to meet the needs and desires of Ignatius of Loyola: "Ignatius hoped that this would satisfy the Pope in regard to the singing of the office.... This was the type of singing that was used in Rome since so many of the students at the Roman College and the German College knew how to sing this way.... [F]alsobordone fitted most perfectly during this period with the Council of Trent's ideas on liturgical music and its performance."[26] With the exception of plain Gregorian chant, which always had the ideological advantage of making the text easier to understand (at least for those in the parish who could understand Latin), a simple singing in one (Gregorian) or two voices (with fauxbourdon) must have proved a great support to missionary work in countries and areas where the polyphonic style of Christian liturgical singing was totally alien to the indigenous population.

The strategy for proselytization adopted by the Jesuits in the Portuguese settlements in Southeast Asia was geared to the teaching of children, since they were the most open-minded and easy to influence. Another report by Padre Francisco Pérez from 21 January 1555 mentions that the children did not live with the clerics but with their families, in order to spread the missionary message among the slaves at home.[27] But the missionaries taught orphans, too. Here the societies of the Jesuits, the Franciscans and the Dominicans functioned on the one hand as supporters of the Portuguese system of conquest and suppression and on the other as Christian humanitarians caring for orphans (who nevertheless were only orphaned because their parents had been killed in battles and skirmishes with the Portuguese). According to Bispo, the convent schools of Cranganor and Santa Fé de Goa permanently taught around eighty orphans of non-Christian parents about Christian belief. As well as the orphans, children of Portuguese origin and the local ruling class also learned at these convent schools, being taught in playing the organ and singing as well.[28]

Since as far as we know no scores or musical manuscripts have survived, it is not possible to know for certain whether the Jesuits in Southeast Asia used methods similar to their colleagues in Brazil, although Coelho refers to a Goan source that mentions the use of harpsichords, trumpets, flutes, shalms and organs together with "instrumentos da terra", that is, local instruments of the native people of Goa.[29] With such a mix of instrumentation, the music would of course have sounded different. The missionaries in Brazil in general and Anchieta in particular "set Christian beliefs to native tunes and ... capitalise[d] on the Indian's [sic] marvelous musical talent".[30] They thereby created an intercultural mix of European Renaissance music and the Tupi culture of the indigenous Brazilians. Such intercultural encounters went so far that the representatives of the Society of Jesus felt forced to intervene: for the clerics it had become unclear who was proselytizing whom — the missionaries the Tupi people, or vice versa.

The first bishop sent to Brazil, Pero Fernandes Sardinha, found these developments alarming. It seemed to him that the Jesuits were being converted to paganism. He wrote a letter to the superior of the Society of Jesus in Lisbon, asking for an immediate remedy, and soon embarked for Portugal in order to sort out the situation.[31]

Such documents are not currently available for a Southeast Asian context. We can therefore only assume that musical practice in Goa and Malacca, and perhaps later in Macau and other Portuguese centres, was of a similar mixture, with the sound characterized by the musical instruments in use in that region. In a liturgical context within a Christian parish at least, musical life may have followed the Portuguese model more strongly than in a missionary or secular context.

The ardour and emphasis with which the missionaries talk about the success of their efforts — especially among the children, who reportedly sang in the streets and in their homes the whole day — was obviously transmitted back to the European brothers: "The key was that music drew people to church, and once in church the Jesuits could preach to them and hear their confessions. Musical activity was almost always referred to in these terms; there are terms that help the apostolic effectiveness of the order."[32] However, the reports and letters from Goa, Macao and elsewhere in Portuguese Asia should be approached with caution. It might be that such behaviour from boys and girls in Goa was true of the mid-sixteenth century, but not over the long term.

CONCLUSION: PERSPECTIVES INTO THE SEVENTEENTH CENTURY AND BEYOND

The German Protestant missionary Johann Christian Sartorius reports from Goa in the year 1735:

> When I came here, our children could only sing three songs that were sung on Sundays, but in such a way that the true melody was hardly recognizable. Our colleagues had already taught them for almost a year ...; however, all efforts seemed to have been pointless ... because they always stayed with their monotony, when they were supposed to sing high, they just sang louder.... We wrote the keys differently and drew everything as a staircase to make them recognise what "high" meant. Item we stood by a staircase and when we sang a tone higher we climbed one step higher, and then down again.
>
> (Als ich hierher kam, konnten unsere Kinder nur drey Lieder singen, welche alle Sonntage gesungen wurden, aber so, dass man von der rechten Melodie wenig hören konnte. Unser Mitarbeiter hatte sie nun schon fast

ein Jahr lang informiret ...; es schien aber alle Mühe vergebens zu seyn ... weil sie immer bey ihrer monotonie blieben, wenn sie hoch singen sollten, nur ein wenig stärcker schryen.... Wir schrieben die claves anders und mahltens als eine Treppe, ob sie es so fassen wollten, was hoch sey. Item wir stelleten uns an eine Treppe, und wenn wir einen Ton höher sungen, stiegen wir auch eine Stufe an der Treppe in die Höhe, und denn wieder nieder.[33]

Obviously, not much of the Portuguese proselytization efforts from the past two centuries had remained among the local people, although Bartholomäus Ziegenbalg, the first Protestant missionary in India in 1706, reports that he had to learn Portuguese to communicate with the local people.[34] Considering the relatively small percentage of the population in Southeast Asia in general and in India in particular that are Roman Catholics, from a long-term perspective the Portuguese presence and especially the missionary work were rather unsuccessful: according to Coelho, "by the early seventeenth century it had become clear that the Jesuits were falling far short of their goal in converting Indians to Christianity."[35] The reasons for this relatively insignificant legacy are diverse and have led scholars to formulate the following main arguments.[36]

First, unlike some areas of South America and Africa, the Asian countries were kingdoms with a clearly defined and working infrastructure long before the Portuguese conquest. Furthermore, the Portuguese mainly stayed along the strategic trade routes and did not occupy whole countries.[37] However, they utilized conflicts between local groups for their own benefit — "benefit" here mainly meaning the fostering and support of trade and economic development. Around the year 1600, the Dutch and the English began to explore their own commercial routes to Asia and thus became serious competitors not only to the Portuguese trading system. Such conflicts erupted into battles and massacres, accompanied by the attempt to proselytize in the region with the new Protestant reformed faith that both the Dutch and the English professed, albeit in different and occasionally conflicting ways.

In his travel reports from India between 1672 and 1674, the French spy Abbé Carré, "an imperial defender of French culture and Christian superiority in the vast, heathen wilderness of India",[38] mentions a concert of former slaves who had been under Portuguese patronage before they were employed by a Dutch nobleman:

They had passed their youth in slavery with some Portuguese nobles, where they had learnt to strum guitar and sing some airs, almost as melodious as penitential psalms.... One tortured a harp, another strummed a guitar, a third scraped on a violin, and two others, having no other instruments but their voices, joined in with the rest in such a way that one could not listen to their harmonies without pity and compassion.[39]

Despite the very arrogant and pejorative tone in Abbé's utterance, some details of the musical practice that was obviously taught by the Portuguese are worthy of comment. The instrumentation of a harp, a guitar (probably the Spanish-Portuguese *vihuela* or *viola*), and a violin plus two singers suggests that the musicians might have played and sung a *villancico* (in Spanish) or *vilancete* (in Portuguese), one of the most important musical genres in Spanish and Portuguese culture at that time, comparable only to the Italian madrigal, though much less discussed, indeed neglected, within current historical musicology. The spread of *villancico* playing and singing among the *fidalgos* has not yet been researched.

The second reason often stated for the lack of an abiding legacy of Portuguese influence in Southeast Asia is political: specifically, the political union with Spain from 1580 to 1640. During that time, and accompanied by the appearance of the mighty Dutch and English, the Portuguese began to concentrate their efforts more and more on their colony in Brazil. This was due to mineral and natural resources that had been found there, such as gold, diamonds, ivory, coffee, sugar and so on.[40]

Third, although Portugal initially led the seaborne expansion of Western Europe in the fifteenth and sixteenth centuries, its resource base was ultimately no match for England, Spain or the Netherlands, especially in terms of the human capital it was able to commit to its huge empire. Some authors assume that this lack of manpower is the real reason for the non-durable influence of the Portuguese in Southeast Asia. The musicologist Margaret Kartomi argues that in the case of Malacca, the Portuguese influence there has lasted longer and more intensively than in other parts of Southeast Asia, especially due to the "policy of the Portuguese government in the sixteenth Century to encourage their men to marry local women and settle down in their new countries".[41] To satisfy their need for musical entertainment, she believes that "the Portuguese had brought large quantities of musical instruments to Malacca, especially plucked and bowed strings, which probably included alto violins called *viola* in Portugal and *biola* in Malay".[42] Such a policy is likely to have been practised in Goa, Macao, and elsewhere as well.

At the end of the day, the lack of manpower of those "purely" Portuguese in origin and Christian in belief as it was taught in Europe might also have had an influence on Jesuit mission work. Although the first Jesuits in Goa and Southeast Asia were mainly of Portuguese and Spanish origin, in due course more and more missionaries from other European countries went to Asia. The worldwide network of the Jesuits thus also manifested itself in a shift in the supply of musical material. A source referred to by Coelho names Giacomo Carissimi as a composer whose music had been played in Goa.[43] Carissimi was master of chapel at the church St. Apollinaris of the Collegium Germanicum in Rome, "to this day one of the most famous Jesuit colleges in Europe",[44] from 1629 until his death in 1674. How his music went to Goa is unknown, but it is likely that it took a direct route from Rome without being received in Portugal or Spain first, especially since there is no entry for Carissimi in the Lisbon index from 1649 or other indices, such as those of Braga, Porto or Coimbra.

Nonetheless, there are of course remnants of the Portuguese presence in Southeast Asia that have survived over centuries, and some of them are musical. Victor Coelho mentions that in Goa, a parish consisting of nearly seventy thousand Christians, persisted until the early nineteenth century.[45] He also states that "the itemised College accounts [for the Colégio de São Paulo] for the last two decades of the seventeenth century show regular payments for an organist, as well as for viol and strings, a combination of instruments capable of accompanying small- and large-scale genres that was used in Spanish and Portuguese churches at home and abroad."[46] Margaret Kartomi has found a still extant synthesis of Portuguese and Malay musical structures.[47] And the tune "Jingkly Nona" of the Kristang culture in Malacca and Singapore is living evidence of intercultural encounters in the past.

Notes

1   A.J.R. Russell-Wood, *The Portuguese Empire, 1415–1808: A World on the Move* (Baltimore: The Johns Hopkins University Press, 1998), p. 9.

2   The quotation "muj-tos tanbores e anafie e cha/ramella" is from *Diário da Viagem de Vasco da Gama* (Porto: Livraria Civilização, 1945), p. 39, cited in Antonio Alexandre Bispo, *Grundlagen christlicher Musikkultur in der außereuropäischen Welt der Neuzeit. Der Raum des früheren portugiesischen Patronatsrechts*, vol. 2 (Rome: Consociatio internationalis musicae sacrae, 1988), p. 544.

3   Ibid.

4   Antonio Ybot León, "Los franciscanos, pioneros de la fé en el Brasil (1500–1538)", in *Actas do Congresso Internacional de História dos Descobrimentos*, vol. 4, edited by José Caeiro da Matta (Lisbon: Comissão Executiva dos Comemorações do V Centenário da Morte do Infante D. Henrique, 1961), p. 142.

5   Fernão Lopes de Castanheda, *História do Descobrimento e Conquista da India*

pelos Portugueses (Coimbra: Imprensa da Universidade, 1924), cited in Bispo, *Grundlagen*, p. 553.

6 Ibid., p. 555.

7 Ibid., p. 559; and Victor Anand Coelho, "Music in New Worlds", in *The Cambridge History of Seventeenth Century Music*, edited by Tim Carter and John Butt (Cambridge: Cambridge University Press, 2005), p. 99.

8 Bispo, *Grundlagen*, pp. 559–60.

9 António Manuel Nunes Pereira, "Die Kirchenbauten in Alt-Goa in der zweiten Hälfte des 16. und in den ersten Jahrzehnten des 17. Jahrhunderts", Ph.D. dissertation, Rheinisch-Westfälische Technische Hochschule Aachen, 2002), pp. 49–51.

10 Ibid., p. 52.

11 Bispo, *Grundlagen*, pp. 560–61.

12 Manuel Carlos de Brito, *História da Música Portuguesa* (Lisbon: Universidade Aberta, 1992).

13 Maria Augusta Barbosa, "Einführung in die Musikgeschichte Portugals bis zur Mitte des 17. Jahrhunderts", in *Ars Musica, Musica Scientia: Festschrift Heinrich Hüschen zum fünfundsechzigsten Geburtstag am 2. März 1980*, edited by Detlef Altenburg (Cologne: Gitarre-und-Laute Verl.-Ges., 1980), pp. 22–29.

14 *The Edinburgh Magazine or Literary Miscellany*, vol. 11 (London: James Symington, 1798), p. 429.

15 Ibid.

16 Gunnshoruiju, *The Record of Yoshitaka Ohuchi*, vol. 13, p. 411, cited in Minoru Takahashi, "A Portuguese Clavichord in Sixteenth-Century Japan?", *The Galpin Society Journal* 54 (May 2001): 116–23.

17 Takahashi, "A Portuguese Clavichord", p. 118.

18 Ibid., p. 123.

19 For an image of this clavichord, see Bernard Brauchli, *The Clavichord* (Cambridge: Cambridge University Press, 1998), p. 74.

20 Takahashi, "A Portuguese Clavichord", p. 123.

21 Coelho, "Music in New Worlds", p. 93.

22 See John W. O'Malley, *The First Jesuits* (Cambridge, MA: Harvard University Press, 1993), p. 122.

23 Letter of Padre Francisco Pérez from 1548, in *Documenta Indica*, vol. 1, *1540–1549*, edited by Joseph Wicki (Rome: Institutum Historicum Societus Iesu, 1975), p. 343, cited in Bispo, *Grundlagen*, p. 605.

24 Cited in Bispo, *Grundlagen*, p. 605.

25 Thomas Frank Kennedy, "Jesuits and Music: The European Tradition, 1547–1622", Ph.D. dissertation, University of California, Santa Barbara, 1982.

26 Ibid., p. 23.

27 Bispo, *Grundlagen*, p. 606.

28 Ibid., p. 621.

29 Coelho, "Music in New Worlds", p. 100.

30 O'Malley, *The First Jesuits*, p. 77.

31 Rogério Budasz, "Music of Missionaries, Natives and Settlers in 16th-Century Brazil", p. 13 in the booklet accompanying *Mil Suspiros Dió Maria: Sacred and Secular Music from the Brazilian Renaissance*, compact disc, Ricercar, RIC 246, © 2006.

32 Kennedy, "Jesuits and Music", p. 33.

33 Johann Anton Sartorius, "An den Editorem", in *Der Königl: Dänischen Missionarien aus Ost-Indien eingesandter Ausführlichen Berichten, Dritter Theil*, edited by Gotthilf August Francke (Halle: Waysenhaus, 1735), pp. 673–74.

34 Bartholomaeus Ziegenbalg, "Ausführlicher Bericht vom 22. August 1708", in Francke, *Der Königl*, p. 1.

35 Coelho, "Music in New Worlds", p. 102.

36 See, for instance, Malyn Newitt, *A History of Portuguese Overseas Expansion, 1400–1668* (London: Routledge, 2005), pp. 174–251.

37 Peter Feldbauer, *Die Portugiesen in Asien, 1498–1620* (Essen: Magnus-Verlag, 2005), p. 168.

38 Pompa Banerjee, "Just Passing: Abbé Carré, Spy, Harem-Lord, and 'Made in France'", in *Emissaries in Early Modern Literature and Culture: Mediation, Transmission, Traffic, 1550–1700*, edited by Brinda Charry and Gitanjali Shahani (Farnham: Ashgate, 2009), p. 96.

39 Abbé Carré and Charles Fawcett, *The Travels of Abbé Carré in India and the Near East, 1672–1674*, 3 vols., translated by Lady Fawcett (London: The Hakluyt Society, 1947–48), cited in Katherine Brown, "Reading Indian Music: The Interpretation of Seventeenth-Century European Travel-Writing in the (Re)construction of Indian Music History", *British Journal of Ethnomusicology* 9, no. 2 (2000): 15. Unfortunately, Brown does not indicate from which of the three volumes the quotation is taken.

40 Russell-Wood, *The Portuguese Empire*, p. 128.

41 Margaret Kartomi, "A Malay-Portuguese Synthesis on the West Coast of North Sumatra", in *O Portugal e o Mundo: O Encontro de Culturas na Música / Portugal and the World: The Encounter of Cultures in Music*, edited by Salwa El-Shawan Castelo-Branco (Lisbon: Publicações Dom Quixote, 1997), pp. 312–13.

42 Ibid., p. 313.

43 Coelho, "Music in New Worlds", p. 95.

44 In the original German: "Dieses Kolleg, eine der bis heute bekanntesten jesuitischen Ausbildungsstätten Europas, war seit dem späten 16. Jh. ein einflußreiches Zentrum der Katholischen Reform." *Die Musik in Geschichte und Gegenwart: Allgemeine Enzyklopädie der Musik*, Personenteil 4, 2nd ed., s.v. "Carissimi, Giacomo".

45 Coelho, "Music in New Worlds", pp. 105–06.

46 Ibid., p. 106.

47 Kartomi, "A Malay-Portuguese Synthesis", pp. 289–350.

PART THREE
Adversity and Accommodation

10

PORTUGAL AND CHINA: AN ANATOMY OF HARMONIOUS COEXISTENCE (SIXTEENTH AND SEVENTEENTH CENTURIES)*

Roderich Ptak

The history of Sino-Portuguese encounters — their initial years in particular — has often been told. Cultural dimensions of the exchanges between the two parties also have been studied repeatedly. While there is no need to reiterate those investigations, we obviously cannot proceed without taking into account some of the known details and therefore we will start out by giving a chronologically arranged synoptic introduction. Not that the events "in themselves" are essentially of interest to us here, but rather the structural principles underlying these contacts; in other words, the conditions which were to shape certain modes of interaction over a long period of time. We must take into account the fact that these principles evidently have been subject to change, that they were not always consistent, and that some of the images that the scholarship has maintained to this day would indeed have

*   This chapter was originally published by the Deutsches Historiches Museum, Berlin, as "Portugal und China: Anatomie einer Eintracht (16. und 17. jh.)", in *Novos Mundos — Neue Welten: Portugal und das Zeitalter der Entdeckungen*, edited by Michael Kraus and Hans Ottomeyer (Berlin: Berlin Deutsches Historisches Museum, 2007). It appears here with the museum's kind permission and in English translation by Regina Robert.

to be redrawn. There is a central element in particular which is pertinent to this: speaking of "China" as an entirely self-contained entity in its own right — in terms of economy and culture — seems only partly correct for the sixteenth and seventeenth centuries. A more useful assumption would be to consider that the Portuguese were in fact facing a number of various local Chinese groups and regions. And something similar applies to the Portuguese side of the matter: the Portuguese-speaking population living in permanent residency in Macao did indeed act and think in quite different ways from those recently arrived from Europe or India. One might almost speak of different identities, though I would not want to go so far as that.

CHRONOLOGY

Let us begin then with a briefly summarized chronology of important events. The first Sino-Portuguese encounters on record took place in Malacca. Several Chinese groups seem to have welcomed the Portuguese conquest of the locale (in 1511) — its part in international trade at the time has been vastly overstated — and henceforth worked together with the Portuguese. Most of the Chinese who put their services on offer apparently originated from the province of Fujian and areas around the city of Zhangzhou in particular. Other sections of the Chinese population, those living in the north of the Isle of Java, were closer to the Islamic princes, and hence supported them against the Portuguese. All their attempts to regain Malacca, however, failed.[1] It is important to realize here that the Chinese "faction" the Portuguese dealt with was in fact rather fragmented.

It was the Fujianese who eventually showed the Portuguese the way to China. The newcomers, it seems, were expected to provide new partnerships in trade and maybe also — bearing in mind a superior European artillery — some defence services. The first "landing" of the Portuguese on Chinese territory however did not occur in Fujian but in the central part of the Guangdong province. Since China was factually "closed", admitting only tributary missions but no free private trade of the kind that the Portuguese had been used to in India and on the African continent, Portugal now aimed to "open up" the Middle Kingdom through diplomatic channels. The delegation sent for this purpose under the vanguard of Tomé Pires failed however (early 1520s), and Pires himself was sent to prison and probably died in Guangzhou, the great southern metropolis of the Ming state (Ming period: 1368–1644). Since Pires's travels to Nanjing and Beijing (the court residences) had been accompanied by some misunderstandings and even a short incidence of Sino-Portuguese conflict down in the far south and off the Guangdong coast, both sides now went separate ways for some time to come. This in fact was true only for the official representatives of the state, rather than the unofficial "ranks". Portuguese tradesmen and adventurers continued to meet their Chinese counterparts — in secret, owing to the Chinese interdiction — either off the Chinese coastline or elsewhere.[2]

Most of the Chinese with whom the Portuguese had contact during this time (1530s and 1540s) seem to have been Fujianese. And this left Guangdong with nothing since its big harbour of Guangzhou remained closed for Portuguese and some others, following the aforementioned incidents. This state of affairs meant less external trade for the province of Guangdong — and more business for Fujian. While the Fujianese rejoiced, the authorities of Guangdong were indignant.

Soon enough, though, a situation of competition arose from the secret contacts between the Fujian Chinese and the Portuguese. Both parties had begun at the same time to expand their influences in several ports in Southeast Asia — Patani for one — where they traded similar goods, pepper in particular, and thus got in each others' ways. The Portuguese presence off the Fujianese coast during the 1540s did not bring about any positive results either.[3]

This is one of the reasons why the third stage in Luso-Chinese contacts led the Portuguese back to central Guangdong. As competitors of the Fujianese, the Portuguese were now no longer unwelcome even though the abovementioned trade restrictions were still in force. Officials in Guangdong were well aware of the technical superiority of Portuguese ships and weapons, and besides, they had come to value their partners' reliability.

To this day there is disagreement as to which were the factors that in the end turned the balance for Guangdong to tolerate the Portuguese at first on a few islands off their coast and finally in the southern half of the Macao peninsula itself. Tradition has it that the Portuguese helped to fight a number of pirates and were given a stretch of Chinese land as a reward. Others speak of bribery. Yet another point of view reminds us that the Chinese court was in constant need of expensive substances — such as ambergris — which the Portuguese knew how to procure; Macao was placed at their disposal for this reason, they say. No such text of a treaty has ever existed nor is it possible to determine whether Macao was "given as a present", "sold", "let out on lease", or handed over in any other possible way. There is even debate about the "founding" date of Macao itself, which probably occurred some time between the years 1555 and 1557. No matter how the land was given away, it seems that the court was informed — that is to say, the provincial administration apparently did not act on its own authority.[4]

Macao's first major lifecycle (the 1550s until about 1640) was characterized by the silk and silver trade. Silver came largely from Japan, silk from the neighbouring Guangzhou, which itself imported silver from Japan. Copper, gold, mercury, precious tropical timber and some other goods played another major role in Macao's foreign relations.[5] In Guangzhou itself the Portuguese competed with Fujianese and others for market shares. The Guangzhou point of view on the matter must have been favourable as prices would surely have been pushed up had the provision of imported goods to the city been largely in the hands of the Fujianese.

Foreign trading soon brought great wealth, which was then either reinvested locally or fed back into the trade. From the 1580s onwards Macao — rather inadvertently — began to cooperate with Manila, though with due caution since Spain, on the one hand, was also partaking in the silk and silver business and was in partnership with the Fujianese, and, on the other hand, Spanish clerics had suggested establishing missionary home territories in China. Some even had dreams of a Conquista-style attack on China, seizing entire coastlines at a time, much to the displeasure of the Portuguese. It was due to their dexterity and diplomacy that the Portuguese eventually managed to keep Spain away from the East Asian mainland.[6]

The aggressively operating Dutch, who were active in these regions from around 1600, could not find a proper gateway into China either. Their presence, however, demanded new investments from the Portuguese: the military fortification of Macao had become necessary. Additional fortresses and buildings had to be erected. A larger workforce was needed. Macao's growth through the export trade thus gave rise to its demographic growth: more and more Chinese immigrants and others arrived who would work in the city by day and travel home to their neighbouring villages in the evening.[7]

When Macao was hit by a number of unfortunate developments around the 1640s — the loss of the Japanese market, the Dutch conquest of Malacca, the temporary interruption of the Macao-Manila trade traffic due to the dissolution of the Spanish-Portuguese dual monarchy — it found itself in a demographic trap: parts of the foreign trade had broken away, but the population of Macao, which, according to various estimations had risen to some 40,000 inhabitants by then, still needed to be fed. Matters were further complicated by the fact that neighbouring China underwent a change of dynasties. The Ming were driven back south by the approaching Manchu forces, Guangzhou came under a different owner twice, and fugitives poured into Macao; hence an economic decline of the city was bound to occur.[8]

The Qing (1644–1911), victors in the internal Chinese conflict, continued to fight the so-called Zheng clan over the following decades, which had control over parts of Eastern Fujian and several territories on the western side of Taiwan. These conflicts temporarily led to some drastic evacuation measures and trade embargoes that affected almost the entire Chinese coastline. In those days the port of Macao was rigidly controlled, free trade became virtually impossible, the city sank into poverty even faster, and many of its former Chinese immigrants now turned their backs on it.[9]

It was not until the Qing had brought about the collapse of the Zheng reign (early 1680s) that the tense situation in South China finally eased. Trade was free now and the seafaring Fujianese in particular came to benefit from this new situation; Macao was only marginally affected. Neither during the remaining decades of the seventeenth century nor at any later time could Macao ever regain the important international role it had played during the first great trade cycle. There was a constant lack of money, ships and the silver that had helped make Macao rich earlier. The eighteenth century saw trading in Southeast Asian commodities and an intermittent trade with tea that largely came from Fujian via Guangzhou, but European competitors coming now from Great Britain and more and more from the Netherlands, France and Scandinavia — as well as the Fujianese seafarers — became increasingly important. Besides, Portugal had suffered the loss of all its outposts in Southeast Asia — with the exception of Timor — that made it impossible for it to strategically link up its different territories in an attempt to bring about economic regeneration.[10]

Yet that is not all there is to tell: when more and more European vessels sailed to Guangzhou in order to pick up tea there during the course of the eighteenth century, Macao faced an entirely new situation. Near the end of the century it happened that Macao — yielding to extraneous circumstances — often found itself accommodating European merchants who were "hibernating" there, waiting for the next trading season in Guangzhou to set in. Since these strangers brought some money with them, Macao now came to supply services. A kind of creeping process of transformation set in: the old trading town turned itself into a place that subsisted not only on commerce but also on rental and other revenues. With a new course being thus set, our brief chronology may come to an end here.[11]

PORTUGUESE, CHINESE AND OTHERS

Let us now consider the structural aspects of these "bilateral" relations. As has been mentioned earlier, the Portuguese were principally concerned with two larger groups, the Fujianese and the Chinese from Guangdong (the overseas Chinese have no relevance here). Fujianese Chinese are active in the maritime trade during the whole period of time. The same applies to the Guangdong Chinese, yet on a far lesser scale. In the early years of their presence on the Macao peninsula itself, the Portuguese came upon representatives of both groups. Some Hakka families (Kejia) probably joined them, although more specific details are not available. One thing is certain however: the Guangdong element is on the increase over the course of time; consequently, the cultural and commercial authority of the Fujianese Chinese in and around Macao is lessened.

Inside the great trading metropolis of Guangzhou itself — and Macao had for a long time served as Guangzhou's most important gateway to the outside world — the Fujianese's importance must have been perceived quite differently, though details sadly must remain in the dark again. A remarkable and very profound development can be determined nevertheless, taking place under the auspices of the Qing: most of the merchants offering tea to the Europeans in Guangzhou now come from Fujian. What is more, as previously indicated, Fujian seems to gradually outrank others as the leading tea-producing region within China. In brief, Fujianese tea finds its way aboard the European vessels via domestic channels, with Fujianese wholesalers controlling the sales price. Since the Portuguese are rarely involved in the business, they might be said to evade the Fujianese in a similar way from what they had done earlier.[12]

Macao, instead, often cooperates with the local populace of the lower stratum — in other words, with the Guangdong Chinese from the backlands of Macao. Even though there is no reliable evidence for it, the following assumption does seem to fit into the picture: from the point of view of the population of Guangzhou — as well as Guangdong — it must have been easier on many occasions to cooperate with the Portuguese rather than the Fujianese, since the latter were obviously in control of a large part of the tea business. And not only the Fujianese were strangers in Guangzhou: the new Manchu rulers whose administrators were heading certain levels within the local administration likewise came from the "outside". It is thus easily conceivable that the population of central Guangdong felt itself under a twofold burden of heteronomy — through the representatives of the Qing court on the one hand, and the wealthy Fujianese entrepreneurs on the other — thus finding the "old familiar" Portuguese presence, which had done well under the Ming, not so aggravating after all. Such deliberations must remain a speculative matter and are rarely found in the relevant literature; however, they do take into account — at least by implication — the fact that during the imperial epoch the coastal areas of China differed from each other and in many ways formed entities in their own rights.

Another interesting situation arose in Macao itself. In the beginning it must have been predominantly the Portuguese who left their mark on the urban population. The entire upper class was Portuguese. This elite was flanked by many individuals coming out of other Portuguese overseas territories such as Malayans, Indians or even Africans. However, due to immigration and miscegenation processes, the Chinese element was on the increase very soon. Within this social stratification, families with Guangdong backgrounds probably were in a majority early on, as has been mentioned before. There were greater fluctuations, though, in the number of Chinese inhabitants as opposed to the resident Portuguese. Economic as well as political reasons — not just within Macao but most of all in the Chinese hinterlands — were ultimately causing these demographic alterations.

We may assume that the statistical "Sinicization" of a once predominantly "Portuguese coloured" metropolis was accompanied by certain acculturation processes. This, however, raises the initial question of which of the two groups "assimilated" to the other and in what direction the assumed acculturation(s) actually did take place.[13] Evidence is hard to come by as the few descriptions of everyday life in Macao of the sixteenth and seventeenth century hardly suffice to support any relevant conclusions. And very rarely do architectural relics or other tangible remains help find a genuine answer to such a question either.[14]

Yet the following farther-reaching consideration should not be ignored: next to a stratum of administrators who thought and acted predominantly "Portuguese" and which initially included only a few persons of (partly) Chinese descent, another group soon came into existence who in today's literature are often called the Macanese. These "mestizos" of Chinese, Portuguese and sometimes entirely different origins communicated in a creole language shot through with Chinese, Malayan and other verbalisms. Born in Macao, they felt obligated to their town. Most of them earned their living as merchants and traders and had mastered Cantonese to that end. Their lifestyle and their Catholic faith connected them with the Portuguese "proper"; they had established themselves between existing "camps", as it were, maintaining the same kind of good contact with the Chinese "proper" in and around Macao.[15]

The latter rather seem to have kept to themselves — just like the "thoroughly" Portuguese often did — although they worked for their Portuguese masters and were adopted from time to time by their masters' families. This apparently was true for Chinese girls in particular. A fair number of contemporaries thus reported some kind of a "surplus of women" for certain epochs, something that could be explained in economic as well as cultural terms.

Assuming that we are in the right picture here, then the obvious suggestion would be that many Chinese immigrants adapted themselves to Portuguese ways of living, that is to say, that an "acculturation" took place accordingly. This process must be distinguished from the above-mentioned ethnic amalgam, even though the passage was probably fluent and we may assume that an acceptance of the foreign did indeed encourage such interconnections.

It is also possible that many of the Chinese from Macao, whose numerical weight, as we know, increased throughout the course of history, remained emotionally tied to their native China — or else developed a unique local identity, somewhat parallel to those circles we would associate with the categories of "mestizos" and "Portuguese proper". One might further complicate the pattern by splitting up the ensemble of Macao-Chinese *in toto* according to their places of origin or clusters of origin. Indications for either of the acculturation variants can be found in the literature, but the overall picture remains blurred, and a quantitative assessment of the different directions the acculturation processes may have taken is thus virtually impossible.

REASONS AND RHETORIC

Modern social science likes to assume that the people living in colonial societies and "diaspora-like" structures were generally and above all interested in the increase of their wealth. This is certainly true for Macao, though it would be inappropriate to leave aside other social dimensions — such as religious life — entirely. Those who ruled Macao and represented it to the outside world could not afford to think only in terms of money and profit; they also — or above all — had to keep in mind the interests of the church that was busy establishing missions and proselytizing in China and Japan. After all, it was Macao that served as a logistical base to both missionary territories. Commercial interests thus had to be put aside as circumstances demanded, so as not to jeopardize the missionaries' achievements. As part of the Padroado pattern, Macao was not only bound to Goa or Lisbon, but also to Rome. With regard to their institutions, the citizens of Macao constantly found themselves facing two superordinated levels at the same time, thus having to bear in mind issues on all sides whenever they had to take important decisions. It is a matter of course that this did not work out every time and could cause temporary domestic controversies.

Apart from the more "European" issue, there was another dimension to be dealt with: Macao in its entirety had to get along with its Chinese neighbours in Guangdong. The task was brilliantly mastered; in order to better understand the circumstances, though, it is necessary to go into further detail.

Confrontations of the kind that took place during the early decades of Portuguese "expansion politics" in the Arabian Sea, off the west coast of India for example, did not fit into the situation of the Far East. Neither Japan nor China was home to Islamic opponents that would need to be antagonized. Besides, the founding of Macao took place in an epoch when the Portuguese part of Asia had long since come to some kind of arrangement with many Islamic powers. The medieval spirit that had spurred the first India travellers to stab their Moorish antagonists in the back had long since blown away.

Moreover, from the beginning, the Portuguese "opening up" of the East Asian markets appears to have been accompanied by overwhelmingly optimistic expectations: China and Japan were believed to be rich; it was hoped that there would be substantial profits to be made; and their respective cultures were soon appreciated even though they remained misunderstood for some time to come. The deployment of military resources would be a mere emergency measure for the authorities of Macao, if anything. Only very rarely did some individuals — often venting their spontaneous frustration about some recent grievances — express their desire to "punish" China. Such proposals were never put into action — with the exception of one short campaign that occurred around the middle of the nineteenth century and led to the temporary occupation of a single Chinese border post.

While it was in the interest of the citizens of Macao and the missionaries to live in peace and harmony with China, China itself was often in controversy over how to handle the Portuguese.[16] That Macao itself had a right to exist constituted an anomaly to the mandarins' point of view, something that seemed to have no place within the Chinese "worldview". Yet central Guangdong came to benefit from the Portuguese presence substantially and the Portuguese repeatedly pointed out that the Chinese state itself had given them permission to colonize Macao. Out of this situation a complex rhetoric arose that both sides made recourse to whenever they felt it necessary to uphold their respective status quo while at the same time having to keep up appearances. Whatever the fulminations were that came out of the heart of China from time to time — and as much as some high officials following their radical inclinations liked to plead for the expulsion of the Portuguese — in the end the moderates on both sides always won, recalling the "old privileges" the imperial court had granted the Portuguese (though the fact is disputed to this day) and reminding their fellow citizens of the advantages of a good neighbourhood in general.

Part of a successful social intercourse lay in the parties' ability to keep their materialistic interests in check. Most Confucian-minded officials had grown up believing that the pursuit of profit was the cause of a "simple" rather than a "noble" man. According to official readings, a merchant did not have much say at all. Thus in bilateral talks, emphasis would not be put on matters of the public interest — much less on trading details — but rather on the positive experience derived from such a long-standing neighbourhood. And the longer Macao existed, the more important this rhetorical element must have become, for the amount of time passing by served as an increasingly reliable guarantee for Portuguese "compliance". In other words: citizens of Macao — most of all those who had grown up in Macao and were familiar with Chinese social manners, that is, the Macanese — had learnt over the years to adjust to Chinese expectations and knew how to make use of their sublime game of gestures and symbols for their own and their town's benefit.

LEVELS OF RELATIONSHIP

It is true that no other part of the entire Estado da Índia had a greater need for tact than Macao. There was no other place that gave diplomacy such priority. One manifestation of this situation, among others, is to be found in the number of different embassies that were travelling to China regularly either from or via Macao. Let us try to "structure" them and understand them within their macrocosm.

Early missions from a time even before the founding of Macao are sparsely documented, although we know there were talks on an "informal level" — talks between Portuguese individuals acting without official approval from Goa and Chinese provincial officials who, according to one of several interpretations, likewise acted on their own account. Fundamentally important for success was their mutual interest in a successful cooperation: the Portuguese appeared to be reliable partners, they supplied silver from Japan, and their presence could help reduce provincial Guangdong's economic dependence on Fujian and other merchants. Just how the Chinese provincial officials managed to enforce their local issues at the central office far up north in Beijing in the end, we do not know, but that they did so is beyond debate.

We may also presume that the "representatives" of Portugal had seen through the pattern in China's domestic affairs at quite an early date, and, moreover, that they knew how to handle things in a highly flexible way. While Tomé Pires, travelling and acting on an official mission, would sadly fail (due to his lack of experience, the adverse circumstances, and the fact that he had to comply with certain objectives), those travelling salesmen who in the end spurred the Chinese into a change of thinking did not have to consider any formal expectations coming from a superior Portuguese authority. This worked to their advantage. They created precedents (Macao was an unofficial foundation) that were then approved *ex post facto* by Goa and Lisbon alike.

Only when the founding of Macao had been accomplished — and after Macao had been given its own administration — did relations with China gradually became "formalized". Soon, three different levels of bilateral exchanges were emerging that remained operative far into the eighteenth century: on the lowest level, the city communicated with functionaries from the neighbouring district of Xiangshan; on a middle level they talked to the provincial government in Guangzhou; and on the top level — the one between two sovereign states — contact was made between Lisbon and Beijing.[17]

Official delegations hardly ever travelled between the two capitals, however. Most of them started from Portuguese quarters with the intention of supporting not only Macao but also the missionaries' work in China. On these travels the above-mentioned special kind of rhetoric was employed: from a Chinese point of view Portugal basically asked for nothing, made presents, and proved itself a thankful "subject". The Portuguese point of view — in far-away Europe — was different: there could be no sign of submission, and the Chinese "worldview" (which allowed for no equality between the powers whatsoever) in fact remained opaque to the European mind. Indeed, the art of creating two possible interpretations — one for local use in Macao and Beijing, and another for Lisbon — was owed to the padres and those sedentary Portuguese — or Macanese — who worked as interpreters and "cultural intermediaries" and had learnt to attune to the diplomatic needs of their respective "clients".[18]

Since Portugal asked for nothing — no further territory, no second colonial base — it was not difficult to find a mutually convenient mode of rhetoric. In other words, their exchange was rarely about anything substantial and more often about formal matters since the old "privileges" that Portugal was in the habit of recalling — even though they might never have been granted lawfully — had long since obtained the status of *fait accompli*. Macao was not hard put to live with not dwelling on the subject and leaving everything as it was. The idea of harmonious coexistence — in fact a fundamentally Chinese notion — needed no clarification.

The situation was slightly different at the lower level. Everyday life in Macao had its share of ethnic tensions; hence, regional Chinese authorities repeatedly interfered in local issues. In a way, they represented their fellow countrymen's interests, though they often did so merely in a symbolic way since life in Macao would take its usual course even without complex regulations; besides, the Macao Chinese may have had their own special identity, as was pointed out earlier. Occasional "interventions" by Chinese bureaucrats were probably due to their own obligation to legitimize their assignment in front of their provincial superiors in Guangzhou from time to time. Some show of dissociation and the occasional threat seem to have been part of their duty and proof of vigilant borderline politics in the eyes of the provincial governors. And it also complied with the provincial administration's own need to justify itself before the next higher level, the court in Beijing. Vigilant subjects in the form of busy local civil officers were a good "seller" there.

The Portuguese administration knew how to put up with all that. Following the notion that it would be better to grant a basically cooperative local officer his occasional bouts of ranting rather than seeing him displaced by a true "hardliner", the administration made concessions accordingly. This is particularly true for the eighteenth century. There were also periods of serious "resentments", for instance on those occasions when Chinese citizens of Macao had been put to death by other citizens and the Chinese administration insisted that their own jurisdiction be applied to the case. Those cases were often played up artificially by an otherwise lethargic local civil service who would take up the opportunity to draw attention to themselves.[19] Generally speaking, though, an attitude of laissez-faire was employed to avoid the pitfalls of difficult constellations since no party was interested in any conflicts arising. Individuals inside the administration of Macao who felt the urge to go against this policy — those who had just arrived from Portugal and had not yet made sense of the rules of the game — were hardly ever able to prevail against those who sought to maintain a harmonious coexistence; the merchants and long-time residents looked to that. Also gifts of money surely helped ameliorate crisis situations and especially the Chinese officials often seem to have shown themselves to be rather susceptible to generous "endorsements".

With transition to the Manchu reign, the gradual blossoming of the tea trade, and the increasing number of European tradesmen arriving in Guangzhou, matters became rather complicated for Macao. We must bear in mind that the Qing government was not Chinese. Macao had merely been one of many entities within its "compartmentalized" multiethnic state. One non-Chinese "bastion" on the underside of the giant Chinese territory within the Qing state could not do much harm, or so one or another court official may have thought, considering that the Han Chinese showed a numeric domination that called for a balance. So when Manchurian officials controlled part of the administration in Guangzhou and Fujianese merchants controlled entire segments within the tea trade, the interests of the local Guangdong population were virtually kept in check. This situation was not unwelcome to the Portuguese who saw an opportunity to live up to old friendships with their partners from Guangdong, to enhance them at the local level, and to continue to nurse them outside the rules, in the shadows of the higher "ranks", as it were. Also, in case of an emergency, Macao could come to the defence of "its" Han Chinese against Manchurian interests, verbally at least, even though it seems to me that such an interpretation would be difficult to substantiate.

Further, the Manchu reign exhibited even more particularities. At the highest level of communication, the Portuguese party deliberately considered the Qing court as the rightful heir to the defeated Ming, in this way discreetly reminding everyone that it would be beneficial to all parties involved if the once-granted rights were to be upheld. Another unvoiced argument held that both sides had Chinese subjects: the infinitesimal Macao, a mere appendage of Guangdong, and the giant Manchu empire to which Guangdong was answerable; no matter how, Macao would look after "its" Chinese, and so everyone was in the same boat. To the Manchu, the situation must have been quite satisfactory.

The Portuguese obviously counted on the fact that along the maritime outskirts of their realm, the Qing would behave similarly to their predecessors, while in Northern Asia and Turkestan they behaved differently, allowing for a certain coequality among the ruling monarchs. The famous treaty of Nertschinsk (1689), negotiated by Russians and representatives of the Manchu (assisted by clerical translators) serves as a classic example hereof. The Jesuits, who had realized that the Qing state was much more internationally minded than the Ming had ever been, now did everything in their power to engage the courtly circles of Beijing for themselves — and for Macao.

Nevertheless, the missionaries' political role during the rule of the Qing should not be overemphasized, bearing in mind that when the controversy over rites broke out, the church came away weakened while Macao was still alive and kicking. The time-proven traditions of the far south as well as the Qing state's very own ancient mechanisms, which would indeed concede a foreigner his own ways, probably were crucial to Macao's ability to master this crisis — as it mastered so many others.

CONCLUSION

Historians have tried to define Macao as an "autonomous zone" under the Qing, as a well-integrated territory within the Estado da Índia, something similar to a colony, as a diaspora-enclave or even as a variant of a *fanfang* — a "foreign quarter" on Chinese soil — but we can easily find arguments against one option or the other.[20] In short, it is indeed impossible to assign Macao to a single category alone. What strikes us, though, is that the city has always been governed in a very flexible way, at times even in an opaque and ostensibly irrational manner, which often made it impossible for another party to "take hold" of it. Moreover, though one aspired to a neat "designation" of the city's own status from time to time — a Portuguese desire, mostly — ultimately this move was wilfully avoided until late into the nineteenth century.

A number of exogenous as well as endogenous factors — with a local government leading the way which often behaved rather independently from Goa and Lisbon — in the end made it possible that Macao went through good times and bad times without ever really being in harm's way. One might almost say that Macao was governed in a "Confucian" style. Most of the time, it assumed an air of modesty — there were no sharp edges to it. Indeed, its contours remained "diluted": the door was left open to every option — and to all parties. It was this very vagueness which made for the extraordinary strength that showed itself in Macao and the Portuguese who truly knew how to contrast pleasantly with the rest of the European powers — and continued to do so until the end, Lisbon showing itself unwilling by all means to follow the sabre-rattling example of the British preachers of "law-and-order" and preferring to put its focus on respect and harmony instead.

Notes

[1]   On the matter of the Portuguese and Fujianese, see for example, Roderich Ptak, "The Fujianese, Ryukyuans and Portuguese (c. 1511 to 1540s): Allies or Competitors?", in *Anais de História de Além-Mar* 3 (2002): 447–67; and Roderich Ptak, "Reconsidering Melaka and Central Guangdong: Portugal's and Fujian's Impact on Southeast Asian Trade (Early Sixteenth Century)", in *Iberians in the Singapore-Melaka Area (16th to 18th Century)*, edited by Peter Borschberg (Wiesbaden: Harrassowitz; and Lisbon: Fundação Oriente, 2004), pp. 1–21.

[2]   The essential events are covered in Rui Manuel Loureiro, *Fidalgos, Missionários e Mandarins: Portugal e a China no Século XVI*, Orientalia 1 (Lisbon: Fundação Oriente, 2000). Important Chinese studies on early contacts are, for example: Stephen Zengxin Zhang (Tseng-hsin Chang), *Ming ji Dongnan Zhongguo de haishang huodong (Maritime Activities on the South-East Coast of China in the Latter Part of the Ming Dynasty)*, pt. 2 (Taipei: China Committee for Publication Aid and Prize Award, 1988); also, several articles in Jin Guoping, *Zhong Pu guanxi shidi kaozheng*, Haohai congkan (Macao: Fundação Macau, 2000), and Jin Guoping, *Xi li dong jian: Zhong Pu zaoqi jiechu zhuixi*, Haohai congkan (Macao: Fundação Macau, 2000), as well as, for example, Jin Guoping and Wu Zhiliang, *Guo Shizimen (Abrindo as Portas do Cerco)* (Macao: Aomen chengren jiaoyu xiehui, 2004), essay no. 2. Publications in English are, for example, Ng Chin Keong, "Trade, the Sea Prohibition and the 'Fo-lang-chi', 1513–1550",

in *Proceedings of the International Colloquium on the Portuguese and the Pacific*, edited by Francis A. Dutra and João Camilo dos Santos (Santa Barbara: Center for Portuguese Studies, 1995), pp. 381–424; see also Roderich Ptak, "Sino-Portuguese Relations circa 1513/14 to 1550s", in *Portugal e a China: Conferências no II Curso Livre de História das Relações entre Portugal e a China (Séculos XVI–XIX)*, edited by Jorge Manuel dos Santos Alves (Lisbon: Fundação Oriente, 1999), pp. 19–37. For readings in German, see for example, Roderich Ptak, *Portugal in China: Kurzer Abriß der portugiesisch-chinesischen Beziehungen und der Geschichte Macaus im 16. und beginnenden 17. Jahrhundert*, Portugal-Reihe (Bad Boll: Klemmerberg-Verlag, 1980).

3   On the matter of the Chinese in Southeast Asia, see for example, Roderich Ptak, "Ming Maritime Trade to Southeast Asia, 1368–1567: Visions of a System", in *From the Mediterranean to the China Sea: Miscellaneous Notes*, edited by Claude Guillot, Denys Lombard and Roderich Ptak (Wiesbaden: Harrassowitz-Verlag, 1998), pp. 157–92.

4   For the most recent works on the foundation of Macao, see for example, Rui Manuel Loureiro, *Em Busca das Origins de Macau (Antologia Documental)* (Macao: Museu Marítimo de Macau, 1997), and Loureiro, *Fidalgos* (2000), chap. 21. See also Tang Kaijian, *Aomen kaibu chuqishi yanjiu* (Beijing: Zhonghua shuju, 1999), pp. 82–130, as well as Tang Kaijian, *Weiliduo "Bao xiao shimo shu" jianzheng*, Aomen congshu (Guangzhou: Guangdong renmin chubanshe, 2004); furthermore, Jin Guoping and Wu Zhiliang, *Dong xi wang yang (Em Busca de História[s] de Macau Apagada[s] pelo Tempo)* (Macao: Aomen chengren jiaoyu xiehui, 2002), esp. essays 3, 4, 5 and 7; and finally, Jin Guoping and Wu Zhiliang, *Jing hai piao miao (História[s] de Macau: Ficção e Realidade)* (Macao: Aomen chengren jiaoyu xiehui, 2001), essay 3.

5   On the subject of Guangzhou-Macao-Japan trade relations, Okamoto Yoshitomo, *Jûroku seiki Nichi-Ô kôtsu-shi no kenkyû* (Tokyo: Rokkô shobô, 1942), was especially decisive. Later on, Boxer came to benefit from him. Otherwise, see for instance, Roderich Ptak, "Sino-Japanese Maritime Trade, circa 1550: Merchants, Ports and Networks", in *O Século Cristão do Japão: Actas do Colóquio Internacional Comemorativo dos 450 Anos de Amizade Portugal-Japão (1543–1993) (Lisboa, 2 a 5 de Novembro de 1993)*, edited by Roberto Carneiro and A. Teodoro de Matos (Lisbon: Centro de Estudos dos Povos e Culturas de Expressão Portuguesa da Universidade Católica Portuguesa and Instituto de História de Além-Mar of the Faculdade de Ciências Sociais e Humanas da Universidade Nova de Lisboa, 1994), pp. 281–311; and Roderich Ptak, "Mercadorias em trânsito em Macau durante o seu período histórico: Seda, prata, sândalo, chá, pimenta, almíscar", in *Os Fundamentos da Amizade: Cinco Séculos de Relações Culturais e Artísticas Luso-Chinesas* (Lisbon: Centro Científico e Cultural de Macau and Fundação para a Cooperação e o Desenvolvimento do Macau, 1999), pp. 61–69. One of the most recent Chinese studies containing extensive data on all of Macao's trade relations is Zhang Tingmao, *Ming Qing*

shiqi Aomen haishang maoyishi (Macao: Aoya zhoukan chuban youxian gongsi, 2004), esp. chaps. 2 and 3.

6   On Manila and Macao, see for example, Benjamin Videira Pires, "A viagem de comércio Macau-Manila nos séculos XVI à XIX", *Boletim do Instituto Luís de Camões* 5, nos. 1–2 (1971): 5–100, as well as Manuel Ollé, *La Invención de China: Percepciones y Estrategias Filipinas Respecto a China durante el Siglo XVI*, South China and Maritime Asia 9 (Wiesbaden: Harrassowitz-Verlag, 2000).

7   On demography and growth in Macao, see for example, George Bryan Souza, *The Survival of Empire: Portuguese Trade and Society in China and the South China Sea, 1630–1754* (Cambridge: Cambridge University Press, 1986), pp. 31–36; also Roderich Ptak, "The Demography of Old Macao, 1555–1640", *Ming Studies* 15 (Fall 1982): 27–35; and Roderich Ptak, "Wirtschaftlicher und demographischer Wandel in Macau: Stadien einer Entwicklung", in *Macau: Herkunft ist Zukunft*, edited by Roman Malek (Sankt Augustin, Germany: China-Zentrum and Institut Monumenta Serica, 2000), pp. 153–86.

8   On the end of the trade with Japan, see most recently Valdemar Coutinho, *O Fim da Presença Portuguesa no Japão* (Lisbon: Sociedade Histórica da Independência de Portugal, 1999). For all other developments, see works mentioned in notes 4 and 5.

9   On this epoch, see for example, John E. Wills, Jr., *Embassies and Illusions: Dutch and Portuguese Envoys to K'ang-hsi, 1666–1687* (Cambridge, MA: Harvard University Press, 1984), and Roderich Ptak, "Der Handel zwischen Macau und Makassar, ca. 1640–1667", *Zeitschrift der Deutschen Morgenländischen Gesellschaft* 139, no. 1 (1989): 208–26; see also Jorge Manuel Flores, "China e Macau", in *História dos Portugueses no Extremo Oriente*, vol. 1, tomo 2, *De Macau à Perifeira*, edited by A.H. de Oliveira Marques (Lisbon: Fundação Oriente, 2000), pp. 215–34; and finally Susana Münch Miranda, "Os circuitos económicos", in *História dos Portugueses no Extremo Oriente*, vol. 2, *Macau e Timor: O Declínio do Império*, edited by A.H. de Oliveira Marques (Lisbon: Fundação Oriente, 2001), pp. 259–88.

10   On these matters, see for example, António Martins do Vale, *Os Portugueses em Macau (1750–1800): Degregados, Ignorantes e Ambiciosos ou Fiéis Vassalos d'El-Rei?*, Memória do Oriente 9 (Macao: Instituto Português do Oriente, 1997), as well as António Martins do Vale, "Macau: Os eventos politicos 2", in Oliveira Marques, *História dos Portugueses*, 2:159–227; see also Jorge Manuel Flores, "Macau: Os eventos politicos 1", in Oliveira Marques, *História dos Portugueses*, 2:71–155, as well as Roderich Ptak, "Die Rolle der Chinesen, Portugiesen und Holländer im Teehandel zwischen China und Südostasien (ca. 1600–1750)", *Jahrbuch für Wirtschaftsgeschichte*, pt. 1 (1994): 89–106. On the demography for this and later periods, see for example, António Martins M. do Vale, "A população de Macau na segunda metade do século XVIII", *Povos e Culturas* 5 (1996): 241–54, or else Susana Münch Miranda and Cristina Seuanes Serafim, "População e sociedade", in Oliveira Marques, *História dos Portugueses*, 2:231–42.

[11]   On the transformation process, see Roderich Ptak, "Macau: Trade and Society, circa 1740–1760", in *Maritime China in Transition, 1750–1850*, edited by Wang Gungwu and Ng Chin-keong (Wiesbaden: Harrassowitz-Verlag, 2004), pp. 191–211.

[12]   Ptak, "Die Rolle der Chinesen", and Ptak, "Trade and Society".

[13]   Roderich Ptak, "China's Medieval *Fanfang*: A Model for Macau under the Ming?", *Anais de História de Além-Mar* 2 (2001): 64–68.

[14]   On architecture, see a recent overview by Pedro Dias, *A Urbanização e a Arquitectura dos Portugueses em Macau, 1557–1911* (Lisbon: Portugal Telecom, 2005). On everyday life and the fine arts, see also, for example, Paulo Drumond Braga, "A vida quotidiana", in Oliveira Marques, *História dos Portugueses*, 2:461–91, and also Alexandra Curvelo with Celina Bastos, "A arte", in Oliveira Marques, *Histórias dos Portugueses*, 2:423–58, as well as Maria Augusta Lima Cruz, "Formas de expressao cultural", in Oliveira Marques, *História dos Portugueses*, 2:343–420.

[15]   Most studies on the Macanese population refer to the twentieth century. Ana Maria Amaro has made some important contributions in this area. Some of the titles, for instance, can be found in the following bibliographical surveys: Roderich Ptak, "Macau and Sino-Portuguese Relations, c. 1513/14 to c. 1900: A Bibliographical Essay", *Monumenta Serica* 46 (1998): 343–96, and also Roderich Ptak, "Twentieth Century Macau: History, Politics, Economics: A Bibliographical Survey," *Monumenta Serica* 49 (2001): chap. 9.

[16]   Several interesting essays on the subject can be found, for example, in Tang Kaijian, *Ming Qing shidafu yu Aomen*, Haohai congkan (Macao: Fundação Macau, 1998).

[17]   Some interesting statements on the subject, which are partly congruent with the analysis presented here, can be found in Jorge Manuel dos Santos Alves, "Natureza do primeiro cíclo de diplomacia luso-chinesa (séculos XVI–XVIII)", in *Estudos de História do Relacionamento Luso-Chinês, Séculos XVI–XIX*, edited by António Vasconcelos de Saldanha and Jorge Manuel dos Santos Alves (Macao: Instituto Português do Oriente, 1995), pp. 179–218; see also Jorge Manuel dos Santos Alves, "The First Decade of Sino-Portuguese Diplomatic Relations Following the Foundation of Macau", in Dutra and Santos, *Proceedings*, pp. 305–13.

[18]   Important studies on the subject of diplomatic missions can be found, for example, in João de Deus Ramos, *História das Relações Diplomáticas entre Portugal e a China*, vol. 1, *O Padre António de Magalhães, S.J., e a Embaixada de Kangxi a D. João V (1721–1725)* (Macao: Instituto Cultural de Macau, 1991), and also in Isaú Santos, "A embaixada de Manuel de Saldanha à China, em 1667–1670", in *As Relações entre a Índia Portuguesa, a Ásia do Sueste e o Extremo Oriente: Actas do VI Seminário Internacional de História Indo-Portuguesa (Macau, 22 a 26 de Outubro de 1991)*, edited by Artur Teodoro de Matos and Luís Filipe F. Reis Thomaz (Macau: Instituto de Investigação Científica Tropical, 1993); see also António Vasconcelos de Saldanha, ed., Mariagrazia Russo, comp., and Jin Guoping,

trans., *Embaixada de D. João V de Portugal ao Imperador Yongzheng, da China (1725–1728)* (Lisbon: Fundação Oriente, 2005); and finally, Wills, *Embassies and Illusions* (1984). On the different Chinese and Portuguese interpretations, see for example, Roderich Ptak, "Chinese Documents in Portuguese Archives: Jottings on Three Texts Found in the Arquivo Histórico Ultramarino, Lisbon", *Zeitschrift der Deutschen Morgenländischen Gesellschaft* 149, no. 1 (1999): 185–90.

[19]   *Cf.* some data in studies by Tang, *Ming Qing* (1998), esp. the essays on pp. 158–84 and 219–40.

[20]   On the subject of *fanfang*, see for example, Wu Zhiliang, *Segredos de Sobrevivência: História Política de Macau* (Macao: Associação de Educação de Adultos de Macau, 1999), pp. 71–84, as well as Jin and Wu, *Jing hai piao miao*, essay 5, and Ptak, "Twentieth Century Macau".

11

"AOCHENG" OR "CIDADE DO NOME DE DEUS": THE NOMENCLATURE OF PORTUGUESE AND CASTILIAN BUILDINGS OF OLD MACAO FROM THE "REVERSED GAZE" OF THE CHINESE

Vincent Ho

After the Portuguese became established at Macao in the mid-1500s, they gradually built up the settlement and developed their residential quarters near Lilau and started self-governance by establishing the Senate, the City Wall, the Holy House of Mercy and fortresses. China's scholar-officials were amazed by all of the infrastructure of Aocheng (澳城; City of the Port) when they visited Macao. The Portuguese king, Dom João IV, bestowed the name Cidade do Nome de Deus (City of the Name of God) on Macao in 1654, which marked its important position. A question arises, however, as to why the Portuguese were able to settle in this port near the Pearl River Delta and construct such a large array of building compounds. In what way did the Chinese people in Macao understand the infrastructure and institutions established by the Portuguese? This study aims to re-examine the so-called "reversed gaze" of the Chinese people as well as the Chinese sources related to the urban development of Macao from the mid-sixteenth to the early nineteenth century with an interpretation of the names of the Portuguese and Castillian buildings used by the Chinese people.[1] Chinese sources, including *Aomen Jilüe* (澳門記略; *A Brief Record of Macao*), local gazetteers, poems, notes, journals and reports of the Chinese officials will be used to illustrate Chinese nomenclature and the actual process of the encounter in Macao between the Portuguese and Castillians on the one hand, and the Chinese on the other. Such records are important to acknowledge as they offer a new and more balanced view of these interactions, relative to the standard Eurocentric perspective. In the discussion below, shorter quoted or summarized text that appears in English will be followed by the original Chinese; for longer passages, the original Chinese appears in the endnotes.

MACAO: "CITY OF THE PORT"

Aocheng (澳城; City of the Port) was the name that usually referred to the walled Portuguese settlement on the southern part of the Macao peninsula. According to *A Brief Record of Macao*, a famous Chinese historical work on Macao written by Yin Guangren (印光任) and Zhang Rulin (張汝霖) in 1751, the City of the Port was created by the Folangji (佛郎機; Portuguese) during the Late Ming period. During the reign of Emperor Wanli (萬曆, AD 1573–1620) of Ming China, the ex-Xiangshan Ling (香山令; ex-magistrate of Xiangshan county), Cai Shanqji (蔡善繼), was promoted to be an official of Lingxi Dao (嶺西道; the western part of the Guangdong circuit). The governor-general who succeeded him, He Shijin (何士晉), took his advice and gave an order to destroy the towers of Aocheng (澳城明季創自佛郎機。萬曆中,蔡善繼由香山令仕至嶺西道,總督何士晉採其言,下令隳澳城臺。).[2] Of course, the Portuguese settlement was not destroyed because this order was not carried out, thanks to the fact that the Portuguese gave the governor-general ten thousand taels (銀一萬兩) to solve the problem.[3]

In 1614, the local officials of Xiangshan (香山) County reported to the Liangguang Buyuan (兩廣部院; viceroy of Guangdong and Guangxi) and the Xunan Yashi (巡按御史; senior inspection official) that they had drafted a document, the "Haidao Jinyue" (《海道禁約》; "Restraints on the Maritime Region") on a stela. The last clause clearly stated the Chinese officer did not allow

[the Portuguese to] build any houses without authorization [from the Chinese government]. All the foreigners' cottages, if they are built already, are allowed to be restored to their original style in case of destruction.

From now on, if the foreigners dare to build any new building, or to add any parts to the existing buildings, or to begin building with even a piece of brick or wood, such constructions of any kind will be destroyed by burning and those who are involved will be seriously punished. [凡 澳中彝寮, 除前已落成, 遇有壞爛, 准照舊式脩葺。此後敢有新建 房屋、添造亭舍、擅興一土一木, 定行拆毀焚燒, 仍加重罪。]4

Of course, such a prohibition was never strictly enforced since many new buildings were constructed afterwards, demonstrating that the threat was not fulfilled; further, the Ming Dynasty fell thirty years later, in 1644.

After overcoming the threat from the greedy local Chinese officials, and during the reign of Emperor Tianqi (天啓, 1621–27), the Portuguese settlement of Macao took the opportunity to develop further after the Portuguese told the Haidao Fushi (海道副使; vice officer of maritime affairs), Xu Ruke (徐如珂), that the Dutch would attack Xiangshan County. The Portuguese then asked for reinforcements, additional money, and a supply of food from the local Chinese government. The Portuguese also asked for the Chinese authorities to provide wood and stone in order to fortify the city wall. As a result, "the Macao city wall was built a hundred *zhang* [丈; 3.3 metres] daily!" [澳垣日築百丈].5 Of course, the actual scale of the development of the city wall was not exactly 330 metres per day; however, this average reflects the fact that the Portuguese were starting to build a stronger defensive wall to protect themselves from any further threat from the Chinese authorities or the Dutch invaders.

It is no surprise that the Chinese people were quite interested to know the details of the military power of the Portuguese settlement of Macao. According to *Aomen ji* (澳門記; *A Report of Macao*), a journal written in 1745 by Xue Yun (薛縕), a Qing literati, there were six forts in Macao previously established by the Westerners, namely, Dong Wang Yang (東望洋; Guia; eastern side of the coast), Ka Si Lan (咖斯蘭; Castilla; St. Francis), San Ba (三巴; Three Hopes; St. Paul's Church), Nan Wan (南灣; Praya Grande; southern bay), Xi Wang Yang (西望洋; Penha; western side of the coast), and Niang Ma Ge (娘媽閣; Mother's Hall; Barra; A-ma Temple). He also knew there were forty-six bronze cannons and thirty-six iron cannons; sixty-one of those were large and fifteen were small. All the "temples" looked like forts; only Three Hopes was elegant and grand.6 Such detailed descriptions were rare in most of the Chinese records on the forts and cannons of Macao. Normally, these observations were made from aboard a boat cruising along the coast.

ST. PAUL'S CHURCH: THE CHURCH OF THREE HOPES

The City Wall that separated the Chinese settlement at the northern half of the peninsula from the Portuguese settlement was not a fully blocked one. There was a main entrance to permit contact between the Portuguese and the Chinese that was located next to St. Paul's Church, which was known as the Sanba Men (三巴門; Gate of Three Hopes). In fact, the term "Sanba" (三巴) has no proper meaning in traditional Chinese usage, even though it can be understood as "three hopes" or "three wishes", an unusual expression or sentiment. The origin of the term is unlikely to be derived from references to the Holy Trinity in Catholic doctrine. Instead, the name of the gate is probably related to St. Paul's Church, which the Chinese called "Sanba" (in Cantonese), an aural cognate based on the first two syllables of "São Paulo" (that is, "São Pau") from the name of the church in Portuguese, Igreja de São Paulo. Such a colloquial way of naming things was common in Macao and often generated many unreliable unofficial names for buildings and locations among the Chinese community.

Undoubtedly, St. Paul's Church was a landmark for the Macao Chinese who came from the rest of China: in 1729, Jiao Qinian (焦祈年) urged visitors to "enter the 'City of the Port', [and] visit the 'Temple of Three Hopes'" (進澳城，入三巴寺).[7] The fact that St. Paul's was located at the most popular boundary district between the Portuguese and the Chinese probably accounts for its standardized Chinese nickname. This beautiful church was dedicated to the Mater Dei (Mother of God or Blessed Virgin Mary) and thus attracted many Chinese visitors. In the eyes of Jiao Qinian, St. Paul's was "extremely grand and beautiful! The size of the building is so big that even horses can run on the floor" (極壯麗!樓可走馬).[8] Interestingly, he was attracted by the sound of the Western musical instruments and the bells of the church: "The foreign organ generated sounds of hitting metals which was really a sound from the remote world of antiquity" (洋琴錚錚，然有太古音。).[9] The following description from *A Brief Record of Macao* clearly describes the pipe organ in St. Paul's:

> There was a pipe organ in the tower of the "Temple of Three Hopes" which was stored in a leather cupboard. Hundreds of pipes are linked with silk stings, and [the player] presses the bottoms from the exterior. The air will be drawn mildly into the pipe organ, after that some voices will come out from the leather cupboard in different melodies in harmony to chorus. The sound was wonderful![10]

Concerning the actual religious function of the temple, the Chinese journal reflects that St. Paul's Church was influential in both Macao and other parts of coastal Southeast China. In 1744, Zhang Rulin, the Xiangshan Ling, banned Christians from the Tangren Miao (唐人廟; Chinese Temple) with great effort and finally achieved his goal. The Chinese Catholics dared not visit the temple, so they moved their worship of God to the Sanba Si (三巴寺; Temple of Three Hopes; St Paul's Church). Some of the worshippers came secretly from the coastal regions nearby to attend. [11]

There is comparatively little detail to be found in Chinese records about the interiors of other churches in Macao, relative to the descriptions of St. Paul's, which suggests that the Chinese literati either were not interested in them or were not allowed to enter them. For example, the account of St. Joseph's Seminary was relatively brief: "At the western part of Macau was Xiao Sanba Si [小三巴寺; Little Three Hopes Temple; St. Joseph's Seminary] whose scale was smaller than St. Paul's Church but more stylish. It was the outer store of St. Paul's Church" (澳西有小三巴寺，規制差約而軒豁過之，三巴之外庫也。).[12]

There are quite a lot of Chinese records about St. Paul's Church. Such detailed descriptions might be due to the fact that some Chinese people had already converted to Catholicism. Another possible interpretation is that this reflects the openness of the church to Chinese visitors, both those who had and had not converted.

ST. FRANCIS'S MONASTERY AND THE CATALONIAN MISSIONARY

Besides the popular St. Paul's, another structure that enjoys wide coverage in Chinese sources is St. Francis's. A comparison of the Chinese records about this monastery with Western records indicates that there were at least three Chinese titles for this entity with homophonic characters of the same entity (or similar) pronunciations in Cantonese: Qie Si Lan (伽思蘭);[13] Ge Si Lan (噶斯蘭);[14] and Jia Si Lan (家斯欄).[15]

Two observations can be made about St. Francis's based on the information found in Chinese sources. First, none of the above Chinese variations on the name of the monastery relates in any way to a saint or a religion. Further, the terms themselves do not make any sense in Chinese. Instead, it appears that the Chinese name was merely an imitation of the first three syllables of the place name "Catalonia", a region in the northeastern part of the Iberian peninsula ("Catalunya" in Catalan; "Cataluña" in Spanish; and "Catalunha" in Portuguese). As it so happens, the first missionary at St. Francis's was from Catalonia, having left his homeland on 2 February 1580. One Chinese source, however, uses the name "Mai Jiasi Si" (賣家私寺; Temple of Selling Furniture) for St. Francis's, but this appears to be an exceptional case.[16]

Second, most of the sources about St. Francis's do little more than record its location on a map, at the south end of the cathedral.[17] Physical descriptions are brief and lack detail about the architectural characteristics of the monastery.

OTHER CHURCHES OF MACAO: FUNCTION AND APPERANCE

The Chinese terms "Miao" (廟; temples or churches), "Si" (寺; pagodas or temples), and even "Tang" (堂; halls) were commonly used for religious buildings of Buddhism, Taoism and even Confucianism. In the case of Macao, Catholicism was something new for the Chinese in South China. For this reason, the Chinese borrowed terms from their own religious traditions in an interchangeable way to refer to the cathedrals, churches, and any building related to the Catholic Church.

According to one entry in *A Brief Record of Macao*, there were eight "temples" (Miao; 廟; churches) in Macao in 1751, namely: (1) Sanba (三巴; Three Hopes [Temple]; St. Paul's Church); (2) Ka Si Lan (咖斯蘭; Castilla [Temple]; St. Francis's Monastery); (3) Taimiao (大廟; the Great Temple; the Cathedral of Macao); (4) Banzha (板樟; Hall Covered by Board; St. Dominic's Church); (5) Longsong (龍鬆; Relaxed Dragon [Temple]; St. Augustine's Church); (6) Fengshun (風信; Windy Message Temple; St. Lawrence's Church); (7) Zhiliang (支糧; Food Supply [Temple]; the Holy House of Mercy); and (8) Fawong (花王; Flowery King [Hall]; St. Anthony's Church).[18]

These churches do not constitute a complete list of all Catholic structures in Macao. In fact, Xue Yun mistook the Holy House of Mercy for being a church. A more comprehensive account of the suite of Catholic buildings in Macao comes from the 1827 *Xinxiu Xiangshan Xianzhi* (新修香山縣志; *New Edition of the Local Gazetteer of Xiangshan*), compiled by Zhu Huai (祝淮) and Huang Peifang (黃培芳). They record that the chief church was the Temple of Three Hopes, or St. Paul's Church, which was located in the centre of Macao. Its stone sculpture was "beautifully made in a special way with nice characters" and there had originally been a Catholic church beneath the statues of the Holy Mother, God and Jesus, once banned during the period of Emperor Qianlong (乾隆).[19] The Little Temple of Three Hopes was located in the western district of Macao. South of St. Paul's was the Temple Covered by Board, described as being "especially magnificent" (壯麗特甚). In the southwest part of Macao was Longsong Miao (龍嵩廟; Temple of Dragon Peak; St. Augustine's Church), also known as the Feilai Si (飛來寺; Flying Temple). The Great Temple was located in the southeast part of Macao and was called Wangren Si (望人寺; Waiting Temple; the Cathedral). It should be noted that the *New Edition*'s predecesor, *The Local Gazette of Xiangshan* (香山), written by Bao Yu (暴煜), erred with respect to these latter two structures, stating that there was another Flying Temple and another Waiting Temple in the city.[20]

Moving on throughout the city, Fengxin Miao (風信廟; Windy Message Temple; St. Lawrence's Church) in the southwest part of the city was "where the foreign ladies prayed for a safe voyage … after the foreign vessels parted for their journey".[21] At the eastern corner of Macao was Jia Si Lan (咖思嚹; Castilla Temple; St, Francis's Monastery), and at its northern corner was Huawang Miao (花王廟; Flowery King Temple; St. Anthony's Church). Zhiliang (Food Supply Temple; Holy House of Mercy), at the southern corner served "just like the system of Orphanage [育嬰堂] on the mainland".[22] Yiren Miao (醫人廟; the Clinic Temple; St. Raphael's Hospital) was located in the eastern part of Macao and offered medical treatment to foreigners "who are not able to get cured themselves". Nigu Si (尼姑寺; Nuns' Temple; St. Clara's Convent), located in the southeast, had its doors "locked by and protected by guards. Once within, [nuns] are not allowed to leave for life; even their close relatives are not allowed to see them."[23] Finally, in the southeast, outside the city, the *New Edition* noted the existence of the isolated Mafeng Si (痲瘋寺; Leprosy Temple; St. Lazarus's Church).[24]

While the above set of names provides basic information on the location of the churches and the Chinese names for them, it does not provide explanations for name choices. For example, why was Longsong Miao (龍嵩廟; Temple of Dragon Peak; St. Augustine's Church), a church located at Gang Ding (崗頂; Peak of Hill]), called the Flying Temple (Feilai Si; 飛來寺)? According to a remark in *Aomen Zashi* (澳門雜詩; *Unclassified Poems of Macao*), written by Wang Zhaoyong (汪兆鏞) and published in 1918, during the early years of the building of Longsong Miao, the name "Flying Temple" was a corrupted form of the name "Longsong Miao". In Cantonese, the pronunciations of Song (嵩; Peak) and Song (鬆; Relaxed) are similar. As it so happened, the roof of the church was almost ruined and may have been covered by palm fronds. Thus, the canopy was loosened and looked like the whiskers of a dragon (髯龍) (初就圮，或覆之以 簑，鬆髯如髯龍), so that was the reason why the name of the church was sometimes written as Longxu Miao (龍鬚廟; Temple of Dragon's Whiskers) since Song (嵩; Peak), Song (鬆; Relaxed), and Xu (鬚; Whiskers) all have similar pronunciations in Cantonese.[25] Actually, all of these Chinese names were suitable to describe the church's appearance with its loosened canopy at its location at the peak of a small hill, thus resembling a dragon's whiskers.

The Chinese name of a street near this structure was Longsong Zhengjie (龍嵩正街; Central Street of the Dragon Peak). In Portuguese, it was known as Rua Central (Central Street), in reference to its location on a small hill in the central district of Macao.

Besides noting the architectural appearance of these buildings, Chinese observers also briefly mentioned the churches when recording some religious activities. For example, both Yin Guangren and Zhang Rulin were aware that there was a temple at the northern coastal corner of the Macao Peninsula where "all the foreign men and ladies who are in love would visit ... to take an oath in front of [the statue] of God. A 'monk' would bless them for good fortune at the end of the ceremony."[26] This church was called Huawang Miao (花王廟; Flowery King Temple; St. Anthony's Church). The name "Flowery King" is not clearly explained by any Chinese records of that time, but it might refer to the wedding ceremony with flowers and Catholic priests; the term "Wang" (王; king) could be a short form of "king of canon", or Fawang (法王), meaning "priest". The Chinese name for St. Anthony's Church means "stable" because of its central location and importance. However, Yin Guangren and Zhang Rulin also knew that St. Anthony's Church was not the only one that offered wedding ceremonies. They pointed out that "only the temples of Flowery King, the Big Temple, and Windy Message Temple divided the foreign residents into three groups and took responsibility for their marriage ceremonies[;] the other temples did not offer such services to them" (廟惟花王、大廟、風信三分蕃戶而司其婚，餘皆否。).[27] Whereas this nomenclature may not be completely accurate, it does indicate an understanding of the function of these churches on the part of the Chinese.

Some public activities such as processions were organized by churches as well. *A Brief Record of Macao* provided the schedule: the procession of San Ba (三巴; Temple of Three Hopes; St. Paul's Church) occurred in the tenth month of the Chinese lunar calendar; the processions of Banzha (Tang; 板樟堂) were in the third month, as was Zhiliang (支糧); and those of the Big Temple (大廟)were in the second, fifth, and sixth months. The processioners would first visit Longsong Miao at night "to take the statue to their own temples with lights on for the whole night. After the people in Macao are gathered, the African slaves would hold the statue of the Suffering Jesus to march in front of the foreign children who read the spells after them."[28] Recorded observations such as these were important to the Chinese as they allowed them to understand the role of each church in different religious events throughout the year.

The term "temple" might sometimes refer to other structures related to the Catholic Church. The Holy House of Mercy is a good example of how the Chinese understood these Western religious institutions. *A Brief Record of Macao* provides a good example:

> At the Southern costal corner of the Macau Peninsula is a temple called "Food Supply". The function of this temple is similar to that of a nursery on mainland China. Next to the entrance, there is a cradle with a small bell. If anyone gives up his or her child, he or she could pull the string to make a bell ring and put the child into the cradle. When the monks heard the bell ring, they would come to take care of the child.[29]

From this record, it is clear that the people who received a "food supply" from the Holy House of Mercy were the orphans who were just babies and badly needed the monks to provide food for them.

In other cases, the term "liang" (糧; food) actually referred to money. Yin Guangren and Zhang Rulin state that the Clinic Temple was located in the eastern part of Macao "with some medical doctors. All the foreigners who are widowers, widows, alone, or orphans suffering from illness and are not able to afford the cost of medical treatment themselves are allowed to visit there to receive medical treatment paid by the Zhiliang Miao [支糧廟; Food Supply Temple]" (別爲醫人廟，於澳之東，醫者數人。凡夷人鰥寡煢獨，有疾不能自療者，許就廟醫，其費給自支糧廟。).[30]

It is worth noting that the Chinese literati might not have travelled all over the whole City of the Name of God but only the central part of it. This is suggested by the fact that only St. Paul's Church, the Holy House of Mercy and St. Joseph's Seminary are mentioned in relative detail. The following are examples of observations recorded about some of the "remote" churches in the central part of Macao. At Fengxin Miao (風信廟; Windy Message Temple; St. Lawrence's Church) in the southwest part of Macao, "when foreign ships went for their journey, the relatives of the sailors waited anxiously everyday for their return. [They] pray for the message of wind here" (此外，西南則有風信廟，蕃舶既出，室人日跂其歸，祈風信於此。).[31] In the northeast of Macao, the doors of Ni Si (尼寺; Nuns' Temple; St. Clara's Convent) were "locked with great caution. Girls under the age of ten would be accepted to this temple. However, they are not allowed to leave for life. Even their close relatives are not allowed to go in for a visit" (尼寺在澳東北,扃鑰嚴邃。女十歲以下許入寺,即入終其身不復出,雖至親不能入視。).[32] In the southeast, outside the city, was Fafeng Si (發瘋寺; Madness Temple; St. Lazarus's Church), where "foreigners affected by leprosy live within. An armed force paid for a monthly guard for the outside" (東南城外有發瘋寺, 內居瘋蕃, 外衛以兵, 月有廩。).[33]

As St. Clara's Convent, St. Lazarus's Church and St. Lawrence's Church were all located outside the centre of Macao, Chinese observations about them are very limited.

THE LOYAL SENATE: "PAVILION FOR DISCUSSION"

Surprisingly, the physical appearance of the Leal Senado (Loyal Senate) building was not widely covered in Chinese documents even though the institution was frequently mentioned in the Chinese records as Yishi Ting (議事亭; Pavilion for Discussion). Unlike the name of the churches, the name of this building described its function rather than its appearance.

Some of the Chinese documents provide brief descriptions on the function of this building as a place for Luso-Chinese communication. *A Brief Record of Macao* also pointed out that the Loyal Senate was the only institution related to the Chinese authority of the Ming Dynasty that was still functioning at the time (今惟議事亭不廢). "Whenever an official or a military officer arrives in Macao, he will sit in the 'Pavilion for Discussion'. After the leader of the foreigners who sits nearby offers a cup of tea to him, if they want to start a conversation, a translator would be there to help with the communication" (凡文武官至澳，坐議事亭上。彝目列坐進茶畢，有欲言則通事傳之。).[34]

In other words, the Chinese documents about the Loyal Senate of Macao mainly focused on its diplomatic nature between the Chinese and Portuguese authorities. The other reason for the Chinese name of the Loyal Senate being the "Pavilion for Discussion" might have been due to its major function as a municipal institution and a place of major decision-making for Macao's self-governance. The Chinese records mention that there were four leaders of the foreigners in the Loyal Senate. If these four made a decision, "the people dared not show any objection" (「眾莫敢違」).[35] The common Chinese people might not have been allowed access to such important Portuguese authorities. Therefore, they could only describe the doors of the entrance. For instance, "when nothing of importance happens on a peaceful sea, the doors would be closed for a long time with an empty pavilion behind" (海上太平無一事，雙扉久閉一空亭。[凡海上事，官紳集議亭中，名議事亭]。).[36] A note in the original text states that "all the maritime issues would be discussed by the officials and gentlemen in the pavilion".[37]

For more detailed descriptions of the interior setting of the Loyal Senate, it appears that the Chinese records were only able to identify those that were somehow related to China. For example, after the death of Wang Chuo

(王綽), a Chinese general who stayed in Macao in 1565, "a spirit tablet of him was put in the Pavilion for Discussion for the foreigners to worship in the Spring and the Autumn" (設位議事亭，番人春秋供祀事焉。).[38] Another example comes from the stela that listed the prohibited issues in Macao: "later on a stela was provided with foreigners' characters in the Pavilion for Discussion and a Chinese version of the stela in the office of the Assistant County Magistrate [of Xiangshan county]" (後乃以番字碑立議事亭，漢字碑立縣丞公署。).[38]

CONCLUSION

The records discussed above, which were written by Chinese literati and officials, are evidence of the nature of the Luso-Chinese encounter. The difference between the original Portuguese or Castilian names and the Chinese names is that the latter were usually just descriptions of the physical appearance of the buildings or the social function of the churches rather than a reference to the deities being worshiped there. Only a few exceptions to this pattern can be found, notably in the records that acknowledged the relationship between St. Paul's College on the one hand and St. Joseph's Seminary and Chapel on the other as the two buildings shared the common name of "Three Hopes". However, the name itself did not reflect the real connection between these two chapels, which belonged to the same Jesuit mission.

How much did the Chinese know about the Portuguese? As most of the Chinese people at that time did not know any Portuguese, they created different names for the buildings in Macao established by Portuguese merchants and missionaries. The existence of several names for the same church with similar Chinese pronunciations documents the oral tradition of the Chinese people. One of the major reasons for this phenomenon of multiple names for the same entity might be that there were at least two important ethnic groups in Macao that spoke different dialects: Cantonese, and Hokkien/Fujianese (閩語; 福建話). The dialect of the Boat People (Tanka; 蜑家) might also have had an impact. Surprisingly, Lilau or the Yapo Jing (亞婆井; Old Lady's Well), which was known as one of the community centres of the Portuguese in Macao, was not mentioned in any Chinese documents from the mid-sixteenth to the eighteenth centuries. No matter how difficult it is to match the names of the particular buildings to the original ones, such records are nevertheless good examples of how the "reversed gaze" of the local Chinese people regarded the activities of the Portuguese in Macao.

Notes

1   For an academic discussion of the concept "reversed gaze", see Kum Kum
    Chatterjee and Clement Hawkes, eds., *Europe Observed: The Reversed Gaze in Early
    Modern Encounters* (Lewisburg: Bucknell University Press, 2008); and Mwenda
    Ntarangwi, *Reversed Gaze: An African Ethnography of American Anthropology*
    (Urbana: University of Illinois Press, 2010).

2   Yin Guangren 印光任 and Zhang Rulin 張汝霖, 趙春晨, *Aomen Jilüe Jiaozhu*
    澳門記略校注 [A Corrected and Annotated Edition of A Brief Record of
    Macao], edited by Zhao Chunchen (Macao: Aomen wenhua sishu, 澳門文化
    司署, 1992), pt. 2 (卷下), "Aofan Pian" 澳蕃篇 [Foreigners in Macao], p. 147.
    For Portuguese translations, see Tcheong-Ü-Lâm 張汝霖 and Ian-Kuong-Iâm
    印光任, trans., Luís Gonzaga Gomes, *Monografia de Macau (Ou-mun kei-leok)*
    [A brief monograph of Macao] (Lisbon: Quinzena de Macau, 1979); and Yin
    Guangren 印光任 and Zhang Rulin 張汝霖, comp., Zhao Chunchen 趙春晨,
    trans., Jin Guo Ping 金國平, rev., Rui Manuel Loureiro, *Breve Monografia de
    Macau* [A brief monograph of Macao] (Macao: Instituto Cultural do Governo
    da R.A.E. de Macau, 2009).

3   Jin Guoping 金國平 and Wu Zhiliang 吳志良, "'Dizuyin Yiwan Liang' Yu
    'Dingliang Yiwan Liang'" (〈「地租銀一萬兩」與 「丁糧一萬兩」〉)
    ["Ten thousand taels of rent" and "Ten thousand liang of food for the people"],
    in *Dongxi Wangyang* 東西望洋 [Eastern and western side of the coast], edited
    by Jin Guoping 金國平 and Wu Zhiliang 吳志良 (Macao: Aomen chengren
    jiaoyu xuehui 澳門成人教育學會 [Association of Adult Education of Macao],
    2002), pp. 182–88.

4   Yin 印光任 and Zhang 張汝霖, *Aomen Jilüe Jiaozhu* 澳門記略校注, pt. 1
    (卷上), "Guanshou Pian" 官守篇 [Official duties], p. 70.

5   Ibid., 2:147.

6   In the original Chinese: 西人於澳内舊設礮臺六座：曰東望洋，曰咖斯
    蘭，曰三巴，曰南灣，曰西望洋，曰娘媽閣。礮：銅具四十六，鐵具
    三十六；大者六十一，小者十有五。凡廟若礮臺，獨三巴爲崇閎焉。
    Xue Yun 薛醖, "Aomen ji" 澳門記 [A report of Macao], in *Xiao Fanghu Zhai
    Yudi Congchao* 小方壺齋與地叢鈔 [Collected texts on geography from the
    Little Square Kettle Studio], edited by Wang Xiqiji 王錫祺, vol. 9 [第九秩]
    (Shanghai: Zhuyi Tang 著易堂, 1877), p. 317.

7   Jiao Qinian 焦祈年, "Yiwen . Ji" 藝文．記 [Arts and literature: Reports],
    in "Xunshi Aomen ji" 巡視澳門記 [An inspection report on Macao],
    in *Xiangshan Xianzhi* 香山縣志 [Xiangshan Gazetteer], edited by Bao Yu 暴煜
    and Li Zhuokui 李卓揆 (Gunagzhou, 1750), p. 45.

8   Ibid.

9   Ibid.

10 In the original Chinese: 三巴寺樓有風琴，藏革櫝中。排牙管百餘，聯以
    絲繩，外按以囊。噓吸微風入之，有聲嗚嗚自櫝出，八音並宣，以和經

吹。甚可聽。Yin 印光任 and Zhang 張汝霖, *Aomen Jilüe Jiaozhu* 澳門記略
校注, 2:172–73.

[11] Zhang Zhentao 張甄陶, "Zhiyu Aoyi Lun" 制馭澳夷論 [On controlling the
foreigners in Macao], in Wang 王錫祺, *Xiao Fanghu Zhai Yudi Congchao* 小方
壺齋與地叢鈔, 9:332.

[12] Yin 印光任 and Zhang 張汝霖, *Aomen Jilüe Jiaozhu* 澳門記略校注, 2:150.

[13] Lu Kun 盧坤 et al., *Guangdong Haifang Huilan* 廣東海防匯覽 [A general
overview of coastal defence in Guangdong] (Guangzhou, 1835), p. 32. This
page is from pt. 2, "Paotai: Yi" (礮臺．二; "Fortress"), sec. 21, Fanglü: Ershi
(方略．二十一; "Strategy"), in chap. 30 (卷三十).

[14] "Yishang" 夷商 [Foreign traders], in *Yuehai guanzhi: jiao zhu ben* 粵海關志: 校
注本 [Guangzhou customs record: A corrected and annotated edition], edited
by Tingnan Liang 梁廷柟, compiled by Yuan Zhongren 袁鐘仁 (Guangzhou
廣州: Guangdong Renmin Chubanshe 廣東人民出版社 [Guangdong People's
Press], 2002), p. 504.

[15] "Yutu" 與圖 [geographical illustration], in *Guangzhou Fuzhi* 廣州府志 [A record
of Guangzhou], edited by Shen Tingfang 沈廷芳 (Guangzhou 廣州: Daoshu
道署 [Government Office], 1758), n.p.

[16] Shen Lianghan 申良韓, rev., Ouyang Yuwen 歐陽羽文, *Xiangshan Xianzhi*
香山縣志 [Xiangshan Gazetteer], vol. 1, *Guan Shou* 官守 [Official duties]
(Shiqi 石岐 [?], 1673), p. 168. This page is from chap. 10, "Waizhi" 外志,
sec. 6, "Ao Yi" 澳彝 [Foreign affairs: Barbarians in Macao]. This work is stored
in the library of the *Xianggang zhongwen daxue* 香港中文大學 [The Chinese
University of Hong Kong].

[17] "Yutu", n.p.

[18] Ibid.

[19] Zhu Huai 祝淮 and Huang Peifang 黃培芳, *Xinxiu Xiangshan Xianzh i* 新修香
山縣志 [New edition of local gazetteer of Xiangshan], vol. 4 [卷四], "Haifang:
Fu Aomen" [海防 • 附澳門; Coastal defence: Plus Macao] (Shiqi 石岐 [?]:
Government Office 本衙 of Shiqi [?], 1827), p. 105.

[20] Ibid.

[21] Ibid.

[22] Ibid.

[23] Ibid.

[24] Ibid. The Chinese text covering notes 19–24 is as follows: 寺首三巴，在澳
之中，雕石綺疏，製殊瑰異，奉天母及天主耶穌像下，舊有天主堂，即
乾隆間所封禁者。澳西有小三巴寺；南有板障廟，壯麗特甚；龍嵩廟在
澳西南，即飛來寺；[《暴志》另載飛來寺誤]。大廟在澳東南，即望人
寺。[《暴志》另載望人寺誤夷人始至澳所建也]；西南則風信廟，蕃舶
既出，蕃婦祈風信於此；東隅則咖思嘮廟；北隅則花王廟；南隅廟曰支
糧，如內地育嬰堂制；醫人廟在澳東，夷病不能自療者就醫；尼姑寺
在澳東南，扃鑰嚴毖，終身不復出，至親不能視；東南城外別爲痲瘋
寺。

25 Wang Zhaoyong 汪兆鏞, illus., 圖譯 Ye Jinbin 葉晉斌, *Aomen zashi tushi* 澳門雜詩圖譯 [Illustrated unclassified poems of Macao] (Macao: Aomen jijin hui 澳門基金會 [Macao Foundation], 2004), p. 56.

26 Yin 印光任 and Zhang 張汝霖, *Aomen Jilüe Jiaozhu* 澳門記略校注, 2:150. In the original Chinese: 北隅一廟，凡蕃人男女相悅，詣神盟誓畢，僧爲卜吉完聚，名曰花王廟。

27 Ibid., 2:155.

28 Ibid., 2:151. In the original Chinese: 歲中天主出遊。三巴則以十月；板樟以三月、九月；支糧三月；大廟則二月、五月、六月凡三。出遊率先夕詣龍鬆廟，迎像至本寺，燃燈達旦。澳眾畢集，黑奴舁被難像前行，蕃童誦咒隨之。

29 In the original Chinese: 南隅有廟曰支糧，如内地育嬰堂制，門側穴轉斗縣鐸，有棄其子者，挈繩響鐸，置轉斗中。僧聞鐸聲至，收而育之。Yin 印光任 and Zhang 張汝霖, *Aomen Jilüe Jiaozhu* 澳門記略校注, 2:150.

30 Ibid.

31 Ibid., 2:150–1.

32 Ibid.

33 Ibid.

34 "Haojing Ao" 濠鏡澳 [Port of Oyster Mirror], in Bao 暴煜 and Li 李卓揆, *Xiangshan Xianzhi* 香山縣志, p. 26.

35 Wang Shizhen 王士禎, *Chibei Outan* 池北偶談 [Notes on the conversation from the northern lake], vol. 22 (卷二一), "Tanyi: Er" 談異．二 [On strangeness: Section two] (Beijing 北京: Zhonghua Shuju 中華書局, 1982), pp. 517–18. These pages deal with Xiangshan Ao 香山嶴 [the port of of Xiangshan].

36 "Aozhong zayong: Qi" 澳中雜詠．七 [Unclassified poems on Macao: Number seven], in Wu Yushan ji Jianzhu 吳漁山集箋注 [A brief annotation of Wu Yushan's collected works], by Wu Li 吳曆 and compiled by Zhang Wenqin 章文欽 (Beijing 北京: Zhonghua Shuju 中華書局, 2007), p. 166.

37 Ibid.

38 Bao 暴煜 and Li 李卓揆, *Xiangshan Xianzhi* 香山縣志, chap. 6 (卷六), "Renwu liezhuan: Wugong" 濠鏡澳 [Biographies: Military officers], p. 85.

39 Ibid.

12

ENEMIES, FRIENDS AND RELATIONS: PORTUGUESE EURASIANS DURING MALACCA'S DUTCH ERA AND BEYOND

Dennis De Witt

The Portuguese and the Dutch were age-old enemies, and remnants of the historical, political and religious competition between the two nations can still be found in the culture and heritage of the Portuguese Eurasian community in Malacca. Margaret Sarkissian said it best when she observed that whenever the history of the Malacca Portuguese Eurasian community touches on the Dutch era, people from this community invoke the brief tale of the cruelty of Dutchmen who "inflicted a period of religious persecution upon the hardy Portuguese, reduced them to subsistence fisherfolk, forced them into the jungle for secret church services, but were unable to crush their spirit".[1]

This is a rather popular point of view that portrays the negative aspects of Malacca Portuguese Eurasians during the Dutch era that is shared by historians and writers from this community, such as the late Bernard Sta Maria[2] and Gerard Fernandis.[3] They, in turn, were much influenced by the views and research of Roman Catholic clerics with whom they had interacted in Malacca. The source of their research is based to a large extent on Portuguese documents, either from primary sources that were translated by those clerics, or from secondary sources obtained by them that were written by Portuguese historians, in the Portuguese language.[4] Although Malacca existed for 160 years under Dutch rule, the disconnection between that community with the

Netherlands since 1825 has caused local historians to be greatly deprived of materials and books that would have given them an alternate point of view, namely, from the eyes of the Dutch.

Therefore, when the history of the Malacca Portuguese Eurasian community is re-examined from a Dutch perspective, it can be seen that the Dutch period was not a time of totally rampant persecution and focused discrimination against this community. In fact, some members of the community even enjoyed economic gains and attained some manner of status when they were associated with the Dutch. It is the purpose of this study, therefore, to bring such a perspective to bear on the subject, in particular one that is informed by Malaccan church documents.

THE HISTORICAL CONFLICT

When Philip II became the ruler of Spain and the Netherlands in 1556, his oppression of the people of the Low Countries and Protestantism led to the Dutch War of Independence in 1568. Spain was then the most powerful European nation. The Roman Catholic Church was the official state church of Spain and did not tolerate Protestantism. In 1594, Philip II of Spain gained the Portuguese throne as a son of Princess Isabel of Portugal, thus subordinating Portugal's sovereignty to Spain. By definition, Spain's enemies became those of Portugal. For that reason, Protestant Dutch merchants were no longer allowed to trade in Lisbon or in any other Portuguese-controlled ports, and the lucrative Asian trade was monopolized by the Portuguese.

As a result, the Dutch *eerste schipvaart* (first shipping) to Asia was organized with the aim of breaking the Portuguese monopoly on Asian spices. Soon, more and more Dutch ships were making their way to Asia, and they successfully returned to Europe with their cache of spices. Dutch sailors began to gain favour among Asian Muslim rulers, and they started to undermine the Portuguese trading presence in Asia. The Dutch used the newly developed trade with Asia as an economic weapon against their enemy and threatened to break the Iberian trade monopoly in Asia by capturing Portuguese forts in the Spice Islands (the Moluccas) and forging friendships with the Malays.

As the Dutch became stronger and bolder, it was inevitable that the two powers would clash in an epic battle. Soon enough, the Dutch were eyeing Malacca, and their first attempt at wresting control of the port from the Portuguese came in 1606 when they besieged the fortress. This event then led to one of the greatest sea battles in the region, known as the Battle of

Cape Rachado.[5] From then on, the two European nations remained fierce competitors and bitter enemies in their attempt to control the Straits of Malacca and the historic port town of Malacca. Portuguese Malacca eventually fell to the Dutch in 1641 after six months of deadly conflict. It was a major blow for the Portuguese, and it marked the beginning of the end of the monopolistic Iberian reign in Asia. The Protestant Dutch, enemies of the Roman Catholic Portuguese, became the new rulers of Malacca.[6] Many Portuguese then left Malacca, but some, mainly descendants of the Portuguese, remained and were governed by the European interloper and their "heretic" enemy for the next 160 years.

To the Portuguese, it was inconceivable that their strong fortress could fall into the hands of their enemy. Blame for it was soon put on one of their own — Manuel de Sousa Coutinho, the Portuguese governor of Malacca. Rumours spread that the fall of Malacca was due to a bribe he received, and he died shortly after Malacca fell to the Dutch.[7] After the conquest, the victors focused on rebuilding Malacca and attempted to rejuvenate its trade relations with neighbouring countries. To achieve this, the presence of a flourishing community and society was a necessary prerequisite. Therefore, the Dutch encouraged the inhabitants of Malacca to settle down to honest work and pledge their loyalty to them. Instead, a group of Portuguese clerics and wealthy citizens requested safe passage to the Coromandel Coast in India. The Dutch invited them to stay and take part in the governance of the town, as long as they agreed to swear loyalty to the new Dutch administration. The priests did not agree to the offer, insisted on leaving Malacca, and thus were allowed to do so.

RELIGIOUS CONFLICT

In Europe, Holland continued to be at war with Spain and Portugal. Therefore, the Dutch continued to be subjected to numerous attempts to deprive them of their share of trade in Asia. For political reasons, the Malacca Dutch administration initially allowed Catholics there to build their churches on private land located outside the town and to conduct Mass. They hoped that by allowing some degree of religious leniency towards the Portuguese descendants of Malacca they could retain many of the indigenous Malacca Portuguese, halt the exodus of these people from Malacca to other Portuguese-controlled locales, and allow them to settle down to honest work. Although the two Christian groups were enemies, the Malacca Dutch administration hoped to establish religious peace between the Dutch Protestants and the Portuguese Roman Catholics. However, this did not stop the Dutch from trying to convert the Portuguese to the Gereformede Kerk (Dutch Reformed Church).

Soon after the capture of Malacca, the Dutch administration intended to attract the Portuguese Catholics to their Reformed Church.[8] However, it became evident that their attempts to convert the Malacca Portuguese Roman Catholics would be futile. Commissary Schouten even admitted that "very few, if any, of the Malacca Roman Christians are likely to be converted to the true Reformed Church even by sermons in the Portuguese language".[9] Such early awkward and feeble attempts at converting the Malacca Roman Catholics were quickly seen as a failure and the Dutch made no further efforts to unify the Christian community in Malacca under the sole banner of the Reformed Church. While only the Dutch Reformed religion was permitted in Dutch territories, the provisions against priests of other religions were rarely enforced in a strict sense.

In a letter dated 6 December 1645 from the Hoge Regering (Supreme Government) at Batavia to Arnout de Vlamingh van Oudtshoon, Governor of Malacca, the Dutch administration began to retract its leniency towards Roman Catholics. Catholic churches were banned and all forms of public worship by the Catholics were halted. All those who refused to give up their Catholic religion were required to leave Malacca. The sudden change of attitude by the Dutch was the result of their distrust of Jesuit priests who were seen as behaving as enemies and traitors towards the Dutch in Malacca. To the Catholic priests who visited Malacca, the Dutch were still viewed as their heretic enemy, and they encouraged their flock to offer resistance against the Malacca administration. On 12 June 1646, through an official public proclamation in Malacca by Governor Balthasar Bort, the Malacca Dutch administration explicitly forbade the coming ashore of Roman Catholic priests, and all priests who were already ashore were required to leave within one month, unless they were willing to desist from wearing their cassocks and refrain from preaching or holding public masses.[10]

In early 1665, the Malacca Dutch administration discovered that while a Portuguese ship was lying in the roadstead, no less than 1,500 people were secretly meeting in a garden near the town to attend Mass. The Dutch *fiscaal* (prosecutor) went to the garden with soldiers, dispersed the worshippers, and brought their religious images back to the fort where they were burned. The priest escaped to Bengkalis on a native ship.[11] The action taken by the Dutch must have infuriated the Portuguese Catholic community in Malacca. As a result, it led to further distrust of the Malacca Portuguese, and their employment as night watchmen at the fort was terminated.[12] Following this event, the Dutch promptly decreed that all Catholic priests were banned from entering Malacca and all forms of public preaching for the Roman Catholic faith were to cease. By 1666, Dutch intolerance towards the Roman Catholics in Malacca reached its climax. On 15 January 1666, Governor Balthasar Bort began to strictly enforce his anti-Catholic legislation.[13]

Religious restrictions by the Dutch did little to dampen the faith of the Catholics in Malacca. The Portuguese Eurasians formed the Irmãos da Igreja (Brothers of the Church), a secret brotherhood of laypeople who were loyal to the Roman Catholic Church, to ensure the continuance of Catholicism in Malacca. Public masses were still celebrated but in secret and at remote areas in Malacca's interior.[14] A French Jesuit bound for China who visited Malacca in 1698 wrote that "Catholics are obliged to go far into the interior of the forest to celebrate the sacred mysteries (i.e., Mass)."[15] Therefore, Dutch persecutions against Roman Catholics were still adhered to up to the end of the seventeenth century.

Despite their religious conflicts, difference in beliefs and cultures, though, the Dutch did not look with contempt upon the Portuguese Eurasians. In fact, Schouten regarded them as "the natural Malaccans" and it was his opinion that this community formed the backbone of Dutch Malacca. Although there were various levels of religious suppression of the Portuguese Catholics in Malacca, it generally did not cause a severe strain on the Dutch-Portuguese social relationship. Portuguese Eurasians were still employed by the Dutch as night watchmen, a position of some importance with regard to the security of Malacca's fortress for the governor and other officials who lived within it.

Members of the Malacca Portuguese Eurasian community were also instrumental in providing assistance to Malacca's Dutch administration in the seventeenth century, especially when dealing with surrounding Malay rulers, due to their knowledge of Malay culture and language as well as their experience in local customs and culture. For instance, Tomas Dias (or Diaz) was a Portuguese Eurasian from Malacca who served as a trusted employee of the United Dutch East India Company (Vereenigde Oost-Indische Compagnie, or VOC). During his unprecedented journey to the Minangkabau highlands of Sumatra in 1684, he served as a diplomat and trade envoy for the Dutch in Malacca to develop contacts between the Dutch and the interior states of Sumatra. It was by his ability to successfully deal with Minangkabau rulers that the Dutch were able to resolve trade rivalries and misunderstandings that had occurred in Siak and to further develop trade there. This was ultimately beneficial to both Johor and Malacca. Although Dias was a mestizo, he served in a diplomatic capacity for the Dutch in Sumatra and was regarded as an important link between Malacca and Sumatra.[16]

At the beginning of the eighteenth century, the Dutch attitude towards the Roman Catholics took a turn. Their anti-Catholic legislation was abruptly discontinued, and the Malacca Dutch administration began to take on a more liberal and tolerant outlook towards the Catholics there.[17] Around the year 1702, Catholics in Malacca built St. Peter's Church at Bunga Raya, located just outside the town and now serving as the oldest functioning Catholic church in Malaysia. Around the same time, Roman Catholics in Malacca established the Chapel of the Holy Rosary, located along the riverbank in Bunga Raya.

INTER-ETHNIC RELATIONSHIPS

In time, the Dutchmen in Malacca and the Portuguese women there intermarried, and as a result, many families from these communities bonded and became interconnected. A deeper bond between the two communities thus emerged, and they eventually shared a symbiotic relationship. An early example of this relationship can be found in the case of Maria Pereira of Malacca and her son, Jurriaan Beek.[18]

Maria Pereira was a young Portuguese Eurasian girl who lived in Malacca more than 350 years ago. She was married to another Portuguese Eurasian named Francisco Da Costa. Between 1646 and 1655, Maria and Francisco had three children. After his death, Maria married Jan Beek, with whom she had a son named Jurriaan. Through unknown circumstances, young Jurriaan was sent to Holland. He never returned to Malacca and never saw his mother again. By the beginning of the eighteenth century, Jurriaan Beek was living in the house that he owned on the upscale Herengracht canal in Amsterdam.

Jurriaan lived alone with his servants until the final days of his life. On 22 May 1714, he made out his last will and testament. A week later, at approximately fifty-four years of age, Jurriaan died and was buried in the Oude Kerk (Old Church) in Amsterdam. In his will, Jurriaan named the Weeskarmer (Orphan Chamber) of Amsterdam as the executor of his will. The main beneficiaries of his properties were his half-siblings — the first three children of Maria Pereira, who were from Malacca. Eventually, the Weesmeester of Amsterdam, acting as the trustees, managed to track down the half-brother and half-sisters of Jurriaan Beek in Malacca. The Weesmeesters of Malacca confirmed that the other children of Maria Pereira were Magdalena Da Costa, Catarina Da Costa, and Joan Da Costa. Unfortunately, Joan Da Costa had died in Batavia, but he had surviving children. Magdalena Da Costa was by then the widow of the *burgerkapitein* (captain of the Civil Guard), Reijnier Broenken. There was no information concerning Catarina, but it is known that shortly after 1717, the entitled beneficiaries received their portions of the inheritance.[19] This is probably the only case in which an inheritance from Holland was transferred to Malacca during the Dutch era. More importantly, it shows that although Jurriaan Beek was far removed from his stepfamily, he was still willing to acknowledge them.

By the eighteenth century, the Dutch community of Malacca was made up of a curious mix of Dutch and Dutch-descent Protestants and Roman Catholics. There were also some Protestant Portuguese Eurasians who practised the religion of the Reformed Church, although a majority of them, mainly from the poorer community, were faithful Roman Catholics. The Dutch records contain a number of entries for mixed marriages, particularly between males of the Dutch settler community and females of the Portuguese Eurasian community. However, there are also the names of three Portuguese Eurasians in various records.[20] Included in the names of Europeans, and classified as Malacca Freeburghers (that is, Free Citizens of Malacca), one finds: Matthias Monteira (that is, "Monteiro") Sr., 1758–1837, of Malacca, hired by the VOC in 1781 as a bookbinder on a salary of fourteen guilders a month;[21] Matthias Monteira Jr., 1798–18??, of Malacca, who was a burgher at Surabaya;[22] and Roemalda Tissera (that is, "Teixeria"), who was born sometime around 1750 at Malacca.[23] All of these individuals are mentioned as being Europeans and were considered to be on par socially with the other Dutch Freeburghers in Malacca.

There is also a 1680 record of a person named Domingos Monteira (that is, "Monterio"), who is listed as a Burgher of Malacca living in the Noorder Voorstadt (northern suburb) with his wife. Both of them were classified as *vrijzwarten* (free blacks) in order to identify them as Portuguese Eurasians but free citizens of Malacca.[24] In 1775, the Portuguese Eurasian named Quintiliano da Graca (that is, "Graça") was appointed as the *wijkmeester* (ward administrator) of Heeren Street, the part of Malacca town where many officials from the Malacca Dutch administration lived.

During the course of the eighteenth century, Malacca began to undergo many social, economic and political changes. As the Malacca Dutch administration began to be more tolerant of the Catholics living there, the city's plural society, consisting of Malays, Chinese, Indians, Peranakans, Eurasians and Europeans were living harmoniously together. The various communities there interacted in administration, trade, and in defence of the town when threatened by external foes. On 13 February 1784, the Bugis leader Raja Haji and his fleet arrived from the south and occupied Teluk Ketapang in the southern part of Malacca. He was soon joined by Malay forces from Selangor and Rembau. Malacca found itself blockaded by the enemy who occupied all the surrounding suburbs and villages. The people of Malacca came together and took up arms to repel the enemy. With each race under its own *kapitan* (captain) and leaders, the Malays, Indians, Chinese and Portuguese Eurasians fought together with the Dutch.[25] Abraham Couperus, who was then the *fiscaal* at Malacca (and later rose to be governor of Malacca), commanded a company of mixed races against Raja Haji's attack on the city.

Towards the end of the eighteenth century, a Mrs De Costa owned a substantial piece of property located northeast of Malacca town and indeed was one of the largest landowners in the area.[26] Her case provides evidence that the Dutch administration held no preference against property owners and allowed Portuguese Eurasians as well as other Asian races to own large amounts of property in Malacca.

GENEALOGICAL LINKS

In time, Portuguese Eurasian women often married Dutch personnel stationed in Malacca. The Dutch felt closer to the Portuguese Eurasians than other groups in Malacca, probably because they were fellow Christians, even though they were from different denominations.[27] As a result, the two Christian communities bonded and became genealogically linked.

Contemporary Portuguese Eurasian writers such as Sta Maria have mentioned the conversion of Dutch citizens to Roman Catholicism in Malacca through intermarriage, a conclusion based primarily upon the marriage records of the registers of St. Peter's Church in Malacca.[28] It would appear that one motive for making this observation was to display the religious resilience and strengths of that community throughout history. However, this research was limited to a consultation of the records of the Catholic Church in Malacca and did not extend to a comparison of the list of marriages found in Dutch records. Significantly, when both of these types of sources are cross-referenced, one often finds that these "mixed marriages" also appear in the Dutch ecclesiastical records of Malacca and in the records of the Malacca Dutch administration.[29] In other words, these alliances were solemnized in both the Protestant and Catholic churches of Malacca. Examples of these mixed marriages are found in Table 12.1.

Little or no research has been conducted to explain why these marriages appear in both Catholic Church records as well as in the Dutch Reformed Church records. This question has been asked mainly by genealogists researching their roots going back to the Dutch era in Malacca. So far, it is presumed that since the bride was Portuguese Eurasian, her family probably held her marriage in a Roman Catholic Church as a means to spiritually

TABLE 12.1
Late Eighteenth-Century Portuguese Eurasian and Dutch Intermarriages Co-solemnized in Catholic and Protestant Churches in Malacca

| | Ecclesiastical Records, St. Peter's Church, Malacca | | Ecclesiastical Records, Dutch Reformed Church, Malacca |
Date	Entry	Date	Corresponding Entry (summarized)
17 Sept. 1774	Nicolao Frandebek, Europiano; Clara Miguel, f. [*filha* / daughter of] Joa [*sic*?] Miguel Semet e Florinda Janse	18 Sept. 1774	Nicholaas van der Beek from Delft was married to a Clara Michielsz Smith of Malacca[a]
4 Nov. 1775	Lamberte Feruve, Europiano, Maria Hes, viuva [widow of] Jannes [illegible]; [witnesses]: Anthonij [illegible], Constantia de Souza	5 Nov. 1775	Lambertus Verhoeven and Maria van Es were married
12 Nov. 1775	David Fanleiven de Gaudo, Europiano, Ursela da Graca, f. Quintiliano da Graca; [witnesses]: Regina D'eldre [illegible], Anthonij Bruijns, A. Gomes	12 Nov. 1775	David van Leeuwen de Gouda and Ursela da Graca were married
24 May 1778	Belom Fan Vanoes, na de [*natural* / native of] Amsterdam, Jozefa Fernandez, f. Jose Fernandez, Suzanna Esteirat	24 May 1778	Wilhelm van Veenhuijsen of Amsterdam and Sophia Fernande[z] were married

Note: A Clara Michielsz Smith was born in Malacca. Her marriage thus shows that some members of the Malacca Dutch were Catholics, not Protestants.
Sources: List of Accessions, Baptisms and Marriages (1986), Ecclesiastical Records of the Church of St. Peter, Malacca, AU/1/V, and List of Accessions (1957–67), Ecclesiastical Records of the Dutch Reformed Church of Malacca, M 245/72, Arkib Negara Malaysia, Kuala Lumpur.

solemnize their union. However, the children from these marriages were baptized in the Dutch Reformed Church, showing that the families practised and perpetuated the religion of their fathers. The children of those marriages were christened in Malacca's Dutch Reformed Church, and their descendants actively remained as members of that church.

In time, it was common to find family connections between Portuguese Eurasian and Dutch-descent families in Malacca as a result of these intermarriages. However, this did not mean that there were only Dutchmen who were marrying Portuguese Eurasian women in Malacca. By the beginning of the eighteenth century, Malacca saw more new arrivals of Europeans who made Malacca their new home and became part of the Malacca Dutch community. By then, the town had its fair share of young ladies of Dutch descent. The newcomers found their wives among the daughters of the Malacca Dutch community and in this way helped maintain the "Dutchness" of the society of colonialists. However, it is interesting to note that in the late eighteenth-century records one finds marriages between Portuguese Eurasian grooms and brides with Dutch-sounding names.[30] Examples of these unions are found in Table 12.2.

From the data in Table 12.2, it can be seen that by the late eighteenth century, there was more acceptance by the Dutch community of Malacca towards their fellow Christians from the Malacca Portuguese Eurasian community. To take this a step further, there were even those from the Portuguese Eurasian community in Malacca who had been assimilated into

TABLE 12.2
Late Eighteenth- and Early Nineteenth-Century Portuguese Eurasian and Dutch Intermarriages in Malacca

Date of Marriage	Name of Groom and His Position (If Stated); and Name of Bride
16 Oct. 1788	Philippe de Melloe, burgher; Johanna Pol
26 Jan. 1792	Jan Nonis, inlands soldaat [soldier]; Isabella Claas
1 May 1792	Manuel Francisco de Soiza, inlands burgher; Wilhelmina Elisabeth Spijkerman
2 May 1793	Domingos Ferdinandus, inlands burgher; Magdalena Velge
17 Nov. 1795	Michel de Santo; Dorothea Barnikkel
13 Nov. 1817	Pedro de Rosairo; Hendrica Minjoot

Source: Trouwboek van E. Commissarissen van huwelijkse en kleine gerechtszaken, De archieven van de Verenigde Oostindische Compagnie, 1602–1795, Nationaal Archief van Nederland, The Hague.

Dutch society and decided to relocate their families to Dutch Indonesia. Such was the case of Matthias Monteira (Jr.) who moved from Dutch Malacca to the Dutch port town of Surabaya in Indonesia, at least by 1829. His descendants fully assimilated themselves through intermarriage with the Dutch in Indonesia and were eventually repatriated to the Netherlands after Indonesia achieved independence. Their descendants who are living in the Netherlands now are part of the Indische Nederlanders (Indo-Dutch) community living throughout that country.[31]

A somewhat similar pattern may be found in the case of the descendant of Peter do Rozario, who was born in 1795 at Malacca. His grandson, Fertuliano George de Rozario, migrated to Batavia sometime during the nineteenth century. Eventually, his descendants also moved to the Netherlands.[32]

The fact of the matter was that in Malacca, as well as elsewhere in other Dutch colonies in Asia, a larger number of Dutchmen who were stationed in the colony married women from the local Portuguese Eurasian community. When the Dutch in Asia began marrying locals and Portuguese Eurasian ladies, the culture that was passed on to the children of these mixed marriages was mostly that of their Asian or Eurasian mother. As the lingua franca in the Malay Archipelago during the seventeenth century was mainly Creole Portuguese — known then as the language of traders — many children of Dutch fathers had a better command of the language learnt from their mothers rather than having fluency in Dutch. Similarly, it was in this way that the ancestral culture of the mother was emulated to a greater degree and perpetuated in many Dutch-descent families.

By the eighteenth century, the Malacca Portuguese Eurasian culture had become well rooted in the Malacca Dutch community. In time, the assimilation of many Dutch families into Malacca's Portuguese Eurasian community and their culture became complete. Even today, there are families with Dutch-sounding names who speak Kristang[33] and practise the culture of the Portuguese Eurasian community. Current generations from families with non-Portuguese surnames such as Danker, Goonting, Hendroff, Klassen, Minjoot, Overree, and Spykerman have attached themselves closely to the Malacca Portuguese Eurasian culture and identify their roots with the Portuguese Settlement in Malacca.[34]

In Malacca, Portuguese Eurasians have received the support of the Catholic Church and Portuguese cultural organizations from Macao and Portugal. The Portuguese Settlement is now not only a major tourist attraction in Malacca but, more importantly, is popularly seen as the bastion of the rich and colourful culture and heritage of all Portuguese Eurasians in Malaysia.[35]

CONCLUSION

The Portuguese and the Dutch began their relationship in Malacca as political enemies and religious competitors. In time, however, the Dutch became dependent upon members of the Portuguese community to act as commercial and political intermediaries for their ability to move easily between the Dutch and the Malay worlds. The relationship between Portuguese Eurasians and the Dutch community in Malacca became a symbiotic one. Their bond became complete through intermarriage between the two groups, and the Portuguese Eurasians gained acceptance by the Dutch who came to regard them as their equals. As the ecclesiastical records examined in this study demonstrate, a more profound understanding of the scope and nature of this relationship can be achieved through further research into and analysis of the data to be found in an expanded field of enquiry into sources associated with "both sides" of this complex social equation.

Today, there are over twenty-nine thousand Eurasians living in Malaysia, the vast majority of whom are of Portuguese descent. The Portuguese Eurasians from Malacca, who refer to themselves as "Christao", have every right to be proud of their unique roots and culture. Nevertheless, their history and heritage are entwined with the other Malaysian Eurasians, and the history of each respective race becomes the collective heritage of Malaysian society at large.

Notes

[1]   Margaret Sarkissian, *D'Albuquerque's Children: Performing Tradition in Malaysia's Portuguese Settlement* (Chicago: University of Chicago Press, 2000), p. 26.

[2]   Sta Maria wrote that although the Dutch, during their 160 years in Malacca, had enticed the Portuguese to stay by exercising tolerance, they had "subtly introduced policies that amounted to social and religious suppression". Sta Maria goes on to postulate that there could have been unrecorded martyrs from the Malacca Portuguese community who may have undergone torture by the Dutch as a result of their stubborn perseverance to sustain their religion. Bernard Sta Maria, *My People, My Country: The Story of the Malacca Portuguese Community* (Malacca: Malacca Portuguese Development Centre, 1982), pp. 24 and 73.

[3]   Fernandis wrote that the Dutch had a poor regard for the "Mestiços", that is, the Portuguese-Eurasians, and also spoke of persecution against their religion. Gerard Fernandis, ed., *Save Our Portuguese Heritage Conference 95 Malacca, Malaysia* (Malacca, 1996), pp. 95–97.

[4]   Through the ardent and unyielding efforts of clerics such as Monsignor Manuel Teixeira and Friar M.J. Pintado, who were learned Portuguese priests serving

the Roman Catholic Church in Malaysia, as well as avid amateur historians and authors, much of the old Portuguese texts on Malacca have been translated and made available in publications. See Manuel Joaquim Pintado, *Survival through Human Values* (Malacca: privately printed, 1974).

5   This refers to the battle between the Dutch fleet commanded by Admiral Cornelis Matelief de Jonge, who attacked Malacca in 1606, and the Portuguese fleet commanded by Dom Martin d'Alphonso de Castro who had arrived from Goa, India to rescue Malacca. Cape Rachado in now known as Tanjung Tuan and is located near Port Dickson in Negeri Sembilan.

6   For a discussion of the decade or so preceding the fall of Malacca to the Dutch, see Anthony Disney, "Malacca in the Era of Viceroy Linhares (1629–35)", in Volume 1 of this work.

7   Dennis De Witt, *History of the Dutch in Malaysia* (Petaling Jaya, Malaysia: Nutmeg Publishing, 2007), p. 55. Dutch records spoke of how the Portuguese governor fought gallantly against them. The remains of the Portuguese governor were buried with full military honours.

8   Sermons were carried out in Portuguese at the New Church in Malacca and Mass was mostly attended by "half castes" and "black" women who were married to Dutchmen.

9   P.A. Leupe, "The Siege and Capture of Malacca from the Portuguese in 1640–1641", *Journal of the Malayan Branch of the Royal Asiatic Society* 14, no. 1 (1936): 120.

10   Nevertheless, Catholics challenged this law, and their priests still came into Malacca to stay and to hold public masses in secret. Even at the height of Dutch intolerance and the implementation of anti-Catholic legislation, Governor Bort was only too aware of the difficulties in eliminating the presence of Catholic priests in Malacca as he reported that the "proclamation was frequently transgressed by the Romish clergy and their adherents here". Balthasar Bort, "Report of Governor Balthasar Bort on Malacca, 1678", translated by M.J. Bremmer, *Journal of the Malayan Branch of the Royal Asiatic Society* 5, no. 1 (1927): 82.

11   W. Ph. Coolhaas, "Malacca under Jan van Riebeeck", *Journal of the Malayan Branch of the Royal Asiatic Society* 38, no. 2 (1965): 180–81.

12   Bort, "Report of Governor Balthasar Bort", p. 82.

13   Although there was strict intolerance towards the Catholics, the Dutch administration of Malacca had never actually banned the Roman Catholic religion in Malacca. Instead, it maintained the ban on Catholic priests entering Malacca, forbade the administration of the sacraments, the Mass and public preaching. In fact, the Dutch administration reaffirmed that Catholics in Malacca were free to believe in their faith within the privacy of their own homes.

14   It is believed that the wooden cross that was found on a hill at Malim (located about six kilometres northwest of Malacca town) was the site of such a secret Mass. A chapel to house the old cross was built at the site in belief of the miraculous powers of the old wooden cross. Until today, Catholics still flock to

the little Malim Chapel to celebrate the feast of Santa Cruz, observed annually on the second Sunday in September, to venerate the old cross kept there.

[15]   Manuel Teixeria, *The Portuguese Missions in Malacca and Singapore*, vol. 1, *Malacca*, 2nd ed. (Macao: Instituto Cultural de Macau, 1987), p. 323.

[16]   Timothy P. Barnard, "Mestizos as Middlemen: Thomas Días and His Travels in Eastern Sumatra", in *Iberians in the Singapore-Melaka Area (16th to 18th Century)*, edited by Peter Borschberg (Wiesbaden: Harrassowitz; and Lisbon: Fundação Oriente, 2004), pp. 152–60.

[17]   This change was due to the War of the Spanish Succession (1701–14). The Dutch Republic entered the war, together with England, on the side of the Holy Roman Empire (that is, the political entity of Europe's Christendom in the Habsburg domains) to check France's plans for expansion in Europe.

[18]   P. C. Molhuysen and P. J. Blok, eds., *Nieuw Nederlandsch biografisch woordenboek*, vol. 8 (Leiden: A.W. Sijthoff, 1930), pp. 67–68, <http://www.biografischportaal. nl/persoon/34180165> (accessed 22 August 2010); and De Witt, *History of the Dutch in Malaysia*, pp. 67–68.

[19]   De Witt, *History of the Dutch in Malaysia*, pp. 67–68.

[20]   P.A. Christiaans, "De Europese bevolking van Malakka onder het laatste Nederlandse bestuur 1818–1825", *Jaarboek van het Centraal Bureau voor Genealogie*, vol. 40 ('s-Gravenhage: Centraal Bureau voor Genealogie en van het Iconographisch Bureau, 1986), pp. 257–87.

[21]   De archieven van de Verenigde Oostindische Compagnie, 1602–1795 (hereafter cited as VOC), 1.04.02, vol. 11694: 1783, fol. 396, Nationaal Archief van Nederland (hereafter cited as NAN), The Hague.

[22]   Monteira was born in Malacca and became commander of the ship *Mastora*. He was mentioned as a burgher (citizen) at Surabaya, Indonesia in 1829. See Christiaans, *De Europese bevolking van Malakka*, p. 268.

[23]   Christiaans, *De Europese bevolking van Malakka*, p. 273.

[24]   Zevende boek: Batavia's ingekomen brievenboek, deel 1: Ambon, Banda, Ternate, Makassar, Timor, Palembang, Malakka, Sumatra's Westkus, 1681, TTTT, De archieven van de Verenigde Oostindische Compagnie, 1602–1795, 1.04.02, vol. 1359, fol. 505v–06, NAN.

[25]   Abdullah bin Abdul Kadir, "Hikayat Abdullah", translated and edited by A.H. Hill, *Journal of the Malayan Branch of the Royal Asiatic Society* 27, vol. 3 (1955): 60.

[26]   J.H. Moor and J.J. Newbold, *Malacca Territory with Muar and Lingee Rivers* (Singapore, 1837).

[27]   Barbara Watson Andaya, "Melaka under the Dutch, 1641–1795", in *Melaka: The Transformation of a Malay Capital, c. 1400–1980*, edited by Kernial Singh Sandhu and Paul Wheatley, vol. 1 (Kuala Lumpur: Oxford University Press, 1983), pp. 210–11.

[28]   It is believed that the Church of St. Peter in Malacca was built in 1710. Its marriage records go back to 1768 and are housed at Arkib Negara Malaysia, Kuala Lumpur, and at the church in Malacca (see notes 29 and 30).

[29]   The *Trouwboek van E. Commissarissen van huwelijkse en kleine gerechtszaken* records the marriages of local Christian Burghers, employees of the United Dutch East India Company (Verenigde Oostindische Compagnie, or VOC), mestizos, Moors and Hindus (Mooren en Jentieven), Chinese (Chineesen), and even Malays (Maleijers). *Trouwboek van E. Commissarissen van huwelijkse en kleine gerechtszaken*, VOC, NAN.

[30]   *Trouwboek van E. Commissarissen.*

[31]   De homepage van Herman Oomen, <http://www.johan-jong.nl/Herman.html> (accessed 25 August 2010). After Indonesia received independence from the Netherlands in 1949, around three hundred thousand people from all ranks and ages, and of mostly mixed descent (Eurasians), who were considered as Dutch nationals, migrated from the Dutch East Indies (Indonesia) to the Netherlands to start a new life in Europe.

[32]   De Rozario Family Tree, <http://members.chello.nl/a.w.de.rozario/index.html> (accessed 25 August 2010). The Malacca Portuguese Settlement community might be interested to know that they not only have ancestral roots in Portugal but that they also have descendants from their community who are living in the Netherlands.

[33]   A Portuguese-derived Creole spoken by the Malacca Portuguese-Eurasian community. For sociolinguistic and linguistic discussions of Kristang, see, in this volume, Alan N. Baxter, "The Creole Portuguese Language of Malacca: A Delicate Ecology"; and Mário Pinharanda-Nunes, "Verb Markings in Makista: Continuity/Discontinuity and Accommodation".

[34]   There currently exist three levels of assimilation from the Malacca Dutch descent community. There is one group that has fully assimilated into the Malacca Portuguese-Eurasian community and has accepted their culture as their own heritage. There is another group that has adopted the Portuguese-Eurasian culture as their own, but they are aware of their Dutch heritage. Finally, there is a group that has never assimilated into the Portuguese-Eurasian community and continues to hold fast to their Dutch heritage. Many from the first group actually reside in the Portuguese Settlement or have close relatives who reside there.

[35]   For a fuller discussion of this phenomenon, see Baxter, "The Creole Portuguese Language of Malacca", in this volume.

APPENDIX
Maps

The maps in this appendix show most — but not all — of the geographic locations mentioned in both volumes of this work. A location name that appears in parentheses represents an alternative name, an alternative spelling, or a name used in the historic past. All boundaries are contemporary, not historical.

	Legend
·—··—··—··—··—·	International boundary
- - - - - - - - - -	State/Provincial boundary
··················	County boundary
▣	National capital
◉	State/Provincial capital
●	Main city/Town
★	Geographic feature
INDIAN OCEAN	Ocean
Arabian Sea	Sea/Bay

The World

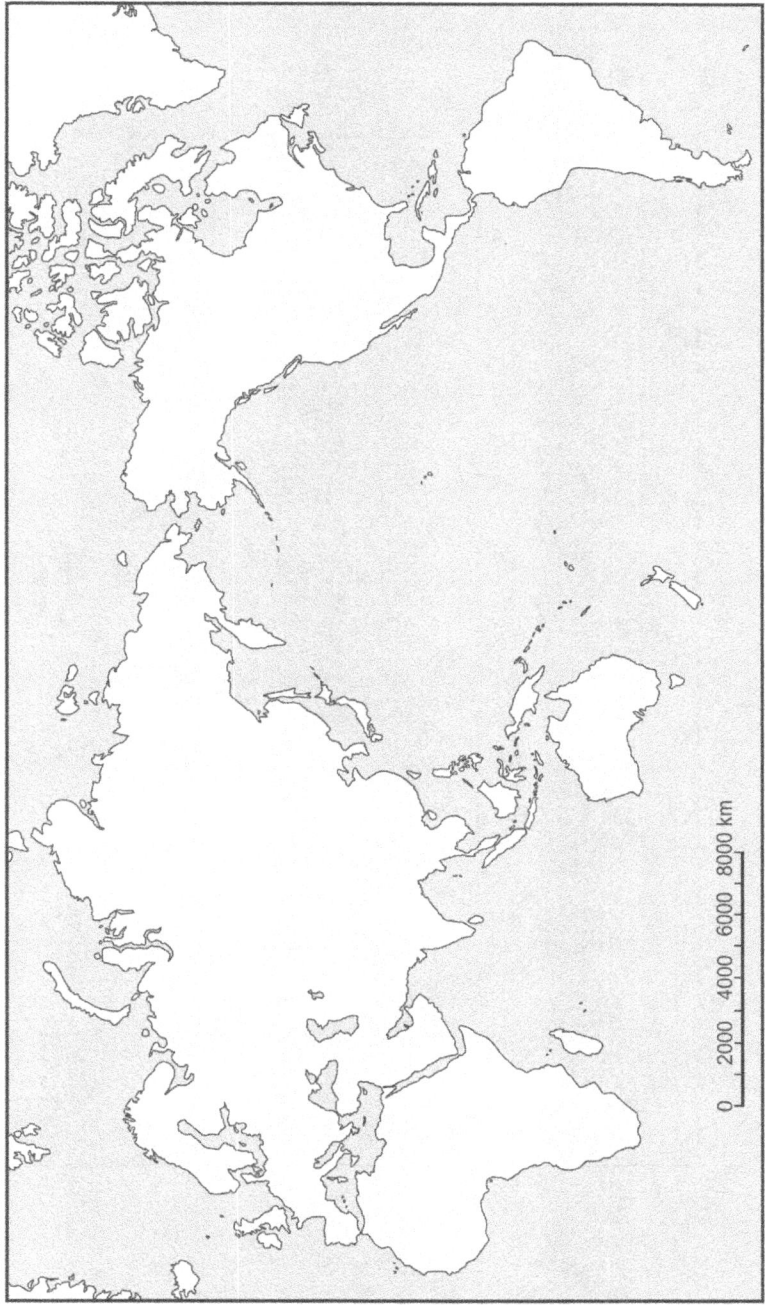

Western Europe and the British Isles

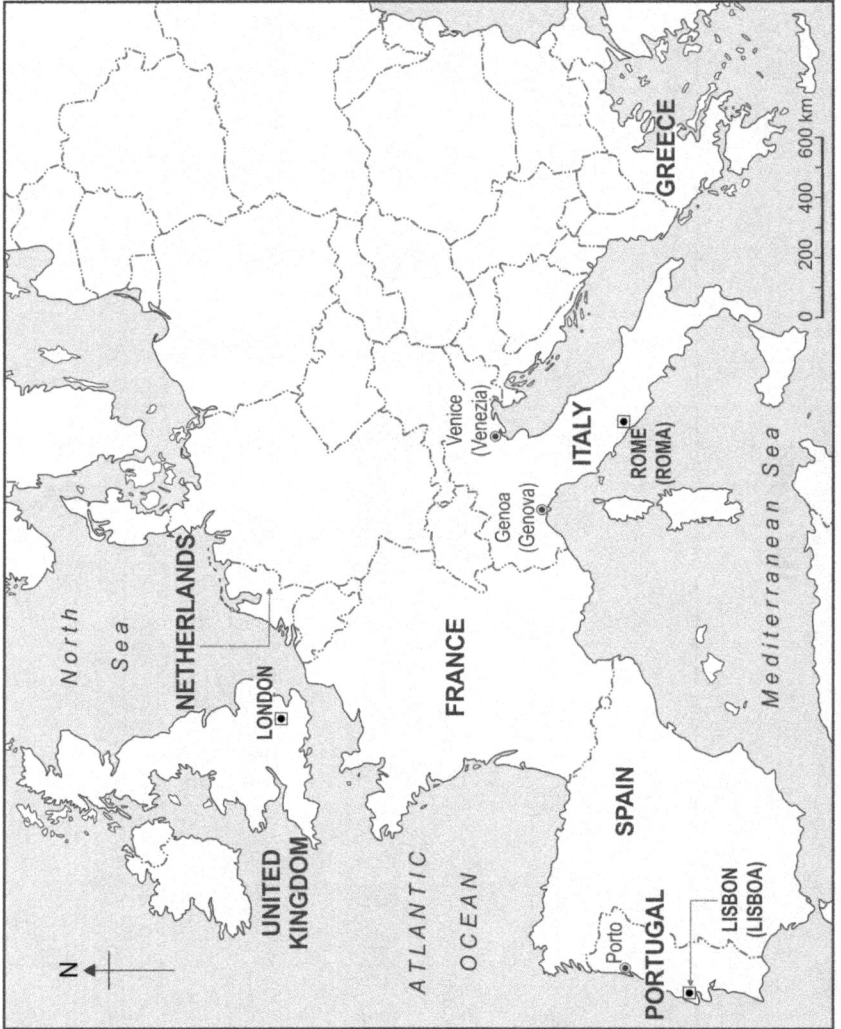

TRADITIONAL PROVINCES AND CONTEMPORARY DISTRICTS OF PORTUGAL: EXPLANATORY NOTE

In 1976, Portugal's traditional provinces were divided into eighteen districts and two autonomous regions (the Azores and Madeira). The list below shows the correspondence between these former provinces, many of which are mentioned in the text, and today's districts.

Traditional Provinces	Current Districts
Algarve	Faro
Alentejo	
Baixo Alentejo	Beja; Setúbal†
Alto Alentejo	Évora; Portalegre**
Extremadura	Lisboa**; Setúbal†; Leiria†
Ribatejo	Santarém**; Lisboa*; Portalegre*
Beira ("The Beiras")	
Beira Litoral	Coimbra**; Leiria†; Aveiro**; Santarém*
Beira Baixa	Castelo Branco; Coimbra*; Santarém*
Beira Alta	Guarda*; Viseu*; Coimbra*
Entre Douro e Mindo	
Douro Litoral	Porto; Aveiro*; Viseu*
Minho	Braga; Viana do Castelo
Trás-os-Montes and Alto Douro	Vila Real; Bragança; Guarda*; Viseu**

*   A small portion of the district was previously part of the province indicated.
**   A large portion of the district was previously part of the province indicated
†   About half of the district was previously part of the province indicated.

Portugal

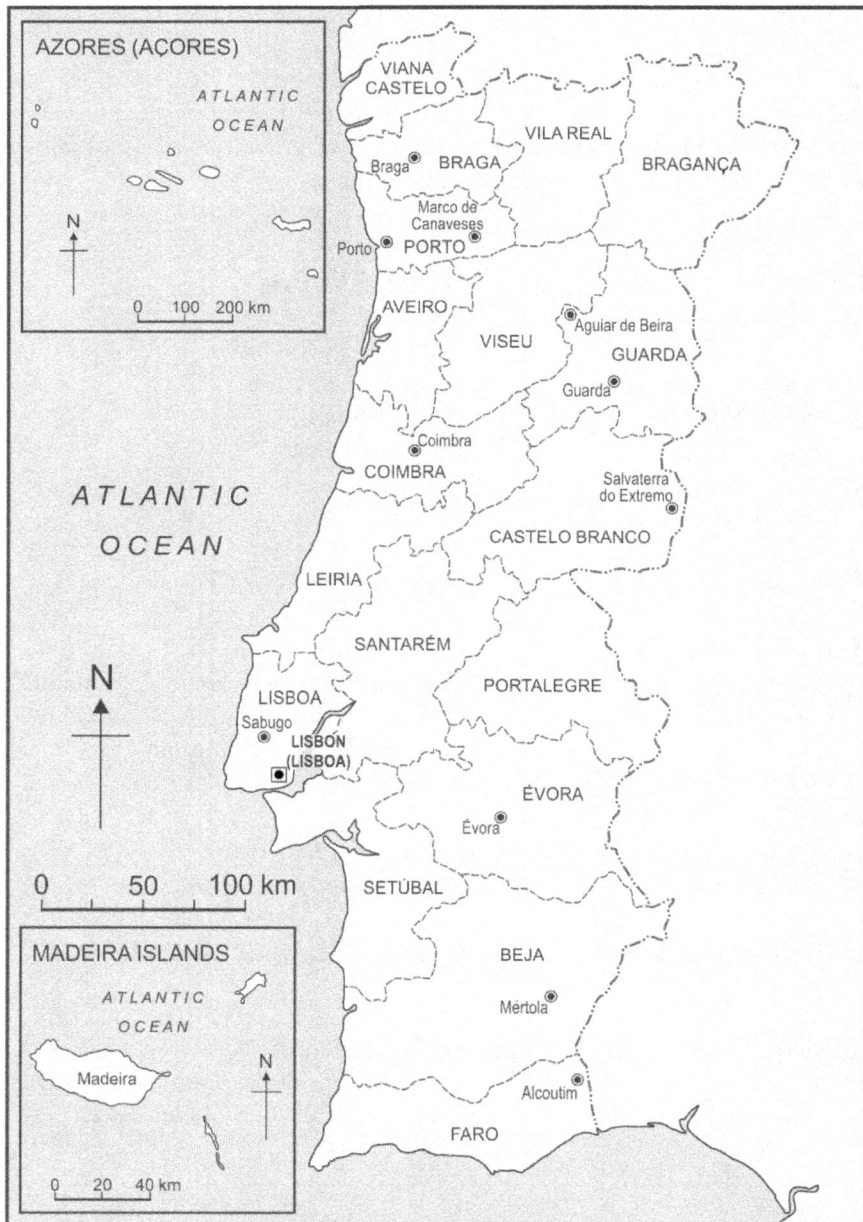

AZORES (AÇORES)

ATLANTIC OCEAN

N

0   100   200 km

VIANA CASTELO

VILA REAL

Braga BRAGA

BRAGANÇA

Marco de Canaveses

Porto PORTO

AVEIRO

VISEU Aguiar de Beira

GUARDA

Guarda

Coimbra

COIMBRA

Salvaterra do Extremo

CASTELO BRANCO

ATLANTIC OCEAN

LEIRIA

SANTARÉM

N

LISBOA PORTALEGRE

Sabugo

LISBON (LISBOA)

ÉVORA

Évora

0   50   100 km

SETÚBAL

BEJA

MADEIRA ISLANDS

ATLANTIC OCEAN

Mértola

Madeira

N

Alcoutim

FARO

0   20   40 km

Africa

N

CABO
VERDE

GUINÉ-
BISSAU

Suez Canal

Red Sea

Gulf of Aden

Gulf of Guinea

SÃO TOMÉ
& PRÍNCIPE

UGANDA

RWANDA   KENYA

BURUNDI   TANZANIA

Mombassa

ZANZIBAR

LUANDA

ANGOLA

ATLANTIA OCEAN

MOZÁMBIQUE

0   1000   2000 km

TANGANYIKA and ZANZIBAR. The former territory and
later independent state of Tanganyika comprised
today's countries of Rwanda, Burundi and Tanzania.
Zanzibar is now a semi-autonomous region in Tanzania.

INDIAN OCEAN

India

N

NEW
DELHI

UTTAR
PRADESH

BIHAR

GUJARAT

WEST
BENGAL

INDIA

DIU

DAMAN

MAHARASHTRA

Bay

of Bengal

ANDHRA
PRADESH

GOA

KARNATAKA

Arabian

Sea

INDIAN OCEAN

TAMIL
NADU
(MADRAS)

KERALA

0   200   400 600 km

West India

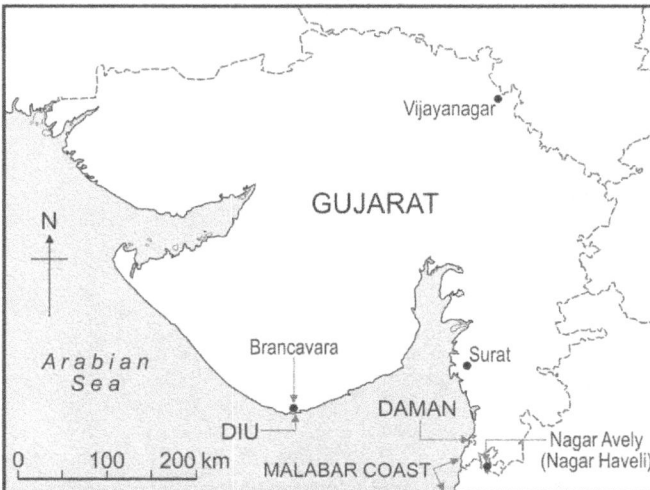

West India, cont'd

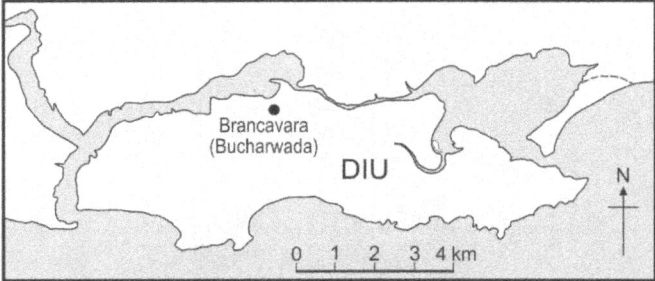

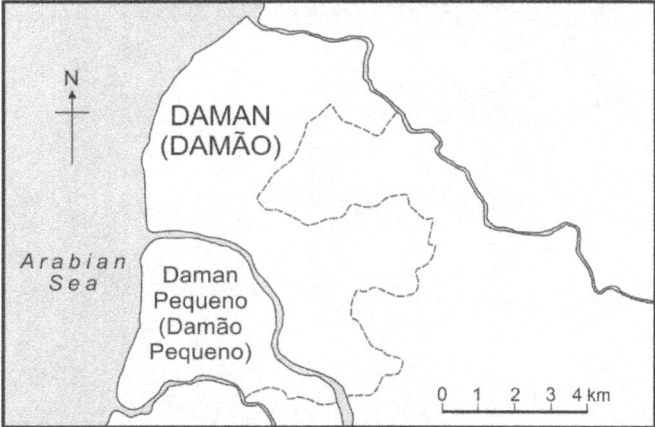

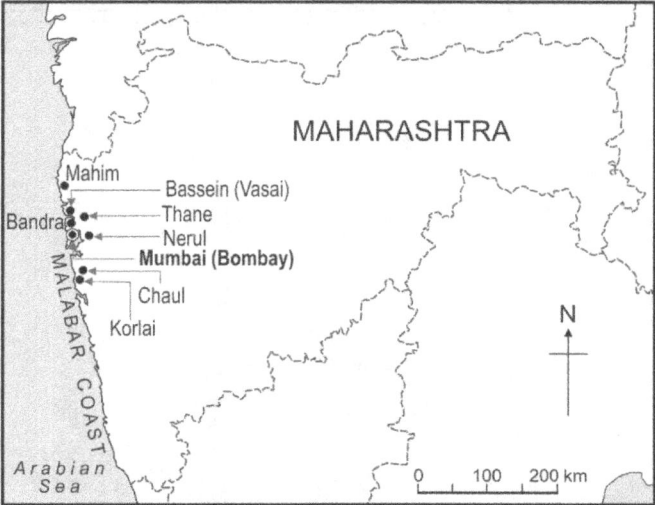

Brancavara
(Bucharwada)

DIU

N

0 1 2 3 4 km

N

DAMAN
(DAMÃO)

Arabian
Sea

Daman
Pequeno
(Damão
Pequeno)

0 1 2 3 4 km

MAHARASHTRA

Mahim
Bassein (Vasai)
Thane
Bandra
Nerul
Mumbai (Bombay)
Chaul
Korlai

MALABAR COAST

N

Arabian
Sea

0 100 200 km

South India

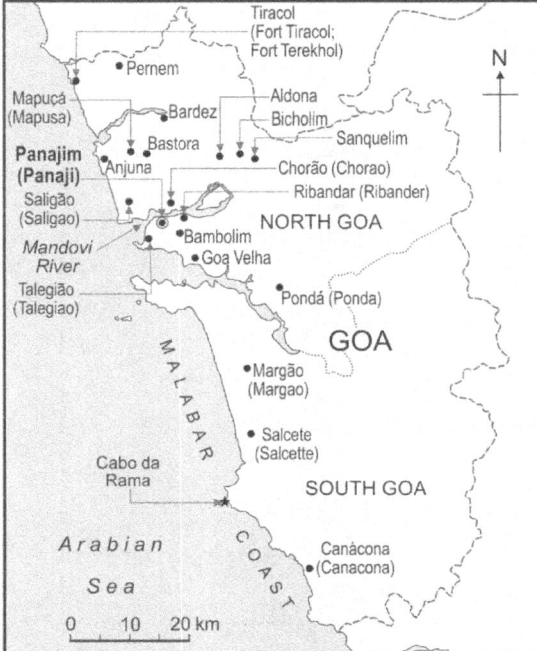

South India, cont'd

South India, cont'd

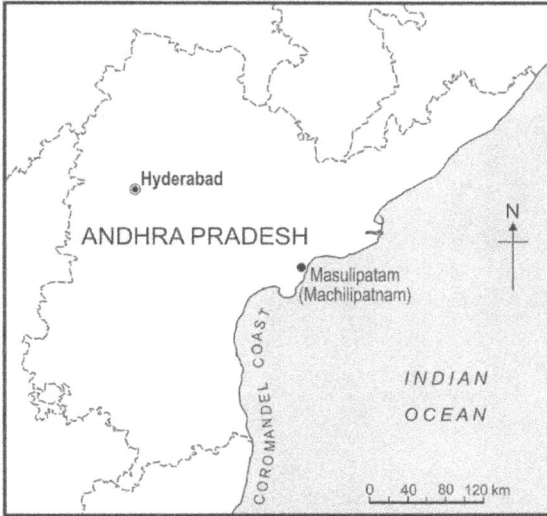

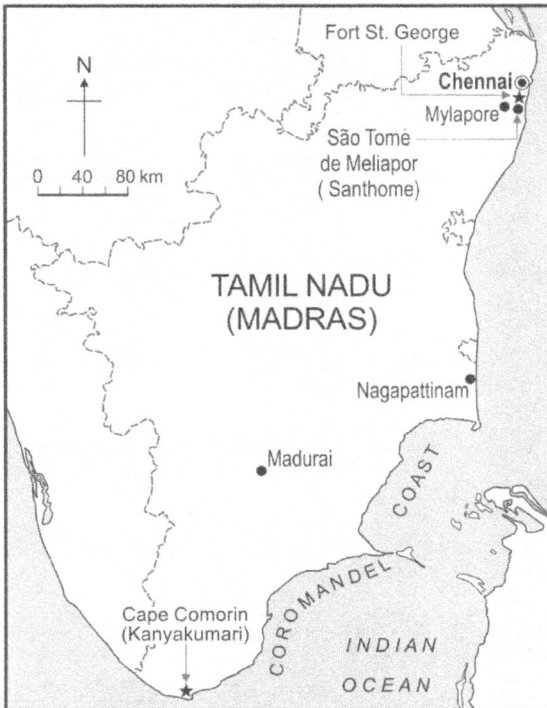

South Asia

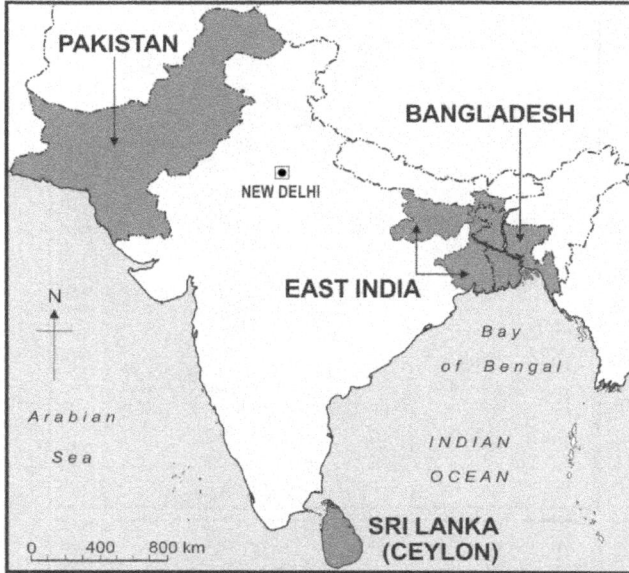

South Asia, cont'd

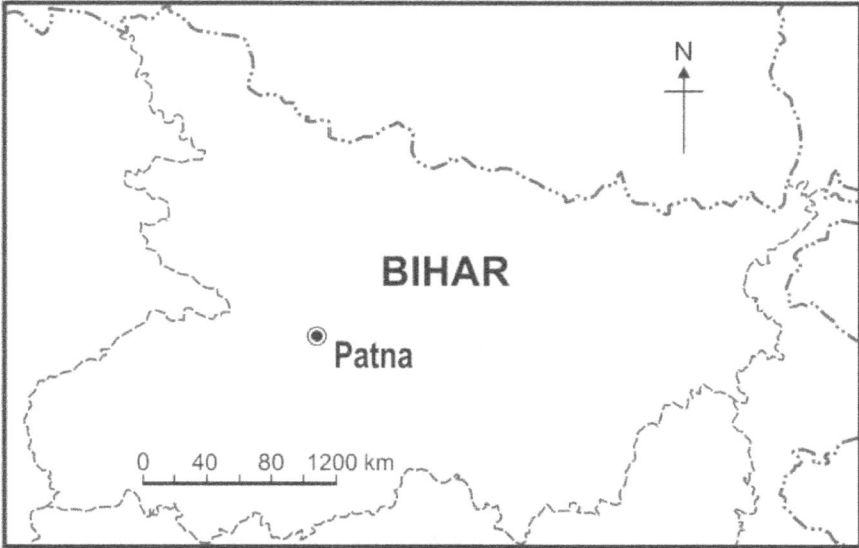

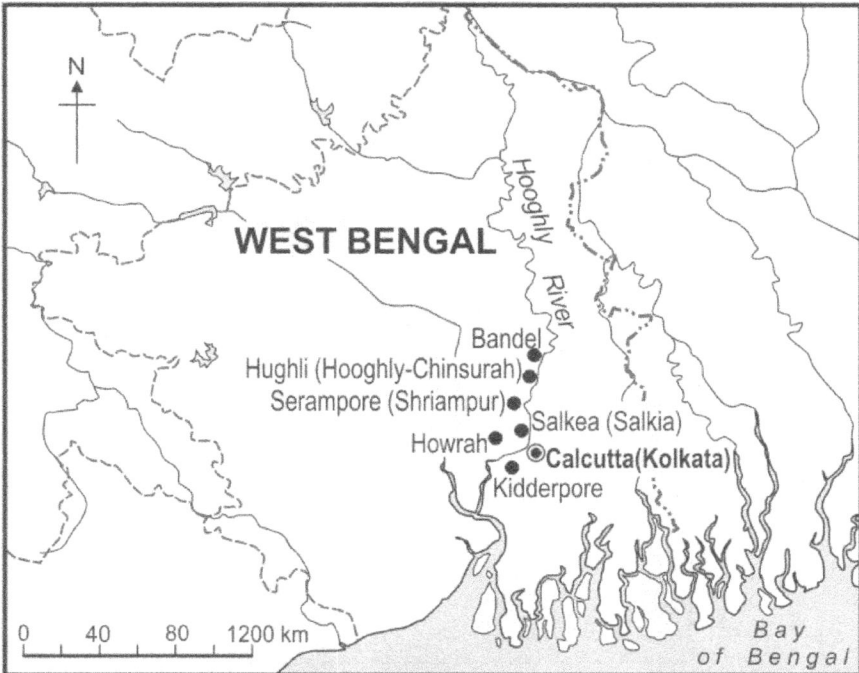

South Asia, cont'd

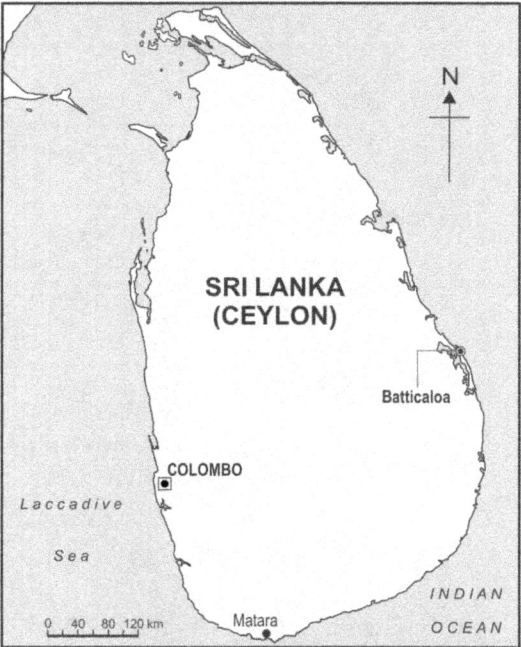

N

BANGLADESH

DACCA
(DHAKA)

Chittagong

Sandwip
Islands

Bay of Bengal

0   40   80 1200 km

N

SRI LANKA
(CEYLON)

Batticaloa

COLOMBO

Laccadive

Sea

INDIAN

OCEAN

Matara

0   40   80 120 km

Southeast Asia

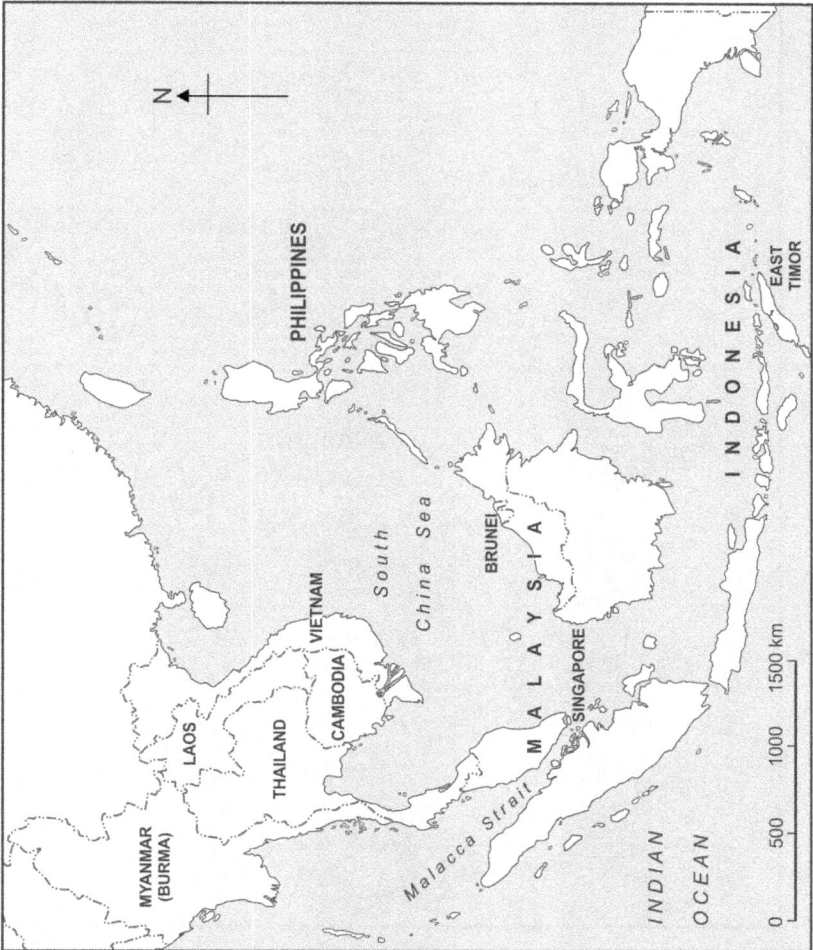

Southeast Asia, cont'd

N

MYANMAR
(BURMA)

VIETNAM

Sittwe (Akyab)

Gulf of
Tonkin

Pegu
(Bago)

Bassein

Da Nang
(Tourane; Turon)

THAILAND

Hoi An (Faifo)

Martaban

Lop Buri (Luvo)

Ayutthaya   Chao Phraya River

Tavoy

BANGKOK

Mergui
Archipelago

Gulf of
Thailand

South

Andaman

China

Sea

Sea

Pattani (Patani)

0   200   400   600 km

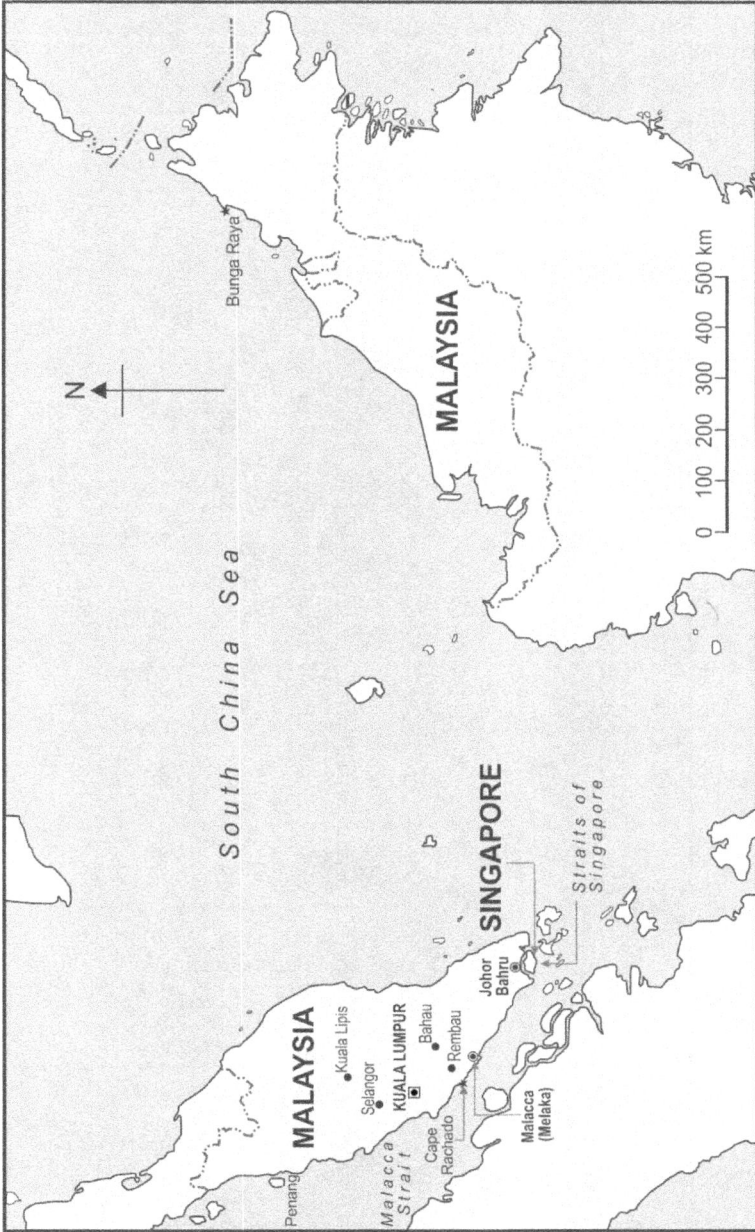

Southeast Asia, cont'd

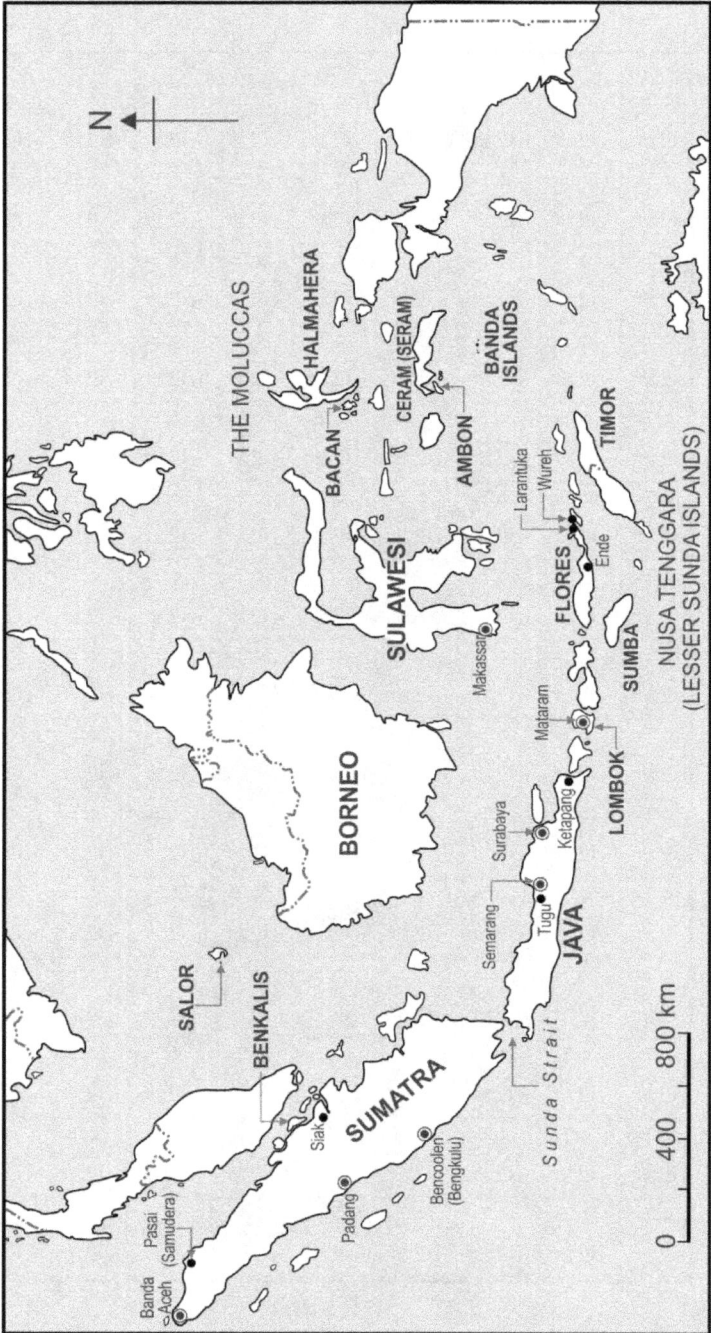

Southeast Asia, cont'd

Southeast Asia, cont'd

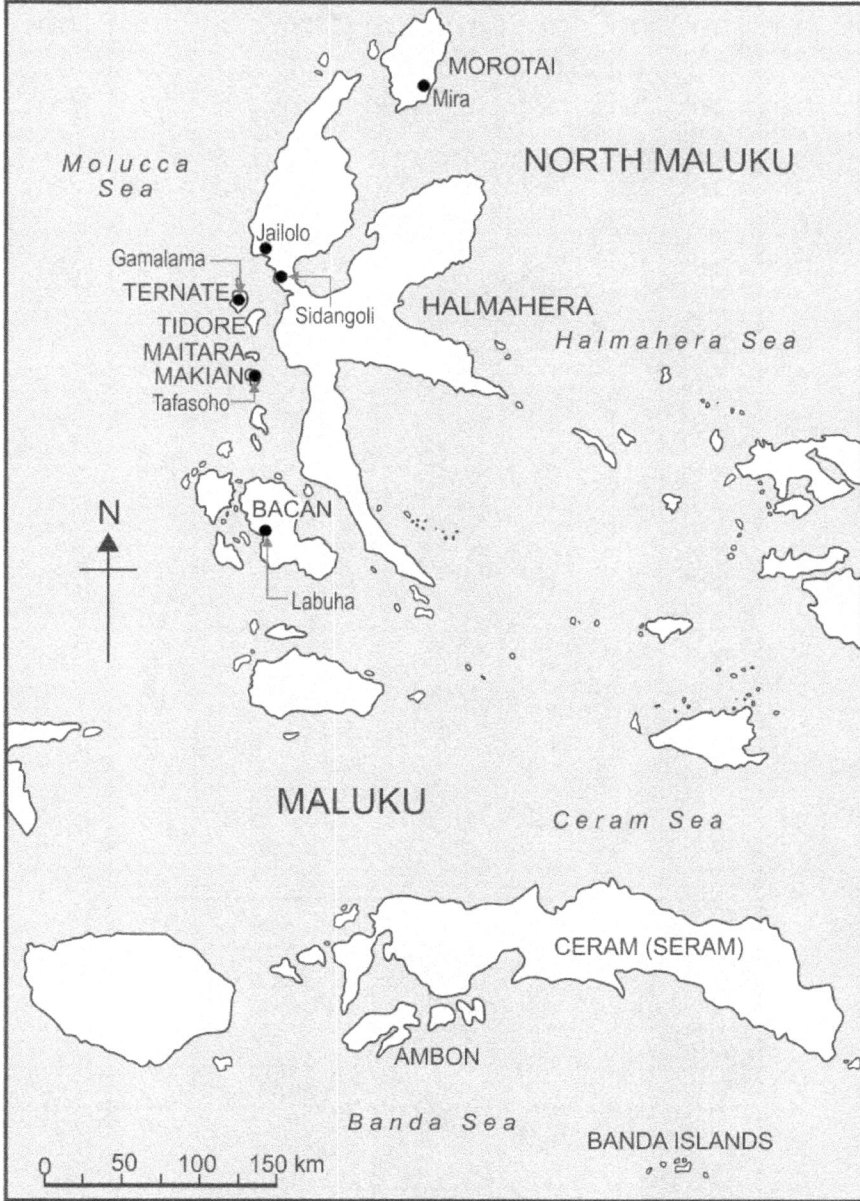

Southeast Asia, cont'd

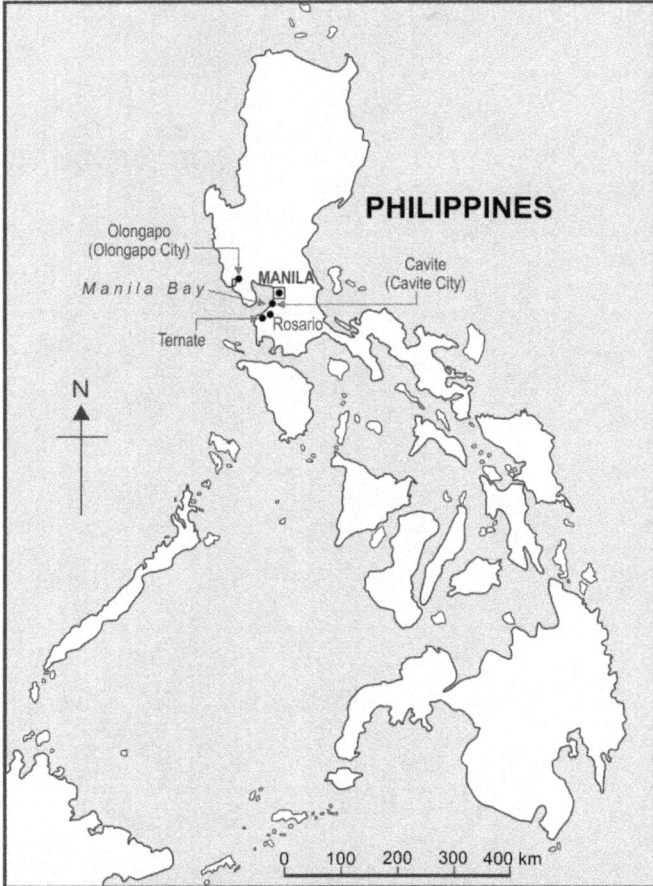

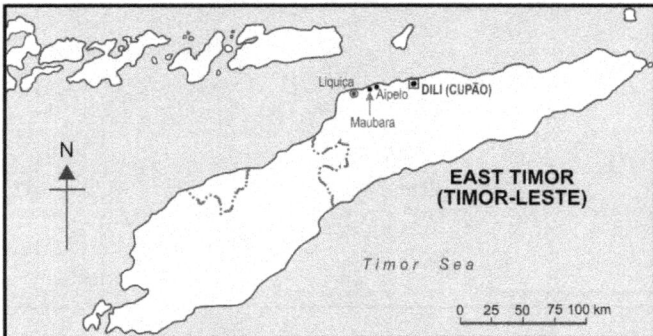

PHILIPPINES

Olongapo
(Olongapo City)

MANILA

Manila Bay

Cavite
(Cavite City)

Ternate

Rosario

N

0   100   200   300   400 km

Liquiça

Aipelo

DILI (CUPÃO)

Maubara

N

EAST TIMOR
(TIMOR-LESTE)

Timor Sea

0   25   50   75 100 km

China, Taiwan and Okinawa (Japan)

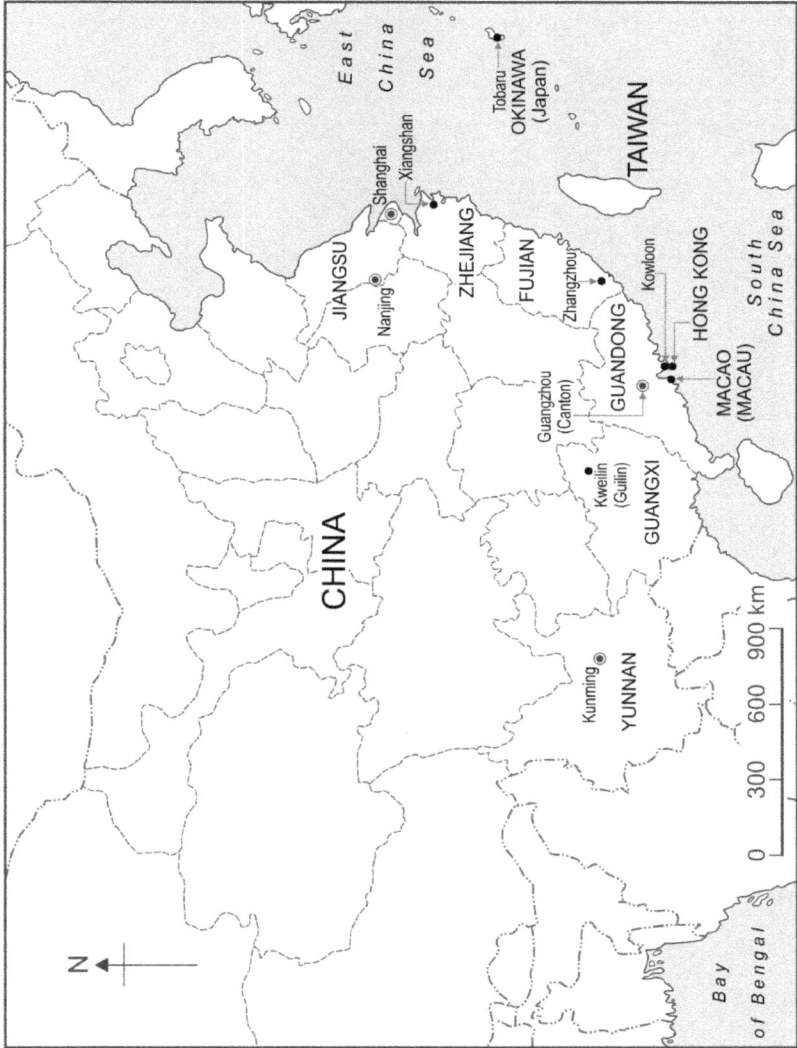

Japan and Korea

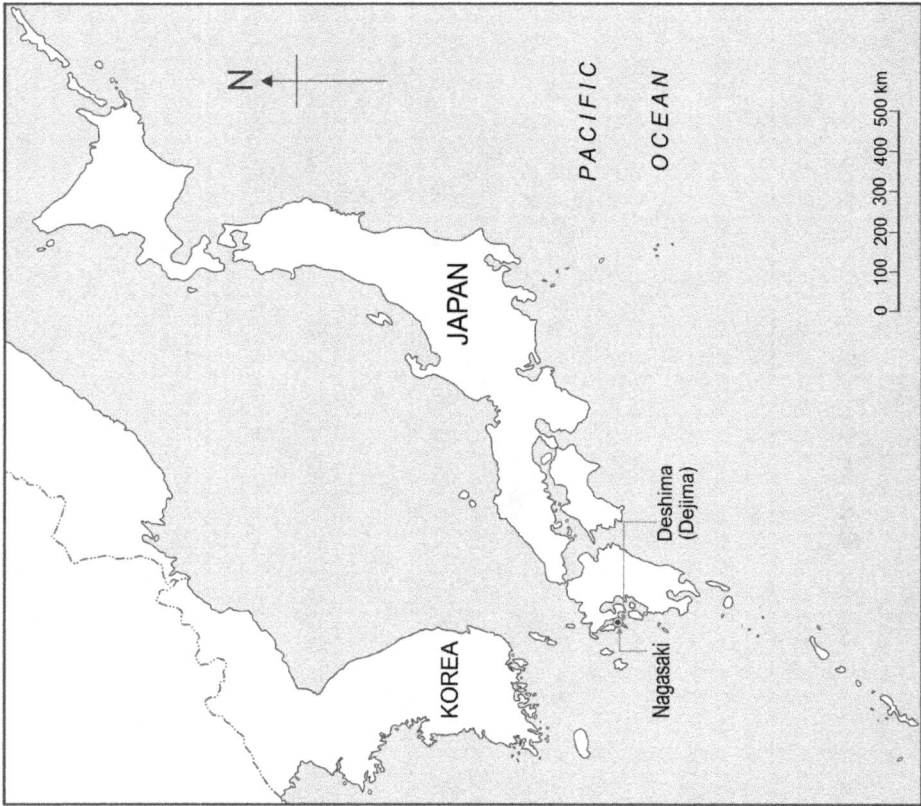

Oceania

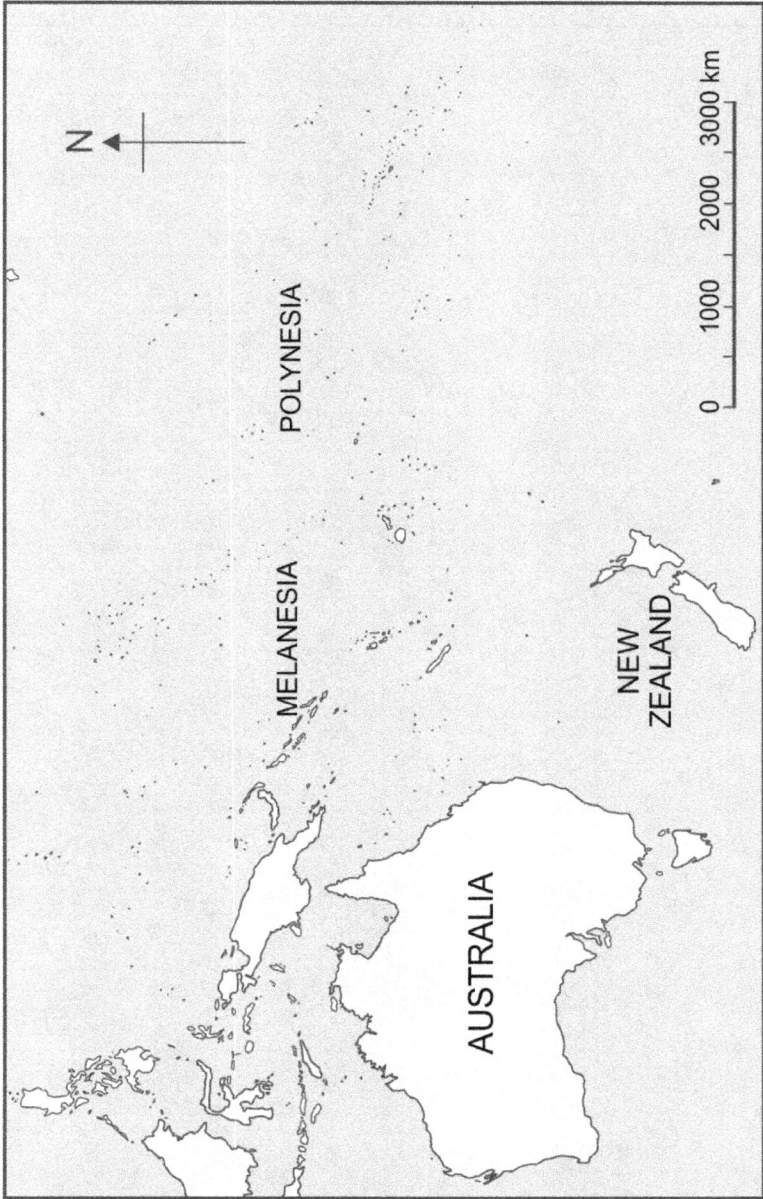

The Americas

BIBLIOGRAPHY

Archival Sources

FRANCE
Archives des Missions Étrangère de Paris
Cochinchine: Lettres 01: 1663–74.
Cochinchine: Lettres 04: 1685–91.
Journal du Tonkin 1: 1667–97.
Tonkin: Lettres, 1666–77.
Tonkin: Lettres, 1677–1714.

MACAO
Arquivo Histórico de Macau
Administração Civil, 1734–1982. (AC)

NETHERLANDS
Nationaal Archief van Nederland, The Hague
De archieven van de Verenigde Oostindische Compagnie, 1602–1795.

PORTUGAL
Arquivo Histórico Ultramarino, Lisbon
Administração Central, Secretaria de Estado da Marinha e Ultramar, 1562–1911,
    Direcção Geral do Ultramar, Macau e Timor. (ACL_SEMU_DGU)
Conselho Ultramarino.

Arquivo Nacional da Torre do Tombo, Lisbon
Corpo Cronológico.
Núcleo Antigo.

Biblioteca da Ajuda, Lisbon
Anno de 1651[.] [A]o Pᵉ Francisco de Tavora da Compª de JESUS assistente em
Roma das Provincias de Portugal e da India. Relação da Nova Missão q' fizerão
os PP Pero de Mesquita e Mᵉˡ Henriques mandados do Collº de Macao a Cidᵉ
e fortaleza de Malaca em 1651, 1650s.
Gaspar Luis, "Annua da missam de Cochinchina anno de 1628", January 1629.
Jesuítas na Ásia.

SPAIN
Archivo General de Indias, Seville
Filipinas.
Indiferente.
Patronato.

VATICAN CITY
Archivio Storico de Propaganda Fide
Congregazioni Particolari (1622–1864) (CP)
Scritture Originali Riferite nelle Congregazioni Generali (1622–1892) (SOCG)
Scritture Riferite nei Congressi (SC), Indie Orientali e Cina (1623–1799)

Secondary Sources

Alexandre, Valentim. *Velhos Brasis, Novas Áfricas: Portugal e o Império (1808–1975)*.
Porto: Afrontamento, 2000.
Allen, Peter M. "The Complexity of Structure, Strategy, and Decision Making". In
Evolution and Economic Complexity, edited by J. Stanley Metcalf and John Foster,
85–107. Cheltenham, UK: Edward Elgar, 2004.
Almeida, Miguel Vale de. "Portugal's Colonial Complex: From Colonial
Lusotropicalism to Postcolonial Lusophony". Queen's Postcolonial Research
Forum, Queen's University, Belfast, 28 Apr. 2008. http://site.miguelvaledealmeida.
net/wp-content/uploads/portugal-colonial-complex.pdf.
Alves, Jorge Manuel dos Santos. "The First Decade of Sino-Portuguese Diplomatic
Relations Following the Foundation of Macau". In *Proceedings of the International
Colloquium on the Portuguese and the Pacific*, edited by Francis A. Dutra and
João Camilo dos Santos, 305–13. Santa Barbara: Center for Portuguese Studies,
1995.
―――. "Natureza do primeiro cíclo de diplomacia luso-chinesa (séculos XVI–XVIII)".
In *Estudos de História do Relacionamento Luso-Chinês, Séculos XVI–XIX*, edited by
António Vasconcelos de Saldanha and Jorge Manuel dos Santos Alves, 179–218.
Macao: Instituto Português do Oriente, 1995.
―――. "Une ville inquiète et un sultan barricadé: Aceh vers 1588 d'aprés le *Roteiro
das Cousas do Achém* de l'Evêque de Malaka". Archipel 39 (1990): 93–112.
Andaya, Barbara Watson. "Melaka under the Dutch, 1641–1795". In *Melaka: The*

Transformation of a Malay Capital, c. 1400–1980, edited by Kernial Singh Sandhu and Paul Wheatley. Vol. 1, 195–241. Kuala Lumpur: Oxford University Press, 1983.

Andaya, Leonard Y. "The 'Informal Portuguese Empire' and the Topasses in the Solor Archipelago and Timor in the Seventeenth and Eighteenth Centuries", *Journal of Southeast Asian Studies* 41, no. 3 (2010): 391–420.

———. "The Portuguese Tribe in the Malay-Indonesian Archipelago in the Seventeenth and Eighteenth Centuries". In *Proceedings of the International Colloquium on the Portuguese and the Pacific*, edited by Francis A. Dutra and João Camilo dos Santos, 129–48. Santa Barbara: Center for Portuguese Studies, 1995.

———. *The World of Maluku: Eastern Indonesia in the Early Modern Period*. Honolulu: University of Hawai'i Press, 1993.

Anderson, Benedict. "The Idea of Power in Javanese Culture". In *Culture and Politics in Indonesia*, edited by Claire Holt, 1–70. Ithaca: Cornell University Press, 1972.

"Aozhong zayong: Qi" 澳中雜詠．七 [Unclassified poems on Macao: Number seven]. In *Wu Yushan ji Jianzhu* 吳漁山集箋注 [A Brief Annotation of Wu Yushan's Collected Works], Wu Li 吳曆 and compiled by Zhang Wenqin 章文欽. Beijing 北京: Zhonghua Shuju 中華書局, 2007.

Araújo, Abílio. *Timor Leste: Os Loricos Voltaram a Cantar*. Lisbon: Trama, 1977.

Argensola, Bartolomé Leonardo de. *Conquista de las Islas Malucas*. Madrid: Miraguano-Polifemo, 1992. First published in 1609.

Ashley, Kathleen and Pamela Sheingorn. "*Sainte Foy* on the Loose, or, the Possibilities of Procession". In *Moving Subjects: Processional Performance in the Middle Ages and the Renaissance*, edited by Kathleen Ashley and Wim Hüsken, 53–67. Amsterdam: Rodopi, 2001.

Augé, Marc. *A Construção do Mundo: Religião, Representação e Ideologia*. Lisbon: Edições 70, 2000.

Backman, Louis E. *Religious Dances in the Christian Church and in Popular Medicine*. London: George Allen & Unwin, 1952.

Bañas Llanos, Maria Bellén. *Islas de las Espécies: Fuentes Etnohistóricas sobre las Islas Molucas, s. XIV–XX*. Cáceres: Universidad de Extremadura, 2000.

Banerjee, Pompa. "Just Passing: Abbé Carré, Spy, Harem-Lord, and 'Made in France'". In *Emissaries in Early Modern Literature and Culture: Mediation, Transmission, Traffic, 1550–1700*, edited by Brinda Charry and Gitanjali Shahani, 85–110. Farnham: Ashgate, 2009.

Barbosa, Maria Augusta. "Einführung in die Musikgeschichte Portugals bis zur Mitte des 17. Jahrhunderts". In *Ars Musica, Musica Scientia: Festschrift Heinrich Hüschen zum fünfundsechzigsten Geburtstag am 2. März 1980*, edited by Detlef Altenburg, 22–29. Cologne: Gitarre-und-Laute Verl.-Ges., 1980.

Barnard, Timothy P. "Mestizos as Middlemen: Thomas Días and His Travels in Eastern Sumatra". In *Iberians in the Singapore-Melaka Area (16th to 18th Century)*, edited by Peter Borschberg, 152–60. Wiesbaden: Harrassowitz; and Lisbon: Fundação Oriente, 2004.

Barreto, Luís Filipe. *Macau: Poder e Saber, Séculos XVI e XVII*. Lisbon: Editorial Presença, 2006.

Barros, João de. *Décadas da Ásia de João de Barros. Década Terceira* [1563]. CD-ROM. Lisbon: Comissão Nacional para as Comemorações dos Descobrimentos Portugueses, 1998. This edition first published in 1778–88.

———. *Década Quarta* [1615]. CD-ROM. Lisbon: Comissão Nacional para as Comemorações dos Descobrimentos Portugueses, 1998. This edition first published in 1778–88.

Barros, Jorge. "A alma Timorense". *Seara: Boletim Eclesiástico da Diocese de Díli* 10, no. 1 (1958): 95–99.

———. "O Lorsán". *Seara: Boletim Eclesiástico da Diocese de Díli* 15, no. 2 (1963): 46–56.

Barth, Fredrik, ed. *Ethnic Groups and Boundaries: The Social Organization of Culture Difference*. Illinois: Waveland Press, 1998, © 1969.

Baustert, Raymond. *La Quarelle Janséniste Extra Muros, ou, La Polémique Autour de la Procession des Jésuites de Luxembourg, 20 Mai 1685*. Tübingen: Gunter Narr Verlag, 2006.

Baxter, Alan N. "Causative and Facilitative Serial Verbs in Asian Ibero-Romance Creoles: A Convergence of Substrate and Superstrate Systems?". *Journal of Portuguese Linguistics* 8, no. 2 (2009): 65–90.

———. *A Grammar of Kristang*. Canberra: Pacific Linguistics, 1988.

———. "Kristang (Malacca Creole Portuguese): A Long-Time Survivor Seriously Endangered". *Estudios de Sociolingüística* 6, no. 1 (2005): 1–37.

———. "O português em Macau: Contato e assimilação". In *Português em Contato*, edited by Ana Maria Carvalho, 277–312. Madrid: Iberoamericana; and Frankfurt: Editorial Vervuert, 2009.

———. "Portuguese and Creole Portuguese in the Pacific and Western Pacific Rim". In *Atlas of Languages of Intercultural Communication in the Pacific, Asia, and the Americas*, edited by Stephen A.Wurm, Peter Mühlhäusler and Darrell T. Tryon, 299–338. Berlin: Mouton de Gruyter, 1996.

———. "Some Observations on Verb Serialization in Malacca Creole Portuguese". *Boletim de Filologia* (Lisbon) 31 (1990): 161–84.

———. "Vestiges of Etymological Gender in Malacca Creole Portuguese". *Journal of Pidgin and Creole Languages* 25, no. 1 (2010): 120–54.

Baxter, Alan N. and Patrick de Silva. *A Dictionary of Kristang (Malacca Creole Portuguese): English*. Canberra: Pacific Linguistics, 2004.

Bentley, G.C. "Indigenous States of Southeast Asia". *Annual Review of Anthropology* 15 (1986): 275–305.

Bispo, Antonio Alexandre. *Grundlagen christlicher Musikkultur in der außereuropäischen Welt der Neuzeit. Der Raum des früheren portugiesischen patronatsrechts*. Vol. 2. Rome: Consociatio internationalis musicae sacrae, 1988.

Black, Christopher. *Italian Confraternities in the Sixteenth Century*. Cambridge: Cambridge University Press, 2003.

Blair, Emma Helen and James Alexander Robertson, eds. *The Philippine Islands: 1493–1898*. Vol. 15. Cleveland: A.H. Clark Company, 1904.

Blair, Emma Helen, Edward Gaylord Bourne, and James Alexander Robertson, eds. *The Philippine Islands: 1493–1898*. Vol. 27. Cleveland: A.H. Clark Company, 1905.

Bohigian, Gary William. "Life on the Rim of Spain's Pacific-American Empire: Presidio Society in the Molucca Islands, 1606–1663". Master's thesis, University of California, Los Angeles, 1994.

Boogaart, Thomas A. II. "Our Saviour's Blood: Procession and Community in Late Medieval Bruges". In *Moving Subjects: Processional Performance in the Middle Ages and the Renaissance*, edited by Kathleen Ashley and Wim Hüsken, 69–116. Amsterdam: Rodopi, 2001.

Borri, Cristoforo. *Relation de la Nouvelle Mission des Pères de la Compagnie de Jésus, au Royaume de la Cochinchine*. Lille: Pierre de Rache, 1631.

Bort, Balthasar. "Report of Governor Balthasar Bort on Malacca, 1678", translated by M.J. Bremmer. *Journal of the Malayan Branch of the Royal Asiatic Society* 5, no. 1 (1927): 1–232.

Boxer, C.R. *The Embassy of Captain Gonçalo de Sequeira de Souza to Japan in 1644–1647*. Macao: Tip. Mercantil, 1938.

———. *Francisco Vieira de Figueiredo: A Portuguese Merchant-Adventurer in South-East Asia, 1624–1667*. The Hague: Martinus Nijhoff, 1967.

Boxer, Charles and Frazão de Vasconcelos. *André Furtado de Mendonça*. Lisbon: Agência Geral do Ultramar, 1955. Reprint, Lisbon: Fundação Oriente; and Macao: Museu e Centro de Estudos Marítimos, 1989.

Braga, Paulo Drumond. "A vida quotidiana". In *História dos Portugueses no Extremo Oriente*, edited by A.H. de Oliveira Marques. Vol. 1, tomo 1, *Em torno de Macau*, 519–60. Lisbon: Fundação Oriente, 1998.

———. "A vida quotidiana". In *História dos Portugueses no Extremo Oriente*, edited by A.H. de Oliveira Marques. Vol. 2, *Macau e Timor: O Declínio do Império*, 461–91. Lisbon: Fundação Oriente, 2001.

Brauchli, Bernard. *The Clavichord*. Cambridge: Cambridge University Press, 1998.

Breazeale, Kennon. "Review of Leonor de Seabra, *The Embassy of Pero Vaz de Siqueira to Siam (1684–1686)* (Macao: University of Macau, 2005)". *Journal of the Siam Society* 97 (2009): 234–37.

Brito, Manuel Carlos de. *História da Música Portuguesa*. Lisbon: Universidade Aberta, 1992.

Brockey, Liam. "Introduction: Nodes of Empire". In *Portuguese Colonial Cities in the Early Modern World*, 1–14. Aldershot: Ashgate, 2008.

———. *Journey to the East: The Jesuit Mission to China, 1579–1724*. Cambridge, MA: Belnapp Press, 2007.

Brown, Katherine. "Reading Indian Music: The Interpretation of Seventeenth-Century

European Travel-Writing in the (Re)construction of Indian Music History". *British Journal of Ethnomusicology* 9, no. 2 (2000): 1–34.

Buc, Philippe. *The Dangers of Ritual: Between Early Medieval Texts and Social Scientific Theory*. Oxford: Princeton University Press, 2001.

Budasz, Rogério. "Music of Missionaries, Natives and Settlers in 16th-Century Brazil". In the booklet accompanying *Mil Suspiros Dió Maria: Sacred and Secular Music from the Brazilian Renaissance*. Compact disc. Ricercar, RIC 246, © 2006.

Cadilhon, François. "Les processions Jésuites en France au XVIIe et XVIIIe siècles". In *Fastes et Cérémonies: L'Expression de la Vie Religieuse, XVIe–XXe Siècles*, edited by Agostino Marc, François Cadilhon and Philippe Loupès, 189–202. Pessac: Presses Universitaires de Bordeaux, 2003.

Cardon, R. "Portuguese Malacca". *Journal of the Malayan Branch of the Royal Asiatic Society* 12, no. 2 (1934): 1–23.

Cardoso, Hugo. "The African Slave Population of Portuguese India: Demographics and Impact on Indo-Portuguese". *Journal of Pidgin and Creole Languages* 25, no. 1 (2010): 95–119.

——. "O cancioneiro das comunidades norteiras: Língua, fontes e tradição". *Camões: Revista de Letras e Culturas Lusófonas* 20 (2010): 105–23.

——. *The Indo-Portuguese Language of Diu*. Utrecht: LOT, 2009.

Castanheda, Fernão Lopes de. *História do Descobrimento e Conquista da India pelos Portugueses*, edited by M. Lopes de Almeida. Vol. 2. Porto: Lello & Irmão, 1979.

Castelo, Cláudia. *O Modo Português de Estar no Mundo: O Luso-Tropicalismo e a Ideologia Colonial Portuguesa (1933–1961)*. Lisbon: Edições Afrontamento, 1999.

Castro, Affonso de. "Notícia dos usos e costumes dos povos de Timor". *Anais do Conselho Ultramarino*, unofficial section, 1863, 29–31.

Castro, Afonso de. *As Possessões Portuguezas na Oceania*. Lisbon: Imprensa Nacional, 1867.

Castro, Alberto Osório de. *A Ilha Verde e Vermelha de Timor*. Lisbon, 1943. Reprint, Lisbon: Cotovia, 1996.

Chan Kok Eng. "A Study in the Social Geography of the Malacca Portuguese Eurasians". Master's thesis, Universiti Malaya, 1969.

Chatterjee, Kum Kum and Clement Hawkes, eds. *Europe Observed: The Reversed Gaze in Early Modern Encounters*. Lewisburg: Bucknell University Press, 2008.

Christensen, Maria. "The Meiji Era and the Modernization of Japan". http://www.samurai-archives.com/tme.html.

Christiaans, P.A. "De Europese bevolking van Malakka onder het laatste Nederlandse bestuur 1818–1825". *Jaarboek van het Centraal Bureau voor Genealogie*. Vol. 40, 257–87. 's-Gravenhage: Centraal Bureau voor Genealogie en van het Iconographisch Bureau, 1986.

Cinatti, Ruy. "Brevíssimo tratado da Província de Timor". *Revista Shell* 346 (Jul.–Sept. 1963): 14–25.

————. *Motivos Artísticos Timorenses e a sua Integração*. Lisbon: Instituto de Investigação Científica Tropical, Museu de Etnologia, 1987.

Cinatti, Ruy, António de Sousa Mendes and Leopoldo Castro de Almeida. *A Arquitectura Timorense*. Lisbon: Instituto de Investigação Científica Tropical, Museu de Etnologia, 1987.

Clark, Robert. *O Nascimento do Homem*. Lisbon: Edição Gradiva, 1995.

Claudius, Gros. *Complex and Adaptive Dynamical Systems: A Primer*. Berlin: Springer, 2008.

Clements, J. Clancy. *The Genesis of a Language: The Formation and Development of Korlai Portuguese*. Amsterdam: John Benjamins, 1996.

Clements, Joseph Clancy. "The Indo-Portuguese Creoles: Languages in Transition". *Hispania* 74, no. 3 (Sept. 1991): 637–46.

Clercq, F.S.A. de. *Ternate: The Residency and Its Sultanate*, edited and translated by P.M. Taylor and M.N. Richards. Digital ed. Washington, DC: Smithsonian Institution Libraries, 1999. http://www.sil.si.edu/digitalcollections/anthropology/ternate/ternate.pdf (accessed 26 Mar. 2007). Originally published as *Bijdragen tot de kennis der Residentie Ternate*. Leiden: Brill, 1890.

Coelho, Francisco Adolfo. "Os dialectos românicos ou neo-latinos na África, Ásia e América: Novas notas suplementares". In *Estudos Linguísticos Crioulos: Reedição de Artigos Publicados no Boletim da Sociedade de Geografia de Lisboa*, edited by Jorge Morais-Barbosa, 1–234. Lisbon: Academia Internacional da Cultura Portuguesa, 1967. First published in 1886.

Coelho, Victor Anand. "Music in New Worlds". In *The Cambridge History of Seventeenth Century Music*, edited by Tim Carter and John Butt, 88–110. Cambridge: Cambridge University Press, 2005.

Colín, Francisco and Pedro Chirino. *Labor Evangélica*, edited by Pablo Pastells. Vol. 2. New ed. Barcelona: Henrich, 1904 (1900–02). First published in Madrid, 1663.

Commelin, Isaac. *Begin ende van de Voortgangh Vereenighde Geoctroyeerde Nederlandsche Oost-Indische Compagnie*. Amsterdam: Jan Jansz, 1646.

Cónim, Custódio N.P.S. and Maria Fernanda Bragança Teixeira. *Macau e a sua População, 1500–2000: Aspectos Demográficos, Sociais e Económicos*. Macao: Direcção dos Serviços de Estatística e Censos, 1998.

Cooke, Nola. "Strange Brew: Global, Regional and Local Factors behind the 1690 Prohibition of Christian Practice in Nguyễn Cochinchina". *Journal of Southeast Asian Studies* 39, no. 3 (Oct. 2008): 383–409.

Coolhaas, W. Ph. "Malacca under Jan van Riebeeck", *Journal of the Malayan Branch of the Royal Asiatic Society* 38, no. 2 (1965): 173–82.

Cooper, Frederick. *Colonialism in Question: Theory, Knowledge, History*. Berkeley: University of California Press, 2005.

Cooper, Frederick and Rogers Brubaker. "Identity". In *Colonialism in Question: Theory, Knowledge, History*, by Frederick Cooper, 59–90. Berkeley: University of California Press, 2005.

Correia, Gaspar. *Lendas da Índia*, edited by R.J. de Lima Felner. Vol. 2. Lisbon: Typographia da Academia Real das Sciencias de Lisboa, 1856.

———. *Lendas da Índia*, edited by R.J. de Lima Felner. Vol. 3. Lisbon: Typographia da Academia Real das Sciencias de Lisboa, 1862.

"Correio das missões: Malaca". *Boletim do Governo Eclesiástico da Diocese de Macau* 86 (1911): 249–50.

Coutinho, Valdemar. *O Fim da Presença Portuguesa no Japão*. Lisbon: Sociedade Histórica da Independência de Portugal, 1999.

Couto, Diogo do. Década Quarta da Ásia. Vol. 1, edited by M.A. Lima Cruz. Lisbon: Comissão Nacional para as Comemorações dos Descobrimentos Portugueses, Fundação Oriente and Imprensa Nacional-Casa da Moeda, 1999.

Cruysse, Dick van der. *Louis XIV et le Siam*. Paris: Fayard, 1991.

Cruz, Maria Augusta Lima. "Formas de expressão cultural". In *História dos Portugueses no Extremo Oriente*, edited by A.H. de Oliveira Marques. Vol. 2, *Macau e Timor: O Declínio do Império*, 343–420. Lisbon: Fundação Oriente, 2001.

Curvelo, Alexandra with Celina Bastos. "A arte". In *História dos Portugueses no Extremo Oriente*, edited by A.H. de Oliveira Marques. Vol. 2, *Macau e Timor: O Declínio do Império*, 423–58. Lisbon: Fundação Oriente, 2001.

Dalgado, Sebastião Rodolfo. *Berço de uma Cantiga em Indo-Português (à Memória de Ismael Gracias)*. Porto: Tip. Sequeira, 1921 (separata da *Revista Lusitana*, vol. 22).

———. "Dialecto indo-português de Damão". *Ta-Ssi-Yang-Kuo* 3 (1902): 359–67; and 4 (1903): 515–23.

———. "Dialecto indo-português de Negapatão". *Revista Lusitana* 20 (1917): 40–53.

———. "Dialecto indo-português do Norte". *Revista Lusitana* 9 (1906): 142–66 and 193–228.

———. *Glossário Luso-Asiático*. Coimbra: Imprensa da Universidade, 1919.

Dauenhauer, Nora Marks and Richard Dauenhauer. "Technical, Emotional, and Ideological Issues in Reversing Language Shift: Examples from Southeast Alaska". In *Endangered Languages: Current Issues and Future Prospects*, edited by Lenore A. Grenoble and Lindsay J. Whaley, 57–98. Cambridge: Cambridge University Press, 1998.

David, Maya Khemlani and Faridah Noor Mohd Noor. "Language Maintenance or Language Shift in the Portuguese Settlement of Malacca in Malaysia?" *Migracijske teme* 15 (1999): 417–549.

Davis, Natalie Zemon. "The Rites of Violence: Religious Riot in Sixteenth-Century France". *Past and Present* 59 (1973): 51–91.

De Rozario Family Tree. http://members.chello.nl/a.w.de.rozario/index.html.

De Witt, Dennis. *History of the Dutch in Malaysia*. Petaling Jaya, Malaysia: Nutmeg Publishing, 2009.

Delumeau, Jean. *Rassurer et Protéger: Le Sentiment de Sécurité dans l'Occident d'Autrefois*. Paris: Fayard, 1989.

Dias, Pedro. *A Urbanização e a Arquitectura dos Portugueses em Macau, 1557–1911*. Lisbon: Portugal Telecom, 2005.

Dickinson, A.H. "The History of the Creation of the Malacca Police". *Journal of the Malayan Branch of the Royal Asiatic Society* 19, no. 2 (1941): 251–83.

"A Discourse of the Present State of the Moluccos, Anexed to the Former Journall [Voyage of George Spielbergen], Extracted Out of Apollonius Schot of Middleborough" [1617]. In *Hakluytus Posthumus or Purchas His Pilgrimes*, edited by Samuel Purchas. Vol. 2, 227–29. Glasgow: MacLehose, 1905.

Dorian, Nancy. "Western Language Ideologies and Small-Language Prospects". In *Endangered Languages: Current Issues and Future Prospects*, edited by Lenore A. Grenoble and Lindsay J. Whaley, 3–21. Cambridge: Cambridge University Press, 1998.

Duarte, Francisco. "Commando Militar de Thiarlelo, 31 Aug. 1896". In *Relatório das Operações de Guerra no Districto Autónomo de Timor no Anno de 1896 Enviado ao Ministro e Secretário de Estado dos Negócios da Marinha e Ultramar* by José Celestino da Silva. Lisbon: Imprensa Nacional, 1897.

The Edinburgh Magazine or Literary Miscellany. Vol. 11. London: James Symington, 1798.

The Eleventh Report of the Anglo-Chinese College: For the Year 1835. Malacca: Mission Press, 1836.

Elias, Norbert. *The Court Society*. Oxford: Blackwell, 1983.

Fauconnet-Buzelin, Françoise. *Aux Sources des Missions Étrangères: Pierre Lambert de la Motte (1624–1679)*. Paris: Éditions Perrin, 2006.

Feldbauer, Peter. *Die Portugiesen in Asien, 1498–1620*. Essen: Magnus-Verlag, 2005.

Felner, Rodrigo José de Lima, ed. *Subsídios para a História da India Portugueza*. Lisbon: A.R.S., 1868.

Fernandes, Abílio José. *Esboço Histórico e do Estado Actual das Missões de Timor e Refutação dalgumas Falsidades contra Elas Caluniosamente Afirmadas por um Ex-Governador de Timor*. Macao: Tipografia Mercantil, 1931.

Fernandes, J.A. *Timor: Impressões e Aspectos*. Porto: Tip. A Tribuna, 1923.

Fernandis, Gerard. "*Papia, Relijang e Tradisang*: The Portuguese Eurasians in Malaysia: *Bumiquest*, a Search for Self Identity". Lusotopie (2000): 261–68.

———, ed. *Save Our Portuguese Heritage Conference 95 Malacca, Malaysia*. Malacca, 1996.

Fernando, Radin. "Metamorphosis of the Luso-Asian Diaspora in the Malay Archipelago, 1640–1795". In *Iberians in the Singapore-Melaka Area (16th to 18th Century)*, edited by Peter Borschberg, 161–84. Wiesbaden: Harrassowitz; and Lisbon: Fundação Oriente, 2004.

Ferraz, Luiz Ivens. "Portuguese Creoles of West Africa and Asia". In *Pidgin and Creole Languages*, edited by Glenn G. Gilbert, 337–60. Honolulu: University of Hawai'i Press, 1987.

Flores, Jorge Manuel. "China e Macau". In *História dos Portugueses no Extremo Oriente*, edited by A.H. de Oliveira Marques. Vol. 1, tomo 2, *De Macau à Perifeira*, 215–34. Lisbon: Fundação Oriente, 2000.

———. "Macau: Os eventos políticos 1". In *História dos Portugueses no Extremo Oriente*, edited by A.H. de Oliveira Marques. Vol. 2, *Macau e Timor: O Declínio do Império*, 69–156. Lisbon: Fundação Oriente, 2001.

Flores, Maria da Conceição. "A embaixada de Pedro Vaz de Siqueira ao Sião em 1684". In *Anais de História de Além-Mar*. Vol. 3, 64–76. Lisbon: Centro de História de Além-Mar da Universidade Nova de Lisboa, 2002.

Forest, Alain. *Les Missionaries Français au Tonkin et au Siam XVIIe–XVIIIe Siècles: Analyse Comparée d'un Relatif Succès et d'un Total Échec*. Vol. 3. Paris: L'Harmattan, 1998.

Forster, Marc R. *Catholic Revival in the Age of the Baroque: Religious Identity in Southwest Germany, 1550–1750*. Cambridge: Cambridge University Press, 2001.

Fox, James, ed. *The Flow of Life: Essays in Eastern Indonesia*. Cambridge, MA: Harvard University Press, 1980.

Fox, James J. "Tracing the Path, Recounting the Past: Historical Perspectives on Timor". In *Out of the Ashes: Destruction and Reconstruction of East Timor*, edited by James J. Fox and Dionísio Babo Soares, 1–27. Adelaide: Crawford House Publishing, 2000.

França, Bento da. *Macau e os seus Habitantes: Relações com Timor*. Lisbon: Imprensa Nacional, 1897.

Galvão, António. *A Treatise on the Moluccas (c. 1544): Probably the Preliminary Version of António Galvão's Lost* Historia das Molucas, edited by Hubert Jacobs. Rome: Jesuit Historical Institute; and St. Louis: St. Louis University, 1971.

Gaudart, Hyacinth. "A Typology of Bilingual Education in Malaysia", *Journal of Multilingual and Multicultural Development* 8, no. 6 (1987): 529–52.

Geertz, Clifford. *Negara: The Theatre State in Nineteenth-Century Bali*. Princeton: Princeton University Press, 1980.

Gentilcore, David. *From Bishop to Witch: The System of the Sacred in Early Modern Terra d'Otranto*. Manchester: Manchester University Press, 1992.

Giles, Howard and Peter F. Powesland. *Speech Style and Social Evaluation*. London: Academic Press in cooperation with the European Association of Experimental Social Psychology, 1975.

Goor, Jurrien van. "Merchant in Royal Service: Constant Phaulkon as Phraklang in Ayutthaya, 1683–1688". In *Emporia, Commodities and Entrepreneurs in Asian Maritime Trade, c.1400–1750*, edited by Roderich Ptak and Dietmar Rothermund, 445–65. Stuttgart: Franz Steiner Verlag, 1991.

Goyau, [Georges]. "Les missions depuis la création de la Propagande". In *Histoire Générale Comparée des Missions*, edited by le Baron Descamps. Brussels: M. Hayez, 1932.

Guedes, Armando Marques. "A complexidade estrutural do nacionalismo timorense". Paper presented at the international conference "Ásia do Sul e do Sudeste em Perspectiva [Séculos XX–XXI]", Instituto Superior de Ciências Sociais e Políticas, Lisbon, 2002.

Guerreiro, Fernão. *Relação Anual das Coisas que Fizeram os Padres da Companhia de Jesus nas suas Missões ... nos anos de 1600 a 1609,* edited by Artur Viegas. Vol. 2. Coimbra: Imprensa da Universidade, 1931.

Guisan, Pierre F.G. "Línguas em contato no Sudeste Asiático: O caso do '*Kristang*' ". Master's thesis, Universidade Federal do Rio de Janeiro, 1992.

Gunn, Geoffrey. "Língua e cultura na construção da identidade de Timor-Leste". *Camões: Revista de Letras e Cultura Lusófonas* 14 (Jul.–Sept. 2001): 14–25.

———. *Timor Loro Sae: 500 Anos.* Macao: Livros do Oriente, 1999.

Guterres, Apolinário. "A identidade cultural timorense: Desafios de futuro". In *Estudos Orientais: O Oriente, Hoje, do Índico ao Pacífico,* edited by António Augusto Tavares, 127–42. Lisbon: Faculdade de Ciências Sociais e Humanas, Universidade Nova de Lisboa, 1994.

Hall, Stuart. *Representation: Cultural Representation and Signifying Practices.* London: Sage, 1997.

Hammond, Debra. *The Science of Synthesis: Exploring the Social Implications of General Systems Theory.* Boulder, CO: University Press of Colorado, 2003.

Hancock, Ian F. "Malacca Creole Portuguese: Asian, African or European?" *Anthropological Linguistics* 17, no. 5 (May 1975): 211–36.

———. "Malacca Creole Portuguese: A Brief Transformational Account". *Te Reo* 16 (1973): 23–44.

———. "The Malacca Creoles and Their Language". *Afrasian* 3 (1969): 38–45.

———. "Some Dutch-Derived Items in Papia Kristang". *Bijdragen tot de Taal-, Land-, en Volkenkunde* 136, no. 3 (1970): 352–56.

"Haojing ao" 濠鏡澳 [Port of Oyster Mirror]. In *Xiangshan Xianzhi* 香山縣志 [Xiangshan Gazetteer], edited by Bao Yu 暴煜 and Li Zhuokui 李卓揆. Guangzhou, 1750.

Harrison, Mark. *Crowds and History: Mass Phenomena in English Towns, 1790–1835.* Cambridge: Cambridge University Press, 1988.

Heine, Bernd and Tania Kuteva. *Language Contact and Grammatical Change.* Cambridge: Cambridge University Press, 2008.

Hinton, Leanne. "Language Planning". In *The Green Book of Language Revitalization in Practice,* edited by Leanne Hinton and Ken Hale, 51–60. New York: Academic Press, 2001.

———. "Language Revitalization: An Overview". In *The Green Book of Language Revitalization in Practice,* edited by Leanne Hinton and Ken Hale, 3–18. New York: Academic Press, 2001.

Hobsbawm, Eric and Terence Ranger, eds. *The Invention of Tradition.* Cambridge: Cambridge University Press, 1992.

Holm, John. *Pidgins and Creoles.* Vol. 2, *Reference Survey.* Cambridge: Cambridge University Press, 1989.

De homepage van Herman Oomen. http://www.johan-jong.nl/Herman.html.

Hsia Po-chia, Ronnie. *The World of Catholic Renewal,* 2nd ed. Cambridge: Cambridge University Press, 2005.

Hull, Geoffrey. "The Languages of East Timor: 1772–1997: A Literature Review".

In *Studies in Languages and Cultures of East Timor*, edited by Geoffrey Hull and Lance Eccles. Vol. 1, 1–38. Campbelltown, NSW: Language Acquisition Research Centre, University of Western Sydney, Macarthur, 1999.

———. "Língua, identidade e resistência". *Camões: Revista de Letras e Cultura Lusófonas* 14 (Jul.–Sept. 2001): 80–92.

Humphrey, Caroline and James Laidlaw. *The Archetypal Actions of Ritual: A Theory of Ritual Illustrated by the Jain Rite of Worship*. Oxford: Clarendon Press, 1994.

Jackson, Kenneth David. "Canta sen Vargonya: Portuguese Creole Verse in Sri Lanka". *Journal of Pidgin and Creole Languages* 2, no. 1 (1987): 31–48.

———. *De Chaul a Batticaloa: As Marcas do Império Marítimo Português na Índia e no Sri Lanka*. Ericeira, Portugal: Editora Mar de Letras, 2005.

———. "The Indo-Portuguese Folklore Text". *Boletim do Instituto Menezes Braganza* 168 (1993): 169–91.

———. *Sing without Shame: Oral Traditions in Indo-Portuguese Creole Verse*. Amsterdam: John Benjamins; and Macao: Instituto Cultural de Macau, 1990.

Jacobs, Hubert. "The *Discurso Politico del Gobierno Maluco* of Fr. Francisco Combés and Its Historical Impact". *Philippine Studies* 29 (1981): 309–44.

———, ed. *Documenta Malucensia*. 3 vols. Rome: Institutum Historicum Societatis Iesu, 1974–1984.

Jacobsen, Knut A. "Introduction: Religion on Display". In *South Asian Religions on Display: Religious Processions in South Asia and in the Diaspora*, edited by Knut A. Jacobsen, 1–12. London: Routledge, 2008.

Jayasuriya, Shihan de Silva. "Indo-Portuguese Songs of Sri Lanka: The Nevill Manuscript". *Bulletin of the School of Oriental and African Studies* 59, no. 2 (June 1996): 253–67.

Jiao Qinian 焦祈年. "Yiwen . Ji" 藝文 . 記 [Arts and literature: Reports]. In "Xunshi Aomen Ji" 巡視澳門記 [An inspection report on Macao]. In *Xiangshan Xianzhi* 香山縣志 [Xiangshan Gazetteer], edited by Bao Yu 暴煜 and Li Zhuokui 李卓揆. Guangzhou, 1750.

Jin Guoping. *Xi li dong jian: Zhong Pu zaoqi jiechu zhuixi*. Haohai congkan. Macao: Fundação Macau, 2000.

———. *Zhong Pu guanxi shidi kaozheng*. Haohai congkan. Macao: Fundação Macau, 2000.

Jin Guoping 金國平 and Wu Zhiliang 吳志良. "'Dizuyin Yiwan Liang' Yu 'Dingliang Yiwan Liang'" (〈「地租銀一萬兩」與「丁糧一萬兩」〉) ["Ten thousand taels of rent" and "Ten thousand liang of food for the people"]. In *Dongxi Wangyang* 東西望洋 [Eastern and Western Side of the Coast], edited by Jin Guoping 金國平 and Wu Zhiliang 吳志良, 182–88. Macao: Aomen chengren jiaoyu xuehui 澳門成人教育學會 [Association of Adult Education of Macao], 2002.

———. *Dong xi wang yang (Em Busca de História[s] de Macau Apagada[s] pelo Tempo)*. Macao: Aomen chengren jiaoyu xiehui, 2002.

———. *Guo Shizimen (Abrindo as Portas do Cerco)*. Macao: Aomen chengren jiaoyu xiehui, 2004.

————. *Jing hai piao miao (História[s] de Macau: Ficção e Realidade)*. Macao: Aomen chengren jiaoyu xiehui, 2001.

Johnson, Trevor. "Blood, Tears and Xavier-Water: Jesuit Missions and Popular Religion in the Eighteenth-Century Upper Palatinate". In *Popular Religion in Germany and Central Europe*, edited by Bob Scribner and Trevor Johnson, 183–202. Basingstoke: Macmillan, 1996.

Jost, Jürgen. *Dynamical Systems: Examples of Complex Behavior*. Berlin: Springer, 2005.

Kadir, Abdullah bin Abdul. "Hikayat Abdullah", translated and edited by A.H. Hill. *Journal of the Malayan Branch of the Royal Asiatic Society* 27, no. 3 (1955): 1–354.

Kantiga di Padri sa Chang: Malaca. Compact disc. Vila Verde, Portugal: Tradisom, 1998. Part of the collection *A Viagem dos Sons*.

Kartomi, Margaret. "A Malay-Portuguese Synthesis on the West Coast of North Sumatra". In *O Portugal e o Mundo: O Encontro de Culturas na Música / Portugal and the World: The Encounter of Cultures in Music*, edited by Salwa El-Shawan Castelo-Branco, 289–350. Lisbon: Publicações Dom Quixote, 1997.

Keesing, Roger M. *Melanesian Pidgin and the Oceanic Substrate*. Stanford: Stanford University Press, 1988.

Kennedy, Thomas Frank. "Jesuits and Music: The European Tradition, 1547–1622". Ph.D. dissertation, University of California, Santa Barbara, 1982.

Ladurie, Emmanuel Le Roy. *Carnival: A People's Uprising at Romans, 1579–1580*, translated by Mary Feeney. London: Scholar Press, 1980.

Lasimbang, Rita, Carolyn Miller and Francis Otigil. "Language Competence and Use among Coastal Kadazan Children: A Survey Report". In *Maintenance and Loss of Minority Languages*, edited by William Fase, Koen Jaspaert, and Sjaak Kroon, 333–55. Amsterdam: John Benjamins, 1992.

Launay, Adrien, ed. *Histoire de la Mission de Siam, 1662–1811: Documents Historique*. Vol. 1. Paris: Anciennes Maisons Charles Douniol et Retaux, P. Téqui, successeur, 1920.

————. *Histoire Générale de la Société des Missions-Étrangères*. 1894. Reprint, Paris: Les Indes Savantes, 2003.

Lawrance, Jeremy. "Black Africans in Renaissance Spanish Literature". In *Black Africans in Renaissance Europe*, edited by T.F. Earle and K.J.P. Lowe, 70–93. Cambridge: Cambridge University Press, 2005.

Lazar, Lance. *Working in the Vineyard of the Lord: Jesus Confraternities in Early Modern Italy*. Toronto: University of Toronto Press, 2005.

Lê Thành Khôi. *Histoire du Viêt Nam des Origines à 1858*. Paris: Sudestasie, 1981.

Lea, Henry Charles. *A History of Auricular Confession and Indulgences in the Latin Church*. Part 1. 1896. Reprint, Whitefish, MT: Kessinger Publishing, 2004.

Lee, Eileen. "Language Shift and Revitalization in the Kristang Community, Portuguese Settlement, Malacca". Ph.D. dissertation, University of Sheffield, 2004.

"Lembranças de cousas da Índia em 1525". In *Subsídios para a Historia da India Portugueza*, edited by Rodrigo José de Lima Felner. Lisbon: A.R.S., 1868.

Leupe, P.A. "The Siege and Capture of Malacca from the Portuguese in 1640–1641". *Journal of the Malayan Branch of the Royal Asiatic Society* 14, no. 1 (1936): 1–178.

Lobato, Manuel. "Fortalezas do Estado da Índia: Do centro à periferia". In *A Arquitectura Militar na Expansão Portuguesa*, edited by Rafael Moreira, 43–55. Porto: Comissão Nacional para as Comemorações dos Descobrimentos Portugueses, 1994.

———. "Implementar a União Ibérica na Ásia: O relato da viagem de Francisco de Dueñas de Manila a Maluco em 1582". In *O Reino, as Ilhas e o Mar-Oceano: Estudos em Homenagem a Artur Teodoro de Matos*, edited by Avelino de Freitas de Meneses and João Paulo Oliveira e Costa. Vol. 2, 785–811. Ponta Delgada and Lisbon: Universidade dos Açores, Centro de História de Além-Mar, 2007.

———. "A Man in the Shadow of Magellan: Francisco Serrão, the 'Discoverer' of the Maluku Islands (1511–1521)". Paper presented at the international seminar "Indonesia and Portugal: Past, Present and Future: In Commemoration of Ten Years of the Reestablishment of Diplomatic Relations", Museu do Oriente, Lisbon, 16–17 Nov. 2009.

———. *Política e Comércio dos Portugueses na Insulíndia: Malaca e as Molucas de 1575 a 1605*. Macao: Instituto Português do Oriente, 1999.

Loureiro, Rui Manuel. *Em Busca das Origins de Macau (Antologia Documental)*. Macao: Museu Marítimo de Macau, 1997.

———. *Fidalgos, Missionários e Mandarins: Portugal e a China no Século XVI*, Orientalia 1. Lisbon: Fundação Oriente, 2000.

Lu Kun 盧坤 et al. *Guangdong Haifang Huilan* 廣東海防匯覽 [A general overview of coastal defence in Guangdong]. Guangzhou, 1835.

Lucena, João de. *História da Vida do Padre Francisco Xavier*, edited by Luís de Albuquerque and M.G. Pericão. Vol. 2. Lisbon: Alfa, 1989.

Manguin, Pierre-Yves. *Les Portugais sur les Côtes du Viêt-Nam et du Campā: Étude sur les Routes Maritimes et les Relations Commerciales, d'après les Sources Portugaises (XVIe, XVIIe, XVIIIe Siècles)*. Paris: École Français d'Extrême-Oriente, 1972.

Marbeck, Joan. *Kristang Phrasebook*. Lisbon: Calouste Gulbenkian, 2004.

———. *Linngu Mai: Mother-Tongue of the Malacca Portuguese*. Lisbon: Calouste Gulbenkian, 2004.

———. *Ungua Adanza: An Inheritance*, translated by Celine J. Ting. Malacca: Loh Printing Press, 1995.

Marini, Giovanni Fillippo de. *Historia et Relatione del Tunchino e del Giappone: Con la Vera Relatione Ancora d'Altri Regni, e Prouincie di Quelle Regioni, e del loro Gouerno Politico; Con le Missioni Fatteui dalli Padri della Compagnia di Giesù, & Introduttione della Fede Christiana, & Confutatione di Diuersi Sette d'Idolatri di Quelli Habitatori; Divisa in Cinqve Libri, Opera del P. Gio: Filippo de Marini della medema Compagni; Alla Santitá di N.S. Alessandro Papa Settimo*. Rome: Vitale Mascardi, 1665.

Martin, Philippe. *Les Chemins du Sacré: Paroisses, Processions, Pèlerinages en Lorraine du XVIème au XIXème Siècle*. Metz: Éditions Serpenoise, 1995.

Martinho, José Simões. *Timor: Quatro Séculos de Colonização Portuguesa*. Porto: Livraria Progredior, 1943.

Mather, Patrick-André. "Second Language Acquisition and Creolization: Same (I-) Processes, Different (E-) Results". *Journal of Pidgin and Creole Langauges* 21 (2006): 231–74.

Matos, Artur Teodoro de. *Timor Português 1515-1769: Contribuição para a sua História*. Lisbon: Instituto Histórico Infante Dom Henrique, 1974.

Matthews, Stephen and Virginia Yip. *Cantonese: A Comprehensive Grammar*. London: Routledge, 1994.

McIntyre, Kenneth Gordon. *The Secret Discovery of Australia: Portuguese Ventures Two Hundred Years before Captain Cook*. Medindie, Australia: Souvenir Press, 1977.

McPherson, Kenneth. "Staying On: Reflections on the Survival of Portuguese Enterprise in the Bay of Bengal and Southeast Asia from the Seventeenth to the Eighteenth Centuries". In *Iberians in the Singapore-Melaka Area (16th to 18th Century)*, edited by Peter Borschberg, 63–91. Wiesbaden: Harrassowitz; and Lisbon: Fundação Oriente, 2004.

McRae, Graeme. "Negara Ubud: The Theatre-State in Twenty-First-Century Bali". *History and Anthropology* 16, no. 4 (2005): 393–413.

Medina Ruiz, Fernando. Untitled editorial. *Seara: Boletim Eclesiástico da Diocese de Díli* 2, no. 54 (1967): 1.

"Mémoires de Bénigne Vachet". In *Histoire de la Mission de Siam, 1662–1811: Documents Historique*, edited by Adrien Launay. Vol. 1. Paris: Anciennes Maisons Charles Douniol et Retaux, P. Téqui, successeur, 1920.

Mendes, Nuno Canas. *A Multidimensionalidade da Construção Identitária em Timor-Leste: Nacionalismo, Estado e Identidade Nacional*. Lisbon: Instituto Superior de Ciências Sociais e Políticas, 2005.

Migge, Bettina. "Substrate Influence in Creole Formation: The Origin of Give-Type Serial Verb Constructions in the Surinamese Plantation Creole". *Journal of Pidgin and Creole Languages* 13 (1998): 215–65.

Miraflores, Marquis de and Miguel Silva, eds. *Correspondencia de Don Gerónimo de Silva … sobre el Estado de las Islas Molucas*. Madrid, 1868.

Miranda, Susana Münch. "Os circuitos económicos". In *História dos Portugueses no Extremo Oriente*, edited by A.H. de Oliveira Marques. Vol. 2, *Macau e Timor: O Declínio do Império*, 259–88. Lisbon: Fundação Oriente, 2001.

Miranda, Susana Münch and Cristina Seuanes Serafim. "População e sociedade". In *História dos Portugueses no Extremo Oriente*, edited by A.H. de Oliveira Marques. Vol. 2: *Macau e Timor: O Declínio do Império*, 229–57. Lisbon: Fundação Oriente, 2001.

Moen, Don. "Korean Hybridity: The Language Classroom as Cultural Hybrid". *Journal of Intercultural Communication* 20 (May 2009). http://www.immi.se/jicc/index. php/jicc/article/view/23/14.

Molhuysen, P.C. and P.J. Blok, eds. *Nieuw Nederlandsch biografisch woordenboek*. Vol. 8, 67–68. Leiden: A.W. Sijthoff, 1930. http://www.biografischportaal. nl/persoon/34180165.

Moniz, António Francisco. *Notícias e Documentos para a História de Damão: Antiga Província do Norte*. Vol. 1. Bastorá: Tipografia Rangel, 1923.

Moor, J.H. and J.J. Newbold. *Malacca Territory with Muar and Lingee Rivers*. Singapore, 1837.

Mufwene, Salikoko. *The Ecology of Language Evolution*. Cambridge: Cambridge University Press, 2001.

Muir, Edward. *Ritual in Early Modern Europe*, 2nd ed. Cambridge: Cambridge University Press, 2005.

Mungello, D.E. "An Introduction to the Chinese Rites Controversy". In *The Chinese Rites Controversy: Its History and Meaning*, 1–14. Nettetal, Germany: Steyler Verlag, 1994.

Die Musik in Geschichte und Gegenwart: Allgemeine Enzyklopädie der Musik. Personenteil 4. 2nd ed. S.v. "Carissimi, Giacomo".

"The Negroes and St. Benedict's Feast". In *The Mission Field: The Diocese of Damaun*, 567–72. Bombay: S.R. Santos, 1925.

Newitt, Malyn. *A History of Portuguese Overseas Expansion, 1400–1668*. London: Routledge, 2005.

Ng Chin Keong. "Trade, the Sea Prohibition and the 'Fo-lang-chi', 1513–1550". In *Proceedings of the International Colloquium on the Portuguese and the Pacific*, edited by Francis A. Dutra and João Camilo dos Santos, 381–424. Santa Barbara: Center for Portuguese Studies, 1995.

Ntarangwi, Mwenda. *Reversed Gaze: An African Ethnography of American Anthropology*. Urbana: University of Illinois Press, 2010.

Nunes, Mário P. "By How Many Speakers, by Whom, with Whom, and for What Purposes, Is Kristang Still Used in the Portuguese Settlement of Malacca?". Paper presented at the 8e Colloque International d'Études Créoles, Guadeloupe, May 1996.

———. "Concepção de tempo e espaço no kristang e no malaio". *Papia* 3, no. 2 (1994): 116–26.

Nunes, Mário Pinharanda. "Os demonstrativos em Maquista: Uma análise morfo-sintáctica constrativa". *Papia: Revista Brasileira de Crioulos e Similares* 18 (2008): 7–21.

Nunes, Mário Rui Pinharanda and Alan N. Baxter. "Os marcadores pré-verbais no crioulo de base lexical portuguesa de Macau". *Papia: Revista Brasileira de Crioulos e Similares* 14 (2004): 31–46.

Ollé, Manuel. *La Invención de China: Percepciones y Estrategias Filipinas Respecto a China durante el Siglo XVI*, South China and Maritime Asia 9. Wiesbaden: Harrassowitz-Verlag, 2000.

O'Malley, John W. *The First Jesuits*. Cambridge, MA: Harvard University Press, 1993.

Ospina, Sofi and Tanja Hohe. "Traditional Power Structures and the Community Empowerment and Local Governance Project: Final Report". Report presented to CEP/PMU, ETTA/UNTAET and the World Bank, Dili, 2001.

Palomo, Federico. *A Contra-Reforma em Portugal, 1540–1700*. Lisbon: Livros Horizonte, 2006.

Paulino, Vicente. "Identidade e Representação: Uma Abordagem da Cultura Timorense". Master's thesis, Universidade Nova de Lisboa, 2009.

———. "Timor entre a fé e a cultura". Talk presented to the grupo 3 nós de jovens de Carnide, Casa dos Irmãos Maristas, 2 October 2008, Lisbon.

Pereira, António Manuel Nunes. "Die Kirchenbauten in Alt-Goa in der zweiten Hälfte des 16. und in den ersten Jahrzehnten des 17. Jahrhunderts". Ph.D. disssertation, Rheinisch-Westfälische Technische Hochschule Aachen, 2002.

Perez, Lorenzo. "Historia de las misiones de los Franciscanos en las islas Malucas y Célebes", *Archivum Franciscanum Historicum* 7 (1914): 198–226, 424–46 and 621–53.

Phan, Peter C. *Mission and Catechesis: Alexandre de Rhodes and Inculturation in Seventeenth-Century Vietnam*. New York: Orbis Books, 1998.

Pintado, Manuel Joaquim. *Survival through Human Values*. Malacca, 1974.

Pires, Benjamin Videira. "A viagem de comércio Macau-Manila nos séculos XVI à XIX". *Boletim do Instituto Luís de Camões* 5, nos. 1–2 (1971): 5–100.

Pisauro, Giovanni Battista Lucarelli de. "Viaggio dell'Indie". In *Sinica Franciscana Volumen II: Relationes et Epistolas Fratrum Minorum Saeculi XVI et XVII*, edited by Anastasius van den Wyngaert, 12–92. Quaracchi, Italy: Claras Aquas, 1933.

Ptak, Roderich. "China's Medieval *Fanfang*: A Model for Macau under the Ming?" *Anais de História de Além-Mar* 2 (2001): 64–68.

———. "Chinese Documents in Portuguese Archives: Jottings on Three Texts Found in the Arquivo Histórico Ultramarino, Lisbon". *Zeitschrift der Deutschen Morgenländischen Gesellschaft* 149, no. 1 (1999): 185–90.

———. "The Demography of Old Macao, 1555–1640". *Ming Studies* 15 (Fall 1982): 27–35.

———. "The Fujianese, Ryukyuans and Portuguese (c. 1511 to 1540s): Allies or Competitors?", *Anais de História de Além-Mar* 3 (2002): 447–67.

———. "Der Handel zwischen Macau und Makassar, ca. 1640–1667". *Zeitschrift der Deutschen Morgenländischen Gesellschaft* 139, no. 1 (1989): 208–26.

———. "Macau and Sino-Portuguese Relations, c. 1513/14 to c. 1900: A Bibliographical Essay". *Monumenta Serica* 46 (1998): 343–96.

———. "Macau: Trade and Society, circa 1740–1760". In *Maritime China in Transition, 1750–1850*, edited by Wang Gungwu and Ng Chin-keong, 191–211. Wiesbaden: Harrassowitz-Verlag, 2004.

———. "Mercadorias em trânsito em Macau durante o seu período histórico: Seda, prata, sândalo, chá, pimenta, almíscar". In *Os Fundamentos da Amizade: Cinco Séculos de Relações Culturais e Artísticas Luso-Chinesas*, 61–69. Lisbon: Centro Científico e Cultural de Macau and Fundação para a Cooperação e o Desenvolvimento do Macau, 1999.

———. "Ming Maritime Trade to Southeast Asia, 1368–1567: Visions of a System". In *From the Mediterranean to the China Sea: Miscellaneous Notes*, edited by

Claude Guillot, Denys Lombard and Roderich Ptak, 157–92. Wiesbaden: Harrassowitz-Verlag, 1998.

——. *Portugal in China: Kurzer Abriß der portugiesisch-chinesischen Beziehungen und der Geschichte Macaus im 16. und beginnenden 17. Jahrhundert*. Portugal-Reihe. Bad Boll: Klemmerberg-Verlag, 1980.

——. "Reconsidering Melaka and Central Guangdong: Portugal's and Fujian's Impact on Southeast Asian Trade (Early Sixteenth Century)". In *Iberians in the Singapore-Melaka Area (16th to 18th Century)*, edited by Peter Borschberg, 1–21. Wiesbaden: Harrassowitz; and Lisbon: Fundação Oriente, 2004.

——. "Die Rolle der Chinesen, Portugiesen und Holländer im Teehandel zwischen China und Südostasien (ca. 1600–1750)". *Jahrbuch für Wirtschaftsgeschichte*. Vol. 1, 89–106. Berlin: Akademie Verlag, 1994.

——. "Sino-Japanese Maritime Trade, circa 1550: Merchants, Ports and Networks". In *O Século Cristão do Japão: Actas do Colóquio Internacional Comemorativo dos 450 Anos de Amizade Portugal-Japão (1543–1993) (Lisboa, 2 a 5 de Novembro de 1993)*, edited by Roberto Carneiro and A. Teodoro de Matos, 281–311. Lisbon: Centro de Estudos dos Povos e Culturas de Expressão Portuguesa da Universidade Católica Portuguesa and Instituto de História de Além-Mar of the Faculdade de Ciências Sociais e Humanas da Universidade Nova de Lisboa, 1994.

——. "Sino-Portuguese Relations circa 1513/14 to 1550s". In *Portugal e a China: Conferências no II Curso Livre de História das Relações entre Portugal e a China (Séculos XVI–XIX)*, edited by Jorge Manuel dos Santos Alves, 19–37. Lisbon: Fundação Oriente, 1999.

——. "Twentieth Century Macau: History, Politics, Economics: A Bibliographical Survey". *Monumenta Serica* 49 (2001): 529–93.

——. "Wirtschaftlicher und demographischer Wandel in Macau: Stadien einer Entwicklung". In *Macau: Herkunft ist Zukunft*, edited by Roman Malek, 153–86. Sankt Augustin, Germany: China-Zentrum and Institut Monumenta Serica, 2000.

Purchas, Samuel, ed. *Hakluytus Posthumus or Purchas His Pilgrimes*. Vol. 2. Glasgow: MacLehose, 1905.

——. Vol. 3. Glasgow: MacLehose, 1905.

Pusat Dokumentasi Arkitektur. *Inventory and Identification of Forts in Indonesia*. Jakarta: Pusat Dokumentasi Arkitektur, 2006.

Quadros, Jeronymo. *Cartas de Diu*. 1st ser. (1902–05). Nova Goa: Tipographia Fontainhas, 1907.

Ramerini, Marco. *Le fortezze spagnole nell'isola di Tidore*, http://www.colonialvoyage.com/molucche/4_fortispagnoli.html.

Ramos, João de Deus. *História das Relações Diplomáticas entre Portugal e a China*. Vol. 1, *O Padre António de Magalhães, S.J., e a Embaixada de Kangxi a D. João V (1721–1725)*. Macao: Instituto Cultural de Macau, 1991.

Rego, António da Silva, ed. *As Gavetas da Torre do Tombo*. Vol. 1. Lisbon: Centro de Estudos Históricos Ultramarinos, 1960.

————. Vol. 3. Lisbon: Centro de Estudos Históricos Ultramarinos, 1963.

————. *Dialecto Português de Malaca: Apontamentos para o seu Estudo*. Lisbon: Agência Geral das Colónias, 1942.

————, ed. *Documentação Ultramarina Portuguesa*. 2 vols. Lisbon: Centro de Estudos Históricos Ultramarinos, 1960–1962.

————. "As Molucas em princípios do século XVI". In *A Viagem de Fernão de Magalhães e a Questão das Molucas*, edited by A. Teixeira da Mota, 75–89. Lisbon: Junta de Investigações Científicas, 1975.

Rêgo, António da Silva and Alan N. Baxter. *Dialecto Português de Malaca e Outros Escritos*, Lisbon: Comissão Nacional para os Descobrimentos Portugueses, Imprensa Nacional, 1998.

"Renwu Liezhuan: Wugong" 濠鏡澳 [Biographies: Military officers]. In *Xiangshan Xianzhi* 香山縣志 [Xiangshan Gazetteer], edited by Bao Yu 暴煜 and Li Zhuokui 李卓揆. Guangzhou, 1750.

Rhodes, Alexandre de. *Relazione de' Felici Successi della Santa Fede Predicata da' Padri della Compagnia di Giesù nel Regno di Tunchino, alla Santità di N.S. PP. Innocenzio Decimo di Alessandro de Rhodes Avignonese della Medesima Compagnia, e Missionario Apostolico della Sacra Congregatione de Propagande Fide*. Rome: Giuseppe Luna, 1650.

Rhodes, Alexandre du. *Divers Voyages et Missions dv P. Alexandre de Rhodes en la Chine, & Autres Royaumes de l'Orient: Auec son Retour en Europe par la Perse & l'Armenie*. Paris: Sebastien et Gabriel Cramoisy, 1653.

————. *La Glorieuse Mort d'André, Catéchiste de la Cochin Chine, Qui a le Premier Versé Son Sang Pour la Querelle de Jésus Christ en Cette Nouvelle Église*. Paris: Sebastien Cramoisy et Gabriel Cramoisy, 1653.

————. *Relation de l'Évangélisation de la Cochinchine*. Paris: Sebastien et Gabriel Cramoisy, 1653.

Ring, Grete. "An Attempt to Reconstruct Perréal". *The Burlington Magazine* 92 (1950): 255–61.

Rodao, Florentino. "Restos de la presencia ibérica en las islas Molucas". In *España y el Pacífico*, edited by F. Rodao and Leoncio Cabrero, 243–54. Madrid: AECI-AEEP, 1989.

Roque, Ricardo. *Headhunting and Colonialism: Anthropology and the Circulation of Human Skulls in the Portuguese Empire, 1870–1930*. Basingstoke: Palgrave Macmillan, 2010.

————. "The Unruly Island: Colonialism's Predicament in Late Nineteenth-Century East Timor". In *Parts of Asia*, edited by Cristiana Bastos, 303–30. Portuguese Literary & Cultural Studies 17/18. Dartmouth, MA: University of Massachusetts Dartmouth Center for Portuguese Studies and Culture, 2010.

Rubin, Miri. *Corpus Christi: The Eucharist in Late Medieval Culture*. Cambridge: Cambridge University Press, 1991.

Rudé, George. *The Crowd in History: A Study of Popular Disturbances in France and England, 1730–1848*. New York: Wiley, 1964.

Ruiz, Fernando Medina. Untitled editorial. *Seara: Boletim Eclesiástico da Diocese de Díli* 2, no. 54 (1967).

Russell-Wood, A.J.R. *The Portuguese Empire, 1415–1808: A World on the Move*. Baltimore: Johns Hopkins University Press, 1998.

Sá, Artur Basílio de. *A Planta de Cailaco*. Lisbon: Agência Geral das Colónias, 1949.

————, ed. *Documentação para a História das Missões do Padroado Português do Oriente: Insulíndia, 1506–1599*. Vol. 1, *1506–1549*. Lisbon: Agência Geral do Ultramar, 1954.

————. Vol. 2, *1550–1562*. Lisbon: Agência Geral do Ultramar, 1955.

————. Vol. 3, *1563–1567*. Lisbon: Agência Geral do Ultramar, 1955.

————. Vol. 4, *1568–1579*. Lisbon: Instituto de Investigação Científica Tropical, 1956.

————. Vol. 6, *1595–1599*. Lisbon: Centro de Estudos de História e Cartografia Antiga, Instituto de Investigação Científica Tropical, 1988.

Sá, Isabel dos Guimarães. "Ecclesiastical Structures and Religious Action". In *Portuguese Oceanic Expansion, 1400–1800*, edited by Francisco Bethencourt and Diogo Ramada Curto, 255–82. Cambridge: Cambridge University Press, 2007.

Saccano, Metelle. *Relation des Progrez de la Foy av Royavme de la Cochinchine és Années 1646 & 1647. Envoiée av R.P. General de la Compagnie de Iesus; Par le P. Metelle Saccano, Religieux de la Mesme Compagnie, Employé aux Missions de Ces Païs*. Paris: Sebastien et Gabriel Cramoisy, 1653.

Saldanha, António Vasconcelos, ed. *Embaixada de D. João V de Portugal ao Imperador Yongzheng, da China (1725–1728)*, compiled by Mariagrazia Russo, and translated by Jin Guoping. Lisbon: Fundação Oriente, 2005.

San Agustín, Gaspar de. *Conquista de las Islas Filipinas, 1565–1615*, edited by Manuel Merino. Madrid: Consejo Superior de Investigaciones Científicas, Instituto Enrique Florez, 1975.

Sandhu, Kernial Singh and Paul Wheatley. "From Capital to Municipality". In *Melaka: The Transformation of a Malay Capital c.1400–1980*, edited by Kernial Singh Sandhu and Paul Wheatley. Vol. 2, 495–597. Kuala Lumpur: Oxford University Press, 1983.

Santos, Catarina Madeira. *Goa É a Chave de Toda a Índia: Perfil Político da Capital do Estado da Índia (1505–1570)*. Lisbon: Comissão Nacional para as Comemorações dos Descobrimentos Portugueses, 1999.

Santos, Eduardo dos. *Kanoik: Mitos e Lendas de Timor*. Lisbon: Serviço de Publicações da Mocidade Portuguesa, 1967.

Santos, Isaú. "A embaixada de Manuel de Saldanha à China, em 1667–1670". In *As Relações entre a Índia Portuguesa, a Ásia do Sueste e o Extremo Oriente: Actas do VI Seminário Internacional de História Indo-Portuguesa (Macau, 22 a 26 de Outubro de 1991)*, edited by Artur Teodoro de Matos and Luís Filipe F. Reis Thomaz, 405–36. Macau: Instituto de Investigação Científica Tropical, 1993.

Sarkissian, Margaret. D'Albuquerque's Children: Performing Tradition in Malaysia's Portuguese Settlement. Chicago: University of Chicago Press, 2000.

Sartorius, Johann Anton. "An den Editorem". In *Der Königl. Dänischen Missionarien aus Ost-Indien eingesandter Ausführlichen Berichten, Dritter Theil*, edited by Gotthilf August Francke, 673–74. Halle: Waysenhaus, 1735.

Schuchardt, Hugo. "Beiträge zur Kenntnis des kreolischen Romanisch: VI. Zum Indoportugiesischen von Mahé und Cannanore". *Zeitschrift für Romanische Philologie* 13 (1889): 516–24.

———. "Kreolische Studien III: Über das Indoportugiesische von Diu". *Sitzungsberichte der Kaiserlichen Akademie der Wissenschaften zu Wien (philosophisch-historische Klasse)* 103 (1883): 3–18.

———. "Kreolische Studien VI: Über das Indoportugiesische von Mangalore". *Sitzungsberichte der Kaiserlichen Akademie der Wissenschaften zu Wien (philosophisch-historische Klasse)* 105 (1883b): 881–904.

———. "Kreolische Studien IX: Über das Malaioportugiesiche von Batavia und Tugu". *Sitzungsberichte der Kaiserlichen Akademie der Wissenschaft zu Wien (philosophisch-historische Klasse)* 122 (1890): 1–255.

Schulte-Nortdholt, H. *The Political System of the Atoni*. The Hague: Nijhoff, 1971.

Schwartz, Stuart B. "Ceremonies of Public Authority in a Colonial Capital: The King's Procession and the Hierarchies of Power in Seventeenth-Century Salvador". *Anais de História de Além-Mar* 5 (2004): 7–26.

Scribner, Robert W. "Ritual and Popular Religion in Catholic Germany at the Time of the Reformation". *Journal of Ecclesiastical History* 35 (1984): 47–77.

Scully, Valerie and Catherine Zuzarte. *Eurasian Heritage Dictionary*. Singapore: SNP International, 2004.

Seabra, Leonor de. *A Embaixada ao Sião de Pero Vaz de Siqueira (1684–1686)*. Macao: Universidade de Macau, 2003.

———. *A Embaixada ao Sião de Pero Vaz de Siqueira (1684–1686)*, 2nd ed. Macao: Instituto Português do Oriente, Fundação Oriente, 2004.

———. *The Embassy of Pero Vaz de Siqueira to Siam (1684–1686)*, translated by Custódio Cavaco Martins, Mário Pinharanda Nunes and Alan N. Baxter. Macao: University of Macau, 2005.

———. "Pêro Vaz de Siqueira, mercador e armador nos Mares do Sul da China". *Review of Culture / Revista de Cultura* 11 (2004): 99–113.

Seco Serrano, Carlos, ed. *Obras de D. Martin Fernández de Navarrete*. Vol. 3. Madrid: Atlas, 1964.

Shen Lianghan 申良韓, revised by Ouyang Yuwen 歐陽羽文, *Xiangshan Xianzhi* 香山縣志 [Xiangshan Gazetteer]. Vol. 1: Guan Shou 官守 [Official duties]. Shiqi 石岐 [?], 1673.

Shils, Edward. *Center and Periphery: Essays in Macrosociology*. Chicago: University of Chicago Press, 1975.

Siegel, Jeff. *The Emergence of Pidgin and Creole Languages*. Oxford: Oxford University Press, 2008.

————. "Mixing, Leveling and Pidgin/Creole Development". In *The Structure and Status of Pidgins and Creoles*, edited by Arthur K. Spears and Donald Winford, 111–49. Amsterdam: Benjamins, 1997.

————. "Morphological Elaboration". *Journal of Pidgin and Creole Languages* 19, no. 2 (2004): 333–62.

————. "Morphological Simplicity in Pidgins and Creoles", *Journal of Pidgin and Creole Languages* 19, no. 1 (2004): 139–62.

Silva, Beatriz Basto da. *Em Malaca: Redescobrir Portugal*. Macao: Direcção dos Serviços de Educação de Macau, 1989.

Silva, José Celestino da. *Instruções para os Commandantes Militares*. Macao, 1896.

Smith, Anthony. *A Identidade Nacional*, translated by Cláudia Brito. Lisbon: Edição Gradiva, 1997.

Smith, Stefan Halikowski. *Creolization and Diaspora in the Portuguese Indies, 1640–1720: The Social World of Ayutthaya*. Leiden: Brill, 2011.

————. "No Obvious Home: The Flight of the Portuguese 'Tribe' from Makassar to Ayutthaya and Cambodia during the 1660s". *International Journal of Asian Studies* 7, no. 1 (Jan. 2010): 1–28.

Sousa, A. Botelho de. *Subsídios para a História Militar-Marítima da Índia (1585–1669)*. Vol. 1, 1585–1605. Lisbon, 1930.

Sousa, Francisco de. *Oriente Conquistado a Jesus Christo pelos Padres da Companhia de Jesus da Provincia de Goa*, edited by M. Lopes de Almeida. Porto: Lello & Irmão, 1978.

Sousa, Lúcio Manuel Gomes de. "As casas e o mundo: Identidade local e nação no património material/imaterial de Timor-Leste". Paper presented at "Etnografia: Actas do III Congresso Internacional", Cabeceira de Basto, Portugal, 13–14 July 2007.

Sousa, Manuel de Faria e. *Asia Portuguesa*, translated by M.V.G. Santos Ferreira. Vol. 2. Porto: Livraria Civilização, 1947.

Souza, George Bryan. "Portuguese Country Traders in the Indian Ocean and the South China Sea, c. 1600". In *European Commercial Expansion in Early Modern Asia*, edited by Om Prakash, 69–80. Aldershot: Variorum, 1997.

————. "The Portuguese Merchant Fleet at Macao in the Seventeenth and Eighteenth Centuries". In *Rivalry and Conflict: European Traders and Asian Trading Networks in the 16th and 17th Centuries*, edited by Ernst van Veen and Leonard Blussé, 342–69. Leiden: CNWS Publications, 2005.

————. *The Survival of Empire: Portuguese Trade and Society in China and the South China Sea, 1630–1754*. Cambridge: Cambridge University Press, 1986.

————. *The Survival of Empire: Portuguese Trade and Society in China and the South China Sea, 1630–1754*. 2nd ed. Cambridge: Cambridge University Press, 2004.

Sta Maria, Bernard. *My People, My Country: The Story of the Malacca Portuguese Community*. Malacca: Malacca Portuguese Development Centre, 1982.

Sudesh, Nicholas. "Language Maintenance and Shift among the Portuguese-Eurasians in the Portuguese Settlement". Master's thesis, Universiti Malaya, 2000.

Takahashi, Minoru. "A Portuguese Clavichord in Sixteenth-Century Japan?". *The Galpin Society Journal* 54 (May 2001): 116–23.

Tambiah, Stanley. *Culture, Thought and Social Action: An Anthropological Perspective.* Cambridge, MA: Harvard University Press, 1985.

Tang Kaijian. *Aomen kaibu chuqishi yanjiu.* Beijing: Zhonghua shuju, 1999.

———. *Ming Qing shidafu yu Aomen.* Haohai Congkan. Macao: Fundação Macau, 1998.

———. *Weiliduo "Bao xiao shimo shu" jianzheng.* Aomen congshu. Guangzhou: Guangdong renmin chubanshe, 2004.

Tarde, Gabriel. *Les Lois de L'imitation.* 2nd ed. 1895. http://classiques.uqac.ca/classiques/tarde_gabriel/lois_imitation/tarde_lois_imitation_1.pdf.

Tardieu, Jean-Pierre. *Destin des Noirs aux Indes de Castille XVIe–XVIIIe Siècles.* Paris: L'Harmattan, 1984.

Taylor, Keith. "Nguyen Hoang and the Beginning of Vietnam's Southward Expansion". In *Southeast Asia in the Early Modern Period: Trade, Power, and Belief,* edited by Anthony Reid, 42–65. Ithaca: Cornell University Press, 1993.

Tcheong-Ü-Lâm 張汝霖 and Ian-Kuong-Iâm 印光任. *Monografia de Macau (Ou-mun kei-leok)* [A Brief Monograph of Macao], translated by Luís Gonzaga Gomes. Lisbon: Quinzena de Macau, 1979.

Teixeira, André. *Fortalezas: Estado Português da Índia; A Arquitectura Militar na Construção do Império de D. Manuel I.* Lisbon: Tribuna da História, 2008.

Teixeira, Manuel. "Batávia". In *Macau e a sua Diocese.* Vol. 6, *A Missão Portuguesa de Malaca.* Lisbon: Agência Geral do Ultramar, 1963.

———. *Macau e a sua Diocese: Missões de Timor.* Macao: Tipografia da Missão do Padroado, 1974.

———. *The Portuguese Missions in Malacca and Singapore (1511–1958).* Vol. 1, *Malacca.* Lisbon: Geral do Ultramar, 1961.

———. *The Portuguese Missions in Malacca and Singapore (1511–1958).* Vol. 1, *Malacca.* 2nd ed. Macao: Instituto Cultural de Macau, 1987.

Thiesse, Anne-Marie. *A Creação das Identidades Nacionais.* Lisbon: Temas e Debates, 2000.

Thøfner, Margit. *A Common Art: Urban Ceremonial in Antwerp and Brussels during and after the Dutch Revolt.* Zwolle, Netherlands: Waanders Publishers, 2007.

Thomaz, Luís Filipe. *Babel Lorosae: O Problema Linguístico de Timor-Leste.* Lisbon: Cadernos Camões, 2002.

———. "As cartas malaias de Abu Hayat, sultão de Ternate, a el-rei de Portugal e os primórdios da presença portuguesa em Maluco". *Anais de História de Além-Mar* 4 (2003): 381–446.

———. "O malogrado estabelecimento oficial dos portugueses em Sunda e a islamização de Java". In *Aquém e Além da Taprobana: Estudos Luso-Orientais à Memória de Jean Aubin e Denys Lombard,* edited by L.F. Thomaz. 381–607. Lisbon: Centro de História de Além-Mar, 2002.

———. *País dos Belos: Achegas para a Compreensão de Timor-Leste.* Lisbon: Instituto Português do Oriente, 2008.

Thomaz, Luís Filipe Ferreira Reis. *Early Portuguese Malacca*. Macao: CTMCDP, 2000.

———. "Os Portugueses em Malaca: 1511–1580". Vol. 1. Licenciatura thesis, Universidade de Lisboa, 1964.

Thomaz, Omar R. *Ecos do Atlântico Sul: Representações sobre o Terceiro Império Português*. Rio de Janeiro: Editora da Universidade Federal do Rio de Janeiro, 2002.

Thurgood, Elzbieta and Graham Thurgood. "Aspect, Tense, or Aktionsart? The Particle *Ja* in Kristang (Malacca Creole Portuguese)". *Journal of Pidgin and Creole Languages* 11, no. 1 (1996): 45-70.

Tinharão, José Ramos. *Os Negros em Portugal: Uma Presença Silenciosa*. Lisbon: Editora Caminho, 1988.

Tomás, Maria Isabel. *Os Crioulos Portugueses do Oriente: Uma Bibliografia*. Macao: Instituto Cultural de Macau, 1992.

———. "The Role of Women in the Crosspollination Process in the Asian-Portuguese Varieties". *Journal of Portuguese Linguistics* 8, no. 2 (2009): 49–64.

Tomás, Maria Isabel Gonçalves. "O *Kristang* de Malaca: Processos linguísticos e contextos sociais na obsolescência das línguas". Ph.D. dissertation, Universidade Nova de Lisboa, 2004.

Torres de Mendoza, Luiz, ed. *Colección de Documentos Inéditos … de las Antiguas Posesiones Españolas de América y Oceanía*. Vol. 6. Madrid, 1888.

Traube, Elizabeth. *Cosmology and Social Life: Ritual Exchange among the Mambai of East Timor*. Chicago: University of Chicago Press, 1986.

U.S. Department of State, Bureau of Democracy, Human Rights, and Labor. "International Religious Freedom Report 2006". http://www.state.gov/g/drl/rls/irf/2006/71342.htm.

Vale, António Martins M. do. "Macau: Uma 'república de mercadores'". In *Espaços de um Império: Estudos*, edited by Mafalda Soares da Cunha, 203–11. Lisbon: Commissão Nacional dos Descobrimentos, 1999.

———. "A população de Macau na segunda metade do século XVIII". *Povos e Culturas* 5 (1996): 241–54.

———. *Os Portugueses em Macau (1750–1800): Degregados, Ignorantes e Ambiciosos ou Fiéis Vassalos d'El-Rei?* Memória do Oriente 9. Macao: Instituto Português do Oriente, 1997.

Vaquinhas, José dos Santos. "Timor: I". *Boletim da Sociedade de Geografia de Lisboa* 4, no. 7 (1883): 307–28.

———. "Timor: Usos – superstições de guerra". *Boletim da Sociedade de Geografia de Lisboa* 4 (1884): 490–91.

Varela, Consuelo, ed. *El Viaje de Don Ruy López de Villalobos a las Islas del Poniente, 1542–1548*. Milan: Cisalpino-Goliardica, 1983.

Vasconcellos, J. Leite de, comp. *Cancioneiro Popular Português*, edited by Maria Arminda Zaluar Nunes. Vol. 1. Coimbra: Universidade de Coimbra, 1975.

Viterbo, Sousa. *Diccionario Historico e Documental dos Architectos, Engenheiros e Constructores Portuguezes*. Vol. 2. Lisbon: Imprensa Nacional, 1904.

"The Voyage of Captaine Saris in the Cloave, to the Ile of Japan, What Befell in the Way: Observations of the Dutch and Spaniards in the Moluccas". In *Hakluytus Posthumus or Purchas His Pilgrimes*, edited by Samuel Purchas. Vol. 3, 357–519. Glasgow: MacLehose, 1905.

Waldrop, M. Mitchell. *Complexity: The Emerging Science at the Edge of Order and Chaos*. New York: Touchstone, 1993.

Walter, John. *Crowds and Popular Politics in Early Modern England*. Manchester: Manchester University Press, 2006.

Wang Shizhen 王士禎. *Chibei Outan* 池北偶談 [Notes on the conversation from the northern lake]. Vol. 22 (卷二一): "Tanyi: Er" 談異. 二 [On Strangeness: Section Two]. Beijing 北京: Zhonghua Shuju 中華書局, 1982.

Wang Zhaoyong 汪兆鏞. *Aomen zashi tushi* 澳門雜詩圖譯 [Illustrated unclassified poems of Macao], illustrated by 圖譯 Ye Jinbin 葉晉斌. Macao: Aomen Jijin Hui 澳門基金會 [Macao Foundation], 2004.

Wango, Robert J.J. *The Logic of Nothingness: A Study of Nishida Kitarō*. Honolulu: University of Hawai'i Press, 2005.

Weber, Max. *Economy and Society*. Vol. 1. Berkeley: University of California Press, 1979.

Wekker, Herman. "Creolization and the Acquisition of English as a Second Language". In *Creole Languages and Language Acquisition*, edited by Herman Wekker, 139–49. Berlin: Mouton de Gruyter, 1996.

Wicki, Joseph, ed. *Documenta Indica*. Vol. 1, 1540–1549. Rome: Institutum Historicum Societus Iesu, 1948.

Wicki, Joseph, and John Gomes, eds. *Documenta Indica*. Vol. 12, *1580–1583*. Rome: Institutum Historicum Societus Iesu, 1972.

———. *Documenta Indica*. Vol. 13, *1583–1585*. Rome: Institutum Historicum Societus Iesu, 1975.

Wiener, Margaret J. *Visible and Invisible Realms: Power, Magic, and Colonial Conquest in Bali*. Chicago: University of Chicago Press, 1995.

Wills, John E., Jr., *Embassies and Illusions: Dutch and Portuguese Envoys to K'ang-hsi, 1666–1687*. Cambridge, MA: Harvard University Press, 1984.

Winius, George D. "Embassies from Malacca and the 'Shadow Empire'". In *Proceedings of the International Colloquium on the Portuguese and the Pacific*, edited by Francis A. Dutra and João Camilo dos Santos, 170–78. Santa Barbara: Center for Portuguese Studies, 1995.

———. "Private Trading in Portuguese Asia: A Substantial Will-o'-the-Wisp". In *Vasco da Gama et l'Inde: Chapelle de la Sorbonne, 11 Mai – 30 Juin 1998*, edited by Maria Helena Mendes Pinto and José Manuel García, and translated by Annie Marques dos Santos, 1–13. Lisbon: Fundação Calouste Gulbenkian, and Paris: Chancellerie des universités de Paris, 1999.

———. *Studies on Portuguese Asia, 1495–1689*. Aldershot: Ashgate, 2001.

Wu Zhiliang. *Segredos de Sobrevivência: História Política de Macau*. Macao: Associação de Educação de Adultos de Macau, 1999.

Wunenburger, Jean-Jacques. "Esthétique et épistémologie de la foule: Une auto-poïétique complexe". In *La Foule: Mythes et Figures; De la Révolution à Aujourd'hui*, edited by Jean-Marie Paul, 18–24. Rennes: Presses Universitaires de Rennes, 2004.

Xue Yun 薛醌. "Aomen ji" 澳門記 [A report of Macao]. In *Xiao Fanghu Zhai Yudi Congchao* 小方壺齋與地叢鈔 [Collected Texts on Geography from the Little Square Kettle Studio], edited by Wang Xiqiji 王錫祺. Vol. 9 [第九秩]. Shanghai: Zhuyi Tang 著易堂, 1877.

Yamashiro, José. *História da Cultura Japonesa*. São Paulo: IBRASA, 1986.

Ybot León, Antonio. "Los franciscanos, pioneros de la fé en el Brasil (1500–1538)". In *Actas do Congresso Internacional de História dos Descobrimentos*, edited by José Caeiro da Matta. Vol. 4, 141–59. Lisbon: Comissão Executiva dos Comemorações do V Centenário da Morte do Infante D. Henrique, 1961.

Yin Guangren 印光任 and Zhang Rulin 張汝霖. *Aomen Jilüe Jiaozhu* 澳門記略校注 [A Corrected and Annotated Edition of a Brief Record of Macao], edited by Zhao Chunchen 趙春晨. Part 2, (卷下), "Aofan Pian" 澳蕃篇 [Foreigners in Macao]. Macao: Aomen Wenhua Sishu, 澳門文化司署, 1992.

———. *Breve Monografia de Macau* [A Brief Monograph of Macao], compiled by Zhao Chunchen 趙春晨, translated by Jin Guo Ping 金國平, revised by Rui Manuel Loureiro. Macao: Instituto Cultural do Governo da R.A.E. de Macau, 2009.

"Yishang" 夷商 [Foreign traders]. In *Yuehai guanzhi: jiao zhu ben* 粵海關志: 校注本 [Guangzhou customs record: A corrected and annotated edition], edited by Tingnan Liang 梁廷枏, and compiled by Yuan Zhongren 袁鐘仁. Guangzhou 廣州: Guangdong renmin chubanshe 廣東人民出版社 [Guangdong People's Press], 2002.

Yoshitomo, Okamoto. *Jûroku seiki Nichi-Ô kôtsu-shi no kenkyû*. Tokyo: Rokkô shobô, 1942.

"Yutu" 與圖 [geographical illustration]. In *Guangzhou Fuzhi* 廣州府志 [A Record of Guangzhou], edited by Shen Tingfang 沈廷芳. Guangzhou 廣州: Daoshu 道署 [Government Office], 1758.

Zhang Tingmao. *Ming Qing shiqi Aomen haishang maoyishi*. Macao: Aoya zhoukan chuban youxian gongsi, 2004.

Zhang Zengxin, Stephen (Chang Tseng-hsin). *Ming ji Dongnan Zhongguo de haishang huodong (Maritime Activities on the South-East Coast of China in the Latter Part of the Ming Dynasty)*. Part 2. Taipei: China Committee for Publication Aid and Prize Award, 1988.

Zhang Zhentao 張甄陶. "Zhiyu Aoyi Lun" 制馭澳夷論 [On controlling the foreigners in Macao]. In Wang 王錫祺. *Xiao Fanghu Zhai Yudi Congchao* 小方壺齋與地叢鈔, 9: 332.

Zhu Huai 祝淮 and Huang Peifang 黃培芳. *Xinxiu Xiangshan Xianzhi* 新修香山縣志 [New edition of local gazetteer of Xiangshan]. Vol. 4 [卷四], "Haifang: Fu Aomen" [海防 • 附澳門; Coastal defence: Plus Macao]. Shiqi 石岐 [?]: Government Office 本衙 of Shiqi [?], 1827.

Ziegenbalg, Bartholomaus. "Ausführlicher Bericht vom 22. August 1708". In *Der Königl: Dänischen Missionarien aus Ost-Indien eingesandter Ausfürhlichen Berichten, Dritter Theil*, edited by Gotthilf August Francke. Halle: Waysenhaus, 1735.

Zika, Charles. "Processions and Pilgrimages: Controlling the Sacred in Fifteenth-Century Germany". *Past and Present* 118 (Feb. 1988): 25–64.

Županov, Ines G. *Disputed Mission: Jesuit Experiments and Brahminical Knowledge in Seventeenth-Century South India*. New Delhi: Oxford University Press, 1999.

———. "Twisting a Pagan Tongue: Portuguese and Tamil in Sixteenth-Century Jesuit Translations". In *Conversion: Old Worlds and New*, edited by Kenneth Mills and Anthony Grafton, 109–38. New York: University of Rochester Press, 2003.

INDEX

Note: The appendix to Chapter 2, "A 'Snapshot' of a Portuguese Community in Southeast Asia: The *Bandel* of Siam, 1684–1686", is an index of names found in *A Embaixada ao Sião de Pero Vaz de Siqueira (1684–1686)*, edited by Leanor de Seabra. Those names are not indexed here.

Titles in the Nalanda-Sriwijaya Studies Centre Series

General Editors: Tansen Sen and Geoff Wade

www.ingramcontent.com/pod-product-compliance
Lightning Source LLC
Chambersburg PA
CBHW021845020426
42334CB00013B/201